CHRISTIANITY AND POLITICS
IN TRIBAL INDIA

G. Kanato Chophy

Christianity and Politics in Tribal India

BAPTIST MISSIONARIES AND
NAGA NATIONALISM

First published by Permanent Black D-28 Oxford Apts, 11 IP Extension, Delhi 110092 INDIA, for the territory of SOUTH ASIA. First SUNY Press edition 2021.

Not for sale in South Asia

Cover design by Anuradha Roy.

Published by State University of New York Press, Albany

© 2021 G. Kanato Chophy

All rights reserved

Printed in the United States of America

No part of this book may be used or reproduced in any manner whatsoever without written permission. No part of this book may be stored in a retrieval system or transmitted in any form or by any means including electronic, electrostatic, magnetic tape, mechanical, photocopying, recording, or otherwise without the prior permission in writing of the publisher.

For information, contact State University of New York Press, Albany, NY www.sunypress.edu

Library of Congress Cataloging-in-Publication Data

Names: Chophy, G. Kanato, author
Title: Christianity and politics in tribal India : Baptist missionaries and naga nationalism
Description: Albany : State University of New York Press, [2021] Includes bibliographical references and index.
Identifiers: ISBN 9781438485812 (hardcover : alk. paper) | ISBN 9781438485836 (e-book) | ISBN 9781438485829 (paperback : alk. paper)
Library of Congress Control Number: 2021944201
Further information is available at the Library of Congress.

10 9 8 7 6 5 4 3 2 1

to the memory of
MILES BRONSON
a maker of
modern north-east India

Contents

	Illustrations and Maps	ix
	Abbreviations	xiii
	Acknowledgements	xvii
	Introduction: One Faith, Many Ethnicities	1
1	The Empire and the Pearly Gates	28
2	The Baptist Highland	71
3	Heirs of the New Faith	117
4	Some Converts are More Equal than Others	166
5	Exotic Natives No More	212
6	Legends, Mystics, and Converts	257
7	The Baptist Intellectuals	303
8	Pragmatists and Idealists	348
9	Guns, the Bible, and the Little Red Book	383
	Conclusion: Naga Baptists 2.0	425
	Bibliography	432
	Index	441

Illustrations and Maps

Illustrations

1. Baptist choir comprising women from various Naga communities performing during the NBCC Platinum Jubilee, April 2012. The Nagas' love for music found new expression in the hymnal singing and choral tradition of the new faith. Courtesy DIPR. — 125

2. Molungyimsen village, late 1870s. E.W. Clark, known as an "apostle to the head-hunters", started the village for followers of the new faith in 1876. Courtesy ABAM. — 133

3. The Naga Hills district headquarters, Kohima, during the British period. This sleepy little town would become a centre of American Baptist mission activity starting from 1881. Courtesy DIPR. — 157

4. Rev. and Mrs S.W. Rivenburg. A successful medical missionary in Kohima, Rivenburg worked with Ronald Ross in Calcutta on Ross' landmark research on malaria. Rivenburg was awarded the Kaiser-i-Hind for his public service. Courtesy ABAM. — 159

5. Sumi Naga believers and evangelists during the Baptist conference, *c.* 1942. Considered more warlike than the "warmongering" eastern Naga tribes in the British unadministered region, the

	ILLUSTRATIONS AND MAPS	
	Sumi Baptists became actively involved in evangelism after their conversion. Courtesy SBAK.	174
6	A play on headhunting being performed during the NBCC Platinum Jubilee celebrations, April 2012. Naga Baptists generally represent the pre- and post-Christian eras through the popular imagery of "darkness and light". Courtesy DIPR.	186
7	Panshong *morung* (bachelor's dormitory) in Wanching showing a wood carving of a modern man with a Bible alongside traditional motifs. Photo by the author.	228
8	A miniature *morung* with a painting of Jesus Christ stands next to an uninhabited traditional *morung* in Changway *khel*, Monyakshu village.	229
9	Rani Gaidinliu meeting Prime Minister Indira Gandhi at her residence in New Delhi, *c.* 1983. Courtesy DIPR.	275
10	Rev. J. Tanquist, a gifted translator (front, right), and Rev. G.W. Supplee, considered the most musically gifted missionary (back, left), with Angami evangelists and converts at the Kohima mission station, *c.* 1930. Courtesy NBCC.	316
11	Sarvepalli Radhakrishnan, president of India, arrives in Kohima in 1 December 1963 to inaugurate the state of Nagaland. He is flanked by Vishnu Sahay, first governor, and P. Shilu Ao, first chief minister of Nagaland. Courtesy DIPR.	322
12	T. Aliba Imti, the first NNC president, 1947–8. Courtesy DIPR.	335
13	A.Z. Phizo, the fourth NNC president, 1950–90. Courtesy DIPR.	337
14	T. Sakhrie, the first NNC secretary, 1946–55. Photo: Khilhu Sakhrie	352

ILLUSTRATIONS AND MAPS   xi

15 J.B. Jasokie, chief minister of Nagaland,
    welcoming L.P. Singh, governor of the state.
    Jasokie, former information secretary of the NNC,
    parted ways with the Phizo-led NNC and went on
    to become chief minister. Courtesy DIPR.   366

16 The Naga political drama witnessed the involvement
    of some illustrious personalities, attempting a
    peaceful solution: (Left) Rev. Michael Scott,
    A. Kevichusa, and B.P. Chaliha; (Right) B.P. Chaliha,
    Rev. Michael Scott, and JP (Jayaprakash Narayan).
    Courtesy NBCC.   368

17 Rajiv Gandhi on a visit to Nagaland, October 1987.
    He inherited the vexing Naga political problem
    from his grandfather Jawaharlal Nehru and mother
    Indira Gandhi. Courtesy DIPR.   369

18 Rano Shaiza, the first Naga woman to be elected
    Member of Parliament. Courtesy DIPR.   372

19 Khrieleno Theruja, a noted Baptist educationist and
    the first Naga woman to hold a bachelor's degree in
    divinity. Courtesy NBCC.   373

20 Naga women taking out a peace procession in
    Kohima organised by the NBCC in February 1996,
    a year before the ceasefire agreement between the
    Naga political groups and the Government of India.
    Courtesy NBCC.   377

21 From left to right: Mowu Gwizan, Khodao
    Yanthan, Kaito Sukhai, Yongkong, Ursula Graham
    Betts, 1962. The four Naga leaders were detained at
    London airport and later released by the Home
    Office. Courtesy DIPR.   392

22 Rev. Yankey Patton, the first chaplain in the
    NNC-Federal government. Courtesy NBCC.   405

23 NSCN (IM) leaders Thuingaleng Muivah and
    Isak Chishi Swu. The two Chinese-trained Naga

leaders gave a second lease of life to the Naga armed struggle from the Myanmar jungles in the late 1970s and early 1980s. Courtesy DIPR. 410

24 Kushe, an itinerant preacher and prophet whose son, Isak Chishi Swu, followed in his footsteps, mixing evangelism with ethnonationalism. Courtesy NBCC. 420

Maps

1	American Baptist Mission Stations by 1955	7
2	District-wise Location of Sixteen Tribes of Nagaland	12–13
3	Divisions of Assam Showing Important Places in American Baptist Mission History	52
4	American Baptist Mission Stations 1836–2000	77

Abbreviations

ABAM	Ao Baptist Arogo Mundang (Ao Baptist churches' association)
ABCC	Angami Baptist Church Council
ABMU	American Baptist Missionary Union
BJP	Bharatiya Janata Party
CBCA	Council of Baptist Churches of Assam
CBCC	Chakhesang Baptist Church Council
CBLT	Chang Baptist Lashong Thangyen (Chang Baptist churches' association)
CNC	Council of Nagalim Churches
CPB	Communist Party of Burma
CRBC	Council of Rengma Baptist Churches
CRC	Christian Revival Church
DIPR	Department of Information and Public Relations
FGN	Federal Government of Nagaland
GPRN	Government of the Peoples' Republic of Nagalim
INC	Indian National Congress
KBA	Kuki Baptist Association
KBBB	Konyak Baptist Bumeinok Bangjum (Konyak Baptist churches' association)
KBCA	Khiamniungan Baptist Churches' Association

KBES	Kyong Baptist Ekhümkho Sanrhyutsü (Kyong Baptist churches' association)
KCC	Kuki Church Council
KLO	Kamtapur Liberation Organisation
KSU	Konyak Students' Union
MBC	Manipur Baptist Convention
NBCC	Nagaland Baptist Church Council
NDFB	National Democratic Front of Boroland
NEFA	North-East Frontier Agency
NHDTC	Naga Hills District Tribal Council
NHTA	Naga Hills – Tuensang Area
NMA	Naga Mothers' Association
NMML	Nehru Memorial Museum and Library
NNC	Naga National Council
NSCN (IM)	National Socialist Council of Nagalim (Isak-Muivah)
NSCN (K)	National Socialist Council of Nagaland (Khaplang)
NWF	Naga Women's Federation
PLA	People's Liberation Army
RSS	Rashtriya Swayamsevak Sangh (National Volunteers' Organisation)
SABAK	Sumi Aphuyemi Baptist Akukuhou Kuqhakulu (Sumi ancestral villages Baptist churches' association)
SBAK	Sumi Baptist Akukuhou Kuqhakulu (Sumi Baptist churches' association)
UNLFW	United Liberation Front of Western South East Asia
ULFA	United Liberation Front of Asom

USBLA	United Sangtam Baptist Lithroti Ashimukhong (United Sangtam Baptist churches' association)
VHP	Vishva Hindu Parishad (Universal Hindu Council)
WSBAK	Western Sumi Baptist Akukuhou Kuqhakulu (Western Sumi Baptist churches' association)
YBBA	Yimchunger Baptist Boru Amukhungta (Yimchunger Baptist churches' association)
ZHA	Zeliangrong Heraka Association

Acknowledgements

THAT THIS BOOK is written in English speaks volumes of my Baptist mission heritage, which owes to the contributions of the Baptist fraternity around the world, past and present. A characteristic feature of the faithful – maintaining archives – has allowed a keen element of historicity to structure my narrative, despite arguments and ideas thematically organised that interrupt a broadly chronological flow.

My great debt is to all the Naga Baptist mission centres for rendering help and support. I owe an equally important debt to many Naga believers, some of whom I have kept anonymous, who have shared the stories and experiences which form one of the ethnographic foundations of this book.

From the commercial hub in Dimapur to remote villages across the international border, my Naga brethren have readily opened their homes to me. In particular, I am grateful to Niketu Iralu, Angh Keamang, Kethoser Kevichusa, Philip Imti, Avuli Chishi, Visakhonü Hibo, and Revds Atsi Dolie, Zelhou Keyho, Joshua Rochill, John Ovung, Tajung Jamir, Sangkap Chang, and Yamyap Konyak.

I owe a great debt to Ramachandra Guha, who patiently read my drafts and gave me invaluable insights. Big thanks to Rivka Israel, who hacked through the chapters and made them lucid and readable; her editing was of immense help.

I had the privilege of working as a Fellow of the New India Foundation (NIF), which funded my research and took responsibility for its publication. My thanks to the NIF trustees, Manish Sabharwal, Srinath Raghavan, Nandan Nilekani, and Niraja Gopal Jayal, for showing faith in this somewhat unconventional book on the history and society of an unusually interesting region of the subcontinent all too often seen as peripheral.

My heartfelt thanks to Rukun Advani at Permanent Black for making this book reach the finishing line. He read the final draft meticulously, removed fluff, fine-tuned the arguments, and arranged copublication at the State University of New York Press via James Peltz – to whom also my thanks for his generous reception.

I have been fortunate in friends and a family who have supported me. In particular, Tokuto Zhimo helped me with the maps and plates; Samuel Vaiphei, Azhoni Krichena, David Hanneng, and Chunthailiu Gonmei gave me critical feedback and insights.

Introduction

One Faith, Many Ethnicities

> They are a very uncivilized race, with dark complexions, athletic sinewy frames, hideously wild and ugly visages . . . They are reckless of human life; treacherously murdering their neighbours often without provocation, or at best for a trivial cause of offence . . . Amongst a people so thoroughly primitive, and so independent of religious prepossessions, we might reasonably expect missionary zeal would be most successful.
>
> – John Butler, *A Sketch of Assam*, 1847

ON EASTER SUNDAY 2010, a group of Naga Christians assembled at sunrise near a famous World War II monument in Kohima, capital of the state of Nagaland in north-east India. It appears that the faithful had chosen this spot since the stone-sculpted structure has at its apex a stately crucifix. The WWII memorial, where an interdenominational "sunrise service" is held on this day every year, is a stark reminder of the ruthless modern warfare that ravaged this once-remote place inhabited by an obscure head-hunting tribe best known for its grisly "trophy collection". The spot is usually pummelled by strong winds at this time of year, and 2010 was no exception, but they seemed only to spur the congregation into a more determined show of devotion on that early morning. Around them was complete silence, except for tall pines that rustled in the wind. Enhancing the melancholy of the scene were hundreds of small white marble tombstones that stretched across an immaculately trimmed lawn, their engravings showing mainly alien names.

On a hillside overlooking the Kohima War Cemetery spreads the expanse of Kohima town. The narrow and winding roads of Kohima – which has a population of 1.15 lakhs according to the 2011 census – are always flooded with people, its busy streets clogged with endless traffic jams. Sundays are the exception, for the Sabbath is when the entire town comes to a halt and the many churches in the state capital come to be packed with worshippers. The day after, life bursts forth in the heart of town, and a flurry of Nagamese – the lingua franca of the streets and commercial transactions – flows unimpeded again. Through the snail-paced traffic, people throng the streets once more to continue everyday tasks interrupted by the day of rest.

But at this moment in the Kohima War Cemetery everything seemed calm and serene, as the gathered believers waited for the sun to rise above the lofty mountain range that dominates the sleeping town.

The congregation consisted of a few hundred, young and old, all dressed for the occasion, some in the latest fashions of the town, others in traditional garb. Now, as the sun's soft rays began to light up the surrounding grass, the crowd sang out exuberantly and in unison – "Up from the grave He arose"; the words were from an old Baptist English hymnal. An elderly Naga gentleman, whose erudition and confidence bespoke decades in the business, led the congregation in worship as intermittent applause, cacophonous prayers, and melodious hymns resonated from this piece of hillside.

The significance of the cemetery as a symbol of the clash of civilisations and the collapse of empires seemed lost on the devotees; the attention of each of those gathered was keenly focused on a Palestinian-Jewish prophet from two thousand years earlier whose teachings had changed their world. From being seen as "much-dreaded" tribes during the British Raj to becoming a pietistic community of Christians at the opening of a new millennium in the Indian republic, their transition, over the span of a mere century, had been uncommonly swift.

About 4 km away from the WWII memorial is the Kohima Cathedral. This is built in a noticeably traditional Naga style of architecture, on the Aradura spur, where the faithful would soon proceed for the Easter Sunday service. The cathedral, also known as Mary Help of Christians Cathedral, boasts of being the biggest place of worship in north-east India. It was built on a budget of thirty million rupees, generously donated by "Japanese people" who wished the cathedral to also serve as a memorial for the Japanese soldiers who had laid down their lives during the Battle of Kohima in WWII. Etched on a memorial stone in both English and Japanese are these words:

> It is with thankfulness that we heard that a Catholic Cathedral was being built at Kohima, where mass would be offered every morning in the memory of the fallen . . .

Rumour has it that there is more to the Kohima Cathedral than meets the eye; an inscription of the "number of the beast", i.e. 666, is said to be imprinted on the crucifix atop the cathedral.[1] Some fundamentalist Naga Baptists are convinced that the papacy is a representation of the Antichrist, soon to reveal its true nature, and along their eschatological beliefs the rumour does not seem fanciful. The Kohima Cathedral, which took half a decade to build and was consecrated in 1991, is a manifestation of Catholicism's success story among the Angami Nagas, the average Angami Baptist considering Catholicism an "upstart" denomination that spread its "devious" tentacles to embrace their tribe within a short span of time, and posing a heretical threat to the true Christian faith. Not so long ago, adherents of the traditional Naga religion harboured

---

[1] This "number of the beast" derives from the Book of Revelation, chapter 13, verse 6, and in general suggests danger to Christianity. It has been variously interpreted as signifying the Antichrist, the Prophet Mohammed, and the Roman emperor Nero. The rumour in the Naga context indicated an antipathy for Roman Catholics and was more widespread among fundamentalist Baptists of the North American variety, the denomination I grew up with.

similar perceptions of the Baptist Church as the "white man's religion", but what good did it do them? The followers of traditional religion were an enfeebled minority in less than a hundred years.

Despite the fact that the Angami Nagas have embraced Catholicism in larger numbers compared to other Naga tribes, misgivings about Catholicism among them are no less than among tribes like the Ao, Lotha, and Sumi Nagas, which also have large Baptist followings. Why this general suspicion toward Catholicism among the Naga Baptists? Is it possible that Baptists have viewed Catholicism in a different light than have other Protestant denominations? The Catholics have not been oblivious to the Baptists' perception: "Up to the eve of the Second Vatican Council, the average American Roman Catholic considered an American Baptist as the 'most difficult of all Protestants to comprehend.'"[2]

Being an admirer of Pope Francis, the first Jesuit pope, I find it baffling that this soft-spoken austere man of the cloth with a socialist outlook can seem to anyone a representative of the coming Antichrist who will dominate the world. Yet, according to fundamentalist Baptists, Pope Francis is a baddie who makes lesser baddies seem pale by comparison. Many Naga Baptists consider the Catholics heretics – such is the complexity of interdenominational relations now in this small Baptist heartland. It puts in perspective the history of sectarian conflict generally, and, nearer our context, that of the global Christian past, when Catholics gloated over Protestants who responded to Jesus' "Great Commission" only as late as the eighteenth century.[3]

II

Baptists are Protestant Christians who practise the complete water immersion of believing adults, this being distinct from the baptism

---

[2] Puthenpurakal, *Baptist Missions in Nagaland*, 15.
[3] Taken from the Gospel of Matthew 28: 18–20, the "Great Commission" is understood as a template for mission activity among the Christians who believe that they are fulfilling the commands of Jesus Christ to make disciples of all nations.

of infants as practised by Protestant denominations such as Anglicans, Brethren, and Lutherans. Tracing their roots to the English Separatist movement in the 1600s, the Baptists are discernible as a denomination by their specific beliefs and practices: the accountability of the individual; the autonomy of local churches; communion; *sola scriptura* (scripture as the sole authority for faith and practice); and *sola fide* (salvation by faith alone).

Baptists are of various shades and their beliefs have fostered an impressive array of perspectives. The American journalist and award-winning writer Robert Wright begins his book *The Evolution of God* by mentioning his Southern Baptist upbringing, and how he outgrew his Baptist roots, when introducing his position as lying between science and faith.[4] The Baptist stance on science and faith has gained for its followers the opprobrium of religious fundamentalism, at least in the Bible Belt of the United States. Yet I have come across individual Baptists who are devout while accepting the Darwinian theory. Their reconciliation of the contradiction takes the shape of a supplementary belief – that natural selection shows selection by the Divine Hand. More common, however, are the established denominational orthodoxies that have made Baptists controversial in an increasingly globalised world.

"What distinguishes a Naga Baptist?" I put this ostensibly simple question to Zelhou Keyho, General Secretary of the Nagaland Baptist Church Council (NBCC), one of the foremost Baptist organisations in India. With a PhD on the Old Testament from the US, Zelhou taught in a popular Baptist seminary in Dimapur for several years before being selected to head the parent Naga Baptist organisation in 2015. According to this charming leader of the NBCC, Naga Baptists can be distinguished by their "belief in being born-again, taking the Bible to be the divinely inspired word of God, evangelical faith and adult baptism – a water immersion ritual that is afforded only after a person can discern between good and evil and decides to follow Jesus Christ."

---

[4] See Wright, *The Evolution of God*, Introduction.

Zelhou's mild version of what makes the Naga Baptist distinctive omits the fact that some Naga Baptist beliefs can be very unpopular, even unpalatable, in a multicultural society. For instance, many Naga Baptists believe in a literal interpretation of the scriptures, the eternal damnation of unbelievers, and that salvation comes exclusively through Jesus Christ and his atonement on the cross. However, Naga Baptists mostly occupy a spectrum less extreme, showing adherence to doctrines that are not different from the fundamental southern Baptist churches in the United States at one end, and an uber-Pentecostal variety of faith at the other.[5] One feature that all Naga Baptist churches share is zeal for evangelism and mission, which I think has not waned since the last American Baptist missionaries left the Naga Hills in the mid-1950s; rather, the sense of mission has not yet peaked, for the inevitable decline, clearly visible in the history of other Christian missions, is not yet in evidence. The Naga Baptists currently send missionaries to various states in India, and to neighbouring countries like Bhutan, Nepal, Myanmar, Thailand, Cambodia, and China. Local churches in Nagaland are self-reliant as the believers who throng them tithe religiously and give generously toward mission; most Baptist churches have a mission department which undertakes to spread the gospel to the "unreached". In fact the success of a Baptist church is measured in terms of missionaries sent out and its sponsoring missions outside the home state. As the general secretary of the NBCC puts it, "the heartbeat of the Naga Baptist churches is mission and evangelism."

I was raised in a conservative Baptist home, so I am familiar with Naga Christian denominational idiosyncrasies and legalistic beliefs, and familiarity tends to naturalise what can seem an oddity to those far removed from contexts they see as alien. The images people in the world outside hold of Naga Baptists are often caricatures, much as are views of Baptists in general in the

---

[5] Pentecostalism is the Protestant belief in direct and personal experience of God via baptism in the Holy Spirit.

Map 1: American Baptist mission stations in the Naga areas by 1955.

West. On a visit to the United States, the country to which the Naga Baptists trace their denominational origins, I encountered so-called secularists making sweeping generalisations about an entire religious community. Frequently, friends and acquaintances in the West raise eyebrows or cringe when they hear that I am a practising Baptist. It is small mercy that they do not see me as the Third World version of a gun-toting Young Earth creationist or a Bible-thumping churchgoing fanatic – that being the usual image of Baptists in popular culture.

Baptists, despite a shared history and doctrinal origins, have diversified over the centuries as waves of Christian movements across the world have changed the contours of the faith. Similarly, Baptist denominations among ethnic Naga groups are not monolithic. In my opinion, no serious scholar of religion can write authoritatively on Naga Baptists without grasping the nuances of nineteenth-century Evangelicalism and twentieth-century Pentecostalism, both of which have had a huge influence on the religious life of ethnic Nagas. These global religious movements have fostered schismatic divisions within the Baptist denomination and have engendered a wide range of beliefs and practices. Also, some aspects of indigenous religious beliefs and practices have continued in the new faith, rendering a distinctive character to the Baptist tradition among the Naga tribes.

Verrier Elwin (1902–1964), an authority on Indian tribal life and culture who began his career in India as a missionary from England, infamously labelled one strain of the Baptist faith – which had spread among the eastern Naga tribes in the "Tuensang Frontier Division" in the post-Independence period – the "RSS of Christianity".[6] It seems to me very unlikely that Elwin could hold the same opinion of Naga Baptists now: the new generations of

---

[6] "Tour Notes of Dr Verrier Elwin for the months of March–April, 1954 on the Tuensang Frontier Division", in File No. 139, Elwin Papers, NMML, New Delhi. "RSS" is now one of the best-known abbreviations in India, denoting the Rashtriya Swayamsevak Sangh, the Hindu nationalist organisation which propagates the hardline version of Hinduism known as Hindutva.

Naga Baptists have been educated in some of the finest seminaries and universities around the globe – no less than Elwin in his own day. I have come across some brilliant Naga theologians and scholars, and I am certain the early Elwin – before he converted to tribal hedonism – would have enjoyed a conversation with Kethoser Kevichusa, an Angami Baptist theologian from his alma mater, Oxford.

I heard this young and erudite preacher in 2010, in a small chapel in Kohima Science College, Jotsoma, about 10 km from the state capital; he is from a family of pioneering Baptist converts. His congregation comprised mainly undergraduate students of the college, among whom there is a witty popular aphorism: "Blessed are the preachers who deliver short sermons, for they shall be invited again." The young do not favour the conventionally lengthy sermon, and, unlike in traditional churches, congregations comprising the predominantly young can turn against the most sagacious of preachers if they grow prolix. But the suave young preacher had gauged his congregation's predisposition and had his listeners in the palm of his hand. At one point they burst out laughing when he joked about meeting the veteran Hindi film director Mahesh Bhatt and confessing to him that he, Kethoser, had seen none of his movies.

The sermon was on forgiveness and reconciliation. Kethoser said: "Without forgiveness there can be no reconciliation," which I quickly jotted down in my field notebook. I could not help but notice the timing, since the Naga armed conflict, which began life as hostility to the hegemonic Indian state, was now going through one of its most turbulent factional phases in decades. After a botched attempt to unify the warring factions, especially the National Socialist Council of Nagalim (IM) and the National Socialist Council of Nagaland (K), their clashes had escalated, resulting in the loss of lives. At the time that I joined Delhi University as a postgraduate student in 2008, word was that the various Naga factions were working to end all hostilities, but by 2010 the olive branch had withered and the internecine war had resumed. During this tumultuous period, I was in the Angami village of Jotsoma for my fieldwork; I was working on a doctoral thesis on the religion and worldview of a Naga tribe. And so I had happened to visit the college chapel where Kethoser was delivering his sermon – it was the chapel I had frequented during my undergraduate days in the same college. And Kethoser had been a sought-after preacher on the campus back then as well.

Kethoser represents, as I said, a new generation of highly educated Naga Baptist elites. Having earned a master's in theology from the University of Oxford and a PhD from the Oxford Centre for Mission Studies (validated by Middlesex University, London), his is a success story from the Angami Naga tribe. Hailing from a historic village, Khonoma, the Kevichusa family produced some of the early Naga intellectuals in the British Naga Hills district, courtesy of the American Baptist mission. Kethoser's great-grandfather, Nisier Angami, was the first convert from Khonoma village to enter the halls of Baptist greats as an evangelist and church planter.[7] Nisier's son, Angami Kevichusa (popularly known as A. Kevichusa), educated in a Baptist mission school, distinguished himself as the first Naga graduate, became a Member of the Most Excellent Order of the British Empire (MBE), and played an instrumental role in emerging modern Naga society. But the family's position among the foremost Naga intellectuals also came at a great cost.

Kethoser is no stranger to anguish and loss; he has lost close relatives to the Naga political conflict. Two of his brilliant uncles were assassinated by Naga rebels, adding to the list of many promising educated individuals who fell victim to violence. Despite these losses and bitter memories, or perhaps because of them, Kethoser travels around the country lecturing on peace, forgiveness, and reconciliation to fellow Indian Christians. Apart from being a devout Baptist and well-known figure in Naga Baptist circles, he

---

[7] "Church planter" is a term used mainly in evangelical Christianity to refer to a minister or pastor who starts a new congregation where none existed.

is a leading Naga scholar in the area of peace and reconciliation studies. His ecumenical approach to Christianity is the new face of the Baptist faith in Nagaland.

A variety of ecumenism is being promoted by a new generation of seminary-trained Naga Christians. Among the Ao Naga tribe toward the north of the Angami area, topnotch Baptist seminarians and theologians are spearheading ecumenical theology. One of the oldest Baptist seminaries, Clark Theological College (CTC; founded in 1972) in Mokokchung district, is at the forefront of theological studies and is affiliated to the Senate of Serampore College – the institution in Bengal founded by a renowned English Baptist missionary, William Carey, a household name among Naga Christians.[8] At CTC, seminary students acquaint themselves with subjects ranging from feminist theology, tribal theology, and other subaltern theologies, to Greek hermeneutics and New Testament studies. Bible colleges and institutes have mushroomed in the state, but seminaries like Clark Theological College and Witter Theological College (founded 1991) in Wokha district are still preferred because of the American Baptist mission legacy.

Ironically, most of what the students learn in these Bible colleges does not tally with social reality: the Baptist churches are having to grapple with new social issues. Kethoser is, as noted, one manifestation of the change; another is the fact that we are now well past the day when native converts considered themselves equipped to save souls with a bare minimum of Bible knowledge; now, the higher learning in theological studies is a popular pursuit among Naga Baptists.

III

Not every Naga is an ardent follower of the Baptist faith. Many have conflicting views on Christianity in general and the Baptist

---

[8] As a pioneering figure (alongside William Ward and Joshua Marshman) in the history of printing technology, who in 1800 founded the Baptist Mission Press in Serampore, Carey is also well known to scholars and students of book history in India.

12 CHRISTIANITY AND POLITICS

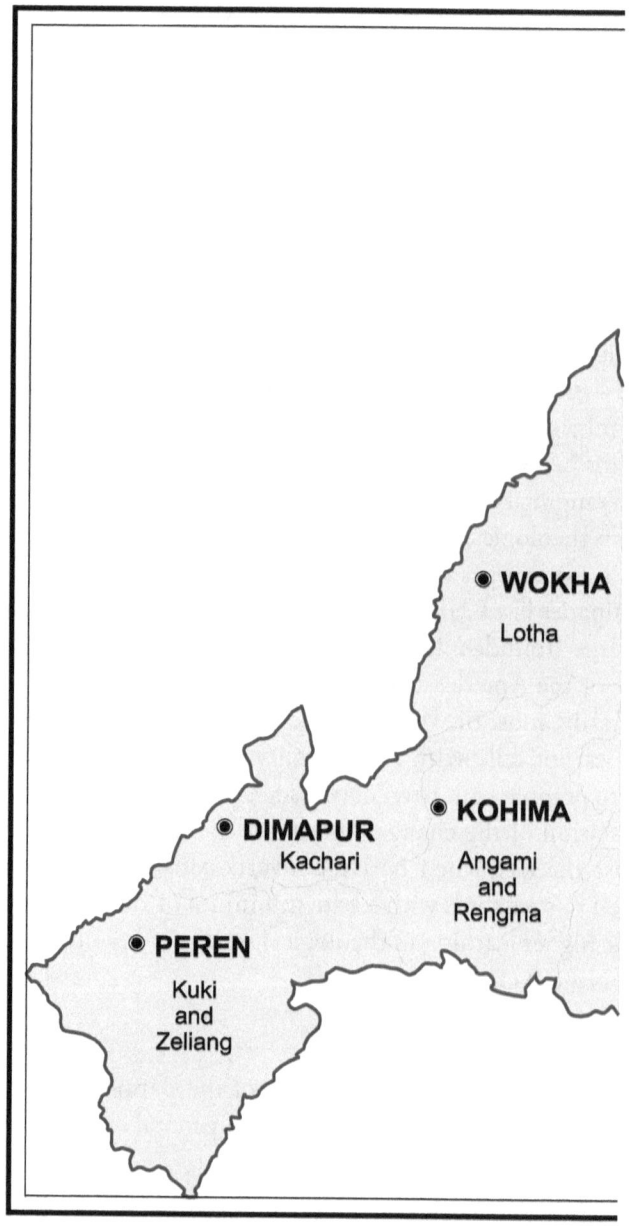

Map 2: District-wise location of

INTRODUCTION

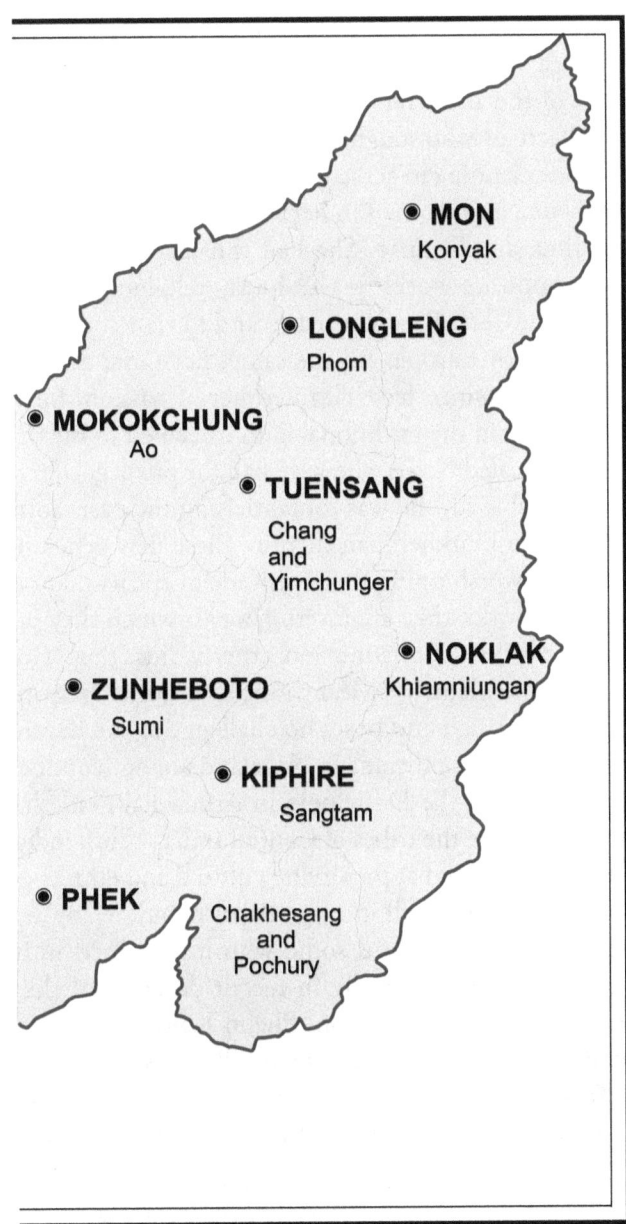

sixteen tribes of Nagaland.

faith in particular. In April 2016, I met the daughter of a well-known Naga writer, now settled in Norway, who claimed to be a follower of the ancestral faith. I had encountered many young Naga intellectuals who sought their roots in the animist past, but rarely anyone claiming to actually practise animism: this intelligent and articulate Naga woman in her mid-twenties was educated in both Kohima and Tromsø. She had thus experienced two diametrically opposite worlds – a zealously religious Naga society, and a far-from-fervid secularised Scandinavian society akin to those in Western Europe. All the same, her more dispassionate world did not seem to have cleansed her of passion, for despite her avid interest in the traditional faith it seemed to me that, like many well-educated Nagas who have had the privilege of travelling and studying abroad, she was romanticising the past. Somewhat in line with the Durkheimian dictum, these new generations of Nagas are not worshipping the multitude of spirits that once inhabited their world, they are revering a past which they presume to be, and valorise as, pristine – in other words, they worship a collective ethnic identity.[9] Meanwhile, traditional Naga religion is heaving its last sigh and poses no challenge to the Baptist faith in the state. Social conditions in Nagaland are not conducive for resurgences such as the Donyipolo in Arunachal Pradesh or the Adi-dharam among the tribes of Central India – both indigenous religious revivals aimed at preserving cultural and ethnic identity.

However, not all is well in Naga Baptist land. Many are disillusioned with the faith and some who have joined university have grown critical, especially in recent decades, of the mode of spreading the Baptist mission. Phejin Konyak, a young Naga independent researcher from Shiong village, is one such. I met her in Kolkata's national museum in 2015, where she was delivering a special lecture on the Konyak tattooing tradition.[10] She

---

[9] Durkheim, *The Elementary Forms of Religious Life*. According to Durkheim, worship of the gods translates into the strengthening of social relationships – the gods being only a figurative representation of society.

[10] Phejin's extensive research on the Konyak tattoo tradition was published two years later. See Konyak and Bos, *The Konyaks*.

had been collaborating with a Dutch photographer to document this fast-disappearing custom among her people. We began our conversation by mentioning the work of the Austrian anthropologist Christoph von Fürer-Haimendorf on the Konyak Nagas.[11] Phejin said her grandfather was with Fürer-Haimendorf during the punitive expedition when British forces – led by a deputy commissioner, J.P. Mills, along with a contingent of Naga warriors and coolies – marched into the unadministered eastern region. They had set out to take action against a recalcitrant village, Pangsha, that had defied British authority; to teach its inhabitants a lesson the village was burnt to the ground. This powerful Khiamniungan Naga village, which once wreaked havoc on neighbouring tribes and villages, is now a hundred per cent Baptist.

Phejin is passionate about the Konyak cultural past, and, like most of my Konyak friends and informants, worries about the progressive loss of their traditions. Educated Konyak Nagas lament that their customs have become showpieces of a fast-fading culture – an instance of this being exquisite Konyak woodcarvings that adorn the drawing rooms of wealthy Nagas in Kohima and Dimapur, far removed from the culture and aesthetics of the Konyak world. Phejin tells me that the disregard for past traditions and the abandoning of indigenous beliefs and practices are a consequence of the Baptist mission, especially in the post-Independence period, when Naga Baptist converts took up the task of preaching to their "unsaved" brethren. This is not a new phenomenon in the conversion of the Naga tribes to a new faith – so, what makes the Konyak Naga experience different from that of other Naga tribes?

Like most Naga tribes, the Konyak are devout Baptists, but the spread of the Baptist faith in the Konyak area is much more complex. The manner of their conversion sticks out like a sore thumb in the history of Naga Baptists, especially the bits showing Naga insurgents, operating from the hermetically sealed region of the Indo–Myanmar border, taking up evangelism along with their

---

[11] Fürer-Haimendorf, *The Naked Nagas*.

ethnonationalism. The evangelical enterprise of these Naga rebels cannot hold a candle to the many decades of the Naga Baptist mission's proselytising in the frontier region, when Naga groups that first came into contact with the American Baptists themselves took up mission work as a divine call. However, the enmeshing of evangelical zealotry with ethnonationalism among a section of the faithful has introduced an element of controversy into Naga Baptist history when viewed in the context of inter-faith relations and political processes in a diverse country like India.

Not every educated Konyak holds Phejin's opinions: a bright Konyak college student named Mercy has a favourable view of the Baptist mission. Both Mercy and Phejin are from the Lower Konyak region and represent second-generation Baptists; both also belong to the Konyak middle class that can afford to send sons and daughters to study in Indian metropolitan cities. Mercy is an undergraduate at one of the premier colleges of Delhi University; she dresses in the latest Western fashion and sports a fashionable haircut; she speaks impeccable English. But we converse mostly in Nagamese, sharing our common identity as Nagas in mainland India. Mercy is also a praise-and-worship leader in a small interdenominational evangelical church, frequented mostly by middle-class students from the north-eastern states, in the university area of north Delhi. She is not very knowledgeable on the Konyak traditional past but outspoken about women's rights and very proud of her heritage. Interestingly, Mercy – like most of my Konyak acquaintances – sees no contradiction between traditional religion and Christianity. I find this intriguing, because the very individuals who critique the British Raj as a manifestation of Western imperialism perceive Christianity as if it were from a different realm. The Nagas are known for their doggedness in political life, but the tenacity of religious belief in their social life is even more compelling. Christianity has taken hold of the Naga mind, entrenched itself firmly in Naga society, and is influencing the future of its next generations.

While in Delhi, I spent some time with Moba Langfhoang at a popular American-brand café in an upscale shopping mall.

Moba is my long-time friend, a graduate in economics from Delhi University and knowledgeable informant on Konyak society. With both of us having studied in Delhi University, our more serious conversations range from the works of English writers much steeped in the Christian worldview – such as C.S. Lewis and G.K. Chesterton – to the works of agnostic postcolonial writers like Edward Said, Frantz Fanon, and Gayatri Spivak. And yet, among educated middle-class Nagas, the encounter with British colonialism – and more importantly the American Baptist missions – evokes multiple perspectives far removed from those of the anticolonial Left. Moba is of the opinion that Nagas would have lagged far behind modern Indian society had it not been for the changes wrought by British rule and the American Baptists. Notwithstanding feelings of resentment against colonialism and disillusionment with the Baptist missions, the modern Naga middle classes were undeniably shaped by the colonial encounter and are beneficiaries of the American Baptist heritage. As Indian citizens within a multicultural nation, Nagas are now striving to find common ground between their traditional cultures and the modern ideals of universal human rights, liberal democracy, the parliamentary form of government, a quasi-British legal system, and an affinity for the English language – all inherited from the West.

IV

Of all the Naga tribes, the Konyak seem to most intrigue those interested in so-called indigenous cultures. What the outside world sees through the aperture of sophisticated cameras belies fast-changing Konyak society and culture. The average reader of expensive coffee-table books may find herself engrossed in glossy high-definition photographs of Konyaks with blackened teeth, body tattoos, exquisite headgear, and colourful tribal dress; what she will not see in these books is teenagers in Levi's jeans and T-shirts dancing to the latest Christian pop songs at the local Baptist church. Like it or not, these are two contrasting worlds that coexist in Konyak villages; also, there are two emerging realities distinguishing those Konyak settled on the Indian side in Nagaland from those on the other side in Myanmar. But, in an indication of increasing apathy among various stakeholders, including academics, the districts of Mon, Tuensang, Kiphire, Longleng, and Noklak, bordering Myanmar, have been clubbed together as "eastern Nagaland", which has become synonymous with underdevelopment, poverty, and backwardness.

Tuensang district remains infamous for its assumed imagery of unruly and warmongering tribes. Known as the trans-Dikhu tribes, or as the unadministered tribes, or euphemistically as the free tribes, the internal doings and affairs of these tribes made the British turn a Nelson's eye in their direction as long as colonial interests were served without threat to the administration. This policy of "splendid isolation" for the unadministered tribes may have been politically strategic, but it also proved crucial in the spread of Christianity. Britain's dual approach to administering the Naga tribes had far-reaching implications in the later years of the Baptist mission, and in the relations between administered and unadministered tribes. I will take up these issues in succeeding chapters, but suffice it to say that the tribes in the administered region inherited from the British a thinly veiled feeling of superiority *vis-à-vis* their eastern Naga brethren.

This state of feeling superior is itself a product of modernity, where education and the embracing of a new faith tilt the scales in favour of Naga groups that were subdued earlier by the British government, as against those subdued later. In the Ao Naga country, where the Baptist faith first took root, the American Baptist mission had pitched its tent even before the British annexed the area, but in retrospect the mission may not have flourished if the British had not come in as conquerors. Overall, the Union Jack had to be foisted on this secluded and "unruly" hill tribe to secure peace – using force if need be – before the American missionaries could preach their message of salvation.

Since Independence, Tuensang has witnessed waves of ethnic conflict which continue to this day. This region, which remained beyond the pale of modernity even years after Independence, became a launchpad for the Naga nationalist A.Z. Phizo to lead an armed uprising. As an administrative unit Tuensang had kept the civil servants of the nascent Indian state on tenterhooks due to the natives' irrepressible desire for freedom. Also at Tuensang, the new Indian state had suffered its first casualty in the theatre of Naga insurgency that ran amok in subsequent years.[12] The state machinery battered the region, and Tuensang was made an example of, for daring to rebel against the Indian state. Importantly, the growth of the Baptist faith in the region went hand in hand with the spread of ethnonationalism among the diverse ethnic groups. Today, Tuensang is a tinderbox. Even a slight misunderstanding can explode into a major ethnic conflict.

Home to Naga tribes like the Chang, Khiamniungan, Sangtam, Tikhir, and Yimchunger, Tuensang district was a fertile Baptist mission field in the post-Independence period. The Baptist mission among the eastern Nagas during these tumultuous years is illustrative of human fortitude, suffering, and perseverance for the sake of religious belief. However, the missionary endeavour in the post-Independence period was no longer the white man's burden; it had become the divine calling of native converts. So, itinerant Ao and Sumi Naga preachers and evangelists preached the gospel to their "less fortunate" brethren whom the fruits of modernity and education had reached late. The phraseology had changed; the eastern Naga tribes were now typecast as heathens: backward, uneducated, and unsaved.

Among the eastern Naga tribes, many first-generation Baptist converts still show the marks of former animist days: intricate faded-green tattoos on their sunbaked and wrinkled skins are a silent reminder of the past. Yet the religious fervour among these elderly Christians is unprecedented, outdoing the religious commitment of second- or third-generation Christians. Prayer and fasting are common, and their seemingly immovable faith in an invisible god is conspicuous. Tuensang district has a substantial number of

---

[12] See Ramunny, *The World of the Nagas*, 74.

first-generation converts, and the narratives of religious conversion here seem to offer a different vantage point on the history and discourse of the Naga Baptists.

Meanwhile, in the Angami and Chakhesang Naga villages in Kohima and Phek districts, the last generation of animists relish their tankards of frothy rice beer. In these villages some Christians, as I was told with a tinge of irony, still brew rice beer clandestinely at the time of important festivals and during agricultural seasons that require heavy work. It seems the sweet, appetising rice beer is too tempting even for Baptists. Nagaland is in theory a "dry" state, but it is also one where the law-enforcement agencies are struggling to curtail bootlegging – all to no avail; the streets of Dimapur, Kohima, and other towns are flooded with Indian made foreign liquor (IMFL). Indeed, the Baptist church faces an uphill battle. It knows full well that many of its baptised members would sell their birthright for a peg of whisky or even spurious liquor. In fact, prayer houses in Nagaland also function as quasi-rehab and de-addiction centres.

Why so much ado about a traditional fermented rice drink? The reason is that teetotalism is a way of life among Naga Baptists, a virtue to be emulated that also amounts to teetotalitarianism. In the early days of Baptist missions, the words "teetotaller" and "non-teetotaller" were used to signify a Christian and a non-Christian, respectively, though the terms "churched" and "unchurched" became popular usage later. So, the consumption of rice beer still raises eyebrows in Naga society. Rice beer is political. It is synonymous with what the Baptists think of as "the sinful days". But the elderly animists won't give up their drinking habit; for many of them, drinking is also an act of dissent.

Critics may condemn the Naga Baptists for inordinate legalism and for their espousal of a religious-fundamentalist attitude toward alcohol. But the elderly generation that had witnessed the ill effects of alcoholism when IMFL began to flood this young Indian state in the late 1960s may give Naga Baptists benefit of the doubt. As for *zu* brewing as a cultural tradition, it will soon vanish like the toothless grins of the last surviving animists, except in the shady alleys of the towns of Dimapur and Kohima for commercial purposes.[13] The wooden wine vats – if the Naga Baptists have their way – will be hauled off to unkempt museums, while the ridiculously large aluminium vessels in shady taverns will evoke guilty memories of the days of a forbidden frothy brew called *zu*.

Among the Sumi and Lotha tribes, who are identified as the earliest settlers in the Doyang area, the spread of Christianity has been comparatively less dramatic and successful. Located in the middle of what was then known as the Naga Hills district, these two tribes were evangelised by missionaries stationed at both Kohima and Mokokchung. The tribes witnessed mass conversion within a relatively short period of time and today the Sumi and Lotha Nagas boast of having achieved 100 per cent Christianity. But this has eventually given rise to schismatic divisions, denominational polemics, and sectarian dissensions that have plagued the church since the post-Independence period. This process has diversified the Baptist faith and religious experience among the Naga tribes. The rise of prayer houses and the popularity of self-styled prophets in Sumi and Lotha Baptist circles have made the religious landscape more exuberant in Zunheboto and Wokha districts. Here, believers are experimenting with new forms of religious experiences, unlike in the traditional Baptist faith.

V

On 14 November 2014, while visiting a Pojoaque Indian reservation in Santa Fe, New Mexico, I was perturbed to see a representation of the missionary encounter with the native population in a small museum there. Modelled in clay a Franciscan friar, with a devilish countenance and holding a Bible, was whipping a bleeding native who knelt for mercy. This harrowing representation made me turn to my American colleague and say, in a momentary outburst of ethnocentrism: "If an American Baptist missionary had

---

[13] *Zu* is an Angami term popularly used for rice beer in Nagaland.

dared to do that to a Naga, his head would have been lopped off." Being familiar with the history of Catholic missions in the New World, and the exploits and religious predilection of Spanish conquistadors like Hernán Cortés and Francisco Pizarro, the striking differences between the Protestant and Catholic missions among indigenous peoples around the world dawned on me. One thing was clear: the distinctive experience of Christian missions among the Naga tribes owes not only to the tribes' cultural uniqueness, but also to the nature of the movements that had converged on their undulating hills.

The progenitors of Protestantism in sixteenth-century North America were dissident Presbyterians and Nonconformists who had fled a majority Anglican–Jacobean England to establish a most formidable religion. Unlike England, with its complex church history interspersed with Catholic and Protestant violence, America was built on Protestant principles: it was born as a Protestant nation, not built on the ruins of a Catholic establishment. This had consequences for the subsequent religious revivalism and reformation there, as well as global implications. The eighteenth century shows the spread of Protestant missions, which was owing to the great evangelical revival that swept most parts of Western Europe and North America. Known as the Pietist movement in continental Europe, the Methodist revival in Great Britain, and the Great Awakening in North America, this global resurgence emphasised salvation via immersion in the personal atonement of Jesus Christ, born-again experiences, the authority of infallible scriptures, and reliance on missionary work rather than sacraments and long-held traditions of the conventional churches. This new missionary endeavour among the Protestants has been pithily outlined:

> Up to the end of the eighteenth century, large-scale missionary efforts were strictly the preserve of the Catholic powers, a point of superiority proudly stressed by Catholic controversialists . . . In the 1790s, however, Protestants took up this challenge. This was

partly a consequence of the evangelical revival and partly due to the unprecedented power and reach of the British Empire.[14]

Until the First Great Awakening between the 1730s and 1740s, America was merely an assemblage of colonies showing not much by way of interconnection and mutual contact, but this great religious revival brought them together. As with most Christian reformations, the flame of the Great Awakening burned for a considerable period, and, by the time it had run its course, thousands of "heathens" in far-off lands had been preached to and "saved". The significant motif of the Great Awakening was "rescue the perishing"; many responded to the evangelical call to go to the ends of the earth to rescue the "lost". But unlike Catholic missionaries to the New World who belonged to the upper echelons of European society, the manpower for Protestant missions more often came from a less privileged background. This class difference would reflect in the missionary–native interaction and the mode of evangelising – at least with the ethnic populations in the northeastern Indian frontier.

The American Baptist missionaries to the Nagas were mostly from the working class. For instance, the Sumi Nagas tell of a Swede orphan born in their farmlands who later migrated to the US for a better life; there he gave his life to Jesus Christ and joined the missionary bandwagon to preach the good news in far-off foreign lands. This was Bengt Ivar Anderson, who brought Christianity to the Sumi Nagas; he is included in the missionary hall of fame along with other pioneers in the region such as E.W. Clark, C.D. King, and S.W. Rivenburg. These individuals belonged to a class of missionaries who carried out their religious duties with the utmost dedication, a consequence of their fervent religious belief, leaving a lasting influence on the natives they converted. Contrary to the image of fiendish whip-wielding friars among Native Americans, Baptist missionaries among the Naga tribes are

---

[14] Jenkins, *The Next Christendom*, 33.

afforded a heroic status. Their busts and enlarged portraits adorn Baptist mission centres and churches in Nagaland.

With respect to the British empire the evangelical enterprise, which can be traced to the Clapham Sect, had little to do with the Crown, the government, or the Anglican church: it initially began as a campaign of dissent. This missionary effort of the Clapham Sect, which began on the north side of Clapham Common, is said to have led to the "moral transformation of the British Empire".[15] Also, contrary to popular belief, the American Baptist missionaries were not directly involved in the project of Western imperialism, nor were they covert agents of the British empire. The nineteenth-century evangelicalism that gave impetus to the American Baptist mission was directed, at least in its own understanding, toward otherworldly aims, even if it left an indelible mark on the mundane world of the Nagas.

The interaction of the American Baptist mission with British colonialists and ethnic Nagas is, in my argument, complicated and therefore requires a more critical examination than through the lens of a conventional postcolonial critique of Christian missions. Official written records and oral history reveal that missionaries were often at loggerheads with the colonial administration and its policies. Many British political agents who wanted to keep the indigenous cultures intact perceived Baptist missionaries as a threat to the status quo, even as the missionaries were single-minded in their aim of readying natives for the impending kingdom of god. If the political life of the Naga tribes was anglicised, their religious life came to be americanised.

VI

The ethnic group known as the Nagas comprises various communities speaking different languages and showing distinct cultural

---

[15] Ferguson, *Empire*, 152. One of E.M. Forster's little-known books, *Marianne Thornton* (1956) – a biography of his great-aunt, a wealthy and devoted member of the Clapham Sect – also contains much interesting information on this influential sect, which included among its members the great social reformer and abolitionist William Wilberforce.

features, but revealing at the same time cultural similarities that cut across these otherwise separable communities. The Naga tribes are distributed across the Indian states of Assam, Arunachal Pradesh, Nagaland, and Manipur, and over the north-western region of Myanmar – all territories that the Nagas claim as their ancestral domain or homeland. Naga-inhabited areas have witnessed a rapid spread of Protestant Christianity, more specifically the Baptist faith, which has deeply influenced the ethnic identity, culture, and socio-political climate of the region. One of the oldest Naga Baptist communities is to be found in the state of Nagaland, and it was from this "Baptist core" that the mission was carried forward to other Naga-inhabited areas.

This book is about the Naga Baptists, their place in history, their response to change, and their ongoing negotiations with the outside world. In recent years, Naga Baptists have been moving out to other parts of India and the globe for work and study, and many have settled outside their native land. The faithful carry their Baptist identity and beliefs with them to these new places, which is not without effect – a large sociological process yet to be explored: even at the time of writing, the First Naga Baptist Church was inaugurated in August 2019 in Dallas Fort Worth, Texas. Naga interactions with varying communities, religions, and cultures have had a noticeable effect on their Baptist faith: the contact has diversified their Baptist beliefs and practices. As noted above, the fundamentalist strain of the Baptist faith is more widespread in rural areas, while among educated Nagas who have interacted with a larger world Baptist beliefs are comparatively mellow.

The influence of cross-cultural contact on adherents is one among several factors that have contributed to the diversity of the Naga Baptist faith and shaped the community; other factors include the colonial encounter, episodic religious movements, distance from the centre of the nation-state, and differential access to modernity. I describe these changes in the following chapters. Notwithstanding the diversity, I consistently argue through this book that there is a definable "Baptist culture" which can be attributed to ethnic Nagas irrespective of external influences.

On the other hand, there can be no gainsaying that Naga Baptists who have settled in parts of India beyond Nagaland and outside the country are developing in varying ways, each according to their own genius. Therefore, great care has to be taken when trying to understand, for instance, Naga Baptists in the Baptist-dominated state of Nagaland and those in the neighbouring state of Arunachal Pradesh: the latter are pulled apart by numerous unapologetic Christian missions, an effervescent traditional reformed religion, and increasingly strident Hindu missions.

Similarly, the Baptist story is different for Naga tribes who have settled in the neighbouring state of Manipur. There they have had to contend with the ethnic Kukis, an expansionist tribe led for generations in the past by powerful chieftains (one among their several distinguishing characteristics). Similarly unique is the Baptist story of the Naga communities of Myanmar, whom the mission reached very late and whose peculiar location – both geographically and within a nation-state – distinguishes them from other Naga Baptists.

While keeping these caveats in mind, I focus primarily on the Nagas who inhabit the state of Nagaland in north-east India. My book aims to understand their religious life, socio-cultural changes, and political dynamics, mainly through an investigation and analysis of their Baptist history. There are sixteen official tribes in Nagaland, and this book deals to varying degrees with all of them.[16] A few are covered more extensively than the others owing to their greater involvement with the American Baptist mission and the British Raj. I have focused the historical and ethnographic

---

[16] The sixteen official tribes of Nagaland are Angami, Ao, Chakhesang, Chang, Kachari, Khiamniungan, Konyak, Kuki, Lotha, Phom, Pochury, Rengma, Sangtam, Sumi, Yimchunger, and Zeliang.

lens on several other variables to shed light on this community that I consider remarkable and uniquely interesting. I also locate the Naga Baptist faithful within larger Indian socio-political life and history, especially in the post-Independence period.

Broadly, the chapters can be divided into three sections. In the first and second chapters the Naga Baptists are located within the history and larger framework of British colonialism, Christian missions, and the rise of new nation-states. The first chapter gives a historical overview of the Baptist mission story against the backdrop of empire-building and clash of cultures to locate the Naga Baptists within the broader framework of "East meeting West". For conceptual clarity, I have used the term "Baptist highland" to understand the transnational character and location of the Naga Baptists in the second chapter.

The next three chapters are devoted to the Naga tribes of Nagaland. The core of these chapters is the Naga encounter with the American Baptist mission; here I explore the Baptist mission story of the different Naga communities and their experiences of a new faith which ushered in momentous changes. Descriptions based on both individual and community accounts have been analysed to understand contemporary issues facing ethnic Naga Baptists.

Chapters 6, 7, 8, and 9 are about the political and cultural changes facing Naga Baptists as seen in the light of modern history. This facet is explored to also highlight the fact that ethnic Nagas are no longer isolated. I contradict popular notions of them as a tight-knit group marooned from unprecedented social and political developments in the rest of India and the world. The chapters in this final section present "quasi-biographies" of Naga personalities who have been shaped by the Baptist faith and who could be considered stars in the Naga Baptist universe.

The book ends with a brief conclusion in which I mention the influence of Naga Baptists on other communities. This sheds some light on a new and wearisome reality of shifting inter-faith and inter-community relations which are of growing concern in Nagaland, as much as in India.

1

The Empire and the Pearly Gates

> The martyr missionary, Winfrid, of Germany,
> is said to have prayed in the eighth century:
> "O merciful God, who willest all men to be saved,
> And to come to the knowledge of the truth,
> Have mercy upon the Assamese,
> Hindus and Mohammedans.
> And all the inhabitants of Assam."
>
> – **Nathan Brown, missionary to Assam, 1890**

> There are certain populations in Europe whose unbelief is only equaled by their ignorance and debasement; while in America, one of the freest and most enlightened nations in the world, the people fulfill with fervor all the outward duties of religion.
>
> – **Alexis de Tocqueville, 1830s**

THE YEAR 1857 was a difficult one for the American Baptist mission in Assam. Grim news of the "sepoy uprising" in northern India had travelled upstream along the Brahmaputra, reaching the furthest Baptist mission station in Upper Assam. The mission had been in Assam for two decades, but its progress with conversions had been slow and laborious, and the number of heathens converted had been negligible. Long sweltering summers, outbreaks of tropical disease, and the death of personnel had put frequent spokes into the mission's wheel. The missionaries of the American Baptist Missionary Union (ABMU) had not heard such ominous news in a very long time.[1] You had to

---

[1] ABMU derives from "The General Missionary Convention of the Baptist Denomination in the United States of America for Foreign Missions", which

think back more than thirty years to recall a disaster as large – to when their brethren in Burma had been thrown into prison by a Burmese emperor during the First Anglo-Burmese War (1824–6): an American missionary duo, Adoniram Judson and Jonathan Price, had been arrested in Ava in 1824 and over the two years of the war the Baptists in America had lost all communication with their Burma missionaries.[2]

And then, only a few years later, in neighbouring British-annexed Assam, the East India Company had disempowered the Ahom dynasty, one of the longest ruling families in the Indian subcontinent. The last Ahom king, Purandar Singha, who in 1833 had been made a "protected prince" of Upper Assam – he paid an annual tribute of Rs 50,000 to the British – was ignominiously dethroned in 1838 and packed off into obscurity, ending a 600-year-old kingdom. The territory had then been annexed and made administratively a part of Bengal. Adding to missionary worries was the local political situation, which was precarious. There were regular raids by "wild" hill tribes and people's loyalties were divided in British-controlled Assam. It was thus no surprise that the American missionaries – who were by then familiar with the history, culture, and politics of the region – had every reason to feel perturbed at news of the 1857 developments in northern India.

---

was formed in Philadelphia on 21 May 1814 and was the foremost Protestant foreign mission organisation to emerge on American soil. Its name was changed to "American Baptist Missionary Union" in 1846, after the Southern Baptists moved out of the society in 1845 following disagreement over the issue of slavery among Baptists in the United States.

[2] Not knowing their fate, George Dana Boardman, who had been appointed as a missionary to Burma, remained in Calcutta for more than a year. After nearly two years of imprisonment the American missionaries returned to their old and now dilapidated mission house in Rangoon. When news of Judson and Price's release reached the Baptists in America, there was great relief and rejoicing. Accounts of the missionaries' hardships and resolute perseverance inspired many young people to join the mission enterprise; their travails had not dampened but rather reignited missionary zeal.

The American missionaries were not alone in their apprehension, for the Assam valley as a whole – which had been home to kingdoms such as the Kamarupa, Chutiya, Kachari, Koch, and Ahom before the East India Company became the sole power – was feeling the tremors of the native uprising in faraway Delhi, Meerut, and Lucknow. British officials of the time, such as Francis Jenkins and Charles Alexander Bruce, who were posted in the Assam region, were not only sympathetic to the Baptist mission, they saw it as an agency for civilising heathens. And the "civilisers", despite their efforts to distance themselves from the worldly realm of politics and empire-building, were often dragged into the conflicts rife in the region. Even the *Baptist Missionary Magazine*, usually parsimonious with words on political affairs in the areas of its foreign missions, had deemed matters serious enough to carry a four-page analysis of "The Revolt in India".[3] Therefore, like their predecessors in the early days of the Baptist mission in Burma, the missionaries in Assam were prepared for the worst.

They waited for the axe to fall in their area: "The streets of Cawnpore and Delhi ran blood, and the missionaries in Assam expected daily to share the fate of their brethren in Hindustan."[4] From the mission station in Nowgong, Miles Bronson wrote to the secretary of the Home Board, Solomon Peck, about religious disaffection among the "Sipahis" as being common to both "Hindoos and the Mussulmans", hinting at a malaise in Assam similar to the one in the mutinous heartland.[5] A Baptist missionary in Guwahati likened the simmering tension in his town to that of "living on the very crater of a smoking volcano".[6] The organ of

---

[3] *Baptist Missionary Magazine* (hereafter *BMM*), Vol. XXXVII, No. 10 (October 1857), 379–82.

[4] Quoted in Chaplin, *Our Gold-Mine*, 313.

[5] Letter from Bronson to Peck, Nowgong, 4 June 1857, in Barpujari, *The American Missionaries*, 63.

[6] Letter from Danforth to Peck, Gowahati, 15 September 1857, in Barpujari, *The American Missionaries*, 67.

the American Baptist foreign mission expressed its apprehensions as well: "The cause of the outbreak was thought at first by many to be simply of a religious character . . . [but sepoys more than] jealous for their religion" were, it had been ascertained, the main cause of the mutiny. The American Baptist missionaries in Assam, it is clear, feared a backlash from natives who, they believed, made no distinction between the agents of a British imperial Company and those preaching a new religion.

Though the British in Assam did not anticipate a full-blown rebellion like the one in north India, suspicion and unease were in the air. The American missionaries, who had finally made some progress after initial setbacks in gaining a foothold, shared the apprehensions of their fellow white men. Ever since the British had hoisted the Union Jack in the plains of Assam, the natives had harboured attitudes ranging from glowering ambivalence to outright hostility. And while the 1857 mutiny storm had not reached Assam, the missionaries feared that violence might engulf the region at any time. So, "for six months, Mr Danforth," the lone Baptist missionary at Guwahati, "drilled daily, in soldier garb, in full view of a large company of mutinous Sepoys, that he might be prepared to defend his family and the mission property to the last."[7] Danforth had joined a volunteer corps at Guwahati which included magistrates, chaplains, clerks, missionaries, and civilians – formed for their protection.[8]

By 1843 the American Baptists had established three mission stations – at Guwahati, Nowgong, and Sivasagar.[9] In the summer of 1857 Guwahati became a place of refuge for missionaries, tea planters, and other white civilians who came in droves to this well-secured British settlement. Fortunately for the American Baptist

---

[7] See Chaplin, *Our Gold-Mine*, 313–14.

[8] An excellent fictional rendering of these scenarios of white people feeling besieged and huddling into enclaves at this time can be found in J.G. Farrell's *The Siege of Krishnapur* (1973).

[9] The first mission was in fact established at Sadiya in 1838, but had to be aborted, as described below.

mission, the Sepoy Mutiny (or the First War of Independence as it was later called) did not have much impact in the Brahmaputra valley. Assam, despite being an important centre of Vaishnavism, had complex ethnic relations, an intricate history, and an intriguing politics all its own. It was distinct from northern India despite the fact that Indic civilisation had flourished in the Assam valley for centuries, and the river Brahmaputra ("son of Brahma"), the source of life for valley dwellers, had Sanskritic origin myths.

No loss of life or property was reported from the Assam Baptist mission stations, but the repercussions of the mutiny debilitated mission work. Rev. Whiting, the missionary at Sivasagar station, feared for his life and remained hidden for a while on the north bank of the Brahmaputra; the Bronsons of Nowgong escaped in a small boat to Guwahati, on their way to America; other missionaries in Assam went on furlough. By 1858 there was only one missionary, Rev. Danforth, left in the Assam mission field.

II

The year 1858 flung more adverse news at the American missionaries of Assam: the Baptist mission, having just recuperated from the perturbation of the sepoy uprising, was asked to close down. It had been twenty years since two Burma missionaries, Nathan Brown and O.T. Cutter, had established the first Assam mission station in Sadiya, in Upper Assam. Their effort had been cut short by an attack on the British garrison there by tribal Khamtis of the region in January 1839.[10] However, as mentioned earlier, by 1843 the American Baptists had three mission stations going in the plains of Assam, and by 1851 there were 3 churches with 85 members and 4 schools with 112 students.[11]

Education had been by far the most successful entry point for the American Baptist missionaries into this alien culture that

---

[10] The circumstances of the attack are more fully described later in this chapter.

[11] See Downs, *The Mighty Works of God*, 34.

they sought to evangelise. Schools formed the vanguard of their mission, imparting reading and writing skills while driving home religious ideas. Over a period of time this dual-pronged teach-and-preach approach had enabled the missionaries to inculcate in the natives a new way of viewing the world. Even among supposedly "wild" hill tribes like the Garo, Singpho, and Naga, the missionaries were able to set up schools without much resistance. Miles Bronson, who was on furlough in America following the sepoy uprising, was disheartened by the thought that the Assam mission field would be shut down; hadn't he started a school among the "Nám Sang Nágas" – spoken of by people in the plains as headhunters – at the request of a Naga chief who wanted the missionaries to educate his sons? It was a separate matter that mission work in the remote Naga village had had to be abandoned because of his illness and the death of his sister and helper Rhoda Bronson. He appealed tirelessly to the Board of Missions not to close down operations in Assam, arguing that the mission would yield a rich harvest in due time. The Assam mission was saved, but it received little support from the ABMU. The crisis, which some Baptist historians would name their "darkest hour", had begun in 1851.[12] The problem was largely the result of severe financial depression in America in the early 1850s, which meant shrinking funds for foreign missions. Baptist contributions toward the Board of Missions fell nearly 30 per cent between 1852 and 1862.[13] Already by 1845 a schism over the issue of slavery had split the American Baptists into Northern and Southern blocs, and the funds for overseas missions had been cut by more than half, with only the Northern Baptists funding the Assam mission. Practically speaking, it would have been reasonable to shut down the Assam mission, which would have meant shutting printing presses and schools as well. It was sheer good luck that the

---

[12] Ibid., esp. Chapter 5.
[13] The precise figures being $108,186.55 in 1852 and $73,770.03 in 1862.

missionaries in Assam happened to be on the right side of history and scraped through this period of crisis. Assam in fact went on to become an American Baptist mission success story, especially among the hill tribes of the uplands.

Disagreements over strategies in alien cultures were almost part of daily discussions in Baptist missions, and a controversy that arose at this time over the instrumental necessity of schools for missionary activity threatened to imperil the mission in Assam. The investment of funds, time, and effort in schools – rather than in preaching and related evangelical activities – became a bone of contention between missionaries in the field and the Board of Missions. Baptist mission strategists in America were not willing to concede that missionaries overseas had to negotiate cultural barriers in order to evangelise natives, and that the New Testament pattern of evangelism in America did not apply in Africa and Asia. Against this view, the missionaries in Burma and Assam argued that educating natives was indispensable for evangelism because schools allowed a long-term relationship with the natives. But, on his visit to Assam in 1854 to settle the issue, the secretary of the Board of Missions, Solomon Peck, decided more converts might have been won had the missionaries not been tied down by school work. The missionaries were dejected by this response to their case studies from all three Assam mission stations, which showed that the road to salvation was best assured by a road through the school. A fallout of this was that the Orphan Institution at Nowgong – the most effective institution of the Assam Baptist mission – was asked to close down, and its founder and caretaker Miles Bronson was asked to continue running a "teachers training centre"; but even for this, funds were not made available.

Nathan Brown, the first Assam missionary, criticised this policy of the Board of Missions. He wrote strongly worded letters to the Baptist churches in America opposing the move, for which his reward was to be recalled home. He resigned from the ABMU while in America – unlike his compatriot Miles Bronson, who decided to carry on with mission work in Assam.

III

Whether in Assam, Burma, or China, the American Baptist mission had to contend with the reigning empire to gain a foothold and then keep a foot in the door. In China the imperial government pursued a policy of excluding foreign missionaries. Even as missionaries were devising strategies to "plant Christianity in the heart of the empire... jealous mandarins were excluding foreigners from the ports."[14] Baptist missionaries in Burma who had their eye on China had to find an alternative route to penetrate the heart of imperium there. Because "there was once a trade route between Sadiya and China",[15] Assam appeared to them a timely gift from, ironically, the very Company that had once driven out American missionaries from their territories in British India.[16] A report from the Assam mission field underscored the significance of a mission station in Upper Assam:

> The first object of opening a mission in Assam was ultimately to reach Northern Burmah and Western China, with the intervening tribes. The Khamptis or Shans, the Singphos and Nagas, living directly on the route to China, have been reached, and some books have been prepared for them. And now just as surveys are being made for a highway from the valley of the Brahmaputra to Western China through Northern Burmah, these people are beginning to ask for teachers, and are more than willing to listen wherever our native preachers go with the Gospel.[17]

The entry of Protestant missions into China coincided with the rise of European powers, especially Great Britain, in the nineteenth century. In 1724, Christianity had been outlawed by the emperor

---

[14] Gammell, *A History of American Baptist Missions*, 212.

[15] Letter from Mr Clark, *BMM*, Vol. LI, No. 12 (December 1871), 442.

[16] The Judsons landed in Calcutta on 17 June 1812 and were baptised in Lal Bazaar Chapel, thereby turning Baptists on Indian soil. However, they had to leave Calcutta on the orders of the British East India Company, which did not want American missionaries evangelising in their territory.

[17] Fifty-Eighth Annual Report, *BMM*, Vol. LII, No. 7 (July 1872), 264.

as an evil cult, which had greatly hindered the religion's spread, and the embargo on the movement of Christian missions had continued. In 1814 – a year after the first American missionary disembarked in Rangoon – the Chinese emperor issued a punitive decree that those spreading the gospel "shall be sentenced to death by immediate strangulation", while native converts were to be sent off as slaves to the "Mohammedan cities".[18]

The Baptist Convention had been deliberating for some time on the possibility of expanding the mission in the East, since they had only one major mission field in Burma and a small outpost in Bangkok, Siam. Interest in the China mission was partly because of success in evangelising the Chinese expatriates of Bangkok by the Baptist missionary John T. Jones. But taking the gospel to mainland China required more strategy than will: the Chinese authorities had closed their eastern coastal cities to foreigners. Their strict vigilance on the eastern coast made the unguarded southern border a possible entry point into the country. Entering China from Burma would have been more feasible than via an outpost in Assam, but the Burmese emperor had prohibited missionary activity in the regions bordering China; this had also prevented missionary work among the Shan tribes of northern Burma. Thus the possibility of an Assam outpost raised hopes among the American Baptists about a China mission. As time passed, however, they realised that the difficulty was not so much the route as ethnic complexity and political challenges in the frontier region: Assam proved as complex and onerous as China or Burma in relation to the mission expansion effort.

Elsewhere in contiguous regions, this was a phase of great optimism for the American Baptist mission, which was basking in its success among the ethnic Karens of Burma, whose receptivity to the gospel had been heartening. A grand Baptist vision for the East is encapsulated in this historical account: ". . . it was expected that a chain of missionary posts might be established among kindred

---

[18] See Maclay, *Life Among the Chinese*, 337.

races, commencing in Siam and stretching through the Tenasserim provinces and the Burman empire into Assam, – and thus circling the western frontiers of China with influences and agencies that must sooner or later penetrate its hitherto impassable barriers."[19] It soon became apparent to the Baptist missionaries that launching an inland China mission from Upper Assam was not feasible. Early in their stay there, they had been put through the test of ethnic and political disturbances in the north-eastern frontier in Assam. As briefly noted earlier, in 1839 one of the Tai-speaking groups, the Khamtis, had attacked the garrison of the new British rulers in Sadiya. In the aftermath of the Khamti attack the American mission had had to abandon their mission station in this British outpost, which they had only recently opened to target "the Assamese peoples, the Kamtis or Shans, and the Singphos".[20]

The reality dawned on these missionaries that with regard to racial composition, language, and beliefs Assam was a microcosm of the Indian mainland. Here were groups speaking languages of the Indo-Aryan, Austro-Asiatic, and Tibeto-Burman families; the history of Hinduism and Buddhism in Assam was as old as the rise of the earliest kingdoms in the Brahmaputra valley; and Islam had arrived during the expedition of Muhammad Bakhtiyar Khalji in the thirteenth century. In the Assam valley a vibrant variety of goddess worship was best visible in the Kamakhya cult, and a Hindu system of social stratification had been in place for centuries. In the fifteenth century a reformist Vaishnavism had swept the land, augmenting the political and religious diversity of the region. In Bengal, English Baptists had had to evangelise a primarily Hindu society, but in Assam American Baptists had to work with two different communities: those weaned on the Sanskritic tradition, and "primitive" hill tribes with varied pantheons and beliefs far removed from Hindu civilisation.

[19] Gammell, *A History of American Baptist Missions*, 213.
[20] *BMM*, Vol. LXXXI, No. 6 (June 1901), 208.

Abandoning the Sadiya station had come as a blow to the Baptist missionaries because "The people among whom they originally designed to establish the mission were the Khamtis, who had been represented as the most interesting portion of the population, and as decidedly superior to the Burmans in intelligence and character."[21] Besides, they had misjudged the linguistic parallelism between Assam and Burma. Linguistic diversity among the ethnic groups would become an issue among native converts, especially with regard to Bible translation. Translation work was at the heart of the Baptist mission undertaking; in fact, the Protestant mission in the East was unthinkable without the printing press. So the American Baptists had made a languge plan for their mission field in Assam:

> The language of the Shyan was similar to the Burman, and might be easily acquired by a missionary who had resided in that empire, while the characters used in printing were essentially the same. The plan seemed also likely to promote a nearer access to the Chinese than had hitherto been attained, under the exclusive policy at that time pursued by the imperial government.[22]

The linguistic element featured prominently in what came to be known as "a great Central Asian strategy in which all of the Baptist centres from there [Sadiya] down to Bangkok would participate."[23]

This grandiose evangelical project targeted a Tai ethnic group known as the Shan; indeed the Baptist mission to Assam that first settled in Sadiya came to be known as the Shan mission. Its main purpose was not merely to evangelise but also serve as an outpost from which to preach the message to the Shan tribes of northern Burma and southern China. Thus, full of hope, the two American missionaries Oliver Cutter and Nathan Brown, after a stopover in Calcutta, spent much of their time learning the Shan language as they travelled upstream on the Brahmaputra to Sadiya in 1836.

[21] Gammell, *A History of American Baptist Missions*, 214.
[22] Ibid., 212.
[23] Downs, *The Mighty Works of God*, 15.

The Baptists had presumed that "an estimated 170 million Shans" shared a more or less common tongue.[24] On reaching Assam they discovered that the Shan they spoke was not understood by the Khamtis and Singphos, and barely resembled the Shan spoken in northern Burma. Also, while the Singphos were accessible from Sadiya, they lived some distance away from the plains. So an immediate request was made to the Board of Missions to send more missionaries to man an outstation close to Sadiya – in today's Changlang district of Arunachal Pradesh – to start work among the Singphos. In response, Jacob Thomas and Miles Bronson were sent as reinforcements to Sadiya. This was to establish American Baptists in the north-eastern frontier of India – an attempt not without hurdles.

By the time the American Baptist missionaries entered British Assam in 1836, the attitude of the authorities towards them had changed substantially from the time of the Judsons' expulsion. It also spoke volumes of the policy change in the British East India Company towards the religion of the natives – for a long time earlier the policy had been non-interference. The reason for the change lay in a fervent religious revival, the epicentre of which was, as noted, the Clapham Sect in London. A British historian later said that "the moral transformation of the British Empire began in Holy Trinity Church, on the north side of Clapham Common."[25] The sect was in fact uncommonly influential and helped alter the Company's religious policy.

IV

In America, the Great Revival or Second Great Awakening at the beginning of the nineteenth century featured various strains of Protestant pietism. In the north-east of the country the revival movement was characterised by preaching, church attendance, prayer, and Bible study – some of the basic Christian virtues.

[24] Ibid.
[25] Ferguson, *Empire*, 116.

Another manifestation of the revivalism was also the emergence of voluntary associations that changed the face of American Protestantism, and of countries in which these associations began to spread the Word. This was a concerted effort to reform society and the world at large. Sending missionaries abroad was likened to a rescue mission which required not only individual volunteers but also a collective undertaking. This outlook, which is the heart of the evangelical worldview, was also the heart of the mission-based organisations that soon proliferated. In America the Great Awakening was a force to reckon with in part because its emergence coincided with a nation – and the West more generally – moving rapidly towards industrialisation and technological development.

Aboard the *Cashmere* in 1834 were sixteen missionaries making the passage to Burma. Twenty years had passed since the first American missionaries had landed on Burmese soil in 1813; now, for the first time, a ship was sailing direct from Boston to Burma without transit through Calcutta. The *Cashmere* was a first-rate vessel, carved out of timber from the Maine forests.[26] Unlike industrialised England, from which it imported most goods, America did not at this point have large manufacturing enterprises. But the country, being blessed with first-grade timber and other raw materials, had set up a large shipbuilding industry that rivalled its British counterpart. In 1773, at the peak of the Great Awakening and the surging interest in evangelism among Baptists, the shipyards of America had built 683 ocean-going vessels that would be perfected over time; more would cross the Atlantic over the decades.[27] The booming shipbuilding industry was crucial to the success of the overseas missions of American Baptists; in fact, Christians in the West generally saw the enabling of evangelism as an outcome of religious belief.[28] Baptist missionaries in places like Assam and Burma perceived Western civilisation as insepa-

---

[26] Howard, *Baptists in Burma*, 16.
[27] See Bureau of the Census, 1955, Vol. 2, Table Z 294.
[28] Stark, *For the Glory of God*.

rable from Christianity: an Assam missionary making cultural comparisons between "the Hill Tribes and the plains peoples" felt "Civilization without God is a very doubtful good. A civilized evil is no better for being civilized."[29]

The *Cashmere* took about 157 days to reach Burma.[30] The time taken was not the chief difficulty; the journey was arduous because of poor amenities and a limited diet; scurvy and disease were common; months of monotonous seafaring took a toll on mental well-being. The diary of Jonathan Wade, a Baptist missionary on board the *Cashmere*, outlines the travails.

> December 3: Still at sea and our circumstances are becoming truly alarming. Four of the men are laid by with the scurvy, and the disease is making sweeping work. Some others of the men are scarcely able to keep up. Our cook is among the number of those laid by. The steward is complaining of the symptoms of the incipient stage of the disease, so are three of the officers (though they are ashamed to own the fact) and the greater part or at least half of the passengers are in the same state, some of whom have been complaining for the last two or three weeks.[31]

What awaited them when they disembarked was often more perilous. Between 1804 and 1825, out of 89 English missionaries who went to West Africa, 54 died and 14 went home ill.[32] Preaching to heathens involved risks, but the number of missionaries killed by natives was negligible; malaria and other tropical diseases killed far more, and those in luck only suffered a nervous breakdown. The saving grace was to be able to attribute all that happened to a divine plan, which allowed many missionaries to persevere and endure incredible levels of affliction.

---

[29] Perrine, "The Value of the Wild Men of India", *BMM*, Vol. LXXXI, No. 6 (June 1901), 212.

[30] By 1884 the time spent at sea was reduced to 58 days, and to 15 days by air in 1944.

[31] See Howard, *Baptists in Burma*, 18–19.

[32] Headrick, *The Tools of Empire*, 63.

The mortality rate among missionaries in the East decreased considerably toward the latter half of the nineteenth century: advancements in Western medicine manifest as antibiotics and quinine could now serve the purpose schools had earlier. Medicines perceived as miraculous enhanced the credibility of miracles by Jesus described in the Bible and played a felicitous role in the bid for converts. "In July I did little besides preaching and doctoring... Many listened to my words with more or less interest, and I know I was able to do much good to the sick. How often have I longed for that divine power which in the early days wrought cures by a word," wrote a missionary in the British Naga Hills on the practical significance of Western medicine.[33]

European empire-builders had battled malaria, but thanks to Ronald Ross' pioneering work Western medicine gradually conquered the mosquitoes in the swamps and wetlands of Asia and Africa. In a remote corner of the Indian north-east frontier, Hattie Rivenburg, the wife of a medical missionary stationed in the Naga Hills district, wrote:

> In Kohima many thousands die or are incapacitated for many months with malaria fever, which exists in its most virulent form. Dr Rivenburg had the great joy and privilege of working in Calcutta with Dr Ronald Ross when he worked out the proof of the theory that mosquitoes carry the germ of that dread disease. So highly did Dr Ross value the services of Dr Rivenburg that he offered to pay all of Dr Rivenburg's expenses in order to secure further help in research work in Sierra Leone in 1907. By draining swamps and pools near Kohima, the scourge of malaria was greatly reduced by the British government in later years.[34]

The improvement in communications which arrived with the invention of the telegraph in 1837 made another big difference. In the 1830s a Baptist missionary in Upper Assam had to wait months for a letter from Calcutta; by 1859 submarine cables from

---

[33] *BMM*, Vol. LXXI, No. 1 (January 1891), 19.
[34] Rivenburg, ed., *The Star of Naga Hills*, 90.

Britain to India transformed imperial communications. In 1868 a missionary from the "Gowahati" mission reported that "The telegraph has been completed to this place, and we are within speaking distance of Boston."³⁵ By the last quarter of the nineteenth century the British were "laying a telegraph line from Kohima in the Naga hills through the Angami Naga country across Manipur and down the Chindwin valley in Burma, to Ava or Mandalay."³⁶

The American Baptist overseas missions were plentifully endowed with abled-bodied men zealous for mission work. Around them was a flourishing seafaring enterprise and a nation with an expanding economy and improving communications system. All this was conducive to exporting ideas, including religious ones. The winds of Christian revival in the West raised scores of volunteers – many the finest products of Western seminaries. But it was centrally the economy that facilitated the extraordinary increase in missionary activity: a Protestant nation was rediscovering the Christian dictum of preaching the Word to all nations (Matthew 28: 18) over a time of economic prosperity, and the new religious fervour was connected to a sense of financial well-being. Charity perhaps always begins at home when times are straitened, but purse strings are more easily loosened when there seems plenty to distribute – when there seems more than enough at home, the poor and the benighted in distant lands come more easily to mind. The religiosity of the Americans with the Great Awakening seems to have surpassed that of the Europeans; de Tocqueville noted that "there is not a country in the world where the Christian religion retains a greater influence over the souls of men than in America."³⁷

To American Baptists the overseas mission was a divine calling, a direct consequence of Christian belief. It was as if having showered them with money, God now wanted them to use it to save

---

³⁵ *BMM*, Vol. XLVII, No. 11 (December 1868), 262.

³⁶ See Assam Mission Jubilee, 1886 conference: paper and discussion, in Ao, *History of Christianity in Nagaland*, 84.

³⁷ de Tocqueville, *Democracy in America*, 314.

the souls of those who hadn't the foggiest who Jesus was. By 1900 there were 5278 American Protestant missionaries serving abroad, in comparison to 5656 missionaries from Great Britain – this despite the fact that it was Britain that dominated substantial regions of the world.[38] And this was, moreover, in a period when the progress of America toward a free-market economy and the powerhouse of capitalism was still to come; America still had "people [who] were poor, and without the resources or the opportunities of financial accumulation which exist in more modern life."[39] The larger context was, all the same, of expansion, growth, technological advance, improvements in travel, and promising medical discoveries. Pockets of poverty have never disappeared altogether and never will; so there was no overpowering deterrent against zealous American evangelicals responding to the call for mission abroad.

The various Protestant denominations in America were not all equally highly regarded:

> Among the people of the United States in 1812 the Baptists occupied a humble position. The social prestige of founders of the State enjoyed by the Congregationalists in Massachusetts, by the Dutch churches in New York, by the Friends in Pennsylvania, and by the Episcopalians in Virginia, belonged to the Baptists only in the small state of Rhode Island; and even here they were torn by divisions on minor points, remnants of which remain to the present day.[40]

Despite these constraints, the American Baptist missions had an inherent advantage: there was little interference by the state in the religious conduct of its citizens. American evangelicals had successfully implemented a New Testament dictum – "render unto Caesar the things that are Caesar's, and unto God the things that are God's" – as a policy for preaching and spreading the faith. Besides, American Baptist missionaries enjoyed full freedom to

---

[38] See Beach, *A Geography and Atlas of Protestant Missions*.
[39] Merriam, *A History of American Baptist Missions*, 4.
[40] Ibid., 3–4.

propagate their religion; in this they had the advantage over British evangelicals, whose work was often impeded by the exigencies of empire-building.

V

One Sunday evening in 1836, Nathan Brown rushed home after his sermon in the English chapel in Moulmein; his infant son William had been ill for some days. The family of four was due to board a vessel for Calcutta early Monday morning. Their final destination was Assam, recently acquired by the British from the Burmese. Baby William succumbed to his illness; he passed away at seven in the morning. The Browns arranged a hasty funeral at twelve noon, presided over by the Burma veteran Adoniram Judson, who not long ago had lost his wife and infant daughter "in the service of Burma" and who comforted the grieving parents at the funeral. At five o'clock that evening, Nathan Brown with his wife Eliza and little daughter Sophia, together with the Cutters, embarked for Calcutta. Nathan Brown had been in Moulmein for almost two years. Since his arrival he had learnt the Burmese language, and it was his knack for languages that had qualified him to be sent to Assam on a mission to the Shan.[41]

Born in Ipswich, New Hampshire, Brown was educated at Williams College and trained at Newton Theological Institution. In 1832 he was appointed by the Baptist Board of Foreign Missions to join Judson in Burma. Two years into the service, Nathan Brown and Oliver Cutter were assigned to the newest mission field to be set up in British territory.

The people they were supposed to evangelise were fiercely independent races along the Himalayan belt, so the new mission venture in the foothills of Assam was fraught with difficulties. From Ava, the "hero missionary" Eugenio Kincaid had travelled to the region: "After obtaining all the information he could

[41] See Downs, *The Mighty Works of God*, esp. Chapter 3.

concerning the position of their county, he conceived the plan of a tour of exploration, to extend, if possible, as far as the borders of China and the frontiers of Assam." Kincaid was advised thus by two Burmese noblemen: "If you wish to go to Assam, go by the way of Bengal; that is a good way." But in 1837 he left for the northern reaches of Burma's unexplored territory to "give books" to the natives.[42] Kincaid's perilous journey would be the last time a member of the American Baptist mission would chart a pathway in an attempt to unite northern Burma, Assam, and China into a single Baptist mission field.

The Burma Baptist missionaries had hopes of their new mission in Assam and beyond. Expressing optimism, Adoniram Judson,[43] the pioneering Burma missionary, wrote home on 11 June 1835:

> Brother Brown embraced the proposal with instant enthusiasm, not merely because of the above advantages; for Assam presents a splendid opening for missionary efforts . . . my heart leaps for joy and glows with gratitude and praise to God, when I think of Brother Jones at Bankok, in the southern extremity of the continent, and Brother Brown at Sudiya in Assam, on the frontiers of China – immensely distant points – and of all the intervening stations, Ava, Rangoon, Kyouk Phyoo, Moulmein and Tavoy, and the churches and schools which are springing up in every station, and throughout the Karen wilderness.[44]

The first Baptist missionaries visualised Assam as a launchpad from where "the Brahmaputra Valley might prove a highway for the gospel of Christ to Western China and Tibet".[45] The British, for their part, were prompted by administrative as well as religious

---

[42] Webb, *Incidents and Trials in the Life of Rev. Eugenio Kincaid*, 87.

[43] Born on 9 August 1788 in Malden, Mass., Adoniram Judson – who was raised as a Congregationalist – was among the core members that initiated the first foreign mission society in American history. As noted above, he and his wife Ann Hasseltine Judson turned Baptists on Indian soil and were the first American missionaries to land in Rangoon in 1813.

[44] Brown, *The Whole World Kin*, 101.

[45] Merriam, *A History of American Baptist Missions*, 129.

motives in inviting the Baptists to Assam. The commissioner and agent to the governor general, Francis Jenkins, had decided to allow American Baptist missionaries to work among the "wild" hill tribes. For generations, the tribes settled in the hilly ranges flanking the Brahmaputra valley had been involved in skirmishes with the kingdoms in the plains. As in Burma, these tribes had been raiding the plains and taking people captive; in one incident, "a single British officer is said to have received and released from the Singphos 5,000 Assamese captured by them for slaves."[46] Slave raiding was not new to these parts; many powerful tribes living in the mountainous region between the Brahmaputra and Chindwin were involved in the trade. And the Khamti, a Tai-speaking people whom the Baptists missionaries intended to evangelise, were notorious for raiding settlements in the plains.

The American Baptist missionaries were divided over the benevolence and contribution of the British; Assam mission stalwarts like Brown and Bronson were critical of the patronage of the British government, which they felt came with ulterior motives. Expressing reservations over the government's patronage of the mission, Nathan Brown wrote to the Board:

> It is true a good deal of interest has been manifested by Capt. Jenkins and other officers of the Government, and liberal donations have been offered by them and also directly by the Government, but I have long since suspected that one great object in urging us on amongst these savage mountain tribes, who have never yet acknowledged their subjection to the English rule, is that we may be the instruments of extending their sway over them. The various presents which the Government are making to the Nagas through the hands of Bro. Bronson will confirm them in their suspicions that we are the agents of the Company, that we cooperate in all their measures, and are the means of bringing them under the yoke.[47]

---

[46] Ibid., 118.
[47] Letter from Brown to Peck, 16 February 1841, in Puthenpurakal, *Baptist Missions in Nagaland*, 53.

Nonetheless, the benevolence of Francis Jenkins and other British residents stationed in Assam proved of great help to the Baptist missionaries. This was especially so during the initial years of establishing the mission in Assam, despite a good number of British political agents disapproving of the Baptist missions. Some administrator-ethnographers would become strident critics of the Baptist mission among ethnic groups like the Nagas, blaming mission influence for eroding tribal cultures and traditional ways of life. As for the English Baptist missionaries in Calcutta, who had in fact forwarded the proposal to the Burma missionaries to start the mission in Assam, their support to their American Baptist brethren was invaluable; their timely help, moral support, and guidance in logistics helped the nascent American Baptist mission. The English Baptist mission at Serampore would become a place of refuge for American missionaries during times of political turmoil and personal loss, and a haven for convalescents.

The objective of the American Baptist mission was to "rescue the perishing", give the "good news of Jesus", and save as many souls as possible. Their core message was about the coming Kingdom of God, not the glory and riches of this world, although they melded social work with evangelism. In essence, this Christian message of a happiness forever impending was otherworldly. The American Baptist missions gained some advantages from the new welcome given them by British rule, but the very nature of their message made it necessary for them to maintain a distance from the worldly affairs of the British empire.

The Company's primary focus on material gain for itself was always in the long run exploitative; even if colonialism stimulated sectors of the economy and benefited some locals, imperial rule basically meant Indians were grist to the British mill. In this respect the missionary endeavour – which provided concrete help to a community via schooling, medicine, and related welfare measures while promising subsequent personal salvation to every individual if only he accepted Jesus as his Lord – was at variance with British political agents and their policies. In some places mission work positively exasperated officials, who accused missionaries of interfering in the recognition by natives that they were now primarily a European Caesar's subjects to whom they had to render what may have once been theirs but was now his; Jesus was the Lord, but allegiance to him came second. Also, some official irritation with the missionaries will have been because, at least before the Clapham Sect became a force to reckon with, British policies had advocated minimal interference in the religion and cultural practices of natives.[48] No British missionary had been allowed to work in British enclaves; in fact the first English Baptist missionary, William Carey of the Baptist Mission Society, initially worked as a manager in an indigo plantation to evade eviction. In 1793, when the news reached the authorities that Carey had crossed the oceans to serve as a missionary, he was transferred from a British ship to a Danish boat, reaching Indian shores as an unwelcome guest, if not an intruder. To work as a missionary he had to settle in the Danish territory of Serampore, the Danish Protestant mission being far away in Tranquebar – non-British territory. News of the undaunted and intelligently evasive efforts of English Baptists and of the exploits of their missionaries, such as Carey, reached their fellow Baptists on the other side of the Atlantic and was unsurprisingly inspiring.

Evidence of the considerable influence of the English Baptist mission on the first American Protestant mission overseas came when, on 6 September 1812, Rev. William Ward of the English Baptist mission baptised Adoniram Judson and his wife Ann Judson in a small chapel at Calcutta. The fame of the Serampore missionaries had spread to the extent that a Baptist mission station along the borders of Michigan, among the Potawatomi tribe, had been named "Carey". The English Baptists were the pathfinders out East; the American Baptists sniffed success for themselves by

---

[48] See Frykenberg, "Christian Missions and the Raj", in Etherington, ed., *Missions and Empire*, 109.

keeping track of "the early movements, trials, and successes of the English Baptist mission in India".[49]

Print, and the culture that arose from the dissemination of printed literature, were among the main thrusts of the mission enterprise. The Massachusetts Baptist Missionary Society, which held its first meeting on 26 May 1802, started the *Massachusetts Baptist Missionary Magazine* to publish mainly reports, correspondence, and letters from missionaries stationed at home and abroad. In its issues were accounts received from, among many, William Carey, Joshua Marshman, and William Ward in Serampore, making it "the chief instrument in fostering the rising enthusiasm for missions among American Baptists."[50] This first Baptist periodical was renamed the *American Baptist Magazine* in 1817, and it then became the *Baptist Missionary Magazine* (*BMM*) in 1836. Reports from Burma and the Assam Baptist missions were regularly published in the *BMM* for readers at home.

VI

To evangelicals, Assam was a land of plenty but debauched, and "likened in old times to a sort of Paphian land, the seat of promiscuous pleasure".[51] The American Baptist mission portrayed the Assam mission field as sitting atop rich natural resources:

> We are in Assam, a country where almost every thing might be done, and nothing is. Its forests offer material for building any thing, from a basket to a temple; its ground holds out perpetual cards of invitation in the shape of petroleum, coal, cotton, grain, spices, tea, and the fruits of both torrid and temperate climates; there are *eri*-trees for silk-worms, and *bargach*-trees for India-rubber, and trees bearing varnish and gums, and dye-stuffs of many colors. No wonder the old Brahmans, when, centuries before, they brought their gods here, fancied that the county took its name from Asama, 'unrivalled.'

---

[49] Merriam, *A History of American Baptist Missions*, 6.
[50] Ibid., 7.
[51] Shakespear, *History of Upper Assam*, 75.

The problem, as the first Baptist missionaries saw it, was that Assam was riddled with the benighted . . .

> . . . a people poor and ignorant, leaving all their thinking to be done by the priests; a priesthood, busiest in reaching out long arms to rake in rupees and annas, and in inventing new falsehoods with which to repay the trust of the people; the whole country one vast Sodom; above it, all the swarm of gods worshipped in costly temples, by rites only less vile than their own histories; and around and binding all, the terrible chain of caste.[52]

With the coming of the East India Company, the territorial area denoted by "Assam" was divided into three distinct regions: the Brahmaputra valley forming the northern part, the Surma valley forming the southern part, and the hill range.

The Brahmaputra valley had been for centuries the domain of three kingdoms – namely the Chutiyas, the Kacharis, and the Koch – before the Ahoms came and defeated them. Upper Assam became the Ahom seat of rule, which diminished over time, with Jorhat being the last Ahom capital. It was in the Ahom heartland, Upper Assam, that the American Baptist mission established its first mission station. It then gradually radiated toward the central region which included Nowgong and Guwahati, the latter an important port on the southern bank of the Brahmaputra. The distance between the Guwahati mission station in Lower Assam and the furthest Baptist mission station in Sivasagar in Upper Assam was roughly 400 km.

Guwahati had been the ancient capital of the Kamarupa kingdom and an important pilgrimage place for the worship of a powerful goddess. Its Kamakhya temple was built, according to legend, on a spot where the most fecund body part of the goddess Shakti fell, making it perhaps the most potent tantric centre in the subcontinent. Stories about human sacrifices made to the goddess of the temple atop a rocky hill overlooking the city naturally could

---

[52] Chaplin, *Our Gold-Mine*, 297.

Map 3: Divisions of Assam Showing Important Places in American Baptist Mission History.

not escape the notice of the American missionaries. Hinduism in Assam had coexisted with Buddhism and become the dominant religion by the ninth century. Some Western observers attributed the tantric Hinduism in the Assam valley to "a blend of Hindu beliefs with the more crude and bloodthirsty rites of the primitive hill tribes, who invaded the valley from time to time."[53] However, Hinduism stopped at the foothills and the Khasi hill tribes who embraced Christianity in large numbers remained unaffected by the potent Kamakhya cult, although they lived in hills close to Guwahati.

A decade after the sepoy uprising of 1857, Ira J. Stoddard, the Baptist missionary at the Guwahati mission station, described the city as "a place of universal beauty, and picturesque in the highest degree. I cannot now name a place on the wonderful Hudson that can surpass it in natural scenery." He noted that "the telegraph has been completed in the city" and so missionaries "are within speaking distance of Boston". Communications had improved in other ways too: "a railroad from Calcutta has been finished shortening the distance, in time, one-half to Gowahati"; and "four steamers a month instead of one a few years ago" now transported goods and people through the Brahmaputra riverway.[54]

Nowgong, birthplace of the neo-Vaishnavite reformer and founder of the Ekasarna Dharma movement Srimanta Sankaradev, came under Burmese rule in 1822 and into British possession in 1826. In 1832 it was carved out as a separate administrative unit. According to one British report, Nowgong showed the presence of diverse faith groups. Its population of over 200,000 was said to be enlightened, "and considerable numbers of them were Mussalmans".[55] The Baptist mission station in Nowgong started toward the close of 1843; schools were opened in all the mission stations, and Bronson, who started the Nowgong Orphan

---

[53] Thomson, *Assam Valley*, 46.
[54] See *BMM*, Vol. XLVII, No. 11 (December 1868), 258–62.
[55] Barpujari, *The American Missionaries*, xxix.

Institution in that year, "aimed at collecting from all parts of the province orphans and destitutes of either sex and to train them up under Christian influence knowledge of useful occupation and of the gospel."[56]

The evangelism and charitable works of the Baptist mission attracted some criticism and suspicion; the missionaries were accused of working hand-in-glove with the British government and enticing people with cash to convert them:

> Gossips, too, are not confined to Christian countries, and there were whispers that the new income tax was to pay for the Bibles distributed by the missionaries; the government and missionaries were in league to destroy caste; that government meant to bring a hundred Christian girls from Calcutta, and compel a hundred Assamese young men to marry them; that a thousand rupees per head had been offered to converts to Christianity.[57]

Sadiya was the northernmost town in Upper Assam. It had remained the third capital of the Chutiya kingdom for nearly three centuries (1248–1524) before being absorbed into the Ahom state in 1673. Situated near the banks of the Brahmaputra and close to the Himalayan foothills, it was an important cultural centre with a long history of trading between the plains and the hills. It was also a centre of Hindu civilisation and the meeting point of northern Burma, southern Tibet, and the Brahmaputra valley.

When Nathan Brown and Oliver Cutter travelled upstream along the Brahmaputra to reach Sadiya in 1836, the town was also the northeasternmost frontier of the East India Company. "Sadiya is beautifully situated in the centre of a spacious plain surrounded by mountains, which form a regular amphitheatre, and bound the horizon on all sides . . . The population, however, is sparse, as is the case with all A'sám, owing to the Burmese and other wars which formerly depopulated the country."[58] The weather here

[56] Ibid., xvii.
[57] *BMM*, Vol. LII, No. 9 (September 1872), 372.
[58] Ibid., 6.

was salubrious "and the soil is extremely fertile and capable of producing almost every variety of fruit." While the place was to the liking of the two American missionaries, it was here that they got the first glimpse of the ethnic quagmire peculiar to Assam.

In the clash of dynasties and kingdoms in Assam, Sadiya would stand out for transfer of power to a "ragtag" group of hill people who "emigrated from a range of mountains bordering on the sources of the Irawaddy river to the valley of Assam, and settled a small colony of fifteen houses in the vicinity of the Tengapanee river" during the reign of Rajeswar Singh in about 1751.[59] These were the Khamtis, Tai-speaking people who filled the vacuum created by the conflict between the Ahom rulers and the Moamarias of Muttock – followers of Moamaria Vaishnavism settled in a tract of land between the Brahmaputra and the Burihiding river. Led by their chief Matibar Bar Senapati, the Moamarias had withstood the onslaught of the Burmese forces during their invasion of Upper Assam.[60]

In 1794 the Khamtis overthrew the Ahom viceroy of Sadiya, traditionally known as the Sadiya Khowa Gohain, and appointed their own chief, adopting the same title and taking possession of the Ahom jurisdiction.[61] "Not content with this usurpation," wrote a British military officer, "they proceeded to reduce the whole of the Assamese population to the utmost verge of degradation; considering them as slaves, only worthy to be spared so long as they continued obedient to the will, and were useful to their masters in cultivating the land, and contributing to their comforts."[62]

Between the Burmese, Singpho, and Khamti thousands of Assamese people were enslaved or taken into captivity. The British wanted to secure their newly acquired territory and pacify the frontier tribes to counteract the possibility of any further Burmese invasion. The Khamtis were forced to accept the suzerainty

[59] See Butler, *A Sketch of Assam*, 39–40.
[60] Goswami, *The History of Assam*, 74.
[61] Gait, *A History of Assam*, 344.
[62] See Butler, *A Sketch of Assam*, 40.

of the new government but no tribute was demanded barring a supply of 40 militiamen, 10 oarsmen, and 20 *paiks*.[63] They were also required to maintain a local force of 200 men trained and armed by the British.[64] However, when the Khamti chief became ambitious and defied British overlordship, the British stripped his powers by terminating the office of Sadiya Khowa Gohain. Antagonised, in 1839 the Khamtis made a daring attack on the British cantonment in Sadiya, where the American Baptist mission work was just starting. "Soon after this, the missionaries removed to Jaipur [Jeypore] (in Dibrugarh). The military followed; then the inhabitants; and Sadiya was abandoned to tigers and jackals."[65]

Upper Assam, from where the Ahom kings had ruled, had become an important centre of activity for preachers of the new religion. In 1837 the American missionary Kincaid, stationed at the capital of the Konbaung kingdom (Burma), had, as noted, attempted to reach Sadiya. He had journeyed to the northern reaches of Burma bordering the Himalayan foothills, where no white man had dared venture. He had barely escaped with his life after being attacked by river pirates and taken to their hideout; plucky preachers like Kincaid and those after him showed that the American Baptist missionaries meant business.

In 1838, the year the Ahom ruling house flickered out, Miles Bronson, who would establish himself as "apostle to the Assamese", moved from Sadiya to Jeypore. Then in 1841 the American Baptists shifted their Upper Assam mission base from Jeypore to Sivasagar, the reasons being a perceived threat from the Singphos and the "insalubrity of the climate" in Jeypore. Broadly, the Ahom sphere of influence – including places like Rangpur, Gorgaon, and Sivasagar – remained culturally important: a region where the

---

[63] In the Ahom kingdom, able males between the ages of sixteen and fifty who were neither noble nor upper caste nor slaves, had to render service to the state. This corvée labour system is known as the *paik* system, and potential labourers as *paiks*.

[64] Goswami, *The History of Assam*, 75.

[65] *BMM*, Vol. LII, No. 9 (September 1872), 368.

"Assamese language is spoken in its greatest purity".[66] The Baptist mission printing press in Sivasagar went on to play a pivotal role in the renaissance of Assamese language and literature.

The Ahom rulers had presided over a vast kingdom, built temples, erected monuments, and constructed the sacred burial place of the royal family in Sivasagar. This important cultural centre and symbol of the former Ahom empire was located close to the former Ahom seat of rule; the capital Rangpur was only two miles away, while Gorgaon, another centre of power near the Dikhow river, was the place to which the king moved during the monsoon.[67] Sivasagar, instead of Jorhat, became the British district headquarters in 1841, and the focus of an indefatigable new religion.

VII

When the British signed a treaty with the Ahoms in 1833 – the Treaty of Gauhati – they included a condition to stop widow burning, even as they flooded the Brahmaputra valley with cheap Akbari opium – a vice that the American Baptist missionaries combated.[68] Several native converts succumbed to opium addiction. In some instances the Baptist mission saw the opium habit in Assam as a greater impediment to evangelism than the caste system: "Caste and opium are the curses of Assam . . . And of the two I think opium by far the most to be deplored. An opium-eater now is not an exception but one who does not eat it is the exception."

One of the foremost Assamese evangelists to the hill tribes, Godhula Brown (born Gendhela Barua), talked of the ruinous effects of opium-eating as part of his message. Remonstrations and advice by native evangelists such as him against superstitions and evil habits among hill tribes struck home easier than missionary

---

[66] Barpujari, *The American Missionaries*, xxviii.
[67] Ibid.
[68] Goswami, *The History of Assam*, 61.

opposition to the doctrines of caste among valley people. When grappling with the resilience of caste beliefs and practices, Miles Bronson excoriated caste as "that legion of evils combined, – that stronghold of [the] devil, – which so boldly defies all our efforts, – all our acts of kindness and love." As in the mainland, the caste system continued a daunting challenge for the Baptist mission, being regarded so dear among the natives that "The dying man refuses our medicine lest he lose his caste."[69] When the American Baptist missionaries entered the Brahmaputra valley, thus, the empire was the least of their concerns: the problem was the manifold beliefs and practices that they considered retrograde, coupled with the ethnic and linguistic diversity peculiar to Assam.

Baptist missionaries whose writings provided cultural and personality sketches of the population groups they encountered joined the ranks of travellers, adventurers, invaders, and traders who wrote up their experiences. The missionaries gradually created a new database of facts about native people, groups, and cultures. In places like Assam and Burma their writings contributed greatly to the development of ethnology as a discipline – "The American Baptists were the pioneers in the ethnological studies in Assam."[70] In addition to descriptions of particular ethnic groups, missionary records of the Assam plains include the geography, history, social institutions, social movements, religious reforms, and commerce of the region. Their often deep knowledge about the places they wanted to evangelise was recognised not only in the evangelical world but also in academia and popular culture. Although not always accurate, this knowledge sometimes rivals that provided by the best British civil servants in South Asia. Of the famous missionary linguist and translator Nathan Brown, the Oxford Indologist Max Müller said: "I should like to write to Mr Brown, and to send him my book on the Turanian Languages, where I have had to quote him so many times. He is one of the few men

---

[69] Barpujari, *The American Missionaries*, 180.
[70] Ibid., xiix.

whose opinion I should like to have on the classifications of these dialects on the borders of India and China which I have attempted there for the first time."⁷¹

Despite their use of Western mission jargon – including words such as heathens, savages, and barbarians which are now politically incorrect or "unwoke", if not deemed downright racist – the Baptist missionaries put a lot of effort into studying the history and culture of their prospective converts. Max Müller was only among the first scholars to realise their value, with many of their works later enriching the archives of Western universities. This profundity of knowledge is visible even in far-flung mission frontiers such as Burma. The Baptist chronicler Ada Chaplin makes a cross-cultural comparison between East and West suggesting a plenitude of experience: "Theatres are common and greatly patronized in Burma; and I have read translations of several plays acted there, in which the Nats figured as largely, and were treated with as little reverence, as gauze or mirrored ghosts in a theatre in New York."⁷²

Assam was administered as a strategic frontier region that was part of the Bengal Presidency, with many government employees there belonging to the English-educated Bengali class. For commoner Assamese-speaking people who lacked the patronage of the new rulers, American Baptist missionaries like Nathan Brown and Miles Bronson became "rescuers" of the ancient Assamese script and language because of their translation work. The mission press was foundational in salvaging the Assamese language and script

---

⁷¹ Letter from Professor Max Müller to Sir Charles Trevelyan, in Brown, *The Whole World Kin*, Appendix D, 602. In his stellar career as a linguist and Bible translator, Nathan Brown made comparative studies of Assamese, Bengali, and Sanskrit along with the Persian, Russian, Latin, and Gothic languages.

⁷² Chaplin, *Our Gold-Mine*, 72. Nats are local spirits worshipped by Burmese people. Nat worship, which was also found among the hill dwellers, was an indigenous faith (preceding Theravada Buddhism) which in conjunction with Theravada Buddhism rendered a unique identity to Buddhism in Burma.

from inundation by Bengali – which the British government introduced as officialese to save the cost of training its native employees in the language of the region. The mission also, in the process, transformed Assamese literature and language. The Assamese were compelled by the new government to use Bengali in administrative set-ups, courts, and schools, completely disregarding the local languages and dialects. The American Baptist mission was in this domain a sterling alternative: it did not need to follow official directives, believing quite correctly that Assamese was a different language. In a letter to the lieutenant governor of Bengal, Miles Bronson wrote:

> The common people do not understand the language written or spoken . . . the first word the new-born child hears from his mother, the first word he learns to lisp, the rude song of the boatman as he plies the oar or spreads his sail, the joyous songs of the reaper as he shouts the 'harvest home', always and everywhere the language used is Assamese not Bangali; and in our humble opinion, the only way to render any plan of education in this Province is to give it to them in their own mother tongue.[73]

Here *Orunodoi*, "a monthly Paper, devoted to Religion, Science, and General Knowledge" – the first periodical in Assamese that the Baptist Mission Press started publishing in 1845 – proved vital. The paper became deeply entrenched in Assamese social and intellectual life, so much so that it became a part of the vocabulary once the Assamese populace began using the word as a generic term for periodicals.[74] The average article in *Orunodoi* discussed scientific topics such as astronomy, geometry, the shape and area of the earth, solar and lunar eclipses, the steam engine, the microscope, and the thermometer. *Orunodoi* also regularly carried features on world history, politics, and current affairs that brought the fresh breezes of modernity into Assam. According

---

[73] Barpujari, *The American Missionaries*, 135–6.
[74] Sharma, "Missionaries and Print Culture", 242.

to William Ward, the mission printer-in-charge in Sivasagar, *Orunodoi*

> is read with usual interest, and, as education advances, the demand for it among the natives seems on the whole on the increase. Whatever prejudices some may have against its religious character, still they have no substitute for it . . . The great aim is to have it read as widely as possible, and we can trust for its usefulness to the great law of influence, which works its own slow but sure result.[75]

In 1867 alone the American Baptist Mission press circulated 115,000 pages of *Orunodoi* in the towns and villages of Assam.[76]

VIII

On 21 January 1842, not long after the American Baptist mission had secured a foothold in Assam, Nathan Brown visited "the last remnant of the Ahom race of kings, who entered Assam about A.D. 1228." It had been four years since the British deposed the last Ahom king, Purandar Singha, who was living in a modest residence in Jorhat, his former capital. The king was bemused that a white preacher should come to convince him to change his religion, but he appeared interested and enquired about Christian doctrine. The king's "twenty-five or thirty-year"-old son was inquisitive about astronomy and geography and asked Brown to open a school in Jorhat. The royal family had lost their former glory but nevertheless seemed aware of a proud heritage befitting a 600-year-old dynasty.

In 1853 Mrs Whiting, wife of the missionary at Sivasagar, was received by Purandar Singha's widow in her royal best, attended by a retinue of kneeling women. She also came across a young prince bedecked in finery and smoking a pipe who felt it was below his dignity to talk to missionaries – his attendants conducted most of the conversation. "What was most striking to the missionaries was that even at their decadent state members of the royal

---

[75] *BMM*, Vol. XLVII, No. 11 (December 1868), 261–2.
[76] Ibid,, 261.

family maintained their earlier pomp and dignity." Whiting felt that, given their state of affairs, they were "too proud and arrogant".[77]

According to *buranjis* – the chronicles of the Ahom rulers – Hinduism was introduced to the Ahom courts by a prince who had been raised by a Brahmin family after his mother died giving birth to him. The prince, whose name was Sudangpha, ascended the throne in 1387 at the age of fifteen, paving the way for the influence of Hinduism under the priestly class.[78] A lofty appellation for the king came into being a century later when Suhungmung (1497–1539), during whose rule the reformer Sankaradeva had flourished, adopted the Hindu title Swarga Narayan or Swargadeo (Lord of the Heavens). One of the greatest Ahom kings, Rudra Singha (1696–1714), who became an orthodox Hindu in old age, installed a famous Sakta priest from Bengal in the Kamakhya temple. However, it was under Sib Singha, Rudra Singha's son and successor, that the last vestiges of Ahom "tribal" beliefs were discarded. The Ahom nobility who had earlier relished a wide variety of meat delicacies began adopting vegetarianism under the influence of the Brahmins at court.[79]

Power tussles within the ruling family weakened the Ahom kingdom, and with kings taking sides in conflicts among the Hindu sects, the downfall of the empire was precipitated. The practice of the popular form of Hinduism that existed in the Brahmaputra valley involved many ostentatious sacrifices where even humans were offered to the gods. Sadiya, which had been the headquarters of the Chutiya kings at the time of the Ahom invasion, was famous for the worship of various forms of Kali, with the goddess being offered both human and animal sacrifices by the ruling house. Naranarayan, the last king of the undivided Koch kingdom of Kamata and one of the greatest kings in Assam's

[77] Barpujari, *The American Missionaries*, 184–5.
[78] Thomson, *Assam Valley*, 48.
[79] Gait, *A History of Assam*, 263.

history, was said to have sacrificed 140 men at the newly restored Kamakhya temple that had been overrun by Muslim invaders.[80]

Long before the American Baptist missionaries came preaching about the excesses of expensive rituals and "meaningless" sacrifices – which found many takers among the hill tribes – there had been a Vaishnavite reformer in the fifteenth century who opposed blood sacrifice, idol worship, and caste barriers, and who preached salvation through pure devotion (bhakti) to Krishna. A contemporary of Chaitanya, the great Hindu reformer of Bengal, Sankaradeva (1449–1569) was born into the Baro-Bhuyans family of Nowgong, a district in Assam where the American Baptists established their most successful mission station in 1841 – manned by Rev. Miles Bronson, who was called the "apostle to the Assamese".

After the death of Sankaradeva in 1569 his followers split into two factions, but under his successor Madhavdev a sect called Mahapurushia continued to spread the teachings of their guru, especially repudiating idolatry and the rule of the Brahmins. The Mahapurushia sect founded centres at Barpeta in Kamrup and on the Brahmaputra's Majuli Island, which the Assamese Baptist evangelist Godhula unsuccessfully tried to penetrate in the third quarter of the nineteenth century before shifting his focus to the hill tribes. The neo-Vaishnavite movement that Sankaradeva kickstarted in the Brahmaputra valley perplexed Swargadeos down the line as they patronised Brahmins at their courts. The kingdom faced less religious dissension under the Ahom king Rudra Singha, who favoured the Sakta sect but was tolerant toward the Vaishnavites and stopped their persecution. However, under rulers like Pratap Singha (r. 1603–41) and the famous Gadadhar Singha (r. 1681–96) the Mahapurushias faced persecution.

By the time the first Baptist missionary to Assam, Nathan Brown,[81] met the last remnants of the Ahom ruling house in

---

[80] Thomson, *Assam Valley*, 47.

[81] Journal of Brown, 21 January 1842, in Barpujari, *The American Missionaries*, 184.

1842, the royal family were fully Hinduised, having endorsed for generations the religion at their court. The Tai-Ahom ethnic group in Assam had relinquished their quasi-animistic tribal religion and adopted the religion of the people they had conquered. As a result, despite considerable investment of human resources, time, and funds, the mission yielded poor dividends among the Assamese Hindus. Would Assam go the way of Burma, where converts to the Baptist faith in the Irrawaddy delta were negligible among the ethnic Burmans following Theravada Buddhism?

The Burma missionaries did find success among the Karens, who were "every where cruelly oppressed by the Burmans among whom they dwell; being compelled to cultivate the land, to pay large tributes, and to perform every kind of servile labor."[82] In fact, one of the first Karen converts who became a seasoned evangelist, Ko Tha Byu, was a former slave whose freedom had been purchased by Baptist missionaries. The Karens, who were widely scattered over the hills and forests in Burma, Siam, and some parts of China originally practised an animistic religion. One of their legends predicted that white strangers from a distant shore would bring them a book containing the Word of God. The legend was so potent that a Baptist missionary found a "'Book of Common Prayer and the Psalms' of an edition printed in Oxford" carefully covered in muslin and venerated by the locals. The book had come into the possession of a sorcerer when a travelling "Mussulman" left it in one of the Karen villages. When the surprised missionary, George Dana Boardman, was shown this mysterious object by the sorcerer, he said:

> [I told them] "It is a good book . . . it teaches that there is a God in Heaven, whom alone we should worship. You have been ignorantly worshipping this book; that is not good. I will teach you to worship the God whom the book reveals." Every Karen countenance was alternately lighted up with smiles of joy and cast down with inward convictions of having erred in worshipping a book instead of the

[82] Gammell, *A History of American Baptist Missions*, 90.

God whom it reveals. I took the book of psalms in Burman and read such passages as seemed appropriate, and having given brief and easy explanation engaged in prayer.[83]

Labelled "wild men" and regarded as being of low status by valley dwellers, the Karens were viewed by the missionaries as "inferior both in physical and intellectual strength" but "in general more industrious, and less addicted to the vices of barbarian tribes".[84] It was among the Karens that the Burma Baptists finally found natives receptive to their message. While with the Burmans conversion came in trickles, "the Karens in their hundreds came forward to be instructed and to be baptized." Till the mid-nineteenth century Burma was a "Baptist country", and with a Christian community of 30,000 and more than "10,000 Church members in full standing", had more converts than India at that time.[85] The Karens formed a substantial proportion of the Christian population in Burma; what was more, the hill tribesmen founded Baptist communities and churches that were self-sufficient and did not depend on the Home Board to dole out funds. By 1931 there were about 611 Karen Baptist schools, almost all of them in villages, and "593 of these do not receive a rupee of mission aid".[86]

Writing decades after the arrival of the Baptist mission in Assam, A.K. Gurney, who came as a missionary to Sivasagar in 1876, observed that the average Assamese was still unimpressed by their message. In dismay, he reported an irrepressible relativism which he called an "accommodating theory", among the Assamese Hindus who would often say:

> Christianity is true, so is Hindooism, so is Mohammedanism. I regard Hindooism as true, you regard Christianity as true: Hindooism is true for me, Christianity for you. "For the European," they say,

---

[83] Ibid., 92–3.
[84] Ibid., 90.
[85] Neill, *A History of Christian Missions*, 250.
[86] Howard, *Baptists in Burma*, 75.

"Christianity is good; for the Hindoo, Hindooism; for the Mussulman, Mohammedanism."[87]

Gurney observed that even those who were convinced would not accept the new faith on account of pressures of caste and family.

The scholarly missionary William Ward, who arrived in Assam in 1848 and died at the Sivasagar mission station in 1873, bemoaned the stunted growth of the mission in Assam: "years and labour almost entirely thrown away because the apparent fruit seemed small." His successor, Edward Winter Clark, who came to Sivasagar to take charge of the mission's printing press, joined other missionaries in voicing discontent with the unresponsiveness of valley dwellers. In 1873 Clark made a brief survey of the mission's effort for the past thirty-seven years in the Brahmaputra valley and found only about a hundred converts, which led to the morose conclusion that only about three converts had been added to the Baptist community per year of work.[88]

S.A. Perrine railed against the plains people of Assam: "The plains people are weighted down, handicapped by the old iron-clad institutions and traditions. For thousands of years these ancient institutions have been tested, and, found wanting, now hang like millstones about the neck of India to sink her to despair." He was quick to point out the "speediest results" among "wild tribes" like the Karens in Burma.[89] These represented a "model self-supporting mission of all the world, of any denomination", in this matter outclassing the men of the plains. Perrine's mission colleague to the Nagas, E.W. Clark, complained of converts in the plains lacking all effort to make their churches self-sufficient and depending on mission handouts. In the estimation of the missionaries, then, the Assam mission field was a failure when weighed against the amount of time, energy, and resources spent. Clark finally wrote

---

[87] Barpujari, *The American Missionaries*, 216.
[88] Puthenpurakal, *Baptist Missions*, 57–8.
[89] *BMM*, Vol. LXXXI, No. 6 (June 1901), 212–13.

to the ABMU: "Must it not be admitted, that the Assamese have been offered the Gospel and have not received it . . . Can it be believed, that Paul or other New Testament evangelists would have spent so long a time on such a field and not tried hard to find a heathen people more favourable to Christianity than the Assamese?"[90]

After this unrewarding mission in the Assam plains, the Baptists found the equivalent of Burma's Karens among the Garos, a Tibeto-Burman-speaking group occupying a hill tract south of the Brahmaputra and about 320 km west of the Guwahati Baptist mission station. It was from Goalpara, a British civil and military station, that the Garos were administered; the lieutenant governor of Bengal saw the work of the American Baptist Mission among the Garos as a civilising effort that would benefit the English government, and so gave permission to the missionaries to operate there. Among the few matrilineal societies in the world, the Garos were said to be

> Fond of making raids into plains and securing bloody heads as proof of their bravery, fond of head and brass ornaments and of puppies roasted alive, but not fond of much clothing, knowing nothing of God, worshipping the stars, the rivers, and the spirits of the hills, sacrificing liquor, rice, flowers, white cocks, sometimes beautiful fat bulls, and on very great occasions human beings, – but hardly knowing to what they sacrificed them – enjoying no feast so well as one eaten from the skull of the enemy.[91]

The Baptist mission in Assam – in the initial days popularly known as the Shan mission after the speakers of this language group – found the evangelising soil rich among other Tibeto-Burman speakers as well, such as the Kukis, Mikirs, and Nagas. Seasoned missionaries to Assam like Bronson, Clark, and Rivenburg found their niche here; the Assam mission would soon shed

---

[90] Ibid.
[91] *BMM*, Vol. LII, No. 9 (September 1872), 372–3.

the hangover from what the early missionaries had envisioned as the "great Central Asian strategy".

In the eyes of the Baptist missionaries the Garos were no less wild than other hill peoples in the uplands of Burma and Assam. They came under the influence of the Baptist mission when some of their tribesmen, working as sepoys for the British government, learnt of the new religion from native Assamese preachers. Two Garo converts, Omed and Ramkhe, would give up their life as sepoys and become tireless preachers to their own tribesmen. Ward spoke of Pastor Omed as a man "probably thirty-five years of age, of mature judgement, sedate and gentle demeanour" who after his conversion lived for two years alone in the "wild jungle" with his wife and "preached to the Garos who passed him [on the way] to the market, or [those whom] he visited . . . in their hills".[92] Omed was to the Garos what Ko Tha Byu was to the Karens; except that Ko Tha Byu was a former criminal and slave who became a seasoned missionary, while Omed was a former military man. Omed and Ko Tha Byu were prime examples of zealous local preachers who garnered more converts to the Baptist fold than the American missionaries. This trend would be observed among other hill peoples like the Chins, Kachins, Nagas, and Kukis, among whom the Baptist mission started spreading slowly. By 1869 the Garo Baptist community had increased to a total of 176 converts, more than the Baptist mission had achieved among the people in Assam plains in three decades.[93]

Even before the British surveyed Sivasagar as a place suitable for growing tea and transformed it into a cosmopolitan town, it was an important economic, religious, and cultural centre that attracted people from various parts of the Ahom kingdom. It was famous for its bazaar, located adjacent to an impressive Shiva temple built by the Ahom kings – as old missionary photographs reveal. The bazaar used to be frequented by a "dreaded" hill tribe whom the

---

[92] Letter from Mr Ward in Ao, *History of Christianity*, 14–15.
[93] Fifty-sixth Annual Report in Ao, *History of Christianity*, 28.

people of the plains called "Naga" (the Assamese pronounced it "Noga"). The Nagas would periodically come down from the thick forested mountains to procure salt, iron, and other items not found in their villages, in exchange for finely woven bamboo mats, baskets, livestock, and forest products.

One of the earliest mentions of the Nagas in history was in the thirteenth century in the chronicles of the Ahom kings; these records show that Prince Sukhapa who moved out from northern Burma faced stiff resistance from the Nagas en route to the Brahmaputra valley. The Nagas, not used to a large contingent of outsiders entering their territory, attacked Sukhapa's force and were met with a strong counterattack and brutality. Oral narratives tell of Ahom invaders using the babies of their Naga foes as projectiles to shake fruit out of trees, and the Ahoms themselves record how the Nagas were force-fed cooked relatives to make them toe the line.[94] Naga groups like the Nocte, Tangsa, and Wancho stood in the way of the Ahom advance, "but Sukapa brought all of them under his control by a policy of blood and rapine"; he carved out a province in the "whole tract between the Daikham and the Patkai" called Khamjang, placing one of his trusted followers there as governor and ordering him to pay regular tributes of local produce.[95] Relations between the Ahoms and Nagas over the centuries veered between the forming of marriage alliances and the sending of expeditionary forces into hill jungles to suppress the Naga chiefs. Trade between them continued, although not with the frequency seen in the plains, and turf battles were fought over brine wells for salt-making. Some Naga men were recruited in the Ahom fighting force, and some members of the nobility to escape infighting at the Ahom court sought refuge in Naga villages in the hills.

It was among these hill villages, over which the British had no suzerainty – in mission phraseology a region where no outsiders

---

[94] Barua, *Ahom-Buranji*.
[95] Baruah, *A Comprehensive History of Assam*, 221.

dared enter – that the Baptist missionaries went on to find their greatest success. A vibrant Baptist movement spread among the ethnic Nagas, which within a few decades became the most successful mission field in the whole of Asia. The persistence of American missionaries against all odds found its rewards among this ethnic community that straddled the Indo–Myanmar border. In terms of the ratio of conversions to total population, the Nagas would surpass the ethnic Karens of Burma and the Garos in the hills of Assam.

2

The Baptist Highland

> The temptation has been strong to compare the Kachin custom and religion with the practices of related tribes such as the Karens, Chins, Nagas, Garos, Mishmis and Abors.
>
> **– Ola Hanson, pioneering Baptist missionary to the Kachins, 1913**

> There are thousands of putative nationalities in the world today; at least sixteen of them are situated on Burma's borders. It is hard to imagine that the inhabitants of these areas would be well served by becoming separate states.
>
> **– Amitav Ghosh, "At Large in Burma", 1995–6**

THE NAGAS ARE A familial group of several ethnic communities occupying the heartland of what I call the Baptist highland: a wide swathe of mountainous territory straddling the international border between India and Myanmar.[1]

---

[1] The etymological derivation of the word "Naga" ranges from the Sanskrit word "*nag*" or "*naga*", which means "hillman" (see Hutton, *The Angami Nagas*, 5; Elwin, *Nagaland*, 4) to the Burmese word "*na-ka*" meaning "ear perforation" (see Sema, *Emergence of Nagaland*, 3; Nuh, *165 Years History of Naga Baptist Churches*, 15). The semantic conundrum aside, the word "Naga" is a generic term used for several tribes spread across three north-eastern states in India and in the north-western Sagaing region of Myanmar. Modern Naga identity formation is very complex, dynamic, and politically charged, and the leading function of ethnic identity mobilisation has been the irrepressible ethnonationalism which is the driving force behind one of the oldest armed struggles in the Indo–Myanmar uplands.

Midway along the Indo–Myanmar border (1643 km), a congeries of tribes called the Nagas occupy parallel folds of high mountains cutting across the region between the Chindwin valley in Myanmar and the Brahmaputra plains in Assam – this being the Indo–Burmese or Indo–Myanmar upland. This mountainous region inhabited by the Nagas merges with the lands of the Chins in the south and the Kachins in the north, forming a contiguous upland, most of which lies 3000 feet above sea level. This long strip of the Indo–Myanmar frontier region was home to a multitude of animistic religions. During the nineteenth and twentieth centuries it was overrun by a Protestant form of Christianity and is now home to one of the largest Baptist followings in the world.

The region identified here as the Baptist highland is known for its ethnic, linguistic, and cultural diversity, but besides its remarkable variety the region shares a common characteristic: the preponderance of the Baptist faith. Ethnic groups like the Kuki-Chins, Kachins, and Nagas inhabiting this region have embraced the Baptist faith in large numbers.[2] And today the Indo–Myanmar frontier region is arguably the most successful legacy of the American Baptist mission overseas.

The Baptist highland remains politically significant because it poses a huge challenge to nation-state building by both India and Myanmar. The region is many things to many people: an El Dorado for anthropologists and historians; a quandary for policy-makers; a whetstone for intelligence personnel; an elusive mission for ethnonationalists; a safe passage for smugglers and drug traffickers; and still a potential mission field for missionaries.

---

[2] The term Kuki-Chin refers to both an ethnocultural entity as well as a linguistic group, and was used widely in missionary writings and colonial reports. The Kuki-Chin tribes are also known by other ethnonyms like Zomi, Khulmi, Mizo, and Chikim. According to Haokip, "The territory inhabited by the Kuki-Chin tribes extends from the Naga Hills in the north down into the Sandoway District of Burma in the south; from the Myittha River in the east, almost extending to the Bay of Bengal in the west." See Haokip, "The Chins in Manipur", 172–5.

With regard to geopolitics, the Baptist highland presents an interesting case, because the region is landlocked, surrounded by a country claiming to be the world's largest democracy, a superpower led by a Communist Party government, a densely Islamic nation, and the longest-military-ruled country in the world. The Indo–Myanmar upland occupied by ethnic Baptists lies at the junction of East, South, and South East Asia, forming a kind of melting pot where the culture, politics, and economy of China, India, Bangladesh, and Myanmar have exerted considerable influence. This peculiar location of the Indo–Myanmar upland poses a unique challenge to its inhabitants, and the most noticeable product has been a tenacious ethnic-based armed struggle across the region. Each country has become involved in the various ethnonationalism projects rife in the region: the Chinese continue to support the Nagas and Kachins, Pakistan (more truly East Pakistan) supported the Naga and Mizo insurgents in the years following Independence, India has been involved with the Chins and Kachins in upland Myanmar, while Myanmar has followed a policy of "Burmanisation" there.[3]

An important development in the Baptist highland is that Christianity has become intrinsic to the cultural expression of various ethnic groups. This is best exemplified among ethnic Naga Baptists in states like Arunachal Pradesh, Manipur, and Nagaland on the Indian side, and among ethnic Chins, Nagas, and Kachins on the Myanmar side. Besides, the Indo–Myanmar upland has become an English-speaking belt by adopting the language of Baptists around the globe and thus bridging the language barriers that separated the various ethnic groups. This is remarkable, because, for example, the language diversity even within a single ethnic group like the Chins of Myanmar has been likened to the Biblical "Tower of Babel".[4] The affinity for things Western is apparent in the Baptist enclaves in this frontier region; one may

---

[3] See Bhaumik, *Troubled Periphery*, esp. Chapter 5.
[4] See Enriquez, *The Races of Burma*, xiii, 52.

even argue that the ethnic groups in the Baptist highland are more sympathetic to Western values because of their American Baptist heritage, although the colonial-period anglicisation of this frontier region cannot be discounted.

The Baptist highland is arguably one of the most successful Christian missionary legacies in the whole of South East Asia. It is remarkable that the American Baptist mission found a foothold in this inhospitable region; in Myanmar the mission (1813–1966) lasted longer than British rule (1885–1948) and would have continued its work if not for the military government crackdown on Christian missions, all foreign missionaries being expelled by 1966. In Myanmar's less undemocratic neighbour, the American Baptist missionaries were tactfully expelled by the mid-1950s as one of their thriving mission fields in the Naga Hills district of Assam became a hotbed of ethnonationalism.[5] By the time the British left the Naga Hills in 1947, the Naga political movement had become the first ethnic-based struggle for self-rule.

In recent times native missionaries have been moving into South East Asian countries, spreading the Baptist faith, which is of great strategic and ideological importance from the perspective of Christian missions. In spite of America's unsuccessful foreign policy in mainland South East Asia in the post-war era – losing ground to communists in places like Myanmar, Cambodia, Laos, and Vietnam – the American legacy in the form of an ardent evangelical Baptist faith has thrived and is very much alive in the Indo–Myanmar frontier region. Through the fervent missionary activity of local inhabitants, it is slowly but buoyantly inching into South East Asia. As Christianity recedes from Western shores, especially in Europe, missionary zeal has gripped the faithful in this part of the world, which was earlier thought of as the untamed outpost of Christian missions. An evangelical worldview,

[5] The Naga Hills district of Assam and the Tuensang Division of NEFA were brought within a single administrative unit named the Naga Hills-Tuensang Area (NHTA) in 1957. NHTA became the sixteenth state of the Indian union, named Nagaland, on 1 December 1963.

comparable to the one that propelled Baptist missionaries to go to the far ends of the earth in the nineteenth century, may be found among ethnic Christians inhabiting this frontier region today.

While the former British colonies are renaming their capitals, important towns, cities, institutions, and memorials in honour of national figures, ethnic Baptists continue to name their mission centres, seminaries, educational institutes, and memorials after pioneering American Baptist missionaries. In the Naga areas, seminaries, schools, and colleges have been named after these revered figures, and their busts and portraits adorn Baptist mission centres.[6] Among the Chins and Kachins too there is reverence for the Baptist pioneers, and, at least in my interaction with ethnic Baptist groups, I have rarely come across the faithful speaking ill of American missionaries. In fact, adherents extol the virtues of the American Baptist mission; for instance, Naga Baptists commonly use metaphors like darkness and light, barbarism and civilisation to describe their situation before and after their encounter with the American Baptist mission. In 1998 Naga Baptists in the state of Nagaland celebrated 125 years of Christianity in their community with pomp and fervour under the theme "From Darkness to Light". Educational institutions are where the American Baptist influence is most strongly felt; literature pertaining to the American Baptist mission is still in circulation, and scores of seminary graduates write theses and publish books on the "positive impacts" of these missions. The Kachin Baptists have named their foremost publication and printing house "Hanson", after Ola Hanson, the Swedish-American Baptist missionary to the Kachins.

Today, among the Nagas on the Indian side, Christianity is practised by about 95 per cent of the population.[7] Among the

---

[6] In the state of Nagaland, Clark Theological College started by the Ao Baptists, Anderson Theological College run by the Sumi Baptists, and Witter Theological College opened by the Lotha (Kyong) Baptists have a strong American Baptist mission legacy.

[7] The percentage of Christians in the state of Nagaland, according to the 2011 census, is 87.93. The Christian population among the fourteen

ethnic Chins in north-western Myanmar the Christian population is an estimated 90 per cent, and about 95 per cent among the Kachins in Kachin state, making them the most Christianised ethnic groups in Myanmar.[8] In these three ethnic groups at the Indo–Myanmar frontier, the Protestant form of Christianity, notably Baptist, has the largest following. The work of the American Baptist missionaries Arthur E. Carson and Laura H. Carson, who reached the Chin Hills in 1899, remains noteworthy in the spread of Christianity among the Chins, while the Kachins were exposed to the American Baptist mission from the late 1870s, with three individuals – William Robert (1879–1913), Ola Hanson (1890–1928), and George J. Geis (1892–1916, 1924–36) – between them spending 108 years in this area. The Nagas' first contact with the American Baptist mission in the late 1830s was short-lived; the mission resumed in the early 1870s and continued till the mid-1950s with a total of twenty-eight American Baptist missionaries serving between 1876 and 1955, at which point the Indian government expelled foreign missionaries from the Naga areas.[9]

The Indo–Burmese upland remained relatively isolated for

Naga tribes indigenous to the state is estimated at 95–98 per cent, of which Nagas following the Baptist faith are believed to comprise 75–80 per cent. The official figure for the Christian population among the ethnic Nagas in Myanmar is not clear since no nationwide census has been held since 1931. But the Naga Baptist missionaries I interviewed estimate 75–80 per cent to be Christian, and this is said to be increasing, although some still practise the traditional religion and some have adopted Theravada Buddhism.

[8] See Steinberg, *Burma/Myanmar*, 57.

[9] The first American Baptist missionary to step on Naga soil was Miles Bronson, who made a three-week visit from 7 to 29 January 1839 to Namsangia village, currently in Tirap district, Arunachal Pradesh. After nearly three decades of hiatus, Godhula Rufus Brown, the Assamese assistant of E.W. Clark, managed to visit an Ao Naga village not far from Sivasagar in April 1872. The duration that the American missionaries spent in the Baptist mission stations in the Naga Hills varied: some were posted there for a few months, while others worked for decades among the Naga tribes.

THE BAPTIST HIGHLAND 77

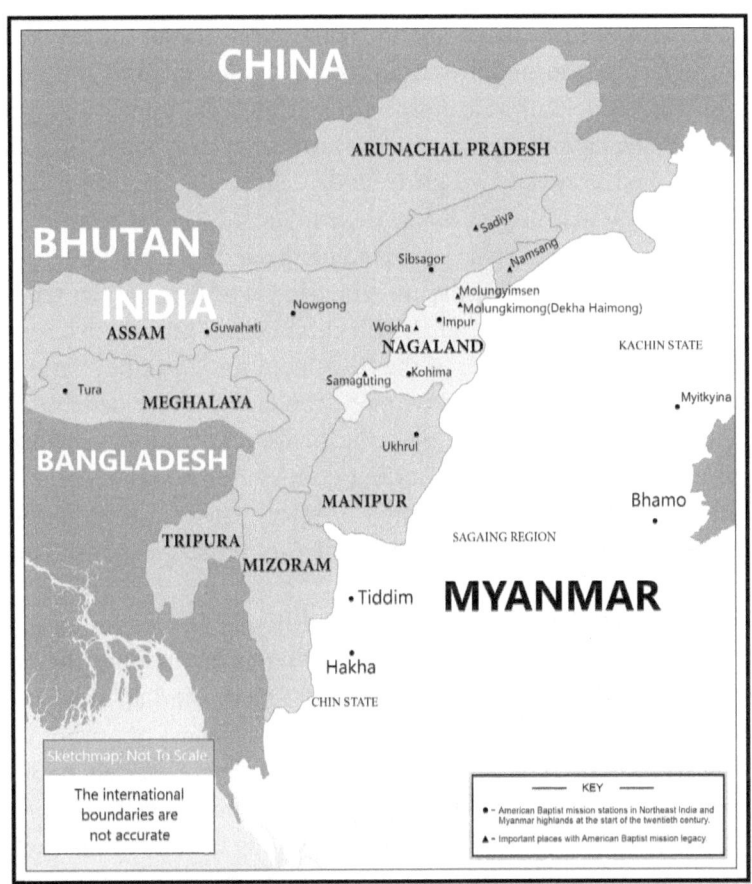

Map 4: American Baptist Mission Stations
1836–1900.

generations, with exchanges confined to barter, raids, and inter-village warfare. Civilisations originating in the valleys kept the surrounding cultures at arm's length, and the important historic trade routes skirted the region. But in the second half of the nineteenth century an Abrahamic faith from a distant shore swept through this inhospitable terrain, changing the religious and cultural landscape within a short span of time. The transformation was momentous because the Indo–Burmese upland had long been sandwiched between two great world religions – Hinduism and Buddhism – that originated in the Indian subcontinent and yet that had for the most part remained unaffected by their influence.

A few American Baptist missionaries, who proved far more resilient than the agents of British colonialism, introduced huge changes in this backwater of the British empire. Zealous missionaries with deep religious convictions could alone have penetrated these locations and lived among ethnic communities long secluded from more advanced surrounding cultures. This was a stateless polity with interactions mostly between villages. Even today, people who claim the same ethnic identity often speak mutually unintelligible languages.

The distinctive ethnic, cultural, and linguistic features of this frontier region were shaped to a large extent by its physical environment and geographical location. On the Indian side, the Baptist highland stretches for almost the entire length of the border with Myanmar. The hills along the Indian side are sparsely populated and densely forested because of heavy monsoon rains, making the upland difficult to access. Ethnic groups in this region challenge the mainstream idea of a nation-state and the international boundary is not strictly adhered to because of persisting claims over traditional homelands overlapping the boundary.[10] Except

---

[10] To ethnic groups, state and international boundaries appear as a colonial-era creation cutting through their traditional homeland. For instance, the Konyak Naga village of Longwa is famous for the international boundary running through the village, where – as the popular saying goes – the *angh*, the village chief, has his meals in Myanmar and sleeps in India, his house straddling the two countries.

for Mizoram, where Baptists are the second-largest denomination after Presbyterians,[11] the Indian states of Nagaland, Manipur, and Arunachal Pradesh, especially in the districts bordering Myanmar, remain predominantly Baptist or are witnessing the rapid spread of Christianity of the Baptist persuasion among their various ethnic groups.[12]

In Myanmar the contiguous horseshoe-shaped range that hems the country on the east, north, and west comprises nearly half of the entire landmass, framing the lowland area of central Myanmar occupied mainly by ethnic Burmans – the region that is the focus of the nation-building project. Given the difficult terrain, the hills here remain sparsely populated, yet support numerous ethnic groups – notably the Karens, Chins, Kachins, Shans, Karennis, Nagas, Akhas, Lahus, Kokangs, Palaungs, and Was. The Baptist highland occupied by ethnic minority groups covers almost one-third of Myanmar's uplands, and it is in the north-western part of these hills that the Baptists are mostly found, in the border regions of Kachin state, the Sagaing region, and Chin state, which share an international boundary with India, extending to the western reaches of the mountainous Chin state and touching China's Yunnan province in the north. American Baptist missionaries also penetrated Shan state in the north-east, as well as Kayin state and Kayah state (with ethnic Karennis) of south-eastern Myanmar, and

[11] Unlike in the Naga Hills, Christian missions entered the Lushai Hills (now Mizoram) only after the British military expedition of 1891. The Welsh Presbyterian mission established a permanent mission station in 1898, while the English Baptist missionaries from the Baptist Mission Society of London soon joined the Presbyterians. After nearly a hundred years of foreign mission presence, the Baptist missionaries were the last to leave Mizoram in the 1970s, following the political uprising among the Mizos. See Pachuau, *Being Mizo*, 158–9.

[12] Except for Anjaw district, which is inhabited by the Mishimi tribe, the other districts of Arunachal Pradesh that share a border with Myanmar have a majority Christian population. The Wancho tribe of Longding district inhabited by the Wancho, the Nocte of Tirap district inhabited by the Nocte, and the Tangsa of Changlang district inhabited by the Tangsa have for the most part converted to Christianity, and the majority are Baptists.

a substantial number of Karen people in the latter two states follow the Baptist faith. People spill across the border from Kayin state into Thailand, taking their Protestant faith with them.[13] Thus if we locate the domicile of ethnic Baptists on a map of Myanmar, it will resemble a curve beginning in Kachin state in the north, bordering China, and stretching patchily toward Kayin state and Kayah state in the south-east of the country.[14] The widely dispersed ethnic Karens are found even in the south-western region of Tenasserim (Tanintharyi) Division. The Baptist highland extends considerably further on the Myanmar side than on the Indian because three major ethnic minority groups – Chins, Kachins, and Karens – became part of the Baptist success story in Burma towards the end of the nineteenth century.

II

When the first Baptist missionaries set foot in the Burmese heartland in the first quarter of the nineteenth century, the Indo-Burmese frontier seemed an unlikely prospect for a new Protestant mission on a small budget. But though by turns wild, barren, and forested it was soon transformed by hardy American Baptist missionaries whose tenacity and passion knew no limits.

Historically, the arrival in Burma of the American Baptist mission preceded British colonialism, but British rule set the larger

---

[13] According to the UNHCR, an estimated 95,681 refugees – mostly Karen and Karenni ethnic minorities – are living in Thailand. Refugee camps in the Myanmar–Thailand border region have become a field of activity for various Christian mission organisations, including Naga Baptists from Nagaland.

[14] The Rakhine Baptist Convention and Mon Baptist Convention are, comparatively, two smaller Baptist associations affiliated to the Myanmar Baptist Convention, the largest Baptist body in the country with headquarters in Rangoon (Yangon). The Rangoon region is the most ethnically and culturally diverse in the country and was long a centre of trading activity as well as an attraction for various religious traditions. It was in Rangoon that the American Baptist mission started work in the Orient at the beginning of the nineteenth century.

stage for the missionary–native encounter. Ethnic groups became americanised in matters of faith, while institutional change in education, the political system, and law and order made them more anglicised. This almost imperceptible but consequential Westernisation process separated the Baptist mission in the Indo–Burmese frontier region from other Baptist mission fields in the Orient. In places like China, Japan, and Ministerial Burma, the religious commitment of converts could not be sustained without durable Western institutions, and with changes in regime and power equations the religion of the "foreign devils" was sporadically eradicated – as during the Boxer Rebellion in China.[15] In the process Western ideas and institutions were often discarded as well, and an anti-Western worldview propagated. While these ancient civilisations selectively appropriated Western ideas and technology, the process of Westernisation remained skin-deep because their cultural heritages could rival those of the West. The East that had sophisticated knowledge of cosmology, elaborate religious traditions, and a well-developed literary culture with a long writing tradition was indigenously equipped to withstand Western cultural encroachment, which is why Western education and the English language – core aspects of Westernisation – did not take root in their areas. In this respect, the hill people of oral cultures in the Indo–Myanmar upland, who were far removed from civilisation, were quite different.

In the Indo–Myanmar highland it was, by contrast, the spread of Protestantism among ethnic groups that ensured the durability of Western institutions and ideas. In the twenty-first century the ethnic Baptists of this region continue to remain pro-West,

---

[15] One of the biggest uprisings against Christian missions in the Chinese mainland started in 1899, where the Boxers started a violent movement to get rid of foreign missionaries whom they labelled "foreign devils". The Boxer Rebellion began as an incendiary anti-imperialist, anti-foreign, and anti-Christian movement, attacking foreign missionaries and native Christian converts. An estimated 30,000 Chinese Christians were killed by the time the rebellion was quelled. For more details, see Fairbank, *et al.*, *East Asia*, 633–40.

not only sharing a sense of common brotherhood with Western Christians but also taking various cues from American popular culture. As such, it is easier for the young here to embrace Valentine's Day in their little urban spaces than for conservative Hindus or Buddhists in metropolitan cities. Christianised ethnic groups in the Baptist highland share a cultural and religious ethos with Christians in the West more than with the majority population of their home country. This has proved a bone of contention even in a diverse country like India, especially at a time when regime change in the centre and several populous states favours a hardline Hinduism that has begun to erode diversity.

In this context the Baptist highland is distinct. British rule brought long-lasting institutional changes in this region, many of which made it conducive for Christianity to continue flourishing despite the tumultuous decolonisation process. This was not so in missionary-intensive places like China, Japan, and even lowland Burma, where Christian missions arrived long before they reached the Indo–Burmese upland. Colonial rule was the first state-like enterprise encountered by this region's ethnic groups. The introduction of institutions – the legislature, bureaucracy, judiciary – and the spread of telecommunications aided the propagation of Protestantism in the region, while the evangelistic work of Baptist missionaries enabled sustainable Westernised institutions to persist in one of the most unlikely places on earth.[16]

The process of colonisation in the Baptist highland differed from that in the rest of India and Myanmar; till the time the British left the region, many ethnic groups were indirectly administered or left alone by colonial agencies. This was despite the British claiming authority and jurisdiction over the vast expanse

---

[16] In a well-researched study, Robert Woodberry attributes the rise and spread of stable democracies in the non-Western world to Protestant missionaries. His thesis suggests that the greater the number of Protestant missionaries per ten thousand native population in 1923, the greater the probability for a nation to have achieved a stable democracy in the twenty-first century. Woodberry, "The Missionary Roots of Liberal Democracy".

of uncharted jungles they acquired as part of their conquests of the more advanced kingdoms in the lowlands – the lowland rulers too had seldom interfered in the affairs of the "wild peoples" of the highlands. Eyeing the British seat of power in East Bengal, Burmese westward expansion into Assam and Manipur (1817–23) skirted the highlands and annexed the Imphal valley and the Brahmaputra valley in the lowlands. After the First Anglo–Burmese War (1824–6), Assam, Manipur, and the provinces of Arakan and Tenasserim were ceded to the British, who extended their influence eastward; the Indo–Burmese highland continued outside the purview of the colonial administration. Even with the complete takeover of Burma in 1885, the Indo–Burmese frontier remained a jungle tract seldom entered, most goods and people wending their way along waterways that connected to the mouth of the Irrawaddy and the Bay of Bengal.

After Burma became a province separate from British India in 1937, the Indian pattern of administration and political expediency served as a template here. Burma was divided into Ministerial Burma – Burma proper, inhabited by the Burmans and directly administered – and the indirectly administered peripheral highlands. This dual form of political control sharpened the ethnic divide between plains and highlands, as well as shaped nationalism based on the idea of a shared ethnic identity. To this day the Burmese blame the British for sowing the seeds of division.[17] Across the present-day border, on the Indian side the uplands were gradually annexed. Yet many of the ethnic communities were ruled indirectly, and the British left the scene before directly administering the "warmongering" tribes occupying the large chunk of jungle-matted mountainous lands eastward of Assam province. As late as the 1930s Fürer-Haimendorf, during a punitive expedition toward the unexplored eastern frontier of the British Naga Hills District,

---

[17] "Burmese" is a term used to collectively refer to ethnic groups like the Chin, Burman, Karen, Kachin, Shan, Wa, etc., who inhabit the state of Myanmar.

observed that "The area further to the east was still unmapped, and the country of these Kalyo Kengyus [Khiamniungan Nagas] had never been entered by any European"; and, "As long as the feuds in the tribal area were restricted to the usual head-hunting raids, a more or less casual affair leading to little loss of life, the British authorities did not usually interfere."[18]

Today, the Khiamniungan Naga "country" is a Baptist enclave, and the much-dreaded village Pangsha (mentioned by Fürer-Haimendorf), on the Indian side of the border, has, as an extension of India's Act East policy, been designated an international trade centre. Aside from being an expression of international ambitions in the South East Asian corridor, the Act East policy aims to enrich the economically backward Indo–Myanmar frontier region; yet a great deal of time and resources go into containing recalcitrant natives suspicious of state-building projects. So far, the Indian government has spent more on intelligence gathering and counter-insurgency measures than on development in the Indo–Myanmar border region. The abysmal human development index and neglect of the region speak volumes of the state's true intentions, though those on the Indian side of the border are comparatively better off.

Starting from the second half of the nineteenth century, the British gradually annexed the Indo–Burmese frontier, but the civilising effort of Pax Britannica could not tame the vast hill tracts along the border; they remained virtually a no-man's-land. Active administration was not achieved, so the British adopted cartographic colonisation and measures to subdue the area's recalcitrant communities, most of whom had come as unwanted baggage with the annexed territories. British "pacification" measures included regular punitive expeditions into the hills, establishing police and military outposts along lines of communication, and opening markets in valley towns – all mostly to protect their own interests in the more populated lowland areas. Still, many ethnic

[18] Fürer-Haimendorf, *Return to the Naked Nagas*, 105.

communities remained pretty much undisturbed and continued with their old ways of life, leaving the conundrum of integration for independent nation-states to tackle after British rule ended.

III

In the post-colonial context the Baptist highland is an anomaly sandwiched between Hindu-majority India and Buddhist-majority Myanmar. After Independence, India chose democracy and diversity while its immediate South East Asian neighbour devolved into the world's longest-military-ruled state built on anti-colonial and anti-foreigner lines. Policies towards minorities in both countries have evolved over the decades after Independence, but the integration process of ethnic minority groups into the mainstream, which has proved complex and messy, owes a great deal to the nations' founding leaders.

The Burmese nationalist leader Aung San, by his sheer personality and a political masterstroke, brought the already fragmented Chin, Kachin, Karen, and Shan peoples into a union with the majority ethnic Burmans. Under this arrangement, officially known as the Panglong Agreement, signed on 12 February 1947, the ethnic minorities were promised full autonomy in internal administration and shared economic resources. In order to pacify the minorities, the post of President of the Union rotated among the more politically empowered ethnic groups; meanwhile, the state's premier was by default a leader within the dominant Burman group. Burma may well have had an ethnic Baptist as President of the Union, since it was the turn of a Kachin to assume the office, but the military coup of 1962 dashed this possibility.[19]

[19] As part of the Panglong Agreement, the first president of the union was a Shan, the next was from a Burman majority, the third was a Karen Christian, and the fourth was supposed to be a Kachin. Given the high percentage of Baptist following among the Kachins – and the fact that Baptist converts were among the first educated middle class – a Kachin Baptist rising to the highest office in the land was a strong possibility.

General Aung San did not live to see his national project come to fruition as he was assassinated on 19 July 1947, some months before Burma's independence on 4 January 1948. His Indian counterpart Jawaharlal Nehru too faced formidable difficulties bringing the frontier ethnic groups within the Indian union; in fact Nehru lived long enough to see an ethnicity-based armed struggle erupting among the Nagas on the Indian side of the Baptist highland. Their ethnonationalism subsequently spilled across the border when the Nagas expanded their "ancestral homeland" territorial claim to include ethnic Nagas living in the Naga Hills in upland Myanmar. This Naga insurgency soon grew into a gruelling issue for India as Naga rebels on its side of the border fought the state with their backs to the impenetrable jungles of Myanmar. In retrospect, Nehru did not fail as a nationalist leader – on the contrary he was arguably the finest popular world leader to emerge among the newly independent nations in the post-colonial period; rather, the Naga desire for autonomy and freedom from the diktat of a subsuming state – a thread common to all ethnic groups in the Baptist highland – was irrepressible even in the face of Nehru's liberal statesmanship and the famed persuasive (occasionally arm-twisting) powers of his home minister, Sardar Vallabhbhai Patel.

The integration policy that followed Burma's independence was disastrous, especially after Aung San's death. Ethnicity-based political movements became a primary hurdle in any attempt at national unity. However, the imbroglio also owed to the change of political regimes in Myanmar. Contrary to what the Panglong Agreement had delineated – "Citizens of the Frontier Areas shall enjoy rights and privileges which are regarded as fundamental in democratic countries" – the fall of the post-independence civilian government following the military coup on 2 March 1962 heralded a new phase in nation-building which changed the political and cultural dynamics of the ethnic groups in the Baptist highland. The process of Burmanisation of ethnic minorities became the order of the day.

Thakin Nu, or U Nu as he is respectfully known, the Burman premier of the post-war civilian government, regarded as a most tolerant and democratic leader, was a devout Buddhist who did not hesitate to use religion for political purposes. Although some argue that it was the problem of ethnicity that spurred the military coup of 1962, ethnic minorities like the Chin, Kachin, and Karen, who during the civilian period included a substantial Christian population, had been antagonised by U Nu's role in introducing Buddhism as Burma's state religion in 1961. To his credit, it should be said that U Nu had also brought in a separate bill to guarantee freedom of worship, but this had not pacified the aggrieved ethnic minorities. The civil conflict over religious differences entered the political arena with the 1962 military coup that brought General Ne Win to power, and thus began an aggressive state-sponsored drive towards Burmanisation. The move for cultural, educational, and religious homogeneity modelled on majority Burman identity alienated non-Burman ethnic groups, more so in the north-western uplands where Christianity prevailed.

Nehru – U Nu's contemporary and close friend – had a special regard for the social category termed "tribes", seeing them as the most disenfranchised of people in independent India. Many of these ethnic indigenous groups were in the division of what in Nehru's day was called the North-East Frontier Agency (NEFA).[20] Trouble was already brewing in the hill district of Assam in the Himalayan foothills. The Nagas, who by then had a substantial Baptist following, especially among the educated elite, were making their desire for self-determination known. India's Cambridge-educated agnostic prime minister, on the other hand, had as his national ideal a secular country where religion did not loom large within a problem seen as fundamentally ethnic. This was a significant difference in the ethnonationalism issue on the Indian side of the Baptist highland. It contrasted with Burma,

[20] In the context of India, the social group "tribe" is regarded as a constitutional category legitimised by Articles 330–340 of the Indian constitution, which sanctions reservations for them in government jobs and educational institutions, a form of "positive discrimination" employed by the state to benefit the tribal and underprivileged caste population in India. For more details, see Béteille, "The Idea of Indigenous People".

where state leaders were not chary of professing a religious tradition and making it clear that Buddhism enjoyed a special status under their charge.

In his foreword to Verrier Elwin's *A Philosophy for NEFA*, Nehru summed up his ideas for integrating tribal communities like the Nagas into the mainstream.[21] He believed "it is always the duty and obligation of the majority to win the goodwill of the minorities."[22] Nehru's was a quintessentially liberal stance to alleviate the problems of a nation divided along ethnic, religious, and linguistic lines. His policy extended to the ethnic communities of the remote Indo–Burmese frontier which the new state was finding difficult to govern. Ethnic Nagas had begun asserting that their shared culture, which they claimed as transnational, was being erased by a geographical boundary drawn in the process of forming nation-states. They opposed such a boundary. The Nagas did not share the nationalist enthusiasm of Nehru and Patel, for whom a well-defined national boundary was coterminous with the idea of an autonomous nation. From the Naga perspective the Indian state, by separating them from their brethren in Burma, was employing much the same divide-and-rule policy as the British.

So policies and relations with ethnic groups in the Baptist highland would become a litmus test for both Burma and India in the post-independence period, with a deadlock persisting well into the twenty-first century, punctuated by violent armed struggle and military interventions. Human rights violations became a common feature in the Baptist highland on both sides of the border; though, all said and done, the Indian state fared better than the Burmese in relation to policies towards ethnic minorities.

[21] See Elwin, *A Philosophy for NEFA*. The author of this widely read book on tribal policy, Verrier Elwin, was an Oxford seminary-trained Anglican missionary turned anthropologist who was also a close confidant of Nehru and his tribal policy advisor. In the foreword, Nehru outlined his policy of tribal development, which came to be popularly known as the tribal *panchsheel*.

[22] Nehru's letter to chief ministers in 1954, quoted in Guha, ed., *Makers of Modern Asia*, 127.

On the Myanmar side of the border, ethnic polemic was fuelled by religious identity as the Burmese state blamed Christian missions for the uprising among hill people. On the Indian side, Christianity – for all its putative arrival in Malabar with Christ's apostle Saint Thomas – was regarded as foreign to Indian soil primarily on account of its association with the British.[23] In Nehru's vision, India had to be built as multi-religious, multi-ethnic, and multilingual; linguistic pluralism was in fact one of his government's legacies. Among the ethnic peoples of the hills, Christian missions had made English the important medium of instruction.[24] Nehru's liberal language policy enabled English – the universal Baptist language – to grow unimpeded in the region. In fact the Baptist highland developed into one of the most literate parts of the country.

Meanwhile the Burmese state began homogenising ethnic minority groups during the 1960s and made this a large bone of contention. In 2017, not long after a commemoration of the Panglong Conference in Naypyidaw led by the State Counsellor of Myanmar Aung San Suu Kyi – though with the "infamous" Tatmadaw (military) still clinging to power – the Swedish journalist Bertil Lintner, a noted Burma expert, observed acerbically that "Using numerology as a guide to national peace and unity in a nation with as many diverse ethnic groups as Myanmar, and where civil war has been raging since independence in 1948, hardly seems like a sensible way forward."[25] The preoccupation with numerology, which draws from the traditional Theravada Buddhist tradition, has been a significant feature of successive regimes, with most heads of state resorting to its esoteric divinations. But such "irrational" rituals are only one facet of the larger national policy of Burmanisation that the state has resolutely pursued over decades.

[23] See Frykenberg, *Christianity in India*, esp. Chapter 4.
[24] The Welsh mission among the Khasis, the Presbyterian mission among the Mizos, and the Baptist mission among the Garos, Kukis, and Nagas are the most notable foreign missions that impacted the region.
[25] Lintner, "A Question of Race in Myanmar".

Today, more than 800,000 Rohingya Muslims in Rakhine state have fled to Bangladesh, with the UNHRC charging Myanmar with ethnic cleansing. Aung San Suu Kyi's handling of the situation has made her unpopular with the very Western media that once idolised her.

The imposition of Burmese as a state-sponsored language affected the ethnic Baptists in Myanmar's north-western upland. Like ethnic Naga Baptists on the Indian side, they had taken to English like a duck to water for the obvious reason that it was their language when acquiring Christianity. American Baptist missionaries had introduced the Roman script for education, proselytising, and translations of religious texts in local languages, thereby transforming an oral society and exposing it to literary culture. While ethnic groups in the Baptist highland spoke diverse tongues originating in the Tibeto–Burman language family, English was taught in all Baptist mission schools. These had become important learning centres, replacing traditional institutions. English had also provided the template for the formalisation of the native tongues – which was often problematic, since inter-village dialect differences within a particular ethnic community were common – and in translations. For instance, Jinghpaw became the first Kachin orthography with translation work done by the Baptist missionary Ola Hanson; the process of Bible translation by the American missionaries led the dialect of an old Angami village, Kohima, to become the template for the Angami Naga literary language;[26] and a language spoken in Wakching, a village made famous by Fürer-Haimendorf's monograph,[27] and where the first Konyak Baptist mission field was established in

---

[26] The headquarters of the British Naga Hills District was established in Kohima in 1878. Originally known as Kewhira, this old Angami village would also become an important base of the American Baptist mission in 1882. The American Baptist missionaries opened their station in the outskirts of Kohima village and sought the help of villagers to learn the Angami language for Bible translation and evangelism.

[27] Fürer-Haimendorf, *The Naked Nagas*.

1950,[28] would become the translation language of the Konyak Baptists.

English education among the Nagas on the Indian side progressed rapidly, with many Nagas earning degrees from the nation's leading universities. Today, their early exposure to this global language has given educated Nagas an edge over most other Indian tribes. It has also made them better represented in the Indian bureaucracy and academia than other ethnic minorities.[29] The literacy rate in Nagaland, according to the 2011 census, averages 80.11 per cent.

Despite Baptist missionaries, English education among the Chin and Kachin tribes of Burma fared poorly by comparison with the Nagas in India. This owed in part to Burmese state policies. The Nagas on the Myanmar side also lag far behind in terms of modern education because no outsiders set foot in the area – not even American Baptist missionaries.[30] Overall, in the Baptist highland, Chin state remains one of the most impoverished regions and has a poor literacy rate. It is common to see Chin students coming to the neighbouring Indian states of Mizoram and Nagaland to be re-educated in schools run by the government, churches, or NGOs. The same is true of Nagas in the Sagaing region of Myanmar, where parents send their children to the Indian side to study in English-medium schools run by the state government and the

---

[28] The Council of Baptist Churches of Assam (CBCA) resolved to open three mission fields among the Konyak Nagas, Abors (Adis), and Meiteis in the late 1940s. Thus, it was that the CBCA appointed its first missionary, Longri Ao, to the Konyak Nagas on 21 September 1950. Konyak, *The Konyak Naga*, 145.

[29] Ramachandra Guha, a leading historian of post-Independence India, observes that educated, English-speaking communities like the Nagas and Meiteis with higher levels of gender equality can access the best jobs all over India, and in such a socio-political context a fight for small, isolated, independent homelands loses its relevance. See Guha, *Patriots and Partisans*, Chapter 1.

[30] In the Naga Hills in Myanmar, headhunting practices continued even as late as the 1980s. See Tucker, *Burma*, 21.

Baptist missions. Mission-minded Naga families in Nagaland support Naga children across the border in Myanmar, enabling them to study in Yangon and other cities within the Burmese education system "to impact the Burmese society".[31] The Kachins also send some of their promising students to Baptist-run schools, colleges, and seminaries in India instead of to poorly run Burmese state schools. "English" education via Baptists means upward mobility. This has pushed Kachin and Chin students across the border to greener pastures in India.

Cross-border cultural similarity of the various ethnic groups in the Baptist highland shows advantages in the perception of students. Such is the porosity of the border and the distance from New Delhi and Naypyidaw that the bulk of ethnic minority students from Myanmar cross over without papers and become part of the ethnic community on the Indian side, staying for years. The interconnectedness of these ethnic groups of the Baptist highland has huge implications for nation-building in the Indo–Myanmar frontier region, since the groups include the rebels.

On the Myanmar side the military takeover in the 1960s severely affected the ethnic groups in the uplands. And in densely populated towns and cities, Christian mission schools were shut down and overseas-born teachers expelled despite the popularity of these schools among well-to-do Burmese. English was the first language removed in learning centres during the state-sponsored education drive; among ethnic minority groups in the uplands the Burmese language was imposed to foster a majoritarian national identity.

To the Tibeto–Burman-speaking Chins, Kachins, and Nagas in the Baptist highland, Burmese, though a Southern Burmish branch of the Sino–Tibetan languages, was a tongue as foreign as German or Swahili. In this matter the Nagas on the Indian

[31] I met a devout Angami couple in Kohima town who support a Konyak Naga boy from Myanmar, whom they have never met. The boy studies in a "good" school in Yangon, and they occasionally receive a letter of gratitude written in Burmese from the Class X student. Many Naga Baptist families donate generously for missions in the Indo–Myanmar frontier states.

side enjoyed an advantage because Nagamese, an Assamese-based pidgin of the Indo-Aryan language family, was developed and continued as a "bazaar" language for commercial purposes. It had been popularised by British political agents when administering natives who often spoke tongues unintelligible to each other despite their geographical and cultural proximity. Besides, the Indian state was laid-back about the ethnic languages of the north-east frontier and did not stifle the language of ethnic minorities as a state-sponsored project.

In Arunachal Pradesh, Hindi has made strong inroads and is considered a successful "Indian" experiment in the post-colonial period, especially among right-wing political parties. Unlike in the neighbouring states of Meghalaya, Mizoram, and Nagaland, where the popularity of English owes mainly to the Christian missions, post-independence state policy insulated Arunachal Pradesh from the missions, although some ethnic groups – like the Adi, Khamti, and Singpho tribes – had come into contact with American Baptist missionaries as early as the second quarter of the nineteenth century. These missionaries were newly arrived from Burma. Before finding success among the Nagas in the Naga Hills district and the Garos in present-day Meghalaya, they had, as earlier noted, opened a short-lived mission station in Sadiya to evangelise the Khamti tribe of present-day Arunachal Pradesh.[32]

In Myanmar's post-civilian government era, the National Language Commission instituted by the military regime decided that the English language be dropped entirely from the school curriculum as a medium of instruction;[33] it would only be allowed as a second language; most popular writings in English were banned, barring a few books such as George Orwell's *Burmese Days*, which was highly critical of British colonialism.[34] This language policy was fatal for the ethnic languages because Burmese was made

---

[32] When the "warlike" Khamtis attacked the British garrison in Sadiya in 1839, the Baptist missionaries soon abandoned the place. See Downs, *The Mighty Works of God*, 17–18.

[33] Cockett, *Blood, Dreams and Gold*, 80.

[34] Orwell, *Burmese Days*.

the sole medium of school instruction throughout the country. Ethnic groups were denied the right to learn and teach their own languages. Burmese as official language meant, moreover, that those who did not speak it were disadvantaged in relation to government jobs, university degrees and diplomas being awarded on the basis of state-monitored curricula. The setback to English-medium educational institutions run by the ethnic Baptist missions was huge. Students saw no point in Baptist learning centres because knowledge of English was of no value in the country's labour market.

In another instance of the state monitoring of languages, the Adaptation of Expressions Law was passed in 1989. Under the garb of decolonisation, this changed the former anglicised versions of names and places in the country to reflect the language of the majority ethnic Burman.[35] Burma became Myanmar, Burmese became Bamar, Karen and Karenni were changed to Kayin and Kayah, respectively, Rangoon was changed to Yangon, Moulmein to Mawlamyine, Tenasserim to Tanintharyi, and so on. This did not go down well with the ethnic minorities; one of the reasons for their taking up arms was the government's relentless Burmanisation project.

IV

The highland inhabitants of the Indo–Burma region were long regarded by the British as "martial races", which led to their recruitment in the military and police and occasionally as mercenaries. Those recruited were from indigenous groups like the Chins, Kachins, Kukis, and Nagas. The idea of "martial races" is

---

[35] The new policy came with General Saw Maung's seizure of power to become undisputed head of state. Saw Maung assumed chairmanship of the State Law and Order Restoration Council on 18 September 1988. The following year the names of cities and important landmarks were changed on the grounds that the names should reflect the original pronunciation and meaning of the "glorious" pre-colonial days.

apparent in the composition of the Burma Army in 1938, which comprised 3040 Karens, Kachins, Chins, and other indigenous peoples, 1587 Britons, 1423 Indians and Gurkhas, and 159 Burmans – when ethnic Burmans comprised two-thirds of the population of Burma.[36]

British military policy subdivided an already fragmented society, a chasm emerging between ethnic groups in the uplands and lowlands. This was accentuated by the new religion brought in by American missionaries. A region dominated by Baptist Christianity in an upland region of "martial races" who had little regard for newly drawn international boundaries came into being. In the post-independence period, when an armed struggle based on ethnic identities began, the division along religious lines took firmer root.

Early in the new-born Indian and Burmese states, the Baptist highland became infamous for people's armed uprisings and counter-insurgency measures by both states, bringing untold misery. Identity-based movements among the ethnic groups were intrinsic to the decolonisation process bequeathed to the new nation-states. Mainstream nationalist leaders blamed colonial rule for the post-colonial political conundrum and ethnic minority leaders believed the British were responsible for the origins of their ethnonationalism. The conventional claim is that the British government betrayed the aspirations of the people by fragmenting traditional homelands. Post-independence India and Myanmar saw tremendous social and political change, but the ethnic leaders of the Baptist highland never forgot the colonial "betrayal". Long after independence, they continued to hope that the defanged Great Britain would intervene in the situation. Until the time of his death in 1990 the Naga nationalist leader A.Z. Phizo, who was then settled in London, continued to appeal to the West, hoping it would support the Naga cause. But in the post-war era, changed geopolitics made the ethnic Naga issue a drop in the vast ocean of

---

[36] Tucker, *Burma*, 32.

a new world. In 25 July 1994 the ageing British politician Enoch Powell wrote in reply to a plea from an elderly Naga nationalist, Khodao Yanthan: "I can understand how you feel; but the fact remains that by the India Act 1947 the United Kingdom ceased to be in any way responsible for India's government or its treatment of its component races." On 10 August 1994 the Naga National Council (NNC) leader fired back:

> In refer. to what you have said: "By the India Independence Act 1947 the United Kingdom ceased to be in any way responsible for India's government or its treatment of its component races." This your statement is of course only an Englishman's lame-excuse, or Pilate who washed his hands claiming his innocence. Because, under whatever Act 1947 India became Independent that was only a matter between Britain and India.
>
> *Please Note Well:* A British control of a Naga territory (bordering Assam) which was called 'Naga Hills' was NOT INCLUDED in the British India. It was a 'Buffer Zone' to protect the administered area of Assam from the Nagas, and later in 1935, it was placed under an 'Excluded Area' i.e. a separate territory from the British Indian Rule. Only one British Political officer (Deputy Commissioner) was kept as a watchdog without interfering in the Naga affair. PARABLE: A traveller once met a man, a friend in need but later the traveller betrayed and sold him to a stranger and then went away. Who was that traveller . . . ?[37]

Khodao Yanthan, a Lotha Naga, had gone to London in 1963 to join the NNC president A.Z. Phizo, who was from the Angami tribe, to internationalise the Naga issue. This was five years prior to Powell's 1968 "Rivers of Blood" speech criticising immigration to the United Kingdom from the Commonwealth countries. Such was the impact of colonial rule that, years after it had ended, elderly Naga nationalists, like many of their contemporaries who had been part of the decolonisation process, hoped to achieve something by raising the issue of Naga self-rule with the British.

[37] See Yanthan, *Wounded Tiger*, 169.

Faith in the British felt by a Kachin WWII veteran, Ho Wa Zan Gam, was also made apparent by a British historian, Richard Cockett, who interviewed him and heard this: "We wanted freedom from the British government, and we looked to the Atlantic Charter [signed between Churchill and Roosevelt in early 1942] that the British would release their colonies. We knew after the war that Burma would have independence . . . so the Kachin from Myitkyina quickly wanted independence from Britain. We were confident about that."[38]

Ethnic leaders in the Baptist highland like Khodao Yanthan – a recipient of the Burma Star and the King George Medal for bravery – and Ho Wa Zan Gam of the Kachin Rangers, a Burma veteran who fought with the Allied forces in WWII to drive out the Japanese, blame the British for turning their backs on them after the war.[39] The experience of these ethnic communities in modern warfare and exposure to military tactics continued to be of use well into the post-independence period over their armed struggle.

The Indo–Burma frontier of the ethnic Baptists would become synonymous with armed rebellion, guerrilla warfare, and unrelenting jungle warfare against the state. A difficult terrain of thick forest has proved a safe hideout for armed rebels, making military operations against them difficult if not ineffective. In response, on either side of the border, the state has heavily militarised the region to suppress ethnic uprising. The Nagas accused the Indian prime minister Morarji Desai (1977–9) of threatening to use his military to overrun their tiny state,[40] but it was during Nehru's

---

[38] Quoted in Cockett, *Blood, Dreams and Gold*, 120.

[39] Besides the "Burma Star" and a "King George the VI Silver Medal", Khodao Yanthan was also awarded the "India Service Medal" for his wartime contribution. Ibid., 15.

[40] In a much-publicised talk between A.Z. Phizo and Indian Prime Minister Morarji Desai, the NNC president accused Desai of threatening to "exterminate all the Naga rebels". The document giving the Naga leader's side of the story was widely distributed, adding Morarji Desai to a list of

time that the infamous Armed Force Special Powers Act (AFSPA) was passed on 11 September 1958 to quell armed rebellion in the Naga Hills district. This act remains in place even now and has been regularly cited as the source of human rights and citizens' rights violations in Kashmir, Mizoram, Nagaland, etc. During the height of military operations in the Naga Hills, there was one soldier for every male native on the Indian side of the border.[41] On the Burma side of the Baptist highland, military dominance has been absolute. The Tatmadaw – as Myanmar's armed forces are collectively called – has in Chin state increased its strength from two to fourteen battalions since 1998, and from twenty-four to forty-one battalions in Kachin state since 1994.[42]

Fear and suspicion have existed between plains and hill people for generations. The Chins inhabited an inhospitable malaria-infested jungle spread over sharp-edged ridges with altitudes as much as 2500 metres and more, falling abruptly to deep ravines where capricious rivers are fed by torrential rains. Strong winds lash the region throughout the year. But more than the formidable habitat, the Chins were dreaded for their "wild" ways. They had plundered their valley neighbours regularly for farm produce and women, and to exact tribute.[43] North of the Chins were the Nagas who inhabited similar jungle-matted hills and were notorious for their headhunting. The Naga tribes were also known for keeping slaves, with more powerful tribes like the Angami, Konyak, and Khiamniungan Naga involved in raiding villages to capture slaves.[44] The Kachins, who inhabit vertiginous mountains north of

---

"unpopular" Indian leaders among the Nagas. See Zinyü, *Phizo and the Naga Problem*, Chapter 29.

[41] By 1956, nearly two divisions and thirty-five battalions of the armed forces were in operation in the Naga Hills district and Tuensang Frontier Division of NEFA. See Mullik, *My Years with Nehru*, 312–14.

[42] Steinberg, *Burma/Myanmar*, 165.

[43] The Chins kept slaves to enhance social status and maintain power. The slave-raiding ventures of the Chins were mainly in the lowlands of Bengal and Burma. See Thakur, "The Institution of Slavery in the Chin Society", 218–19.

[44] See Sema, *British Policy and Administration*.

the Nagas, were no less warrior-like and fiercely independent, and considered by armies of lowland states useful only as mercenaries.[45] They were known for plundering their lowland neighbours, and for exacting tribute from weaker communities and villages. The strip of mountainous land straddling the Indo–Burmese border was therefore virtually isolated. Invading armies, kings, and empire-builders preferred skirting the highlanders during their expansionist projects. The Burmans and Shans had left the Chins undisturbed in their unwelcoming country; the Kachins were not confronted before the British intervened with a far superior military to pacify them; the Nagas – who occupied a far more barren habitat in terms of natural resources like semi-precious stones, coal, and natural gas – remained untouched by successive waves of invading armies. Migrating populations too steered clear of this inhospitable hilly region.

Armed struggle was the driving force of ethnonationalism among the indomitable Baptist highlanders, and guerrilla warfare their modus operandi. Allied with the difficult terrain this meant they could only be overcome by a brutish military strategy and remorseless counter-insurgency measures. In the post-independence period rape, torture, forced labour, extrajudicial killing, and internment camps became common here. In General Ne Win's Myanmar in the 1960s, the Tatmadaw implemented a counter-insurgency strategy called the "four cuts" – aimed at cutting off armed rebels from their jungle base by depriving them of food, funding, information, and new recruits. The trial run for this was the Kachin and Naga area. On the Indian side the military had already applied the four-cuts strategy in the Naga Hills starting in 1957; under this programme, the mass relocation of villagers from their traditional villages into military-designated sites known as "Progressive and Protected Villages" was the bedrock of counter-insurgency. Commonly called "concentration camps", or more mildly "army grouping" by the Nagas, this strategy to isolate Naga rebels brought untold misery to ordinary villagers.

[45] Tucker, *Burma*, 20.

An Angami Naga historian who, as a little boy, left for the jungle in 1956 after his village was burnt down in the military operation, pensively recalls:

> The jungle experience was a defining one – and also a dividing one. At first people did not talk about it. It was too traumatic and so the pain was buried. But now people want to remember . . . I have since spoken with the Karen of Burma, who also lived in the jungle after the Burmese Army burnt their villages, and they tell their stories with great pain and sadness. So do other refugees I have met . . . they [the Nagas] do cry when talking about the experience . . . during those years in the jungle: the torture, rape and killing of their loved ones.[46]

My own parents were, as children, relocated to internment camps during the "army grouping" in 1963, faint memories of which they harbour to this day.[47] Among Naga Baptists who faced these difficult years, harsh military intervention was an impetus for a renewed Christian pietism and a new-found religious experience that coincided with the Charismatic movement – a movement that spread outside the landlocked hills. This new religious movement emphasised the Holy Spirit and propagated a form of mysticism by which the Christian deity became experientially accessible to seekers. It restructured the traditional Baptist faith and sparked off a new discourse on indigenous forms taken by Christianity.[48]

Meanwhile, the military intervention antagonised many mission-school-educated Nagas who gave up the prospect of plum jobs in the state government to join the Naga national cause, further alienating Naga society from the nascent Indian state. Some of these educated Naga leaders became seasoned theoreticians and

---

[46] Sanyü with Broome, *A Naga Odyssey*, 61–2.

[47] In 1963 an army convoy was ambushed by Naga guerrillas about 25 km from the Zunheboto headquarters, killing a number of Indian army personnel. After this incident the nearby villagers were all sent off to the internment camp in the Atoizu Circle. The incident of the ambush is mentioned in Dev, *Nagaland*, 60–3.

[48] See Chophy, *Constructing the Divine*, esp. Chapter 7.

skilled guerrilla tacticians. To achieve their political objective they were happy to deploy religious rhetoric, and their Baptist education came in handy for furthering the cause of ethnonationalism. India was projected in Biblical terms as pharaonic Egypt, and its lawmakers as pharaohs repressing powerless but god-chosen Nagas. These Old Testament analogies were intended as morale boosters during difficult jungle warfare by legitimating Naga nationalism as a mandate from heaven. However, the fallout of a struggle impelled by religion made it seem "jihadic" and sowed suspicion among the Indian political class and policy-makers. Even Nehru, a most secular man, held the Baptist missions culpable for inciting trouble: certain foreign missionaries "in the northeast encouraged separatist and disruptive movements" was how he put it.[49] His closest aide on tribal affairs, Elwin, observed that

> Orders were early issued by the Naga military organisation that every Company should have a pastor and it is said that most of the marching songs had a Christian motif. In 1956, an order was circulated by the Chief of the "Country Guard Government of Nagaland" that "God ought to be included in every practical field of the Nagas and, therefore, as many pastors as possible should be appointed to prepare the war affairs". Services were regularly held in the various hide-outs and there was a great deal of propaganda that since Nagaland was to be the first completely Christian State in Asia (today Naga churches are placarded with posters saying "Nagaland for Christ") it was the duty of Christians to fight the "Hindu Government" in order to preserve their religion.[50]

The Indian authorities, long suspicious of foreign missionaries in the Naga Hills, became more so, attributing the armed uprising to the "dubious" handiwork of American Baptist missionaries. During their frequent "combing operations" the Indian armed

[49] Jawaharlal Nehru's letter to chief ministers dated 17 October 1952. See Khosla, ed., *Letters for a Nation*.

[50] Elwin, *Nagaland*, 62–3. The slight irony in Elwin's observation here is that Elwin himself came to India as a Christian missionary. See the early chapters of Guha, *Savaging the Civilized*.

forces burnt down churches, beat up church workers, and even killed Baptist ministers, though their motivation was not hostility to Christianity per se; attacks on the faithful and the church establishment were part of the state's counter-insurgency measures. A retired Sumi Naga Baptist pastor who was twice relocated to an army internment camp related how the Indian military allowed believers to attend an annual Baptist conference in the mid-1960s in a far-off village in the eastern Sumi region, despite the faithful being kept in a "concentration camp" under strict vigil.[51] State policy did not single out Naga Baptists for their religious affiliation; it was just that there was no escaping the fact that Naga Christianity was seen as responsible for the political unrest. The consequence was a vicious cycle from the perspective of the Indian state, and possibly a virtuous cycle from the perspective of the Naga Baptists, because the Naga rebels made use of the sufferings of the natives – who were then converting to the Baptist faith in huge numbers – as an augmentation of their ethnonationalist rhetoric. During the height of armed violence in the late 1950s the publicity wing of the Naga underground government alleged that

> Over 400 hundred Churches have been destroyed. Like many of the Villages these have been built, destroyed, rebuilt, and so on many times at risk of torture and death. Naga worshippers are forced to shout "Jai Hind" (Victory to India) outside the churches, otherwise they are not allowed to enter ... On many occasions, Indian troops have marched into churches and broken up the services at rifle point. Pastors are forbidden to visit their congregations in their homes, or in the outlying villages, the reason given being that they are messengers of the rebels, so many village churches are neglected and empty.[52]

---

[51] The Baptist minister from Lotisami village was sent off to an internment camp in Rotomi in 1963. It was in the winter of that year that the Sumi Baptist annual conference was held in the eastern Sumi village of Khukishe, which was attended by thousands despite fierce fighting in the jungle between Naga rebels and the Indian armed forces.

[52] Naga National Council, *The Naga National Rights*, 107. The publication is a compilation of letters, documents, and news reports relating to the NNC-led political struggle.

Naga nationalist leaders were unapologetically Baptist and had no qualms using Christian motifs and messages as propaganda. These infused meaning and direction into an incendiary but rudderless ethnic pride in a warrior tradition passed down through the generations, which became in turn a contributing factor in ethnonationalism. Men like A.Z. Phizo were devout Baptists; his clansmen from Khonoma – an Angami Naga village known for its warriors and famous battles – still pride themselves for having raised illustrious Baptist converts. Stories of Khonoma men standing up to the might of British "invaders" were not without effect. Phizo was said to have been weaned on stories of "courageous warriors and famed fighters from Khonoma". When Phizo began his career as a politician and statesman, his distinct style of advocating ethnonationalism melded ethnic pride with Biblical rhetoric:

> Someone may tell us that Nagas are Christians following a foreign religion. The Indians publicly say this. We do not take Christianity as foreign religion any more than we consider the light of the sun as foreign origin from outer world. There is a father-Creator (Ukepenopfü) as we call it. He is God. The message of the Gospel fulfills our Naga conception of religion – Nanyü – which literally means "anguish of mind" for which we do worship.[53]

Such Naga rhetoric is a part of tradition. Though the first modern Naga institution, the Naga Club formed in 1918, did not explicitly allude to Christian motifs since the signatories comprised both Baptists and animists, they employed them adroitly while submitting a memorandum to the Simon Commission on 10 January 1929 to assert their "unique" history: "Our language is quite different from those of the plains and we have no social affinities with the Hindus or Mussalmans. We are looked [down] upon by the one for our 'beef' and the other for our 'pork' and by both for our want in education, [which] is not due to any fault of ours."[54]

---

[53] Phizo's address in Kohima at the Naga plebiscite on 16 May 1951. See Zinyü, *Phizo and the Naga Problem*, Appendix VI.

[54] Memorandum of the Naga Club to the Simon Commission, 10 January 1929. See Chasie, *The Naga Imbroglio*, 183–5.

In their propaganda and writings, Naga nationalists like A.Z. Phizo, T. Sakhrie, and Khodao Yanthan are overtly and proudly Christian, often militantly so. This took a more radical direction in Phizo's former foreign secretary in the Naga underground government, Isak Chishi Swu, who later became chairman of the NSCN(IM) and propagated the idea of a Christian state. Swu saw Naga nationalism as a divine call. For his predecessors, Christianity was a means to an end, but for Swu his devout Baptist faith was an end in itself. Naga leaders were not averse to experimenting with new political ideologies if these aided the cause of a Naga nation, but Swu envisioned a theocratic Naga nation. This did not go down well in mainstream India, especially hostile being Hindu right-wing groups who attributed insurgency woes in Nagaland to external forces and found much-needed arsenal for propaganda in their effort to make India Hindu. The Baptist faith, like Islam, had not originated within South Asia. For right-wing Hindu nationalists keen on countrywide religious homogeneity, Christianity as a rabble-rousing faith was an impediment to national integration and synonymous with the Baptist highland.

V

The Baptist highland is a textbook example of the ethnic quagmire, but in relation to nation-building in the post-colonial period the Burmese and Indian states were grappling with a religious problem: the challenge of a supposedly unholy alliance between Christian missions and armed insurgency. This was the apprehension manifest, for example, in Baptist Nagas being seen by the Indian Central Bureau of Intelligence as more unmanageable than the Roman Catholics.[55]

The Indian state has not formally linked Naga "separatism" to the Baptist faith, but there are political organisations alleging

[55] See Dhar, *Open Secrets*, esp. Chapter 9. According to Dhar, India's intelligence considered Baptist Christians lesser "Indian" nationalists than Catholics.

such a nexus and arguing that the Baptist highland harbours a "missionary conspiracy" to weaken the Indian state from within. Armed struggle has, in this view, less to do with a complex history, peculiar geography, and specific ethnic diversity in the Indo–Myanmar upland. Because Christians make up just 2.3 per cent of the total Indian population in the 2011 census and exceed 80 per cent in Nagaland, the idea of a Naga Christian conspiracy is likely to persist for the foreseeable future. However, the low national ratio of Christians to Hindus, alongside the far higher ratio of Muslims to Hindus, and the concentration of Christianity only in far corners of the country (the far north-east and the far south) are factors reducing the threat preception.

By comparison, in Myanmar the Christian minority suffers state repression, and the Tatmadaw has been accused of church burnings and the oppression of religious minorities. In the Baptist-majority Chin state the regime has been accused of promoting Buddhism and building pagodas using forced labour. Here the ethnic Christian minorities therefore retaliate with assertions of religious identity. Richard Cockett observes that "The modern identity of Kachin is bound up with a very Victorian brand of martial Christianity, and the most important difference between the Kachin and Burmans to this day is still religious . . . Here, the Christian faith is not just a matter of religious observance; it has become a vital, living expression of Kachin culture, identity and autonomy."[56]

The connection of Naga ethnonationalism with Christianity in the Baptist highland is historically contingent; arguably, it would have arisen and persisted in the region even without the American Baptist faith, and its discourse then would have taken a different form – as for instance it has among the Buddhist-majority ethnic Shans and Mons, the animist ethnic Was in Myanmar, and the Hindu-majority Meitei and Ahom people in north-east India.[57]

[56] Cockett, *Blood, Dreams and Gold*, 116.
[57] Some scholars argue that the Naga political movement was the "root"

In fact, a peculiar feature of what I term the Baptist highland has been its politically anomalous nature seen from the perspective of nation-states in the post-colonial period. The Baptist highland overlaps a more broadly troubled region of India commonly called "the north-east". Despite being ethnically, culturally, and linguistically an uncommonly rich and varied part of the country, northeast India has been reduced in Indian thinking and parlance to a kind of geopolitical backwater. The region now holds the attention of majoritarian rule because even "advanced" Hindu communities in the Assam and Manipur valleys – strongly influenced by Vaishnavism – have clambered onto the insurgency bandwagon.

If seen as a geopolitical zone within South and South East Asia, the Baptist highland may be considered a part of a larger "Southeast Asian massif", which James Scott calls "the largest remaining nonstate spaces in the world". Such identification as a "nonstate space" is not, however, straightforward, since the defining characteristic of this particular "nonstate space" has been resistance to "projects of nation-building and state-making".[58] The state-making processes of the surrounding nation are in the Baptist highland marred by ethnic uprisings and violence, with political disputes leading to armed insurrection. The success of a monotheistic faith here has exacerbated identity politics since Christianity has made ethnic identities more amenable to Western influence. Conversely, ethnicity has shaped religious beliefs, giving rise to newer forms of Christianity.

Baptist identity in the Indo–Myanmar frontier is not monolithic despite shared origin and history. In addition to the experience of colonialism, surrounding cultures have significantly determined the contours of Baptist identity among ethnic groups like the Kuki-Chins, Kachins, and Nagas. Among Nagas, the spectrum of Baptist Christian identity ranges from an American fundamentalist

---

of the ethnic-based identity struggle in India's north-east. See Nibedon, *North-East India*, esp. Chapter 2.

[58] See Scott, *The Art of Not Being Governed*, Preface.

type to an amalgamated nativist type, with a Pentecostal variety in between. Differing Christian perspectives are apparent among Naga Baptists from their interpretations of nationalism as well as Christianity. Critics charge that this American brand of Protestantism fosters anti-national and secessionist tendencies, but there is sufficient contradictory evidence showing that many Naga Baptist intellectuals resist blending ethnonationalism and religious ideology.

The continuing involvement of the Naga Baptist church in the peace process between the Indian government and the Naga rebels has to some extent allayed apprehensions of a link between Baptist Christianity and ethnonationalism. As the leading Naga Baptist theologian Kethoser Kevichusa astutely remarks, "there is a clear danger in ethnic identity becoming idolatrous". Drawing from the Old Testament, he says bluntly that "like all idol worship, worship of ethnicity also requires blood offering". He attributes the decades of violence in the region to "an unfettered and unreflective struggle for ethnic-nationalism". Many Naga Baptist thinkers like Kethoser draw a connection between bloodshed and the failure of the Baptist faith in Nagaland. Naga Baptists are not universally cheerleaders of the faith; they have serious critics within. With regard to armed violence, the broad consensus is however that the problem is related to their ethnic identity struggle and not their religious affiliation.

VI

Today, upland Baptists spread their influence and add more converts to their fold, especially from kindred ethnic communities who still follow traditional religion on both sides of the international border. The brand of Christianity in this region is not the diffident and politically correct version of mainstream Western Christianity. In its zealous commitment to the traditional Christian teachings on mission and evangelism it is perhaps closer in its worldview and ethos to the Latin American variant. A distinct evangelical worldview has been inherited and is responsible for the spurt in adherents. This rediscovery of evangelism is a major contributing factor in the rise of Christianity over the "global south".[59]

The most vibrant and thriving Baptist community in the Baptist highland is, as I see it, of the Naga Baptists, and from this hub radiate effects felt afar. Baptist Nagas are now found in Assam, Arunachal Pradesh, Nagaland, and Manipur, and in the northwestern frontier of Myanmar bordering India in the Sagaing region, but in terms of cultural and political dominance Nagaland remains the model Baptist homeland. The Baptists here account for about 75 to 80 per cent of the entire Christian population of the state, making it the world's largest Baptist-domiciled state in percentage (not absolute) terms,[60] surpassing even the Baptist-majority states of Mississippi and Texas in the United States.

Naga Baptists are establishing mission stations and running schools and institutes in Assam, Arunachal Pradesh, Andhra Pradesh, and West Bengal, besides "church-planting" in diverse areas of the country. Young Naga Baptist missionaries work as far away as the Burma–Thailand border and in China's Yunnan province – a region that both enticed and eluded foreign missionaries for generations.[61] Naga Baptists on the Indian side bordering

---

[59] The global South refers to Africa, Asia, and Latin America. Out of the 2 billion Christian population in this category, 510 million live in Latin America, 390 million in Africa, and about 300 million in Asia. And by 2025, Africa and Latin America are expected to become the most populous Christian continents. See Jenkins, *The New Faces of Christianity*, 8–10.

[60] According to the census of 2011, Christians comprise 87.93 per cent of Nagaland's population, of which the NBCC official report estimates the Baptist population to account for 75 to 80 per cent.

[61] Ethnic groups living in the Baptist highland still maintain an oral tradition about their history and migration (albeit vague) from Yunnan province in China. Presently, China has one of the fastest-growing Christian populations in the world despite a harsh crackdown on organised religion by the state. The Baptist presence is still not felt in China, but there is the possibility of a sustainable Baptist community in Yunnan province. This province

Myanmar's Sagaing region have been sending missionaries to convert their brethren. Kachin Baptists are committed to evangelising Myanmar and planting churches in the mainland. The diaspora from the Baptist highland is a growing Baptist community and has adherents settled in the USA, UK, Australia, Scandinavia, etc. It has even begun to seem possible that this increasing evangelical immigrant Christian population from the Baptist upland may help invigorate the time-worn and "tepid" Christianity of the West, especially in Western Europe.

As seen in the preceding section, Naga Baptist church leaders and intellectuals distance themselves from any link between their ethnonationalism and the Baptist faith. Zelhou Keyho, General Secretary of the Nagaland Baptist Church Council (the Naga Baptist parent organisation), says of the protracted Indo–Naga peace process: "Naga independence is not our [NBCC's] business. Reconciliation among warring Naga factions must precede the political settlement, whether be it sovereignty or finding solution within the Indian Union." When questioned further on why Nagas take up arms against the Indian state, he categorically says that "peacemaking with the Indian state is the only viable solution". This is not the only view prevalent among the Naga Baptists. Some have sought solutions in indigenous theology, which is a variant of liberation theology. And some staunch ethnonationalists, though a minority, have swerved in favour of a totalitarian Christian state. On the whole, the Indian democratic state has not viewed the Naga issue as a Christian minority *vs* a Hindu majority problem, even if it frequently suits right-wing Hindu groups to employ anti-Christian and anti-Westerner polarising rhetoric. On the Myanmar side of the Baptist highland, religious differences play out differently. Ethnic minorities like the Chins and Kachins charge the state with religiously motivated persecution. As the state has long been in the hands of majority ethnic

---

of China remains a fertile mission field and has attracted native missionaries from the Kachin, Naga, and Chin areas of the Baptist highland.

Burmans predominantly following Buddhism, the state has in turn blamed Christian missions for political unrest in the uplands. The coming of the American Baptist mission to Burma is seen to have contravened a popular notion: "to be Burman is to be Buddhist". This moment in history had a significant influence quite separate from the impact of British rule. The first American Baptist missionary couple, Adoniram and Ann Judson, arrived in the Burman heartland in Rangoon in 1813, but it was not until six years later that they had their first convert on Burmese soil: a young man called Moung Nau got converted in a *zayat* and was baptised.[62] As in the Assam province of British India, where conversion was infrequent among the dominant races, the response of ethnic Burmans toward the Baptist mission was negligible. Burmans availed themselves of the benefits of Western education and medicine but also harboured contempt for the Westerner. As the Baptist institution eclipsed the *sangha* (community of monks), thereby weakening an age-old symbiosis between laity and religious elites, Burman hostility to Christian missions increased: converting the minorities and marginalising the Buddhist monasteries no longer seemed a negligible issue. This apprehension gathered steam because indigenous ethnic groups like the Chins, Kachins, Karens, and Nagas of the uplands embraced the new religion most ardently, so that a region of the Burmese nation was now conspicuously non-Buddhist in its identity, traditions, and social institutions.

When the Burmese government declared Buddhism the state religion in 1961, it alienated ethnic groups that had converted to Christianity. The Kachins took up arms against the Burman state "to protect their religion", and Christianity became an important identity assertion for them in their opposition to the majority Buddhist Burmans. Then, once English was banned as the medium of instruction, Baptist churches and institutions became not only centres for English language learning but also safe havens to promote Kachin language and culture: the Baptist

---

[62] See Neill, *A History of Christian Missions*, 249–50.

mission had translated religious texts into local languages and promoted Kachin culture, history, and traditions through local writings and publications. In counteracting the imposition on them of the official Burmese language, the Kachins swung vigorously into producing textbooks in their own language – which was taught mostly in Christian-oriented schools – and theological colleges grew into important training grounds where new Kachin elites "were raised with the combined rhetoric of Christianity and ethnonationalism as if they were bloodlines".[63]

British rule had brought in a legal system, formal education, a political system, Western medicine, and telecommunications. These were institutions and knowledge systems that the American Baptist missionaries shared in common with their transatlantic cousins. The conventional argument goes that the Christian mission was a handmaiden of British imperialism. However, in the consciousness of ethnic groups in the Baptist highland there has long been a separation of Christian mission narratives from British colonialism, as among the Karens and other smaller ethnic Baptists in Myanmar.

As the Baptist missionary-anthropologist Harry Ignatius Marshall tells it, the ethnic Karens already had a folk belief about a "white brother" bringing a book that their ancestor had lost a long time ago to rescue them.[64] The Karens, comprising 7 per cent of the total population of Burma, embraced the Baptist faith in large numbers, and although Christians comprise only about 15 per cent of the total Karen population, most Karen leaders are Baptists. Ethnic Karens claim they were better off under British rule, though, as we have seen with the Nagas, they feel betrayed by the British not keeping their end of the bargain after WWII. Interestingly, the Baptist faith has aided ethnic groups like the Karen to assert their differences from majority Buddhist Burmans, even though a larger percentage of Karens practise Buddhism than

---

[63] Quoted in Cockett, *Blood, Dreams and Gold*, 124.
[64] Marshall, *The Karen People of Burma*, 304.

Christianity. Because Baptist churches and missions are viewed as subversive, the Karen are trying now to negate their disillusionment with colonialism and the ongoing crisis with the Burmese state by coming up with a new, mellower narrative of the Baptist faith which informs their daily life.

VII

The Indo–Myanmar frontier region is crucial for India's Look East (now Act East) policy, adopted in 1991 to augment India's expanding influence in the Asia–Pacific region. The policy brought the north-eastern frontier into focus as a strategic asset to India's geopolitical ambitions in the region.[65] The idea was to counterbalance China's rising influence in the South East Asian corridor, secure natural energy requirements, strengthen relations with South East Asian countries, and contain political unrest in the north-eastern states; but for successful policy implementation, India must work its way out of the political constraints posed by this frontier region.

Since it considers the Bay of Bengal and the Indian Ocean littoral as its dominion, India is investing in the Burmese port of Sittwe to safeguard its waters and curtail China's offshore influence. Although it lost out to China for access to natural gas reserves on the Rakhine coast of Myanmar, India has set its eyes on Myanmar's strategic offshore resources. One of the reasons for investment in Sittwe is to connect Chin state with Manipur and the rest of north-east India, to facilitate trade and economic development, and to thus mitigate separatist sentiments in the region. India is also seeking to promote cross-border trade by establishing international trade centres at places like Avankhu, Dan, Moreh, and Zowkha. To connect with the South East Asian countries India has taken up large-scale international highway projects like the Moreh–Tamu–Kalemyo Road, and national highways to connect

---

[65] See Grare, *India Turns East*, esp. Chapter 4.

the interiors of the north-east states. However, the Chinese investment in energy, infrastructure, and military hardware outperforms the Indian.[66] Besides the economic advantage, China enjoys more influence in Naypyidaw's corridors of power, and for decades has had the upper hand in subterranean relationships with ethnic rebel groups on the Indo–Myanmar frontier, which can make or break Myanmar and India's influence in the region.

Geographically, India's Act East policy cuts through the heart of the Baptist highland. India cannot afford to alienate their side of the Baptist highland because the Chinese influence on the Myanmar side is unprecedented, and they can still sway the ethnic rebels on the Indian side of the border to suit their geopolitical interest. This political predicament will always be intrinsic to the Baptist highland, and the issue of separatism will metastasise to newer forms. At the time of writing, the United Liberation Front of Western South East Asia (UNLFW) – the association of Northeast separatist groups comprising NSCN(K), ULFA, KLO, and NDFB (Songbijit) – operates mainly from the Naga Self-Administered Zone in the Sagaing region of Myanmar. More importantly, the Naga separatist group NSCN(K), which has a strong base in the Sagaing region, was declared a "terrorist organisation" by the Indian government in 2015 under the Unlawful Activities (Prevention) Act, 1967, leaving Naga insurgents ripe for the Chinese taking. Meanwhile, the Myanmar civilian government has entered into an agreement with the NSCN(K) as part of the new governmental reforms to bring minorities into the mainstream, although military policy toward the ethnic rebel groups is bound to change depending on the interests of international players like China and India.

While on the Indian side the central government has a policy in place to fence the border in the Naga-inhabited area, the natives say they will be denied access to land and resources they

---

[66] See Kanwal, "A Strategic Perspective on India–Myanmar Relations", 142–3.

have enjoyed over generations. They do not want a man-made boundary to come up in the middle of their ancestral land.[67] Nagas on the Myanmar side increasingly face security checks while coming to buy basic commodities from the Indian side.[68] Naga insurgent groups, especially the NSCN(K), have always stressed the transnational nature of Nagas as the main agenda of their armed struggle and are gaining mileage out of this border imbroglio. From the viewpoint of India's international interests and the Chinese factor looming large, the Baptist highland remains indispensable to success in Indo–Myanmar relations. This landlocked region crossed by international boundaries in all directions can either play a decisive role in India's relation with South East Asian neighbours, or it can prove the dampener curtailing India's influence. Any policy designed for the region will have to take into account international concerns such as immigration, terrorism, environmental depredation, human trafficking, illegal arms smuggling, and cross-border drug trafficking.

In a globalised world that is erasing traditional cultural spaces and boundaries, the idea of cultural zones with socio-political and economic relationships significantly aids understanding of geopolitics and human society at large.[69] The Indian anthropologist Irawati Karve is said to have pointed out that if we divide

[67] In June 2018 I spoke at length with village council members and Baptist church leaders in Dan village in Noklak district. In an incident on 5 May 2018, villagers had chopped down the check gate that the Assam Rifles had put up when a mini-truck was stopped from crossing the border to fetch firewood in their "ancestral forestland".

[68] The Indian Khiamniungan Nagas living at the border bemoaned that "their brethren" from the Myanmar side of the border are asked to produce an Aadhaar card – carrying the 12-digit unique identity number obtained "voluntarily" by citizens of India – without which they are harassed by Indian soldiers stationed at the borders, especially when the situation becomes tense following skirmishes between Naga insurgents and Indian armed forces.

[69] Anthropologists who mostly specialise in ethnography – a micro-study of particular cultures – also mull over cultural zones where a good number of ethnicities, languages, and cultures populate large swathes of land with

India diagonally, the upper half is the wheat-eating zone and the lower half the rice-eating zone.[70] The wheat-eating zone showing cultural relatedness extends north-west up to the Fertile Crescent, while the rice-eating zone includes most of south India, eastern India, and the north-east frontier, and extends on to the countries of South East Asia which are rice-intensive. What I have denoted as the Baptist highland falls in the rice belt.

Rice cultivation which includes both settled cultivation on the same plot year after year, and rotational swidden (*jhum*) agriculture, is found in the Baptist highland and this means of livelihood stretches across the entire South East Asian corridor. If we use economic livelihood as our criterion, it is possible to circumscribe the entire South East Asian region, which houses a multiplicity of languages and ethnic groups, into a conceptual cultural zone; and if we take other social, historical, and political factors as criteria, the possibility of studying South East Asia as a variegated geographic-cultural zone becomes possible. The Baptist highland is one such geographic-cultural zone, distinct in its location and development, and shaped historically by the global movement of religious ideas.

In *The Art of Not Being Governed*, James C. Scott includes the Indo–Myanmar frontier within a larger conceptual geopolitical zone in South East Asia called "Zomia", which includes "all the lands at altitudes above roughly three hundred metres all the way from the Central Highlands of Vietnam to northeastern India and traversing five Southeast Asian nations (Vietnam, Cambodia,

---

usually similar ecological dispositions. We can draw comparisons between James C. Scott's concept of the "Zomia" highlands of South East Asia, and the social anthropologist Ernest Gellner's work on the Berbers of the High Atlas Mountains. Gellner, "Tribalism and the State in the Middle East", 109–26.

[70] My teacher of prehistoric archaeology, the late D.K. Bhattacharya, first introduced me to this concept during my postgraduate studies at the University of Delhi. His hypothesis, building on Irawati Karve's concept, was that worship of the feminine deity is common among people of the rice belt, while male deity worship is more prevalent in the wheat-eating zone.

Laos, Thailand, and Burma) and four provinces of China (Yunnan, Guizhou, Guangxi, and parts of Sichuan)." He identifies "statelessness" and the resilience of ethnic groups who resist their surrounding dominant cultures as the distinguishing feature of "Zomia".[71] This concept, "Zomia", owes to the Dutch scholar Willem van Schendel, who hypothesised it in connection with marginalised ethnic groups with a noticeable distance from the state.[72] Ethnic groups inhabiting the region that I have identified as the Baptist highland fit this concept because they are marked by disenfranchisement, poverty, and comparatively smaller populations – their peculiarity being a Protestant brand of faith unique to the region. This has empowered the inhabitants of this specific Zomia and represents the most important aspect of the present study.[73]

---

[71] See Scott, *The Art of Not Being Governed*, Preface and Chapter 1.

[72] Schendel, "Geographies of Knowing", 20–6. The Dutch scholar Willem van Schendel first advanced the concept of Zomia in 2002, which is now popularly used in borderland studies. His other notable work is on the Indo-Bangladesh border in the Chittagong Hills. Schendel, "The Invention of the 'Jummas'", 26.

[73] What I have described as the Baptist highland fits aptly into Scott's thesis in terms of the socio-political milieu and the attitude of the inhabitants toward state-making projects in the post-colonial period, but is changing substantially in the twenty-first century.

3

Heirs of the New Faith

> I always had the greatest reverence and love for missionaries; I heard and read much about them when I was a child, and for a long time I wanted to be a missionary myself.
>
> – Max Müller, letter to Sir Charles Trevelyan, 1854

> Not infrequently the Missionary blames the trader for the harm that occurs. But it is to be remembered that it is often the Missionary, with his "civilizing" aims who creates a market for the trader.
>
> – J.P. Mills, Deputy Commissioner, Naga Hills, 1926

KIDIMA IS A SIZEABLE Angami village with a proud tradition. The majority of its inhabitants are Baptist, though in the twenty-first century the Catholic and Christian Revival churches have increased the size of their followings. While most southern Angami villages lie along National Highway 29, Kidima is about 10 km from the highway, which makes it off the beaten track for tourists and travellers. NH29 is the lifeline connecting Imphal and Dimapur; it passes through the heart of Kohima and is as old as British colonialism.

At a tri-junction leading off the state highway to Kidima in one direction, Pfutsero town (the Chakhesang Baptist Church Council headquarters) in a second, and Chakhabama (an old Indian army headquarters) a third, the Baptist church deemed it fit in 2015 to construct a small memorial park to commemorate seventy-five years of Christianity in Kidima. Adjacent to this jubilee park across the road is a huge memorial stone on which is etched a line from Ruth 1: 16, "And thy God my God". Unveiled by the general secretary of the Nagaland Baptist Church Council "in the presence of Japanese and Korean Christian dignitaries", the inscription on the monolith reads:

> In January 1832, the first known expedition of British army led by Captains Francis Jenkins and R.B. Pemberton with 700 soldiers and 800 load bearers first entered the Kidima Village of Naga Hills, earlier untraveled by any other explorers in search of a route between Manipur and Assam . . . The British soldiers from a Christian country who were the staunch believers of Jesus Christ arrived at Kidima Village, set foot on the soil and had even walked across the land. Indeed, it would have been a different story had we been able to communicate, befriend, acquaint and be a good host to you then from Christian perspective. If so, Kidima Village would be one of the pioneers not only in spirituality, educational but also in all round development among the Nagas. However, we have not done that at an opportune time for which we regret even to this day.

The jubilee monolith commemorates an event in January 1832 when "Captains Jenkins and Pemberton led 700 Manipuri troops with 800 coolies from the Manipur valley, via Popolongmai, Samoogoodting and the Dhunsiri to Mohung Dijooa on the Jumoona. They had literally to fight their way through the whole Kutcha and Angami Naga country."[1] Though based on the oral tradition of the natives, the inscription describes a historical event; it is a reconstruction of history from the viewpoint of devout Angami Baptists in our time.

It cannot be ascertained whether the "British soldiers" who crossed Kidimia territory back then were in fact "staunch believers of Jesus Christ". Of the two British officers who became the first white men to enter the Naga area, little is known about Captain R.B. Pemberton or his religious beliefs, but Captain Francis Jenkins did play a role in the history of the American Baptist mission in Assam. In 1834, two years after he led the first European expedition

---

[1] Mackenzie, *The North-East Frontier of India*, 101.

into the Naga area, he was appointed "Commissioner and Agent to the Governor General of Bengal" in Assam and posted to Guwahati. Jenkins was believed to be sympathetic toward Christian missions and was in a way instrumental in letting the first American Baptist mission reach the "Namsangia Nagas" in Upper Assam (present-day Arunachal Pradesh).

II

Namsang is a small nondescript village in Tirap district of Arunachal Pradesh, close to the Assam plains. The Naga villages in these hills are distant from the emerging urban centres of Arunachal Pradesh, and Assam still functions as their economic lifeline. The nearest town is Jeypore in Dibrugarh district, which is about 30 km from Namsang. Jeypore, which was the site of an American Baptist mission station for a short period before it shifted to Sivasagar (also "Sibsagor" or "Sibsagar"), is sparsely populated and still known for its lush green tea gardens and rich biodiversity.

The Baptist mission station had, as earlier noted, shifted from Sadiya to "Jaipur [*sic*], centre of growing tea cultivation, in anticipation of increase in population and having access to the Khamtis, the Nagas and the Singphos."[2] From Jeypore, Miles Bronson set out for Namsang village to begin the mission work which Naga Baptists have recorded as the first missionary–Naga contact. Bronson was born on 20 July 1812 in a small town called Norway in New York State and educated at the Hamilton Literary and Theological Institute. He set sail for Assam at the age of twenty-four and first set foot on Naga territory in January 1839, when he trekked up to Namsang village, to natives whose "great fear was that I was a servant of the Company". They took him to be a government spy.[3] Ill health, coupled with the death of

[2] Barpujari, *The American Missionaries*, xvi.
[3] Ibid., 233.

Rhoda, his sister and helper in the Naga mission, made Bronson leave the hills and relocate to Nowgong in 1841, despite a plea from the local people that he continue his work, especially the running of the school.

The American Baptist mission's first Naga contacts were the Nocte, who are ethnically related to the Konyak Nagas and designated a Scheduled Tribe in Arunachal Pradesh. There is a tacit understanding among the Konyak people that the Nocte and Wancho of the erstwhile Tirap Frontier Tract of NEFA belong to the larger Konyak group, and that there is shared ethnic and cultural identity among these cognate tribes spread across Arunachal Pradesh, Nagaland, and the Sagaing region in Myanmar. In early missionary writings the term Nám Sáng Nágas was used to designate the Konyak Nagas. The Konyak and related ethnic groups were spread across the Indo–Burmese frontier, and, on account of its proximity with Upper Assam, Namsang became the first Naga village to be evangelised by the American Baptist mission. At the time of writing, this village has a small Baptist community of ten families among its 113-odd households. Baptist adherents in Namsang are expected to increase since the Ao Naga Baptist mission looks after the church in the village.

Devout Konyak Baptists believe that had the American Baptist mission work continued unimpeded in Namsang in the nineteenth century, the Konyak would have been the most advanced of all the Naga tribes. They attribute historical events to God's divine plan, especially with regard to their encounter with the American Baptist mission. The Naga tribes that first came under the influence of the mission reaped greater political and socio-economic dividends in the post-independence period – the Ao, Angami, and Tangkhul Nagas being cases in point. A sense of spiritual entitlement would become a part of the Naga Baptist worldview: that the first converts were, *ipso facto*, bequeathed God's blessing. So there exists the idea of "firstborn" believers – members of a village, ethnic group, etc. that first witnessed conversion – who are reverentially acknowledged by the faithful.

The first religious literature in the Naga language to be translated by missionaries using the Roman script was in the native language spoken in Namsang. Villagers now, recent Baptist converts included, rarely know of this development; they had to be reminded by Baptist missionaries from Nagaland, who had come to evangelise them, of their "privilege". In 1839 Bronson prepared the first "Naga" catechism and primer in the Nocte language. In hindsight, the discontinuation of mission school and translation work was a severe blow to inhabitants on the cusp of modernity. Conversely, critics of the Baptist mission might say that its exit from Namsang saved a traditional culture from being wiped out. Modernity *vs* tribal culture is a thorny issue that has vexed the faithful because Christianity is seen as inseparable from Westernisation and Naga Baptists are accused of a predilection for things Western. However, the process of Christianisation has varied significantly from one place to the next; and, as for the Nocte Naga Baptists in Namsang, their experience of Christianity is going to be different from that of other Naga tribes who encountered the new faith through American missionaries. Converts in Namsang will experience the cultural baggage that comes with the Naga Baptist mission, just as their fellow Nagas a century ago experienced the new customs and idiosyncrasies of white missionaries.

Mission records show Nagas, in the early days of contact, marvelling at simple appliances and finding even the menial chores of the whites strange.[4] A missionary in Impur writes: "Time seems to have no value to the Nagas. It is a common practice for several men to come to the missionary's bungalow, where they will sit around in the most contented fashion and watch the missionaries in all they do."[5] This specific strangeness will not be faced by the new generation of native converts in Namsang, but, though the

[4] Alva Bowers mentions Ao Nagas who descended to the plains in Sivasagar around the 1860s marvelling at the printing machine. They were also surprised by the sight of children being taught in a mission school. See Bowers, *Under Headhunter's Eyes*, 197.
[5] Smith, *The Ao Naga Tribe of Assam*, 10.

method of evangelism has not changed much from that of their American predecessors, Ao Baptist missionaries preach a gospel coloured by their own cultural peculiarity.

The mission language in Namsang today is Nagamese. Since the villagers here can speak Assamese, it is convenient for Baptist missionaries from the neighbouring state of Nagaland to evangelise in this pidgin Assamese language. Among the Nagas who spoke different languages across tribes, regions, and villages, the development of Nagamese achieved some degree of uniformity amid the diversity. Certainly, Nagamese as a commercial and administrative language became institutionalised under British colonialism; but long before it became dominant in the Naga Hills, American missionaries and Assamese evangelists were laying the ground for this linguistic phenomenon to develop. As early as 1841 an American missionary reports: "The Nágas, who speak the Nám Sáng language, according to the nearest estimate Br. Bronson can make, amount to no more than about 6300, and of these, a large portion can already speak the Assamese language with ease."[6]

English became a primary medium of exchange for succeeding generations of Naga Baptists once they interacted with the outside world, but the road to multilingualism, which is a universal feature among present-day Naga Baptists, was set in motion by the missionary encounter. Barring a few Nagas who picked up the market creole in the plains of Assam and Manipur, the majority spoke village-specific dialects, and in some cases the languages of neighbouring tribes. Arguably, Assamese was the first outsider language that Naga converts learned with the coming of the Baptist mission and British colonialism; among ethnic Nagas who spoke the Tibeto-Burman languages, and who showed some propensity for language acquisition, developing an Indo-Aryan pidgin for popular usage came naturally. In the post-independence period Nagamese grew as an important mission language for the spread of the Baptist faith among this diverse group of people.

[6] Barpujari, *The American Missionaries*, 252.

Not unexpectedly, there is indifference to the American Baptist heritage in Namsang; villagers barely remember Miles Bronson, elsewhere famous as "apostle to the Assamese". Certain vague stories persist about a white missionary coming to live in the old village some generations ago; the site of the village where Bronson began his mission and opened a school has been abandoned, the village has shifted a few kilometres to a lower altitude. Had Bronson proved successful in starting the first Naga Baptist community there, Namsang would now be a pilgrimage centre for Naga Baptists. Instead, what remains of Bronson's memory is a small memorial on the old village site, now overgrown with vegetation and occasionally visited by the faithful from neighbouring states.

In Namsang even the names of the first Naga converts, who normally enjoy celebrity firstborn status in the Naga Baptist universe, do not register in collective memory. The first Naga convert, a young Konyak boy called Hubi, possibly from "Namsanghea", was baptised by the Assam missionary Nathan Brown on 12 September 1847 and died within a month of his baptism.[7] And a duo called Aklong and Amlai, who were also baptised by Brown in Sivasagar in 1855 and went to preach in their native village Namsang, are believed to have died at the hands of the villagers who feared the new teaching would sow discord in the community.[8] They are now merely names in the Baptist archives, and mostly in the West; in this they too are unlike many other Naga converts who were baptised much later. Namsang became a case of "what if" and "if only" in the Baptist mission story, the first Naga converts being relegated to a vague memory.

III

The Nagaland Baptist Church Council (NBCC) headquarters, located in the heart of Kohima town, represent the foremost church organisation in the state and one of the largest and most influential

---

[7] See Downs, *The Mighty Works of God*, 53.
[8] Quoted in Philips, *The Growth of Baptist Churches in Nagaland*, 51.

in north-east India. The Council has achieved the notable feat of bringing together various ethnic Baptists of diverse cultural and language backgrounds under one umbrella. For the NBCC the assumption of a shared Baptist identity is taken as foundational for the organisation of a society with members whose interests often clash.[9] Since its inception in 1937, the NBCC has intervened on numerous occasions to settle ethnic disputes in the state and continues to engage with the protracted Naga political issue.[10]

When crises erupt, ethnic and clan affiliations tend to demote the shared Baptist identity, which only makes the NBCC's role as potential arbiter vital. There is arguably no other modern Naga organisation that holds as much sway over social, cultural, and particularly religious life as the NBCC. Its authority does not erase the autonomy of local churches – church autonomy being a universal Baptist phenomenon; however, certain issues pertaining to culture and politics transcend the individual church and fall under the purview of the NBCC. The NBCC is not free of criticism; member churches and the faithful inevitably disapprove of the parent organisation's stand on some issues, but this is the Baptist way of functioning. Baptists do not agree on many things; as Kethoser Kevichusa said to me wryly, "The difference between a Baptist and a terrorist is that one can negotiate with a terrorist, but not with a Baptist."

The general secretary of the NBCC, Rev. Dr Zelhou Keyho, is a mild-mannered man in his fifties. A third-generation Baptist

---

[9] In addition to the Naga Baptist church associations, the Kuki Baptist Association, Association of Gorkha Baptist Churches, and Nagamese Baptist Churches Association are members of the NBCC.

[10] The idea of an association of all Baptist churches in the Naga Hills is traced to the mid-1930s and the leadership of American missionaries like J.E. Tanquist. The Naga Baptist Church Council, which was reorganised in 1953, was renamed the Nagaland Baptist Church Council after the state of Nagaland was created in 1963. For more details, see Nagaland Baptist Church Council, *One New Humanity*, 15–16.

Ill. 1: Baptist choir comprising women from various Naga communities performing during the NBCC Platinum Jubilee, April 2012.
The Nagas' love for music found new expression in the hymnal singing and choral tradition of the new faith. Courtesy DIPR.

minister in his family, Zelhou received his doctorate in Old Testament Studies from Trinity Evangelical Divinity School in Illinois, USA, and had a long career in both academia and church ministry before becoming the head of this largest of Baptist bodies in 2015. Zelhou appeared to me a non-controversial figure as he patiently and circumspectly answered my many questions on culture, politics, religion, and nationalism. "I am not against yoga, but making it compulsory in government institutions and educational centres is problematic," he said. He was more tongue-in-cheek about the larger saffronisation agenda of the right-wing government at the centre. He denied the culpability of the Baptist faith in Naga ethnonationalism while conceding that most Naga nationalist leaders were practising Baptists. "The NBCC since the beginning have been working toward a peaceful political solution. Nationalism and sovereignty is not the church's agenda. Our commitment is towards non-violence and lasting peace whether

Nagas become independent or have a settlement under the Indian constitution," he argues.

As head of the NBCC, the general secretary's words and actions are widely disseminated and discussed. For instance, the NBCC press release during the state legislative assembly elections in 2018 was portrayed by several mainstream media houses as indicative of a bigoted and undemocratic religious organisation.[11] The general secretary of the NBCC had appealed to Naga Christians in general and Baptists in particular to remain vigilant against the ideology of right-wing Hindu parties at the centre: he said political parties in the state should be wary of "Hindutva forces". While some believed the press release could have been more carefully worded, the NBCC said it was their constitutional right to oppose every "chauvinistic" ideology that discriminated against tribals and religious minorities. However, democratic politics is a two-way street; no religious organisation can openly endorse any particular political party or dissuade its members from voting for a party that disagrees with it ideologically. So, this clearly political stance was new for the Baptist church; it had hitherto mostly concerned itself with issues within the home state. The culture war and related struggle within a country claiming to uphold diversity and democracy had reached the doorstep of the Nagas.

Besides its influence on culture and politics in Nagaland, the Baptist church is at times charged with infringing on the personal space of citizens, particularly in regard to the contentious issue of the Nagaland Liquor Total Prohibition (NLTP) Act, 1989. Many educated Naga Baptists, though aware of the ravages of alcohol in modern Naga society, think that a blanket ban on liquor is not for the church to support. Meanwhile, elderly Baptist leaders who spearheaded the protest feel the younger generation does not understand why the church led a campaign to ban alcohol in the state. The NBCC and Naga Mothers' Association (NMA) led a

[11] "NBCC Sounds Battle Cry against Hindutva Forces", *Nagaland Post*, 10 February 2018.

massive campaign against "alcoholism" in the late 1980s. Leading Baptist ministers and church workers went on a hunger strike, sitting in front of the state legislative assembly in Kohima; some had to be hospitalised. The state government held consultations with various stakeholders and the NLTP Act was finally passed.

The NBCC holds the view that the NLTP Act was well intentioned but not well implemented. Cases of alcoholism, the influx of spurious liquor, and bootlegging continue unabated. Disagreements over social and cultural issues seem to be increasing between old and new generations of Naga Baptists.

The role of the NBCC in making Nagaland a "dry state" reveals the influence of the Baptist church. Many would say that the liquor ban is an abysmal failure, but in the eyes of the world Naga Baptists have secured their image as conscientious teetotalers. This does not mean that all practising Naga Baptists strictly enforce teetotalism as part of their religious duty – some argue that that would be to impose a kind of Pharisaical legalism on the Baptist community. Nevertheless, one of the distinct features of Baptist culture remains its puritanical attitude toward alcohol.

IV

Unlike the Ao, Lotha, Sumi, and Rengma Nagas, who claim to have achieved 100 per cent Christianity, among the Angami Nagas a substantial number are followers of the traditional religion, called Kruna, the term used both for the faith and its adherents. In 1950, when the Ao and Sumi Nagas had a total baptised membership of 20,593 and 16,100, respectively, the Angami Nagas – whom the American Baptist mission first reached in 1878 and whose native preachers played an important role in evangelising neighbouring tribes like the Sumi, Kuki, and Zeliang – had only 4000 baptised members.[12] In Kohima the missionary to the Angami, S.W. Rivenburg, bemoaned in 1891: "I long to see some souls saved. The

---

[12] See Eaton, "Conversion to Christianity among the Nagas", 19.

lack of converts greatly depresses me."[13] The Kohima missionaries lamented that "Five years" had passed "and not a single convert for the Kohima Baptist church."[14] Rev. Dr Atsi Dolie, executive director of the Angami Baptist Church Council (ABCC), told me that the reluctance of the Angami Nagas in embracing the new faith had to do with their social institutions, especially the decision-making body comprising village elders.

The stronghold of Kruna is the southern Angami area which shares a boundary with Manipur state. Here, Viswema village has the largest following of Kruna with a thriving community of believers – a rare spectacle in any Naga village today. Like most Angami Naga villages, Viswema is also known for its splendid terraced fields and impressive church buildings on the choicest spots in the village, usually at a stone's throw from each other. Kruna adherents comprise the fourth-largest religious community in Viswema, after Baptists, Catholics, and Revivalists. Though comparatively the smallest religious group, they retain their distinct identity in present-day Angami society. In Angami villages with similar denominational distribution and demography, Kruna have the option of converting to any of the three Christian denominations but mostly prefer Catholicism to the Baptist faith since Catholics are much less firmly opposed to the consumption of alcohol. Ironically, the catechist in Kigwema says that while the church asks new converts from Kruna to give up drinking *zu*, it does not ask the same of Baptists and Revivalists who shift to Catholicism.

Puthaho, the youngest son of Viswema's *phichü* – the eldest member and custodian of the traditional faith – decided to join the Catholics because he wanted to continue drinking local rice brew after his conversion, although his siblings had joined the Baptist and Christian Revival churches. Their 82-year-old father, Pungon Kikhi, had just assumed the office of *phichü* some months

---

[13] Rivenburg, "The Naga Mission", 445.
[14] Rivenburg, ed., *The Star of Naga Hills*, 85.

before I visited him during the winter of 2017. Pungon Kikhi had taken over from another elderly man of failing health. The home of the *phichü* had, as expected, lots of relics of the past, but half the house was a concrete structure with an inbuilt granary jam-packed with items such as a large wooden vat still in use for ripening *zu*, gigantic bamboo baskets for storing paddy, unused wooden platters, a defused mortar and metal helmet from WWII, and a couple of Japanese ceramic sake bottles.

The day was 19 December, marking a new year according to the traditional lunar calendar for Kruna adherents in the village, after the celebration of Sekrenyi, the traditional Angami festival. Ovole Kikhi, the wife of the *phichü*, was still brewing *zu* in her hearth, which is a virtual identity-marker for Kruna, but Pungon had stopped drinking rice beer for health reasons, though *zu* is indispensable in social and religious transactions among Kruna. In one Kruna home what caught my eye was a calendar showing the indigenous names of months on one half and Sanskrit names on the other. No wonder the Angami Baptists were wary, believing the long arm of Hindu right-wing organisations had penetrated even the remotest of Angami villages. This was not the case a decade or two ago, but, as my Angami guide that morning said, "the Nagas are no longer isolated from the politics and culture of the mainland."

A well-known Angami couple from the area acted as my guides to the inter-faith dynamics in southern Angami villages. The wife, Visakhonu, was from Viswema and married into a neighbouring village, Khuzama. She is an evangelical Christian, and the *phichü* had to bear with her brief witnessing of Christ even that morning; it was rather surreal observing an educated, devout Angami Baptist woman talking about a first-century Jewish teacher to an elderly Kruna Angami man who was prepared to breathe his last in the ancestral faith. "Christianity is complicated; it's full of do's and don'ts," Pungon said. He said it was loyalty to his forefathers that made him continue in the old faith, while Ovole's decision to continue in the old faith was due to respect for her husband and tradition. The elderly Kruna couple were not remotely bothered about life after death. Pungon thoughtfully reasoned that "if Jesus is God then he will be compassionate to those who don't follow him." However, the Baptist message of hellfire does resonate among Kruna, even if they do not embrace the new religion.

Visakhonu's husband Viraho Hibo listened attentively and explained the words of the *phichü*, and at regular intervals interjected with his own interpretations. Viraho is an exemplary Baptist raised in a traditional Christian home; moreover, his village Khuzama takes pride in being 100 per cent Christian. His Hibo clan had moved out from Viswema and founded a new village, Khuzama, a few kilometres away. If not for Christianity, Viraho would have been the incumbent *kemovo* (first settler and head of ceremonies) of the village, since it was the prerogative of the village founder's close bloodline to assume this indispensable office performing crucial rituals for the entire community.[15] But the tradition was abandoned a generation ago; Kedupral Hibo, Viraho's grandfather, was the last *kemovo* of the village before the Baptists overran the Kruna in Khuzama.

The house of the *kemovo* in the village is in ruins, no one has occupied it since the demise of the last incumbent; the ceremonial stone – which was believed to forecast critical community events relating to agriculture, hunting, and war – lies unattended and irrelevant, enclosed by a foot-tall brick enclosure. Except for metal roofing, the house has retained its original structure; the interior is almost empty, with a few prized items of the past gathering the dust of irrelevance. Hibo clan members, including the Baptist pastor in the village, Kevisezo Hibo, have decided to renovate the old house and preserve it as a museum, and for this they have chosen

---

[15] A *kemovo* played an important role in the establishment of a new village, and thereafter. As the first settler, it was his job to propitiate capricious spirits at the risk of his own life and ascertain that the spot was propitious before others joined him. His descendants continue to maintain a delicate balance with the spirit world, and head important rituals and ceremonies in the community.

Visakhonu, who had married into the Hibo clan, as convener. This seems unusual since women in Angami traditional society are sidelined in decision-making, but as Visakhonu, who holds a doctorate in sociology, put it: "Modern education has somehow levelled the playground and bridged the gender barrier."

Both Visakhonu and Viraho are educationists serving as principal and vice principal respectively of a Baptist-run college about 20 km from Kohima town. Nestled in the foothills of Japfu, the second-highest peak in the state at 3084 metres, Japfu Christian College is a model institute imparting the "Christian way of living" along with formal education. On entering the college premises, visitors are greeted by a signboard emblazoned with their vision statement: "to impart God-fearing quality education for all round development of individual to serve humanity, with faith and work ensuring success." The Naga Baptists here seem to have emulated the strategy of the American missionaries – education and evangelism go hand in hand. This residential college maintains a typically Christian environment, with hundreds of young people graduating from it every year.

Though southern Angami villages still have sizeable numbers of Kruna, this may not last long given the strong evangelical presence of devout Baptists like the Hibos, unless a new generation of Kruna can reinvent their religious identity and overhaul the traditional faith. They will else succumb to the evangelical juggernaut of the Angami Baptists, or of the native Catholics whose evangelical fervour matches that of the Baptists. Still, some Angami and Chakhesang Naga villages appear to be holding out as the last Kruna bastions; and their traditional religion has, with the coming of the new faith, itself witnessed considerable changes over the years.

V

Molungyimsen has an important place in Naga Baptist history. It was established in 1876 as a Christian village by the pioneering missionary Edward Winter Clark. To reach Molungyimsen one has to travel the entire length of Mokokchung district before entering Tuli, which is a small town with a humid climate in the foothills bordering Amguri town in Sivasagar district. As a general rule, traditional Naga villages are located on hilltops and spurs, but the elevation of Molungyimsen is exceptional even by Naga standards. A neglected road winds its way up the mountain, but the old missionary trail – which is trod presently by pilgrims to re-experience the travails of missionaries – is a shorter and less circuitous route requiring a strenuous climb up a narrow and steep path. At the hilltop is the present mission compound, the site of the first Christian settlement started by Clark.

The first American Baptist mission to the "Namsangia Nagas" in 1839 ended abruptly with Bronson's departure from Namsang village in 1841, and it was nearly thirty years before the mission picked up again. This time it was Clark, a graduate of Brown University and a product of the Newton and Rochester Theological Seminaries, who was posted to Sivasagar in 1869. Here he was helped by his pertinacious wife Mary Mead Clark. Together the two revived the Naga mission here, turning it into the most successful Baptist mission in the Indian subcontinent. While overseeing printing works in Sivasagar, Clark became so engrossed with the possibility of a mission to the Nagas that he was even willing to pay the expenses involved out of his own pocket, and if need be leave the Missionary Union, to reach his target. He began by engaging the services of "a man for these Nagas".[16] Godhula, the son of an Assamese convert called Kolibor who was a washerman in Sivasagar, had studied in the Orphan School started by Bronson at Nowgong; now he came under the mentorship of Clark and went on to lay the groundwork for the Naga mission starting in 1871. Godhula worked as a teacher in Sivasagar, helped missionaries learn Assamese, and then became a successful evangelist to the Ao Nagas.

By 1872 Godhula Rufus Brown, known to native converts as Godhula Babu, had visited the hills at least five times, becoming

---

[16] Letters from Mrs Clark in Ao, *History of Christianity in Nagaland*, 48.

the first outsider to penetrate the deep jungles that people of the plains had not dared enter. This rather mercurial Assamese evangelist converted a handful of Ao Nagas and brought them down to Sivasagar to be baptised by the American missionary. These converts were counted as baptised members of the church at Sivasagar, starting the first Naga Baptist community.[17] On 1 March 1876 Clark moved to the hills from Sivasagar; his wife joined him in 1878.

About 5 km from Molungyimsen, on a lower mountain range, is Molungkimong. Known as Dekha Haimong in missionary writings, Molungkimong became the first Naga village to be evangelised by the American Baptist mission in 1872 through the steadfast efforts of Godhula, and was first visited by Clark on 10 February 1876. Soon after, on 1 March, Clark left Sivasagar to take up residence in this village.[18] However, by the winter of the same year he had to leave Dekha Haimong with his converts because of increasing opposition from followers of the old faith. The converts started a new settlement, Molungyimsen, which came to be known as Dr Clark's Village among the natives.

Ill. 2: Molungyimsen village, late 1870s. E.W. Clark, known as an "apostle to the head-hunters", started the village for followers of the new faith in 1876. Courtesy ABAM.

[17] Puthenpurakal, *Baptist Missions in Nagaland*, 65.
[18] Ibid., 66.

On a clear sunny day, looking down from Molungyimsen, settlements in the Assam plains appear flickeringly in sight and the Brahmaputra is clearly visible flowing towards the horizon. Viewing the rolling hills from the plains of Sivasagar, Clark says in 1871: "We want a man for these Nagas, upon whose mountain homes our eyes daily rest. They have some crude and indefinite conceptions of a Great Spirit, and an evil one; farther than this, they have no religion."[19] Five years after Godhula's first visit there, Clark had moved to the "mountain", heralding the beginning of the most successful American Baptist mission work in the whole of north-east India.

At present, the old site occupied by the mission has been converted into a kind of religious heritage installation where a jubilee monolith, memorial building, guest house, and even a tree have been marked with noticeboards connected to Clark. Visitors, overwhelmingly Baptist, come to the village from near and far, seeking tangible evidence of the first white missionary who lived in these parts more than a century ago. The pastor says hardly a day goes by without visitors to Dr Clark's Village. A native of the village, Rev. S. Tajung Jamir, has been serving as pastor of the Molungyimsen Baptist church since 2016. An enlarged photograph of his grandfather Samar, the first evangelist from the village, hangs on the wall alongside those of early American missionaries.

Inside a rectangular whitewashed and spacious room named "Pilgrim Home" are enlarged images printed on flex material; and old photographs are displayed on the wall in sequence, highlighting the Naga encounter with the Baptist mission. The magnified photographs serve as a kind of visual essay for people entering the room, the images including an assortment of American missionary couples and the first native converts and evangelists. For me personally the most striking is a photograph of Molungyimsen taken in 1876, the year of its establishment. Naked children with rotund bellies (probably a result of kwashiorkor) and prominent

---

[19] Letter from Mrs Clark in Ao, *History of Christianity*, 48.

foreheads with the traditional inverted-bowl haircut, and a few adults dressed in traditional attire, pose for the camera, with traditional thatched houses in the background. The photograph highlights the staggering change over the century and a half since it was taken. Today, one sees healthy children neatly dressed in school uniforms, and well-groomed teenagers.

A photograph of an English bungalow in Sivasagar – where Clark spent a night – was the only thing British in the collection.[20] There is also one of an impressive Hindu temple in Sivasagar, with some Naga men passing by in the foreground. Apparently this mandir was where Godhula Babu first met Subongmeren from Molungkimong; there used to be a bazaar outside the mandir and villagers went down to it to trade. It is said Godhula was intrigued by men dressed in traditional attire and on enquiring about them was told they were Nagas. After a time Godhula befriended Subongmeren and asked him if he could go with him to his village; taking a stranger to his village was risky so Subongmeren was not willing at first, but he finally agreed. Thus in 1871 the Assamese evangelist Godhula made his first trip to Dekha Haimong. He was not allowed to enter and a small temporary shack was built for him outside the village stockade where he prayed and sang hymns. After gaining the confidence of the inhabitants, Godhula kept visiting Molungkimong, before Clark finally joined him in 1876.

A tall and lush litchi tree next to Clark's memorial building is the only surviving object from the time when the village was established, apart from some movable missionary artefacts preserved on the third storey of the heritage museum. The famous litchi tree has been reproduced in several Baptist souvenirs and publications, and the missionary artefacts, most of which are kept inside glass cases, are impressive and well preserved. They range from photographs and early works of translation to printing

---

[20] The bungalow looks like the one that Colonel Buckingham occupied in Amguri in the foothills. Clark is said to have rested here the night before entering the hills in 1876.

equipment, old fabrics, musical instruments, weapons, carpentry tools, and kitchenware. Most items are what some call "missionary junk". Artefacts preserved in the centres where American Baptist missionaries once stayed attract the Baptist faithful, though these museum collections do not highlight the lives of the natives. At the heritage museum in Molungyimsen the only tangible evidence of the first Baptist community is a set of ten rules which the missionaries had framed for believers when the village was established. The rules – including "We shall not carry on headhunting" – preserved on a marble stone must seem far-removed from their lives to native Christians, but they offer a small glimpse into the early life of a new Baptist community in the second half of the nineteenth century. The sheer commitment of the American Baptists to their mission seems clear from this memorial.

It was only in 1885 that the English government assumed suzerainty over the Ao Naga tribe. For almost ten years after setting foot in Dekha Haimong, Clark lived in the "wild" country without protection from the British government in Assam. The ubiquity of internecine tribal warfare which early missionaries faced is also evident in the museum collection at Molungyimsen. The glass cases include old Naga spears 4 to 5 feet long that came from Tamlu village in present-day Longleng district. However, "the spear which slightly injured Dr Clark's foot was removed from the case at the request of the Tamlu believers," the pastor told me sheepishly. According to the story of this incident that I was told in Molungyimsen, Dr Clark and his companions were on a tour to Tamlu village when they were suddenly confronted by warriors who thought them enemies; one of the men instinctively hurled a spear that injured the missionary on his toe.[21] This spear was put on display and visitors to the museum would point out the weapon. The faithful in Tamlu did not want their habitat to be remembered as the village where a spear had been flung at a venerated missionary, injuring him. So, Pastor Tajung said, the

---

[21] Ibid., 111–12.

spear that injured Clark is now "kept safely out of sight". The event took place well over a hundred years ago, but for Naga Baptist believers these missionary legends and reliquaries are no less significant than are similar sacred memorabilia to devout Catholics in Europe and Latin America.

The traditional culture of the Nagas is fast disappearing, the state has done very little to record it, and the part of the past that has been preserved is the work of Baptists who have painstakingly noted landmarks and retained relics relating to pioneering missionaries. Preserving a cultural heritage is a way of arousing feelings for the past, and the Naga Baptist effort has resulted in a deep religious attachment to the work of those who introduced Baptist Christianity here. A pathway which missionaries once trod has mnemonic significance and also serves as a symbol of the faith. In 1888 Clark built a suspension bridge "two hundred feet span and forty feet or more above high-water mark" over Milak River.[22] This lay along the missionary trail between Molungyimsen and Amguri in the foothills. The natives call it Dr Clark's Bridge and it is still in use; except for concrete pillars supporting sturdy metal wires, the villagers have tried to keep the bridge as it is – because of nostalgia – a nostalgia that is itself an outgrowth from the Baptists' larger effort to keep the past alive. The footpath leading to the village from the suspension bridge has also become an attraction for the Baptist faithful: it is an old missionary trail that Clark is said to have surveyed after his arrival in Molungyimsen, and which became a lifeline connecting the village with the plains of Assam. This well-trodden path, known for its precipitous climb covering a distance of 14 km, is a popular "pilgrim walk". Believers put themselves in the shoes of Clark in his "arduous climb to bring the gospel to the Nagas". Pastor Tajung says the main purpose of the pilgrim walk is to identify with the sufferings of missionaries when first bringing the "good news" of Christ to the Nagas.

[22] Ibid., 129.

The pilgrim walk is perhaps the poor man's version of what the faithful do in Jerusalem; so be it. Not many Nagas can reach Israel, but they more than make do in places designated sacred within their own environs. Their walk here is an act of pure devotion, it is not meant for the average visitor or tourist. Those who undertake it are provided a brief description of the life of E.W. Clark and the founding of the first Naga Baptist village. It usually ends with a prayer meeting in the Pilgrim Hall. A mission route taken by Miles Bronson from Jeypore in Upper Assam to Namsang village in Tirap district in Arunachal Pradesh is also now a pilgrim walk that has attracted Naga Baptists, but Clark's route attracts many more due to its proximity and more relatable history. Clark's 1876 path from Sivasagar up to Dekha Haimong along an old trade route has also been popularised as a "prayer walk".

VI

Impur began as a mission centre in 1894 when the American Baptist mission shifted base from Molungyimsen. The missionaries S.A. Perrine and F.P. Haggard shifted with their wives to the new site, while the Clarks stayed back at the old village to support the church there. The opening of a Baptist mission base in Impur had two advantages: first, it was about 160 km from Kohima, headquarters of the British Naga Hills, and only 16 km from Mokokchung, the British subdivisional headquarters; second, the mission station in Impur made the missionaries accessible to two other large Naga tribes, the Lotha and Sumi Nagas. By the time Impur was selected, there was a bridle path connecting Mokokchung with Kohima via Wokha and on to the military station in the plains of Assam. Mokokchung had a police outpost and a government mail service incoming every two days.[23]

The Ao Naga country, present-day Mokokchung district, became the first American Baptist mission regional hub from

[23] Clark, *A Corner in India*, 147.

where the mission spread to neighbouring tribes. For many years Impur served as the foremost American Baptist mission base in the Naga Hills, although the Baptist mission centre at Kohima fared remarkably well in evangelising Naga tribes other than the native Angami Nagas. The American missionaries handed over the Impur mission station to Ao Naga Baptists in the 1950s, when they were asked to leave the Naga Hills. Native church workers and evangelists proved worthy successors: the number of Nagas who converted under them far surpassed that under the American missionaries. Today, Mokokchung – district headquarters of the Ao Nagas – is home to the largest Baptist following in the state.

The Ao Baptist Arogo Mundang (ABAM; i.e. the Ao Baptist churches' association) now occupies the Impur mission station and the administration of Ao Baptist churches is carried on from here. In Impur, E.W. Clark remains among Ao Baptists the most popular past American missionary: memorial halls and landmarks in the Impur mission centre are named after him, and his memorabilia are religiously preserved and cherished. The Impur Baptist mission centre opened its first Vernacular Bible School in 1955 to train natives as pastors and evangelists. The Bible school has since its inception produced hundreds of missionaries and church workers. The Vernacular Bible School is comparatively affordable and focused on mission works in rural areas, unlike the more expensive Baptist seminaries in towns more academically oriented; from the Baptist mission's perspective this is an effective strategy for training grassroots church workers who will bring more converts into the Baptist fold.

Ao Baptists send missionaries and teachers to countries like Bhutan, Cambodia, China, Myanmar, Lao, Nepal, and Thailand. The ABAM mission has pulled off the difficult feat of opening a school in China to teach the English language, art, and music. The opening of such learning institutes provides an avenue to teach religion. The Ao Nagas, being the first recipients of the American Baptist mission, have an advantage in terms of English education, besides having inherited a musical tradition from the missionaries –

as their superior church choirs and youth praise-and-worship bands attest; and they have put these talents to use in bolstering mission efforts.

Ao Naga Baptists are taking the lead in reviving what is known as the "Shan mission", the idea of Burma missionaries in the first half of the nineteenth century to use Assam as an entry point to reach areas in northern Burma and adjacent parts of south-western China.[24] The Shan mission strategy was abandoned because the diversity proved too complex, and for historical reasons. The ABAM has initiated a joint venture for the Shan people; and various front organisations of Naga Baptists, including the Ao, Sangtam, Chang, Phom, Konyak, Khiamniungan, and Yimchunger, calling themselves sister churches, have taken up this venture in recent times. The Naga Baptist leaders behind the Shan mission are determined to fulfil their American predecessors' original vision.

The landscape of Impur has been transformed. While most Naga villages can be called Baptist settlements, the appearance of Impur, with well-planned landscaping, has the aura of a Baptist mission centre with a long-surviving tradition. The Impur mission centre represents what an ideal Baptist settlement should look like; the stakeholders have inadvertently created a living Baptist museum. In the middle of the mission compound is a Christian heritage site named Pilgrim's Park where the life story of Jesus Christ, depicting events and places, is reproduced on a sizeable hillock. In an online world with every image visible at the click of a button, only a community intensely and pervasively devout would want a park of scenes from the New Testament world.

For visitors to Impur, the Baptist heritage museum is a must. The old house that has been renovated and converted into the ABAM Heritage Museum in 2018 was first constructed in 1907 as a mission training school with a grant from the "East India Company and American Baptist Foreign Mission". A great deal of planning has gone into the museum's display, the thematic

---

[24] Downs, *The Mighty Works of God*, 15.

portrayal of the life of American missionaries being the highlight of this oldest and grandest Naga Baptist museum. Its airtight glass cases contain missionary memorabilia left behind or donated later by families, all meticulously displayed in chronological order. They include an array of objects, from massive printing machinery to faded handwritten letters.

Besides the villages of the Konyak Nagas, whom the Ao Naga Baptists converted in large numbers, the Ao Naga area remains arguably the foremost Baptist stronghold, no other denominations in evidence in any of their villages. Naga tribes like the Angami, Sumi, and Lotha also had mission stations manned by American missionaries, but, unlike other Naga Baptist groups that witnessed a substantial shift to other denominations in the second half of the twentieth century, the Baptist stronghold in the Ao Naga heartland could not be breached. According to a popular story, the Anglican mission in Assam during the colonial period sought permission from the deputy commissioner to enter the Ao area, but the Ao replied they would not practise polygamy (i.e. follow any other denomination). A huge chunk of the Naga Baptist story comes from the Ao Baptist mission, and it was with the Ao Nagas that the American Baptist missionaries worked the longest – eighty years – without leaving the mission station unmanned. From Clark, who came to an Ao Naga village in 1876, to the last missionary, R.F. Delano, who left the Impur mission centre in 1955, nineteen American missionaries worked among the Ao.[25]

The Baptist dominance is not because the Ao remain secluded from other denominations. Among those who studied outside the state, there have been those who brought back new religious ideas to their native places. Thus, denominations like Assemblies of God, Pentecostals, Seventh-Day Adventists and Roman Catholicism were introduced to the Baptist heartland. The Ao Nagas

---

[25] R.F. Delano was posted in the Aizuto Sumi mission centre from 1950 to 1955, but his last few days were spent at the Impur mission station, from where he departed for the United States – the last American missionary to do so.

remained steadfastly Baptist, though there is a sprinkling of them, confined mostly to the towns, along with the Christian Revival Church. This denominational dynamic among the Ao bucks the trend – in other Naga tribes Baptists have shifted to other denominations.

VII

In January 2018 thousands of Sumi Naga Baptists from 169 churches spread across Dimapur district gathered at Zukihe village in Niuland subdivision, where the Western Sumi Baptist Akukuhou Kuqhakulu (WSBAK, i.e. Western Sumi Baptist churches' association) had organised a three-day religious gathering known as revival hour. During his sermon the executive secretary of the WSBAK said to a fired-up congregation: "The revival visited the Nagas in the 1970s and has waned among other tribes, but for the Sumi Naga the revival flame is still burning."

A revival hour is usually an ecstatic religious meet, in contrast with monotonous and sombre Baptist worship services. The highlights of revival hour are singing locally composed revival songs (also known as born-again songs), synchronic dancing, fiery sermons, divinations, and spiritual rejuvenation. Ecstatic devotional singing and dancing seem more a practised style than a spontaneous religious experience; and though the faithful during the worship service were considerably impassioned, as was expected during such a spiritual reawakening meet, the divine experience – attributed to the Holy Spirit – visited only a select few. Most of those affected were young people swooning and being carried out of the big tent raised for the occasion. Many were confessing their sins and repenting, while a few remorseful "sinful" youths were bawling and being consoled by prayer counsellors; one girl in particular could not be calmed when she raised an agonising cry outside the tent. My curiosity got the better of my traditional Baptist upbringing and I rushed out with other fellow "philistines" to witness the spectacle. The girl was surrounded by prayer counsellors dressed in long white coats imprinted with a crucifix on the back, and they had the girl pinned down. They began to recite from the Gospel of Mark 16: 17–18, "And these signs will accompany those who believe; in my name they will drive out demons . . ." The counsellors attributed the girl's uncontrollable experience to the work of evil spirits. Her condition worsened and finally she had to be carried away by stewards since the worship service inside was getting disturbed. From the pulpit a well-known charismatic Baptist preacher made fun of the reprobates who had rushed out from the tent: "Those who ran out to witness the commotion are the non-revivalists," he said in jest; the congregation roared with laughter.

Those attending the spiritual awakening included the faithful from villages in Upper Assam. The Sumi are the most widely dispersed tribe in Nagaland, having settled in at least eight districts. During the colonial period a group of Sumi Nagas went off to settle far up north in what is now the Assam and Arunachal Pradesh border. The Assam government in Tinsukia district has recognised six Sumi Naga villages: Balijan, Lalpahar, Lontong, Paharpur, Tsaliki, and Tingukupathar. The last train station in Assam is Ledo (famous for Stillwell Road during WWII), and these Sumi villages are connected to it.

The peculiar accent of Baptist pastors from Upper Assam gives away their years of contact with their Assamese-speaking neighbours. The Sumi villages in Tinsukia district have given up *jhum* cultivation and adopted a new mode of livelihood, especially tea cultivation and coal mining. The cultural gap between the old and new generation has widened, with the young assimilating into mainstream Assamese society; however, their shared Baptist faith connects Sumi groups that might otherwise have lost touch with each other. The Upper Assam Sumi Baptist churches are associate members of the WSBAK, and the Baptist parent body appoints pastors for them. It is through the church network that common ethnic ties are reinforced and the Sumi language promoted through Christian education and literature. In a way, the Baptist church ministry is preserving an indigenous language which would very likely have been swallowed up by the language of the dominant group. Most importantly, believers in Upper Assam are coming under the influence of a fervent "charismatic" variety of the Baptist faith which is widely popular among the Sumi Naga.

The blueprint of the American Baptist mission was the nineteenth-century evangelicalism that emphasised "rescue of the perishing". To be "born again" means escaping eternal damnation: this was at the heart of Naga Baptist belief and has continued well into the twenty-first century. However, in the second half of the twentieth century a mass spiritual awakening, invariably called the revival, occurred simultaneously across Nagaland's Baptist churches. This revival movement was localised, though it had parallels with the global charismatic movement, also known as twentieth-century Pentecostalism, emphasising renewed pietism and personal empowerment by the Holy Spirit – which is known as the Second Baptism.

The effect of the revival movement is still felt among Naga Baptist groups, with varying degrees of complexity. In the case of the Sumi, the movement split the Baptists into two opposing groups – namely, charismatic Baptists and conservative Baptists – with two separate front organisations and mission centres. The general perception in the conservative Baptist group is that the revival movement is only charismatic Christianity sugarcoated as a movement of the Holy Spirit. When the two disputing parties parted ways in 1993 after more than two decades of church debate that had spilled into social life, the charismatic Baptists established a new mission centre in Zunheboto town; meanwhile the conservative Baptists remained in the Aizuto mission centre, which had been established by the American Baptist missionary B.I. Anderson in 1938. The revival wave breached the fortress of the conservative Baptists – who still claim they are the true inheritors of the American Baptist tradition – and over time they became a clear minority. After the split, their funds were considerably reduced, and the oldest Sumi Baptist mission station in Aizuto became less active compared to the two other premier American Baptist mission centres in Impur and Kohima.

The conservative Baptist camp maintains to this day that the revival movement led Sumi Baptists into spurious religious beliefs and questionable spiritual experiences. "Some self-styled prophets in the prayer houses are even fixing marriages for couples telling them it is from the Holy Spirit," a prominent Sumi conservative Baptist minister charged. He was voicing his displeasure against the phenomenon of "prayer houses" manned primarily by prophets and faith-healers – a contentious issue among Naga Baptists. The conservative Baptist leader argued that charismatic Baptists are making themselves susceptible to syncretism, especially with the traditional faith. The accusation of syncretism can hurt the sentiments of charismatic Baptists, if not infuriate them, but it is a talking point among conservative Baptists. Clearly, not many Sumi Baptists subscribe to the conservative Baptist leader's belief.[26] In fact, conservatives are in a minority among Sumi Baptists.

Rev. Yehoto Chishi, the seniormost evangelist in Aizuto mission centre, says the Sumi Baptist conflict took an ugly turn within a decade of the American missionaries leaving an inchoate Baptist community to decide its own future. The two contending groups tried to gain exclusive control of the mission centre, and in 1985 their conflict grew so severe that the deputy commissioner of Zunheboto district imposed CrPC 144 in the mission centre.[27] Conflicts of interest and internal disputes are common to all Naga Baptist groups, but no other group had had curfew imposed in their mission centre. The NBCC got dragged into the Sumi Baptist church controversy, but even this parent Naga Baptist organisation failed to reconcile the two groups. Conservative Baptist preachers like Yehoto hold to their fundamentalist viewpoints, seeing them as distinguishing them from charismatic Baptists.

[26] The three Sumi Baptist organisations, SABAK, SBAK (Nito Mount), and WSBAK are more inclined towards the Charismatic viewpoint.

[27] Section 144 of the Criminal Procedure Code (CrPC) of 1973 empowers an executive magistrate to act in urgent cases of apprehended danger. Section 144 is often used to prohibit the assembly of four or more people when unrest is anticipated.

The seminary in the Aizuto mission centre, upgraded from a Bible school, is named Anderson Theological College. On the college premises is a bust of Rev. Bengt Ivar Anderson; it was unveiled in 2003 during the Sumi Baptist centenary celebrations. In the mission compound, landmarks and memorials remind visitors of the legacy of Baptist missionaries; however, for Sumi Baptists the land itself, which was purchased by the Missionary Union, is the subject of native Christian folklore. According to legend, when Rev. Anderson bought the land and started clearing the jungle, evil spirits ran helter-skelter from this haunted spot. Such legends of missionaries are popular not only among Sumi Baptists but Naga Baptists in general and have become part of the state's folk Christianity. Naga Baptists may not have made patron saints of the pioneering missionaries – it would go against their denominational belief – but their reverence for them remains exceptional.

VIII

Wokha town could have been the ideal headquarters of the British Naga Hills district: this was the view of Rev. John Ovung, former executive secretary of the Kyong Baptist Ekhümkho Sanrhyutsü (KBES, i.e. Kyong Baptist churches' association). Its location within a wide expanse of low and unvarying hills gives a rather lowland appearance to this beautiful town, which is now the district headquarters of the Lotha Nagas.[28] The Kyong, who are also called Lotha Nagas, inhabit this central district of Nagaland. During the colonial period Wokha was of strategic importance to both the British government and the American Baptist mission. This was because it was only a day's walk from Furkating, Assam, to which by the 1880s there was a connecting bridle path, and which had equidistant access to three other large tribes, the Ao, Angami, and Sumi.

[28] According to Mills, the Lotha Nagas "call themselves *Kyong*, meaning simply 'man,' the name Lhota, of which I have been unable to discover any derivation, being that by which they are known to Government." Mills, *The Lhota Nagas*, 1.

Before Kohima became the headquarters of the British Naga Hills, a new subdivision had been created in 1875 in Wokha to administer the Lotha and neighbouring tribes. As in other British settlements, working-class people from the plains came in to live and became inhabitants, and along with them came an American missionary couple, the Witters. Reporting in 1886, Rev. W.E. Witter highlighted the mixed populace of the Wokha outpost: "For some time past our bungalow has many times been actually flooded with visitors. These are of the most heterogeneous descriptions; shopmen and Naga scullions, representing many different languages, Assamese, Hindustani, Gorkali, Garo, Khasi and Angami, Sehma, Lhota and Rengma Nagas."[29]

It was the indefatigable E.W. Clark who had seen the suitability of Wokha and even considered settling there himself to start a new mission station. Clark solicited the Missionary Union to send a missionary to the Lotha Naga. This large Naga tribe living in the Lower Doyang region had "long been in contact with the Assamese" and the Ahom rulers.[30] J.P. Mills, deputy commissioner of the Naga Hills, pointed out that some Lotha Nagas were influenced by the Hindu tradition in the plains of Assam.[31] However, no Hindu priest or peripatetic sadhu had been known to attempt entering Lotha precincts; and in the Lotha oral tradition there is no evidence of any influence of Hinduism or Buddhism.

Over the colonial encounter the Lotha Naga fitted the image of a "primitive tribe". In an early portrayal, Robert Brown wrote: "On seeing the Rengmah Nagas, I concluded that the extremity of uncleanliness had been reached; but a look at the Lhota convinced me there was a lower depth still."[32] In the present day, in Lotha villages where the Baptist faith is paramount, it is difficult to conceive of the conditions of former days as portrayed by American

---

[29] Witter, "The Naga Mission", 23.

[30] Mills, *The Lhota Nagas*, 1.

[31] Ibid., xi–xii.

[32] Brown, "Narrative Report of the Progress of the Survey Party, Naga Hills, Season 1874", 335.

missionaries and British political agents. John Butler reported that some Lotha men had killed a slave "and pieces of the body [were] sent as presents to various villages"; naturally, believers remember this no more.[33] The sermon on being born again, preached for more than a century in Baptist churches, is not without effect; it has seeped deep into the psyche of believers. The Naga Baptists rarely suffer guilt on account of the past.

Toward the second half of the nineteenth century, American missionaries recognised the Lotha Naga country as a potential mission field because it was under British control and enjoyed superior communications; however, as the Lotha Baptist leader Rev. John Ovung put it, the Lotha Naga were struck by a series of misfortunes.

> Captain John Butler had surveyed the region and wanted to start the British headquarters at Wokha, but he was speared near Pangti village while on duty with his survey party, and so the Lothas missed that out. After some years the Home Board sent Rev. Witter to Wokha in 1885, and he opened the first mission school, and since he was an education missionary we would have benefited immensely, even surpassing the Ao Naga in terms of education, but he left in 1887 never to return.

John Ovung served as executive secretary of the KBES for eight years (1993–2001). As a former teacher in Bible College, what he regretted most was that the mission school in Wokha had ended prematurely, before the natives had understood its importance. John has been the head of 139 Lotha Baptist churches with –

---

[33] Major John Butler reports an incident where Lotha men flayed a slave boy alive and gave "a piece of flesh to each man in the village to put into his dolu, a large corn basket. By this they suppose all evil will be averted, their good fortune will return, and plentiful crops of grain will be ensured." See Butler, *Travels in Assam*, 189. However, Mills adds that "Nagas are always ready to give garbled, not to say scandalous, accounts of the customs of their neighbours, and there can be little doubt that Major Butler was misled by his Angami informants." See Mills, *The Lhota Nagas*, 230, Appendix C.

according to the 2016 NBCC census – 67,614 baptised members spread across Wokha district as well as other district headquarters in Nagaland. Mainstream Lotha Baptist beliefs and practices do not differ much from those of other Naga Baptists; but for the language barrier, any Naga Baptist could enter a Baptist church across Nagaland and feel at home with the liturgy, worship style, and hymnals, not to mention the lengthy sermons. Lotha Baptist ministers like John belong to an old-school Baptist faith which is evangelical in outlook, independent in church functioning, and traditionalist in the reading of scriptures – and they form the Baptist majority. However, a new class of Lotha Baptists are emerging who are painstakingly pietistic, exhibit Pentecostal characteristics, and are inordinately millenarian in outlook.

My enquiry into competing beliefs within the Lotha Baptist faith led me to Rev. Dr Ezamo Murry, a leading Lotha Baptist theologian. Murry is of the generation that saw the fag end of American Baptist mission work and the takeover by natives in the post-independence period. Like most of his contemporaries, he distanced the American Baptist mission from British colonialism. He was critical of British administrator-ethnographers like J.H. Hutton and J.P. Mills. Ezamo said that the British political agents had a genuine interest in the Naga tribes, but most of them were no admirers of the American Baptist mission. In his argument the merits of the Baptist mission outweigh the drawbacks, and that criticism will not impede the faithful seeing the American Baptist mission as their saviour.

When compared with the Ao and Angami Nagas, among the Lotha and Sumi Nagas mission schools started much later. In the case of the Lotha Nagas, the Witters began a school with three Naga boys on 25 August 1886 but they left Wokha in 1887.[34] Later, in 1922, R.P. Longwell started a school for the Lotha Nagas in Furkating, Assam. Students had to walk two days from Wokha to study in it. Only in 1928 was a separate mission station for the

---

[34] Puthenpurakal, *Baptist Missions in Nagaland*, 101–2.

Lotha Nagas started in Vankhosung under the initiative of the American missionary Dr J.R. Bailey. Ezamo was in the first batch of Lotha Nagas to be educated in the mission school here in the postcolonial period; unlike the American Baptist missionaries, he said, "The British were not passionate in educating the Naga tribes although they gave a grant-in-aid from time to time."

Ezamo is one of the first Naga seminarians to earn a master's degree in Christian counselling. Like most of his contemporaries among the early Naga educated class, he has lived an interesting life. He joined an emerging class of educated Naga Baptists who epitomised the rising individualism of the day and broke away from the dictates of traditionalism because modern education had brought them a new-found independence. During the time of his conversion the denominational conflict among the Lotha Naga Baptists had begun; this was a new development; hitherto, the conflict had been between Baptists and adherents of the old faith.

One of the first ruptures in a predominantly Baptist community in fact happened in the Lotha Naga area. In the second half of the twentieth century there had come about an increase in the number of new denominations, such as the Assemblies of God, Roman Catholicism, Nagaland Christian Revival Church, Pentecostals, and Seventh-Day Adventists. The post-independence period signalled a momentous change; with increased communication and the opening up of the Lotha area to the outside world, the Baptist dominance was, for the first time, being challenged. This marked a new phase in Lotha religious life. Ezamo said the schism among Lotha Baptist churches was due to a leadership crisis, and also because of the revival movement that inexorably swept away traditional churches. He related the revival movement in the Lotha Baptist churches in the 1950s to the global charismatic movement and said the revival wave first came from Mizoram during the 1950s, but the religious experience was contagious and spread very quickly. Others contend the revival movement was of indigenous origin. While the Sumi Naga Baptists viewed themselves as a binary – i.e. conservative or charismatic, which was colloquially called revivalists or non-revivalists – Lotha Baptists positioned themselves along a spectrum of expanding religious experiences. Thus, unlike the Sumi Baptists, the Lotha Baptists did not split into two distinct groups because they had internalised varieties of spirituality and religious experience within the same Baptist fold.

At the Lotha Naga Baptist mission centre in Vankhosung, the executive secretary of the KBES, Rev. Nyanchumo Lotha, said there had been supernatural claims in the Lotha Baptist churches, but as there were 140 churches within the KBES it was difficult for the association to monitor each case to examine the Biblical standpoint. The executive secretary occupies the old missionary bungalow, named Houston Cottage after the American Baptist missionary Rev. Howard Houston, the last foreign missionary resident in Vankhosung.[35] Except for the Baptist heritage cottage, which is slated to be converted into a kind of Baptist museum, there are no missionary landmarks or memorabilia preserved for pilgrims and visitors. Among the Naga tribes who were first evangelised by the American missionaries, the Lotha Baptists seem to have undergone the most rapid transformation. The executive secretary of the KBES confirmed that the Lotha Nagas have achieved 100 per cent Christianity, with Baptists comprising about 90 per cent.

The Lotha Baptist faith is evangelical and they have from the start been fervently mission-minded. The mission effort was strengthened and formalised with the formation of the Lotha Baptist Church Association in 1923, which began with twelve village churches after a meeting of believers in Okotso village. From its inception, according to Rev. L.L. Kikon, mission secretary of the KBES, the association initiated a strategy called home mission to evangelise fellow "animists" and neighbouring Naga communities. The mission secretary has himself worked in the Assam field and

---

[35] Howard Houston worked among the Lotha Nagas in Wokha from 1947 to 1954.

wears it as a badge of honour. He worked as a missionary from 2012 to 2016 in Sonitpur district during the second phase of the Lotha Baptist mission in Assam that began in 2006. According to Rev. Kikon, "The rate of conversion in Sonitpur was fast; by the time we phased out on 15 June 2016, there were fourteen churches and 3000 believers."

From 1923 to 1978, Lotha Baptists had no outreach mission; it was only in 1979 that the KBES sent a missionary to Karbi Anglong in Assam. The association gradually started sending missionaries and opened mission schools in places like Manja, N.C. Hills, and Hawaipur. By the time the KBES mission was phased out after thirty years in January 2009, there were 145 churches and 12,600 baptised members. According to the 2016 mission census of the KBES, the number of converts brought into the Baptist fold by Lotha Baptists alone was nearly twice the size of the Naga Baptist population in 1921.[36]

The Lotha Baptist mission in Assam has worked zealously among a diverse group of people. They initiated a third mission phase on 7 July 2017 in Ralan subdivision near the Assam border, and within ten years have targeted the planting of 100 churches, appointing 100 evangelists and pastors, and their plan is to "bring 5000 people to the Lord". Like other Naga Baptist missions, the Lotha Baptists have weaned themselves off foreign funding. Nevertheless, their work is not without complications. The mission secretary says he faced difficult questions on the issue of conversion and cultural contact, but the faithful believe they are following what Jesus commanded in the Gospel of Matthew 28: 19 – to make disciples of all nations. If there is an American Baptist trait among the Naga Baptists that has not waned over the century, it is a fervent desire to convert and "save". Lotha Naga Baptists have filtered into Myanmar, China, Bhutan, Malaysia, and Thailand; and within India into Assam, Arunachal Pradesh, Andhra Pradesh, Sikkim, and West Bengal.

[36] *Census of India, 1921, Assam*, Vol. III, Pt 1, 26, 61.

IX

Chumukedima is a fast-growing town in the foothills on the outskirts of Dimapur township. Human habitation has expanded considerably over the past three decades or so, but, unlike most sleepy towns in Nagaland, which are largely the domicile of a single ethnic group, Chumukedima is the face of a new urban space distinguishable for its multi-ethnic composition. It is home to many affluent Nagas with private villas and bungalows. And, as in any Naga settlement, Chumukedima is noticeable for its thriving Christian community with more than thirty churches belonging to almost all ethnic groups in the state. If one walks up the nearest hill and gazes down upon Chumukedima, the view is spectacular; and amid the growing settlement what stands out are the crucifixes atop church buildings.

The American Baptist missionary C.D. King, who opened a mission station in the hills about 5 km from the present habitation, would not have envisaged this predominance of Baptists. King was ordained in 1874 and reached Samaguting on 11 July 1878 to start the Angami Naga mission, succeeding Clark who was overseeing the Ao Naga mission and who had persistently appealed to the Missionary Union to send a missionary to this large tribe. King's endeavour in Chumukedima – known as Samaguting during the colonial period – was not a success story, but after his death the Baptist mission that he had been part of completely won over the descendants of the first settlers of Samaguting. Samaguting (Chumukedima) became one of the last Angami Naga villages to be evangelised by the Baptist mission.

The town began as a village settlement in the foothills and gradually expanded over the years. In the 1970s the majority of its inhabitants moved down from the old village to the plains. Razhuvotuo Khroitsu's family was the last to shift in 1982, after the demise of his father. The old village, which was once a British settlement, became forested again; and if not for descendants like Razhuvotuo (chairman of the Chumukedima council) who keep the tradition alive, the former site would, like most relocated Naga villages, have been forgotten. Overgrown with vegetation, there are no traces now of the former settlement except a memorial stone erected to commemorate this old British headquarters. But in its vicinity is a crucifix, nearly 12 feet tall, erected by Baptist descendants of the village in memory of C.D. King.

The Kings' stay at Samaguting did not last even six months: they had to rush down to the plains to seek refuge in Sivasagar when the Angami uprising happened in 1879. In 1880, when the dust had settled, they moved into the interior of the hills of Kohima, the new district headquarters of the Naga Hills, and worked there till 1889, notwithstanding failing health and a poor conversion rate among the tenacious Angami Nagas.

Samaguting had become the headquarters of the new Naga Hills district in 1866, when the British government decided to pursue an active policy to rein in the recalcitrant Nagas. In what used to be a British police checkpoint known as Nichuguard, Nagas descending to the plains had to hand over their spears to the authorities.[37] Now, National Highway 29 cuts through this old British checkpoint, which has been swallowed up by the rapid expansion of Chumukedima town. Memory of the checkpoint has been overshadowed by a huge monolith, erected by Angami Nagas recalling their past glory, with these words inscribed in upper case on the stone:

> MR. GRANGE THE SUB-ASSISTANT COMMISSIONER
> OF THE BRITISH INDIA GOVT. STATIONED
> AT NAGAON ENTERED INTO A WRITTEN
> AGREEMENT WITH THE TWO GAON
> BURAS/VILLAGE CHIEFS
> MR. YASIELIE AND MR. LHOUZEIRU OF CHUMUKEDIMA
> (SAMAGOOTING) IN THE YEAR 1840
> WHERE LANDS EAST OF MHUNG DIJOOA
> WERE PROMISED TO THEM AND ELEVEN
> NAGA PRISONERS WERE RELEASED.

---

[37] Mackenzie, *The North-East Frontier of India*, 121.

Despite ambivalence towards British rule and general disapproval of the colonial representation of the Nagas, British official records are taken as reliable evidence whenever a dispute arises or historical veracity is required. The words from the settlement have been inscribed on the monolith at Nichuguard not just to commemorate the historical event but also to send an important political message about the ascendancy of the Angami Nagas in colonial history.

A well-known Angami public intellectual, Niketu Iralu, remarked: "Angamis cannot dwell in the past glory and achievements, we need to move ahead"; nevertheless, memories of past exploits have echoed down the years and are recounted by the new generation. Razhuvotuo, who claims descent from the founder of the village, says "Oral tradition tells that the village was established around 1000 AD, and Dzüvi Khroitsu and Viselu Hama were the founders of Chumukedima, which came to be known as Samaguting." He says evangelists from Khonoma first came preaching during the 1960s, about eight decades after King's departure, and some villagers embraced the new faith. Medolie Seikha became the first convert from the village and is a household name among believers. Razhuvotuo points to something distinctive here: "We were the first village to be visited by the American Baptist missionaries, but became the last to be converted." Home to many descendants of the old Samaguting, the Baptist following grew exponentially in Chumukedima over the years.

The takeover of Samaguting as a British outpost brought tremendous change to the region.[38] Naga belligerence was monitored from this first small outpost in a lower mountain range of Angami Naga country, which had been sporadically occupied between 1846 and 1851. Samaguting, according to J. Johnstone, a political officer posted there, was an unsuitable site chosen in haste as the headquarters of a new district by an officer who wished it "as a speedy road to promotion, and subsequent transfer to a more

[38] Ibid., 121–2.

favoured appointment."[39] The Naga contempt for alien rule was implacable, so political officers posted here administered with an iron fist. Johnstone would hold a loaded revolver while hearing cases "in case of any wild savage attempting to dispute my authority".[40] This was the political milieu when the first missionary to the Angami pitched his proverbial missionary tent in Samaguting to evangelise the powerful Angami Naga tribe.

Amid Samaguting's "unwholesome" environment and unforeseeable political climate in 1879, the American Baptist missionary couple settled alongside a motley crew of sepoys, traders, and labourers from the plains. C.D. King knew he had come to a southern Naga tribe with proven credentials as the most troublesome to British interests in Assam. Not long after the Kings reached, a major native uprising in 1879 almost derailed the mission effort. The battle of Khonoma, as it is famously known, significantly influenced Naga identity and consciousness well into the twenty-first century. When the uprising began and the Kings left for the safety of the plains, the mission temporarily ended, then shifted base to Kohima in 1881 after the uprising was quelled.

Kohima was originally named Kewhira, which natives (who are known as Kewhimia) believe came from Whinuo, the legendary founder of the village. Elwin quotes a British report of 1874 which states: "Kohima is situated on the summit of a ridge, about 5200 feet above the sea, and is of considerable size, containing upwards of 900 houses."[41] Following the policy of actively administering the Naga tribes, "In March 1878 the Chief Commissioner reported that after personal exploration, he considered Kohimah the best site for the headquarters of the Political Officer . . . Kohimah was occupied, without opposition, on the 14th November 1878."[42]

---

[39] Johnstone, "My Experiences in Manipur and the Naga Hills, 1896", 26.
[40] Ibid., 30.
[41] See Brown, "Narrative Report of the Progress of the Survey Party, Naga Hills, Season 1874", 32–3.
[42] Elwin, ed., *The Nagas in the Nineteenth Century*, 182–3.

Ill. 3: The Naga Hills district headquarters, Kohima, during the British period. This sleepy little town would become a centre of American Baptist mission activity starting from 1881.
Courtesy DIPR.

The mission compound, which is presently the ABCC headquarters, is on a hilltop overlooking Kohima town. S.W. Rivenburg's description hints that the mission station was walking distance from the British cantonment: "We are above the military station. I can hear the orders of the officers as they drill . . . In the far distance, we hear the rattle of the men firing at a target on the rifle-range."[43] The township of Kohima began in the present-day Naga Bazar area, which is about 1 km downhill from the mission compound. The first township, which was under the protection of the British garrison, used to be called Manipuri Market, since traders from Manipur had for the first time set up shops in the area, bringing with them a monetised economy.

[43] Rivenburg, ed., *The Star of Naga Hills*, 73.

Angami conversions under King in the Kohima mission station, though insignificant, laid the foundation for his successor, Rivenburg. However, as "first missionary to the Angami Naga" King remains a household name among Naga Baptists. The popular view is that he had more amicable relations with British officers than did Rev. Rivenburg, "who was often harassed by the British government". The part about King appears true as Mary Clark reported "Rev. C.D. King, of Kohima" came to a meeting of missionaries "accompanied by several native police and a hundred Naga coolies."[44] This escort of armed policemen was a privilege that missionaries rarely enjoyed. However, Rivenburg's harassment by the colonial authorities is less certain; he was awarded "the Viceroy's silver Kaisar-i-Hind Medal (Sovereign of India), granted by the British ruler to civilians in recognition of their services to the people of India."[45] Rivenburg's award is common knowledge among Angami believers, but stories of disputes between the Baptist mission and the British government also find an important place in missionary narratives. In the Naga Baptist world a persecuted missionary elicits far more admiration than one influential in worldly affairs. The martyrdom corpus of Christendom informs the minds of Naga Baptists and they relate the travails of both American missionaries and pioneering native converts within the larger history of Christian missions.

The first missionary to be buried in the Naga Hills was Rivenburg's wife Hattie, a native of Bridgewater, Pennsylvania, who died on 22 March 1908 in the Kohima mission station. Decades later, in 1997, Mrs Rivenburg's remains were exhumed from an old cemetery defaced by landslides and reinterred in the mission compound. "Our dear mother Hattie, for the love of God's son,

---

[44] See Clark, *A Corner in India*, 151.

[45] Rivenburg, *The Star of the Naga Hills*, 137. The other Baptist missionary to be awarded the Kaisar-i-Hind was Rev. William Pettigrew of the Ukhrul Baptist mission. Born in Edinburgh, Scotland, the Anglican-raised Pettigrew worked for the American Baptist Foreign Mission Society, and became a Baptist while in India. Pettigrew took 2000 Labour Corps from Manipur to France, earning a wartime medal as well.

Ill. 4: Rev. and Mrs S.W. Rivenburg. A successful medical missionary in Kohima, Rivenburg worked with Dr Ronald Ross in Calcutta on Ross' landmark research on malaria. Rivenburg was awarded the Kaiser-i-Hind for his public service. Courtesy ABAM.

Jesus Christ, you gave your whole life to us, to the service of your God's people. As long as we live here, we the mothers would love to remember you. Because of you we know Christ" is the epitaph (in Roman letters) on her tombstone in Tenyidie. It is followed by this in English:

> How beautiful upon the mountain
> are the feet of those who brings good news.
> Isa 52: 7

> This memorial is raised
> in remembrance of
> Hattie Elizabeth Tiffany
> (Wife of Dr Sidney W. Rivenburg, MD)
> whose mortal remains
> are re-interred here

> The distant hills where you lie buried
> were but a stepping stone
> faithful servant, as you carried
> your cross unwaveringly home.

The re-interring of missionary remains was not without controversy. "I know they kept it for memory to inspire the believers, but if it were during my time I would not have allowed it," maintained Visasieü Dolie, a former women's secretary of the ABCC. Apparently, those who exhumed the remains of Hattie Rivenburg kept her wedding band as an exhibit in the ABCC museum. When relatives of the Rivenburgs visited the mission compound, native Baptists explained their well-intentioned reason for placing the ring in the museum. Removing objects from a place of burial is taboo in Naga society; and the Angami Baptists in some villages still maintain the past tradition of grave goods, trifling with which is considered inauspicious. The moving of Mrs Rivenburg's remains and more so the removal of her ring, though necessitated by recurring landslides, would have been unthinkable in normal circumstances. But as Atsi Dolie, the executive director of the ABCC, reasoned: "It was not a sign of disrespect, but the women's department wanted to preserve the wedding ring to inspire an upcoming generation of Baptist women through the sacrifices and lifework of Hattie Rivenburg." Hattie Elizabeth Tiffany, a native of Pennsylvania, has been long forgotten in her place of birth, but the memory of her life is preserved in the distant hills of Nagaland.

X

The Angami village of Khonoma stands as a fine specimen of a Naga settlement with a rich cultural heritage and a history of irrepressible independence and self-reliance. Stories of Khonoma standing up to British forces are much told among the Naga tribes. Interestingly, my first glimpse as a boy of the history of this village was through a lurid story told by an elder of my tribe. The story dramatised the masculinity of Khonoma warriors in a surreal manner and went like this: a group of warriors chasing British soldiers found the latter stuck thigh-deep in freshly ploughed squelchy terrace fields; the warriors cut down the soldiers and, intrigued by the whiteness of their flesh, boiled the victims to taste it. Notwithstanding their headhunting practices, cannibalism has not existed among the Naga tribes, but in this very rare case J.H. Hutton, one of the foremost experts on the Naga tribes, says "it is reported . . . that at the time of Mr Damant's death and the consequent punitive expedition some young men of Khonoma tasted the flesh of a British officer because it looked so good to eat."[46]

On my first visit to Khonoma in 2010 I sheepishly asked a well-known village elder, Visebi Dolie, about this stewing of the white man, but he did not recall it. I did not persist in my enquiry since Nagas like myself, living in metropolitan cities, are irritated by notions of us as predatory savages gorging indiscriminately in jungles. Of course, mutual ethnic prejudices and caricatures exist among the Nagas, and other Naga groups perceive the Angami as a tribe with relatively adventurous taste buds, but to seek confirmation of the rumour of forefathers slurping up white-man stew is to stir a controversial pot. Khonoma village has had enough trouble brewing!

The Damant affair is still recounted by many, but for the Naga Baptists this was an important incident because it affected the nascent American Baptist mission. On 14 October 1879 Damant was shot outside the gate in Semoma *khel* in Khonoma: "of the 65 police who accompanied Mr Damant 25 were found to be killed or missing, and 14 more were wounded, and of the 20 military 10 were killed or wounded."[47] The incident sent shock waves across the British domains in Assam. A novel by Easterine Kire which pivots on the Second Battle of Khonoma has this: "It was headed by no less than Brigadier General Nation, Charge of

---

[46] Hutton, *The Angami Nagas*, 96, footnote.
[47] See Mackenzie, *The North-East Frontier of India*, 135.

Affairs, who commanded the forces brought from Assam, Manipur and Shillong. Under his charge were 1000 rifles, 2 mountain guns and a rocket battery. Colonel Johnstone's 2000 men joined in the attack. From Chumukedima, Major Evans arrived with 200 rifles."[48] The Khonoma uprising of 1879, as the British called it, became fertile ground for the seeds of Naga nationalism. Narratives of the battle became widespread among Naga tribes asserting their right to self-determination. It is no surprise that the well-known architects of Naga nationalism came from Khonoma.

Khonoma is well known as a must-visit tourist village, and one can see the imprint of commercialism in its outer embellishments, though with undercurrents of ardent Christian faith and deep-rooted ethnic nationalism. Compared to most Naga villages, which are witnessing the rapid loss of traditional ways of life, this historic habitat has done a commendable job of preserving some of its cultural past – the most striking being woodwork and stone workmanship. Most pavements are laid out with blocks of quartzite with a well-maintained narrow drainage system giving the village a clean appearance. A middle-aged woman in Dimapur who grew up in Khonoma during the 1960s described it as a less attractive village in those days, especially its poor sanitation; of course she immediately attributed the improved sanitation and personal hygiene to the spread of the Baptist faith in the village.

On entering the village, two institutions greet the eye: the Baptist church and a state-sponsored eco-tourism centre. These face each other, separated by a sloping road leading up to the church, both a reminder of the far-reaching influence of the Baptist faith and the long arm of the Indian state even in relatively secluded Naga villages. The eco-tourism office is more recent; the Baptist church was constructed in 1973 on land donated by the family of an early Baptist convert from the village. The local Catholic cathedral, which has the second-largest following, is on a site overlooking the Baptist church some distance from the village,

---

[48] Kire, *A Village Remembered*, 119.

and a Christian Revival Church that dates only to the beginning of the new millennium is out of sight from this strategic point in the village. The Baptists have the best site in the village, as they do in most Naga villages.

The Baptist church exhibits modern-day architecture at its best, with steps leading up to immaculately maintained premises. A small administrative office remains out of sight behind the church building. Rev. Tsolie Chase, an experienced Baptist minister, welcomed me into his small office, which he shared with the associate pastor, Vibilie Chase. A burly and soft-spoken man in his eighties, Tsolie is a native of Khonoma and has been pastoring the church for twenty years since 1998. Before that he worked as treasurer for fifteen years with the NBCC, and so is well informed about Baptist organisations and churches in Nagaland. He is among the few Naga Baptist ministers today to have never attended a seminary. Presently, qualification from a seminary is becoming a requirement among pastors, although lay pastors were common during the Baptist beginnings. Tsolie is among the earlier generation of Nagas educated outside the state and who, on returning, got caught between the avenues of employment created by the new Indian state and the struggle of the Naga educated class for self-determination. He got a BA from Shillong and returned to work as a schoolteacher before joining the church ministry. After his matriculation he served as secretary to Khrisanisa, the first president of a Naga underground outfit called the Federal Government of Nagaland. He was twice arrested by the Indian army but friends came to his aid and he decided to pursue higher studies. Living a quiet life has its own rewards; Rev. Tsolie Chase's name might not go down in history in the footsteps of some of his village contemporaries, but he seems content with his life as a low-profile Baptist minister watching his children prosper: "Two of my sons are now working as medical doctors," he says, beaming with pride.

Khonoma is typical in showing a thriving Baptist community, though Catholics and the Christian Revival Church have been giving the Baptists a run for their money. "The Baptists are about 60–65 per cent and the next majority is the Catholics," the associate pastor Vibilie Chase said. "There are less than ten people in the village still believing in the old religion," he added. Adherents of the old faith are not conscientious in observing its rites and rituals; their reason for remaining in the traditional faith, according to the young pastor, is their fondness of the traditional brew, which the Baptist church frowns upon.

The Naga national movement apart, Khonoma is known for spreading the Baptist faith to neighbouring communities and villages. It boasts of producing early evangelists and church workers like the Reverends Nisier, Kekhulhu, Pelesato Chase, and Megosieso Savino. Baptists had secured their foothold here by the turn of the twentieth century despite a slow start. Native believers speak of the first converts being beaten and shunned by the villagers, but the village did not oppose the Baptist faith as violently as they did British rule. Atsi Dolie, a native of Khonoma and the incumbent executive director of the ABCC, explained the growth of the Baptist faith among the Angami: "The functioning of the Baptist church fits well into the idea of a village republic, where the local church enjoys autonomy. It is a typical Naga characteristic where everyone wants to be involved in decision-making; Baptists are democratic and the basic Baptist tenets allowed this participation."

In present-day Angami villages denominational pluralism seems a common feature in religious life, but Baptist culture still retains its hold on community life. "The Angami Catholics are more Baptist in their beliefs and practices when compared to Catholics in places like Philippines and other South East Asian countries," Atsi argued, and "They also talk of salvation through grace and being born again, and possess an evangelical outlook not very different from the Baptists." This US-educated Angami Baptist leader provided a sociological explanation, saying that clan membership determines affiliation to a denomination, at least in his village. "In Khonoma village, Merhema and Semoma *khels* are largely Baptist while Thevoma *khel* is largely Catholic."

The Naga tribes traditionally exhibit varied political systems, ranging from autocratic chieftainship to loosely based democratically governed village councils. Theirs is a society of proud and fiercely independent people surviving in one of the most difficult places on earth; in their confined world the authority and influence enjoyed by some village autocrats might be seen to rival that of medieval European monarchs.

In the post-independence period, Naga areas came to be relatively closed once again to the world beyond. Relentless armed struggle became the order of the day, and the rest of the world remained oblivious of the mass conversion movement in Naga areas. The next chapter provides an account of those lost years.

4

Some Converts are More Equal than Others

> Education and Litigation, doubtful apparitions, are usurping his [the native's] place; the old beliefs wither under the shrivelling touch of Civilization, and the voice of the Missionary is heard in the land.
>
> – J.H. Hutton, Deputy Commissioner, Naga Hills, 1921

> More and more in the future the church in missionary lands will become indigenous in the proper sense of the word, as certainly it should be, and that will mean that it will not be financed with foreign money, or conducted by foreign workers, or projected and patterned on a foreign-made ecclesiastical system.
>
> – William Ernest Hocking, *Re-thinking Missions*, 1932

IN THE FIRST DECENNIAL census of 1951 conducted after independence, the total population of the Naga Hills district of Assam was 205,950, of which the Christian population stood at 93,423 or 45.7 per cent. The proportion of Christian population in the next census in 1961 had increased to 52.9 per cent (195,588 in a total population of 369,200). By 1961 the census operation provided district-wise population data of the Naga Hills–Tuensang Area (NHTA), an administrative unit carved out in 1957 because the political landscape had changed.[1] The

---

[1] On 26 January 1954, the North-East Frontier Agency (NEFA) was divided into six divisions that included Tuensang division. On 1 December

British government had identified natives living beyond the Dikhu river north-east of the Naga Hills district as trans-Dikhu tribes, or frontier tribes. To the administered tribes in the Naga Hills, the inhabitants of this "indirectly administered or unadministered" region came to be known as eastern Nagas, or prejudicially as "backward tribes" in the post-independence period.

In the two former British administrative headquarters Kohima and Mokokchung, the Christian population in 1961 had increased to 41,690 and 108,272 at 38.2 and 85.9 per cent of the total population, respectively. In Tuensang, which was first established as an outpost of Mokokchung in 1948, the total population was 134,275 with a Christian population of 45,626 at 33.9 per cent in 1961; importantly, the converts in Tuensang were overwhelmingly from a region that the British government had categorised as "controlled" areas, as against "unadministered" areas. Opening an outpost in Tuensang meant the presence of the state in this "wild" tract. Though following the Great War the Baptist mission spearheaded by native evangelists and itinerant preachers worked tirelessly in these parts, the opening of an Indian government outpost in the heart of the "warlike" Chang Naga country in Tuensang, with armed police on standby, became a perk for the American Baptist mission that had just outlived the British Raj.

In the post-independence period the eastern Nagas – comprising the Chang, Khiamniungan, Konyak, Phom, Sangtam, and Yimchunger – and occupying the new administrative region named Tuensang, became a mission field for Naga tribes that had been first evangelised by American Baptist missionaries. There was a huge gap in the mission encounter between the eastern Nagas and other Naga tribes. For instance, around the time the Ao Nagas in the Impur mission station were gearing up for the centennial celebration of the coming of Christianity in 1972, a case of headhunting had been reported among the Khiamniungan Nagas in

---

1957, Tuensang was separated from NEFA and attached with the Naga Hills district to form the Naga Hills–Tuensang Area (NHTA).

Tuensang division in the mid-1960s.² These so-called advanced Naga tribes took upon themselves the burden of evangelising the eastern Nagas. Their strategy did not differ much from that of the American Baptist mission but marked a significant new chapter in the history of Naga Baptists.

After Indian independence the Naga tribes, who were collectively in a political deadlock with the new Indian state, crossed a new milestone. The Naga Hills–Tuensang Area (NHTA) became Nagaland, the sixteenth state of the Indian union, on 1 December 1963. In undivided Assam the Naga desire for self-rule, which was spearheaded by educated natives from mission schools, had been the first of its kind among the hill tribes. The success of the American Baptist mission among "animist" Nagas was seen as a problem by the administration. During British times, political agents had expressed displeasure at the new religion for irrevocably changing traditional ways of life; in the post-independence period many political leaders of the new Indian state saw it as a rabble-rousing faith, and thus an impediment to national integration.

The mission field in the Naga areas post-independence was ripe for the taking. A good number of natives had been trained as teachers and preachers in mission schools and vernacular Bible schools. However, political developments which culminated in foreign missionaries being expelled from the Naga areas deeply vexed the American missionaries. The mission to the Nagas was gaining momentum, but not completed: a large number of "heathen" tribes clung to their ways. American missionaries found solace in the fact that able native converts took over the mission. Evangelists from tribes like the Ao, Angami, and Sumi were not untried, since they had largely shouldered the responsibility of grassroots work, but they had hitherto been supervised by American missionaries. "Cometh the hour, cometh the man" luckily came true and native Baptists proved their mettle; in fact, a mass conversion movement developed under their watch.

---

² Ganguli, *A Pilgrimage to the Nagas*, 256–7.

While the American Baptist mission saw a world of difference between Christian and non-Christian Nagas, the British government made a distinction between administered and non-administered Naga tribes, buttressing the notion of natives basking under Pax Britannica. The administered tribes included a section of the Konyak Naga (presently called the Lower Konyak), and tribes like the Ao, Angami, Lotha, Sumi, and Rengma occupying what was known as the British Naga Hills.[3] These were deemed more "docile" and forthcoming, as compared to the "warmongering" tribes east of the Naga Hills. "Involuntarily my eyes always reverted to the white patches on the map . . . Until recently all Nagas were inveterate head-hunters, and even now, outside British rule, head-hunters they remain," said Fürer-Haimendorf of the eastern Naga tribes beyond the pale of civilisation.[4]

The objectives of the two Western enterprises differed substantially with regard to "civilising" the natives. According to the pioneering missionary Mary Mead Clark, "From the beginning it was never contemplated stopping alone with these tribes bordering on the frontier; but on and on, conquering and to conquer, beyond and still beyond, until these mountains should be spanned and the kingdom of our Lord extended from the Brahmaputra to the Irrawaddy, and from the Irrawaddy to the Yangtse."[5] Several British political agents viewed the mission as causing irreparable damage to the traditional Naga way of life. To J.P. Mills the Baptist faith not only heralded the demise of traditional culture but also a dissipating sense of purpose and meaning: "The objectless existence of the 'civilised' Naga is an important point . . . He has acquired new tastes, but not the wherewithal to gratify them. The result is discontent and lack of interest in life."[6] Fürer-Haimendorf was equally critical of the Baptist mission, describing the Baptist

---

[3] In 1913, an outpost had been opened in the Lower Konyak region in Wakching, mainly to control headhunting raids. See Elwin, *Nagaland*, 28.

[4] Fürer-Haimendorf, *The Naked Nagas*, 4.

[5] Clark, *A Corner in India*, 135.

[6] Mills, *The Ao Nagas*, 423.

faith in an Ao Naga village as having created a cultural wasteland.

> People with sullen faces came out of the chapel; they seemed to me mere shadows of Nagas, or, even worse, caricatures of Europeans. There was the "pastor", a skinny young man in khaki shorts and a mauve coat. Some of his flock had also adopted shorts as a most important symbol of a good Baptist – it was, no doubt, taken for faith . . . The Aos' most cherished and valued possessions, the pride of generations, lay unheeded and scattered in the jungle.[7]

Contrary to Western observers, these "sullen faced" native converts took it upon themselves to continue the white man's burden and evangelise their brethren; and, by and large, the whole history of Naga Christianity would seem to suggest this gave native converts a sense of purpose and meaning in their new-found faith. The American Baptist mission had bequeathed to native missionaries and believers an evangelical fervour that transformed the social and cultural landscape of the Nagas.

Missionaries and British agents had, given the colonial context of racism, regularly asserted their civilisational superiority. This attitude the native converts subtly inherited from the Westerners. Which in turn led to labels such as uncouth or civilised, scientific or superstitious, advanced or backward, churched or unchurched, and so forth. When the so-called advanced Nagas took the mission to the eastern Nagas, they perceived their brethren there as embodiments of all the negative terms above.

Tuensang, hitherto a populous and ethnically diverse district, was one of the three (along with Kohima and Mokokchung) formed at the time of statehood in 1963. The Tuensang area was anomalous, a problem facing missionaries and the Indian state. Except for some Konyak Naga villages in the Lower Konyak area (near the plains of Upper Assam), a greater part of Tuensang district had remained outside British administration till 1947. But the

---

[7] Ibid., 55.

government had opened some distant outposts in Tuensang at the request of villagers wary of inter-village wars, headhunting raids, and slave raiding from Burma.[8] It was from the British headquarters in Mokokchung that the trans-Dikhu tribes were controlled. Land disputes remained a thorn in the flesh for the Baptist church and district administration in Tuensang, since conflicts over land and resources erupt from time to time, and this continues into the present.

Since the American Baptist mission could not move east of the Naga Hills, the area that was beyond British administration became synonymous with backwardness. The American missionaries opened mission stations and schools only in the region identified as the British Naga Hills. This was not for lack of trying, it was because the British government stopped Baptist mission activities beyond the Dikhu river. In many instances, British officers felt that the Naga tribes subdued by the administration were in their warring ways no different from the eastern Nagas. Hutton remarked that "The Sema villages of Seromi and Tichipami [administered villages] were allowed free intercourse with any of the women in the Sangtam village of Charr, as the men of that village wished to improve the stock by an admixture of more warlike blood, Charr being rather an inferior village with warlike neighbours."[9] This would be unpalatable to a modern Naga; however, it is true that before their conversion the Sumi Nagas, whose missionaries played a role in spreading the Baptist faith in the Tuensang area, were considered more warlike than their eastern Naga neighbours.

In the eyes of Naga Baptist missionaries the eastern Nagas whom they sought to evangelise were "uncouth" tribes that had to be "civilised" and rescued by the gospel. Educated Naga Baptists now saw in their eastern Naga brethren a reflection of themselves before their own conversion. After the British left the Naga Hills, the natives blamed colonialism for the problems of

[8] Elwin, *Nagaland*, 30–1.
[9] See Hutton, *The Angami Nagas*, 170–1, footnote.

ethnonationalism under the new Indian state. On the other hand within the new Baptist milieu a new class of luminaries emerged in the Naga tradition of hero-worship, drawing new elements into Naga legends. This new class included American missionaries and pioneering native Baptist converts. Among the eastern Naga tribes, native missionaries and preachers now became household names.

II

Yehozhe Yepthomi was in the team of eight Sumi Naga Baptist missionaries who in 1958 went to spread the new religion in the Yimchunger Naga area. Being the first person in his village to attend school, he had converted while studying in the government-run school. After passing the fourth standard he was for two years at a vernacular Bible school in Aizuto and went on to serve as preacher-cum-teacher among the Yimchunger for seven years, from 1958 to 1965. At the start, he worked mainly as an interpreter for senior colleagues; he could speak Yimchunger fluently because his village, Ngozubomi, which was then under Tuensang division of NEFA, shared a boundary with the Yimchunger Naga area.

Yimchunger Nagas were said to be living in a "dreadful" and "pitiable" condition when the native missionaries first visited them. Yehozhe elucidated the terrible state of affairs: "Headhunting was still in practice when we went there to spread the gospel. People were still engaged in internecine warfare; villages were fortified with sentries manning the posts, and at night wooden gates furnished with bamboo spikes would be closed after sunset. During our time we could still see rotting human heads raised on bamboo poles or head trees festooned with skulls."

The consensus among the Naga Baptist missionaries is that the mission not only empowered natives, it also rescued communities from their pitiable existence, especially in the poorer villages. "Looking back you cannot romanticise the living condition of villages in the Yimchunger area; life was extremely harsh. What good is culture and tradition if people are killed frequently and villages raided for the sole purpose of taking away human heads?" This was Yehozhe's irritated question when I pressed him on the loss of tradition because of his mission; he says it took great determination to preach the good news to a tribe so hostile to outsiders. He provided details:

> The Yimchunger occupied a lowland area surrounded by the Sumi and Sangtam Naga. They were pressed from all sides but the eastern Sumi villages like Satami, Melahumi, Ngozubomi, and Phisami pushed the Yimchunger much further; in fact, these conceited Sumi villages used to call the Yimchunger area their head-harvesting field. Also, due to constant raids, people could not cultivate their land and so they had sold off their lands to the neighbouring Sumi villages. And if it were not for the coming of the Baptist mission the Yimchunger area would have shrunk even further . . .

In 1921 Hutton had pointed out that "The Yachumi (Yimchunger) are less warlike than the Semas, who dominate the nearer villages and take tribute from them."[10]

The evangelist Yehozhe, a village chief himself, had an interesting insight on the dynamics of the village political system and the Baptist faith. "The problem with the Naga tribes like the Sumi, Sangtam, Konyak and Yimchunger, who had a hereditary chieftainship system, was that the chief played a decisive role in the acceptance of the new faith. If a chief decided to follow a new religion the entire village would follow suit. This problem of the masses following the village chief was also responsible for nominalism." Rev. Akhum, a veteran Yimchunger Baptist leader and pastor of the Yimchunger Baptist church in Tuensang town, said the problem of "backsliding" was more recurrent among those Naga tribes who converted en masse to the Baptist faith – a phenomenon that contemporary Naga Baptist theologians call the "mass movement". Like the Sumi Nagas, the Yimchunger Nagas witnessed such a mass movement. Atsi Dolie, head of the

---

[10] Ibid., 377.

Ill. 5: Sumi Naga believers and evangelists during the Baptist conference, c. 1942. Considered more warlike than the "warmongering" eastern Naga tribes in the British unadministered region, the Sumi Baptists became actively involved in evangelism after their conversion. Courtesy SBAK.

Angami Baptist Church Council (ABCC), said Naga tribes like the Angami and Ao, whose polity is a loose form of the village republic, withstood the Baptist influence much longer because their elected village elders made the decisions and often categorically rejected the new faith.

Rev. Akhum said that the chiefs in Yimchunger villages were not as powerful as Sumi chiefs and Konyak *anghs* (village autocrats), and so did not play a pivotal role in conversion. A first-generation convert himself, Akhum said it was the message and practices of the new religion that appealed to Yimchunger Nagas, who were hard pressed by exorbitant rituals and exacting taboos. Forsaking spirit worship and rice beer were compensated for by freedom from financially burdensome traditional rituals.

Older-generation Baptist leaders like Akhum did not face the dilemma of cultural loss with which the new-generation Baptists grapple, since Naga society was long isolated from conflicts in the wider world over culture, religion, and ethnicity. The issues facing the new generation of Yimchunger Baptists are very different from those that confronted the forefathers first preached to by Naga Baptist missionaries. The new crop of Baptists face an uphill battle against emerging social realities that determine what is trendy; the days are far gone when native missionaries asked them to give up animal sacrifice and rice beer.

The elderly Akhum, the first Yimchunger Naga to earn a bachelor's degree in theology, still holds a comparatively liberal view of traditional culture despite being an old-school Baptist.[11] He said some of the missionaries who came to the Yimchunger area have been accused of confiscating traditional bead necklaces and other ornaments thought incompatible with Christian ideals. Critics of the Naga Baptist mission accuse native missionaries of cultural chauvinism for depriving eastern Nagas of their traditional culture. This is despite the fact that Baptists are more liberal in integrating traditional culture with their faith when compared to other millenarian charismatic groups that are giving the Baptists a run for their money. The Christian Revival Church (CRC), the second biggest denomination in Nagaland, has adopted a fundamentalist stance towards Naga traditional culture; many of its preachers have denounced it as part of the "pagan" past. Interestingly, the majority of non-Baptist Nagas are "dissidents" who moved out of the Baptist fold as the Naga area opened up to other Christian denominations.

Today, the Yimchunger Naga Baptist mission centre is in Shamator, 55 km from Tuensang town. The baptism of the first Yimchunger convert took place in 1947, so the Yimchunger Naga Baptists have celebrated seventy-five years. What Yimchunger Baptist believers invariably share is respect for the Ao and Sumi Naga missionaries who first brought Christianity to them as pastors, teachers, and Bible translators. The names of these native missionaries are commemorated during jubilee celebrations and important church-related events.

---

[11] Rev. Akhum received his Bachelor of Theology degree (1977–81) from Clark Theological College in Aolijen, Mokokchung.

However, the Baptist mission to eastern Naga tribes such as the Yimchunger is not free of blemish. The most serious criticism levelled against them is cultural hegemony. Ao Baptist missionaries have been accused of promoting the Ao language at the expense of the Yimchunger. "As late as 1985 in Shamator town, Yimchunger children would sing Ao songs and recite scripture from Ao Bibles and the Ao pastors would preach in their own language; also for those Yimchunger wanting to study in Impur Bible School, learning Ao language was made compulsory in the first year, without which getting admission was difficult," a young Yimchunger Naga seminary student said. A Yimchunger pastor from Kiphire district told me: "In 1958, the Ao Baptist mission in Keong range and the Sumi Baptist mission working in Mango range were asked to leave the Yimchunger area on the charge that the Ao missionaries were imposing their language and culture on the Yimchunger tribe."

The Baptist mission came to the Yimchunger Nagas from two directions: from the Ao Naga area beyond the Dikhu River, and from the Sumi Naga area adjoining the Yimchunger. The cultures of both crept into the Baptist mission venture. The Ao Baptist mission viewpoint is that in translating the Yimchunger Bible and hymnal they in no way imposed their culture and language on the Yimchunger Nagas. "My father, Rev. Tsukti Sanglir, served as the pastor in Yimchunger Baptist church in Kiphire town for forty-five years. He gave sermons in Yimchunger language and carried out the church sacraments in the same," Rev. Tsukti's daughter Talijungla told me. A church worker herself, Talijungla pointed out that a dominant tribe bringing the gospel would speak its own language for convenience as it would be counterproductive to be overassertive: "When Christianity was preached to a new cultural group, the Bible and hymnals had to be taught to them; so in such a situation the converts had to learn the language of the missionaries."

Evidently, the eastern Naga culture partially assimilated the culture of the evangelising Nagas. The early Naga Baptist missionaries also invested time and resources in translation work – an American Baptist legacy. The Yimchunger are among the latest Naga Baptist groups to get a complete Bible in their native language; the Old Testament was published as recently as 2009. The Yimchunger Nagas speak six languages, which their forebears said had emerged from a place called Kimifü.[12] The Bible and hymnal translation is in the Langa language, which is spoken by the majority. The New Testament translation in Langa came out in 1975.[13]

Today, the Baptist church dominates every Yimchunger village, the practitioners of the traditional faith having either died out or converted.[14] To quote a conservative estimate, the Yimchunger are about 90 to 95 per cent Baptist, although in recent years some have shifted to Catholicism and Seventh-Day Adventism.[15] The Yimchunger area is no longer a mission field; in fact they themselves are striving to send out missionaries. The Yimchunger Baptist mission is focusing on adjoining areas in Myanmar where the Makhori and Moyu Nagas greatly resemble the Yimchunger in Nagaland. Yimchunger Baptists are also supporting missions in Thailand and Khamti in Myanmar.

III

The Khiamniungan Nagas who settled mostly in Noklak district – which was carved out from Tuensang district in 2017 – have

---

[12] The Yimchunger Nagas speak at least six languages, namely Chirryu, Langayu (Langa), Longpuryu, Mukuryu, Phunungyu, and Thikiryu.

[13] Rev. Lanu, an Ao missionary from Warumong, played a major role in the translation. Rev. Lanu had also translated around ten works of literature into the Yimchunger language. As for the Old Testament, it was Rev. Z. Thsankiu, a Yimchunger Baptist theologian, who did the translation.

[14] According to the NBCC 2016 census, there are a total of ninety-six Yimchunger Naga Baptist churches under the Yimchunger Baptist Boru Amukhungta (YBBA; i.e. Yimchunger Baptist churches' association) distributed mainly in Tuensang district.

[15] Information given by Rev. Akhum, former executive secretary of the YBBA.

a large Baptist community in Tuensang town. This large eastern Naga tribe is predominantly Baptist, with fifty churches in Nagaland and more than sixty in the Sagaing region of Myanmar; all these Baptist churches come under the purview of the Khiamniungan Baptist Churches' Association (KBCA) with its headquarters in Noklak town. The Khiamniungan Naga Baptists provide a classic example of the transnational character of the Baptist mission, uniting through religious ties an ethnic group separated by national boundaries. Amid the 110+ Khiamniungan Baptist churches spread across the Indo–Myanmar border, the one in Tuensang town stands out for its wealth, mission work, and the size of its educated middle-class following.

This church is in the area where Khiamniungan Nagas are concentrated. A distinctive feature about Tuensang township is that localities can be identified by their ethnic composition and the location of ethnic Baptist churches that have become the wellsprings of social interaction. The Khiamniungan Baptists are no less mission-minded than other Naga Baptist groups, but their distinctive location straddling the Indo–Myanmar border makes their mission unusually transnational.

In 2010, Peshia Lam, associate pastor of the Baptist church in Tuensang town, led a team of Khiamniungan Naga Baptist pastors and church workers on a mission trip across the Myanmar border. From what he told me, I inferred that the Naga Baptists on the Indian side enjoy greater religious freedom and are better off in all aspects of human development despite remaining one of the most impoverished tribes in Nagaland. The spread of the Baptist faith among the Khiamniungan Nagas on the Indian side is comparatively recent: it was only in the 1970s that many first heard the Christian message. Peshia's parents were converted in 1976 and were among the first in Pathso Nokeng village to become Baptists. The first conversion in the Khiamniungan area was on 18 May 1947 when a man named Müzo from Noklak village became a Christian, but it was not until the 1960s that Ao Naga missionaries from the Impur Baptist mission station entered the Khiamniungan Naga area.

In the post-independence period, the Saramati watershed became a natural demarcation dividing the Khiamniungan Nagas. This undulating mountain ridge, acting as international border, has partitioned the Khiamniungan into two nationalities. On the Indian side they occupy the easternmost frontier; on the Myanmar side the Khiamniungan along with other Naga groups occupy the north-western mountainous tracts. In addition to their shared culture, history, and livelihood pattern – and even their language across border villages – the topography and climate along the Saramati range are more or less the same. Because they straddled a border, groups like the Khiamniungan and Konyak Nagas were affected by the rise and upsurge of nationalism, nation-states, and related political developments. The varying national destinies of India and Myanmar have greatly impacted frontier tribes and are reflected in their education system, electoral politics, state bureaucracy, and quality of life.

The Indian Khiamniungan Baptists have unified under the same Baptist fold an ethnic group speaking at least five cognate languages and dispersed over more than 110 villages.[16] Those settled in the region from Tuensang town in Nagaland to Khamti town in the Sagaing region use the same Bible and hymnal translated into the Noklak language. This is because the group speaking this dialect on the Indian side first came into contact with and was educated via the Baptist mission. The bond across the border is getting stronger, with the expansion of mission work reinforcing the idea of a common identity. "The Khiamniungan, fortunately or unfortunately, got separated by the international border, and our shared history and kinship ties would have been erased if not for the Baptist mission. The common Baptist faith has not only rejuvenated the ethnic ties but has also fostered a relationship far stronger than the ethnic identity in the form of a new religious community," says Rev. Pinglang, Secretary, Finance and Development, KBCA.

[16] The five different types of Khiamniungan languages (on the Indian side) that can be classified on the basis of region are Pangsha, Noklak, Nukho, Pathso, and Peshu.

The Khiamniungan Baptist mission centre, which was established in 1964, is on the outskirts of Noklak town. The centralisation of Khiamniungan Baptist churches is noteworthy since the spread of the Baptist faith and the consolidation of ethnic identity have gone hand in hand. The Khiamniungan are the only Naga Baptist group to have all churches from both sides of the international border under one Baptist association. The Konyak Nagas settled on both sides of the Indo–Myanmar border are converting to the Baptist faith in large numbers, but they do not have a centralised authority like the KBCA. Educated Khiamniungan credit the Baptist mission for maintaining the transnational character of their identity.

On 9 January 2011 the Khiamniungan Baptist leadership decided to split the mission centres between Noklak in India and Khamti town in Myanmar. Till 2011 the Khiamniungan Baptist mission centre in Khamti had remained a sub-centre under the KBCA in Noklak. According to Pinglang,

> The split had nothing to do with doctrinal difference or leadership crisis; it was for security reasons and also for convenience sake. The Khiamniungan Baptist believers in Burma were under military rule, and they were being monitored and harassed as well; so KBCA decided to adopt a different strategy and divide the centre, although a joint mission and common ties are still maintained... The KBCA formed a new association, United Khiamniungan Christian Conference, where Khiamniungan Baptists from across the border meet once every five years for a big conference. KBCA send representatives every year to Khamti during their annual Baptist conference, and they also send representatives to Nagaland. Even now the Executive Secretary in Khamti Baptist mission centre is a Khiamniungan from India – Rev. Liang from Sanglao village under Thonoknyu circle in Noklak district.

Post-2011, the regime change in Naypyidaw impacted minority relations, subsequently affecting the Baptist mission in the furthest region of north-west Myanmar. "After the Aung San Suu Kyi government came to power, there was a slight improvement in schools and other developmental works, and so we had to change our mission policy," said Munno, Secretary, Christian Education and Literature, KBCA. He has crossed the border on foot several times for mission trips and church visitations. "In 1992, the KBCA had opened an English primary school up to Class IV in Tsonniu in Burma, but we closed it down after twenty-five years, since education improved after the coming of the new government," Munno said.

Recently, Khiamniungan Baptist missionaries from the Indian side have been encouraging their fellow tribesmen in Myanmar to get educated in their own state-run schools and colleges and move up the social ladder; but even with the regime change the Naga tribes in Myanmar suffer disadvantages when compared to their Indian counterparts. Munno laments that

> Schools in Naga areas in the Sagaing region of Burma are of very poor quality; these government-run schools do not equip Naga students for higher education, and most of them drop out in high school. The problem lies with the curriculum. English is made an optional subject at school level, and teachers who barely speak English teach the children, who learn very little about the subject. But in the tenth standard, these Naga students have to clear the English exam to pass the board examination; and the questions set in the tenth standard English exam are for advanced learners, not for students raised in remote village schools . . . One of the reasons we closed down the lone mission school in Burma was because children educated in mission-run English schools do not have employment prospects in Burma. The Naga children getting educated in English-medium schools in India cannot enter the workforce once they return to Burma. It seems they have to register themselves with the Burmese government and remain loyal to the state for at least ten years before they can get any employment. This is nothing less than state indoctrination.

When probed about the ulterior motives of Baptist mission schools, Munno defended the efforts of the Baptist mission.

> Opening of schools is a good mission strategy, since teachers can spend longer time with the students; and it is also because of schools

that many students are coming to Christ, but for the Khiamniungan Baptist mission, our main aim of opening schools is not a ruse to convert people, but dedicated missionary-teachers are giving their best to bring education and development to the region. The Khiamniungan Naga on the Indian side have understood that education is the only way to uplift and empower their brethren in Burma, the majority of whom are still underprivileged.

The closing of the mission school in Tsonniu, Sagaing region, was part of the mission strategy. The KBCA had done preparatory work to open a hostel for the children of Baptist church workers in Khamti, an expanding river port town which the Khiamniungan Nagas claim as their ancestral domain; but the business class in Khamti all belong to the Chinese, Burman, and Shan groups. "The main purpose of the hostel is to support Naga students studying in Burmese schools. During daytime, students can study in the Burmese school, but after their classes are over, they will be taught English language and scriptures," Pinglang said, and added:

> By foot it takes at least six days to reach Khamti town from Noklak, but Khamti has a growing Naga Baptist community. The Naga Baptist Convention there comprises believers from tribes like Pangmi, Mukhori, Lainong, Khiamniungan, Heimi and Somra [a sub-tribe of the Tangkhul Naga]. Among the Naga groups the Baptist faith is growing, but it is very difficult to convert the Shans and Chinese, who own all the business establishments in Khamti town. However the main objective of the KBCA is to co-ordinate with other Naga tribes in Burma to expand the mission.

Mass conversion among the Khiamniungan happened in 1977–8, and as of today the KBCA has estimated that 98 per cent of the Khiamniungan in India are Baptists; even on the Burmese side, the Khiamniungan Nagas are converting to the Baptist faith in large numbers. "At present under the Khamti mission centre, there are total sixty-eight churches and fellowships, although not all of these are full-fledged churches, since the Baptist churches cannot function openly in some villages," the experienced evangelist Pinglang told me.

When the Ao Naga missionaries brought Christianity to the Khiamniungan in India, they did not have to contend with a state machinery since Naga groups as a whole enjoyed some degree of autonomy with respect to religion and customary practices; but on the Burmese side government troops posed an impediment to the Baptist mission. Metsio Thai, a native of Pangsha near the Indo–Myanmar border, worked as a missionary in Myanmar for eight years. Presently, pastoring a Baptist church in Dan, which has been recognised by the Indian government as an international trade centre, Metsio is still involved with the Baptist mission, and because of his years of service in Myanmar remains a go-to person on the subject of mission across the border. He said to me:

> While I was the pastor in Kinphu village, I was arrested by the Burmese army and they took me to the forest and asked where the Naga National Council (NNC) camp was. I replied that I had no connection with the Naga army whatsoever, and that I just was an ordinary pastor working for the poor villagers . . . The persecution of the church by the Burmese army is known to everyone; in my years of associating with the Burma mission, the worst persecution happened in the period between 1999 and 2001. In all the Naga villages, there are state-appointed Buddhist monks who not only seek to convert people, but they are also known to act as government spies. So whenever Baptist missionaries come to the villages, these monks report to the Burmese army, and under the pretext of operating against the Naga underground, the Burmese soldiers harass the villagers. The persecution is more biased against Naga villages with a large Baptist following, because Christians are seen as divisive and working against the Burmese government.

Thus, it is not only on the Indian side that the Baptist church has to distance itself from the vexing issue of ethnonationalism; across the border, the Naga Baptist mission, which is relentlessly spreading the faith, is charged with an anti-state agenda. "The Burmese army is very suspicious of the Baptist faith; and the monks, who are stationed in the Naga villages, see the spread of Baptist faith as a threat to the country's Buddhist majority,"

Metsio said, raising the issue of inter-faith relations. "There are nearly ten Khiamniungan villages where the Baptist missionaries are not allowed to enter by the government-controlled village councils; other than that the Naga Baptist mission has reached almost every Khiamniungan village in Burma," he added.

Metsio said a small percentage of Khiamniungan Nagas (in the Sagaing region), about 2 per cent, have become Anglicans. "The Anglican mission came from the Burma side; also a small percentage of Khiamniungan are Buddhists, otherwise the majority of the Khiamniungan in Burma are now Baptist." According to this Baptist pastor "the Anglican converts are permissive when it comes to smoking and drinking, and even their priests drink occasionally." The Baptist faith in the Indo–Myanmar frontier is part of the American Baptist mission's legacy: evangelical and fervently pietistic.

IV

The township for the eastern Nagas was established on land belonging to Tuensang village, a large and powerful Chang Naga village. The eastern Naga tribes that did not fall under the direct purview of the British direct administration settled here, slowly building up a unique ethnic composition. The diversity in the new township paved the way for changing ethnic relations that posed fresh challenges for the district administration. Tuensang has by far the greatest number of ethnic Baptist churches in the state, since this sprawling township became the headquarters of five Naga tribes. Established in 1948, it is one of the first planned towns in the state.

The first Christian community in Tuensang comprised mostly people from outside who were not natives of this new administrative outpost. It was the largest of all the Naga administrative units, such that four new districts, on the basis of ethnic composition, were carved out of it: Mon, Kiphire, Longleng, and Noklak. Tuensang town is a microcosm of various ethnic Baptist groups whose lives revolve around the church. All the eastern Naga tribes have built large Baptist churches in this ever-growing town. Stately Baptist churches add to the charm of this district headquarters once dreaded by administrators, and by even the most courageous of missionaries.

The first church in Tuensang town began on 17 November 1948 when a small Christian community from various Naga groups started a multi-ethnic interdenominational fellowship. "There were only a few Christians in Tuensang at that time, and so the Naga district administrators and other government employees started a small fellowship to gather on Sundays," Rev. Sangkap Chang, says the pastor of the Tuensang Baptist church. Tuensang is still plagued by incendiary land disputes, pitting communities against each other. The Baptist churches in Tuensang were affected by the ethnic conflict in 2015–16 between the Chang and Yimchunger Nagas; the churches are often left perplexed during outbursts of ethnic conflict. Enraged mobs can cast aside their Baptist identity for an overriding ethnic identity, often forgetting Sunday pulpit teachings on turning the other cheek when push comes to shove. Sangkap was in the thick of the conflict that almost tore apart the two communities in Tuensang. "The association of Baptist pastors in Tuensang town intervened when the conflict broke out in 2015; we urged the congregations in the churches not to give in to evil and to refrain from violence," he said.

The problem with a multi-ethnic town like Tuensang is that diversity is a problem for the Baptist church. Unlike other district headquarter towns, which have been established around the Naga groups inhabiting them, in Tuensang at least six self-identifying Naga tribes were brought together for administrative expediency, making it a post-independence experiment not only for the state machinery but also for the church. Maintaining and asserting their ethnic differences has been a way of life for the congeries of eastern Naga tribes, and outbursts of ethnic conflict are the result. Baptist church leaders like Sangkap express anguish over the ethnic conflicts in Tuensang district, but they have to live with a phenomenon that existed long before the Baptist faith's appearance.

Ill. 6: A play on headhunting being performed during the NBCC Platinum Jubilee celebrations, April 2012. Naga Baptists generally represent the pre- and post-Christian eras through the popular imagery of "darkness and light". Courtesy DIPR.

In the past, the Chang Nagas have been no less "notorious" than the neighbouring tribes for their warring ways and penchant for headhunting. The Chang Naga, like all the eastern Naga tribes, also had a tattooing tradition with deep roots in headhunting; but such body etching was one of the first cultural traits to disappear when the Baptist mission arrived. It was only in the post-independence period that the Baptist faith began to spread widely in the Chang Naga heartland, though Ao Naga missionaries had visited the neighbouring Chang villages in the early 1930s and the first Chang Naga converts to the Baptist faith dated to 1936.[17] A husband-and-wife duo, Loyemju and Longkongtola, converted when they were, as the faithful tell it,

---

[17] The influence of the Baptist mission first reached the Chang Naga country in Yaongyemti in 1932, when the pioneering Ao Naga evangelist Rev. Supongwati visited the village thrice between 1932 and 1934, during his preaching tours to the eastern Nagas.

healed of a debilitating disease. The Chang Nagas record the day of their baptism on 5 September 1936 in Impur as the start of Christianity in Chang land. Ao missionaries played a pivotal role in spreading the new faith in the Chang Naga area; an Ao Naga was the first executive secretary of the Chang Baptist Lashong Thangyen (CBLT; i.e. Chang Baptist churches' association) when it was formed in 1949.[18]

The Chang Baptist mission centre in Tuensang town has a large compound with a Bible school and a large administrative set-up. The CBLT presides over fifty-six churches spread across villages and towns in the state. Chang Baptist churches have a centralised system: individual churches manage their own local affairs, following the cardinal Baptist principle of autonomy for local churches; at the same time they all come under a common association largely on account of shared ethnic identity. This feature of ethnicity is unique to Naga Baptists because elsewhere varying doctrinal stances, traditions, and schismatic divisions largely define Baptist associations and sects. Naga Baptists know full well that the church is inseparable from daily life, and that division in faith can prove detrimental to social relationships. Ethnic ties run deep and this influences the nature of ethnic-based churches where the Baptist communities develop in line with their own genius.

The first church in Tuensang town brought all the Naga Christians under a common platform. The church service used to be held in Nagamese and information on it was given in the relevant Naga languages. But as the number of Naga tribes increased it became difficult to continue with a single church. In 1974 the Chang Baptists separated and started their own, and this greatly enlarged the Chang following.

The words "Tuensang Baptist Church" are written in bright red at the entrance of the Chang Naga Baptist church. Overlooking a vast mountain range, this was the first church in town and began

---

[18] Rev. Aosangba of Noksen was appointed the first executive secretary of the CBLT in 1982 and passed away in 1988 while still in service.

life humbly. On my visit in the summer of 2018 it was colourfully decorated with artistically designed banners broadcasting an ongoing youth evangelist camp. The pastor of the church, Rev. Sangkap, who has been in the pastoral ministry for nearly two decades, guided me through several topics: "We are trying to make the church relevant to the young people; the Chang Baptist church recently conducted the True Love Waits programme under the initiative of the NBCC's youth department," he said, expecting me (a registered Baptist) to know the nitty-gritty of the "purity" movement championed by Naga Baptist churches.

True Love Waits is a popular youth movement that focuses exclusively on the Christian understanding of love, sex, and marriage; here young people take a pledge to remain chaste until they are married. This "purity" movement began under the aegis of the Southern Baptist Convention in 1993 in the United States, becoming a global phenomenon within a few years. In due course the movement reached distant Nagaland. Within Naga Baptist circles it is not uncommon to see pious teenagers and young adults wearing purity bands indicating adherence to this abstinence movement, which has become a fad among urban church youth.

Baptist teaching on sex and marriage has been unswervingly conservative since the days of American missionaries. Converts were expected to be strictly monogamous; adultery and extramarital affairs were frowned upon, the penalty being excommunication. Many early converts fell short of this ideal moral standard, kept the gossip mills running, and became a source of conflict among missionaries. For instance, the first Baptist church in Molungyimsen was disbanded in 1894 (and resumed later), since native converts could not live with such stringent rules of conduct. E.W. Clark records that Haggard, his missionary colleague, kept "a long list of questions designed to probe every weak point in the native character."[19]

Not even powerful polygamous chiefs and the wealthy in some Naga communities were exempt from Baptist marriage rules. This

[19] Quoted in McFayden, *Traveling in Time with Pioneers of Our Faith*, 61.

was difficult in a society where courting and romantic liaisons added zest to an otherwise harsh existence. Fürer-Haimendorf writes of romantic liaisons as commonplace in bachelor dormitories in Konyak Naga villages: "Between men and women of intermarrying clans or *morung*, there prevails on the other hand the fullest freedom to 'talk sex' and jokes with which the young people amuse each other at the nightly gatherings in the girls' clubs."[20] Other tribes also had vibrant dormitories. The Baptist mission represented in this sphere a paradigm shift. While the West reaped the fruit of a sexual revolution – most noticeably in the hippie countercultural movement of the 1960s and '70s – Naga Baptist teachings on sex and marriage remained unchanged, and in fact saw a pietistic revival. True Love Waits teaches nothing new in the context of Naga Baptists: an old teaching is packaged with a new appeal to attract the contemporary evangelically inclined young. Many such movements, large and small, whether of local origin or from the West, have changed the contours of the Naga Baptist faith.

V

The revival movement of the 1970s in eastern Nagaland brought sweeping changes. The main pioneers were Ao Baptist evangelists and freelance preachers who initiated mass conversion drives. A renowned Ao Naga missionary who spearheaded the revival movement in the late 1970s in the eastern part of Nagaland writes: "More than hundred years after the gospel entered Naga soil, the great spiritual awakening and revival took place in Nagaland in 1976. It all started in the Tuli area in Ao Baptist churches."[21] The revival, which was sparked off in a small foothill settlement in Mokokchung district, soon fanned out into the eastern Naga areas where hundreds were daily converted. In some Yimchunger Naga villages the number getting baptised was so large that the pastors

---

[20] Fürer-Haimendorf, *Return to the Naked Nagas*, 186.
[21] Luen, *The Fire of Revival*, 19.

had no time to break for lunch. An Ao Naga Baptist evangelist enthusiast observes: "During the three-days Revival Hour at Sangphur village inhabited by Yimchung tribe, in the Sangphur Baptist church, 126 families comprising 1004 non-Christians came to Christ and accepted him as their Saviour."[22]

The Baptist following in eastern Nagaland saw a sharp increase in the 1960s. According to the 1961 census the Christian population in Tuensang was 45,626 at 33.9 per cent, which increased to 97,923 at 56.6 per cent by the 1971 census, a 22.7 per cent rise over the decade. The increase accelerated in the late 1970s. American Baptist missionaries had never achieved anything on this scale. Naga Baptists attribute this exceptional spread to the work of the Holy Spirit, whereas experts offer secularly sociological explanations, one Namierite suggestion being: "Today at least 90 per cent of the Nagas are Christians. Some of the reasons for the spread of Christianity have been touched on: the possibility of escaping obligations and the lure of a clerical job for an educated Naga."[23] There could be something in this, but a less cynical reason seems to me more plausible: the American Baptist missionaries had come preaching salvation through faith in Jesus Christ; however, during the revival period in the 1970s the Naga Baptist missionaries preached not merely salvation but also empowerment through the Holy Spirit. This had a far-reaching impact on beliefs and practices among the eastern Nagas who embraced the Baptist faith during the revival. The traditional Baptist faith was conformist, but the new Baptist faith that emerged as a result of the revival movement was experimental, nonconformist, and ebullient. Traditional Baptists were puritanical, whereas renewed pietism and faith in mystical experience became the point of departure and enthusiasm among new Baptists.

The revival movement shared many similarities with the twentieth-century global Pentecostal movement known for reli-

---

[22] Ibid., 103.
[23] See Jacobs, et al., *The Nagas*, 154.

gious experiences such as healing, prophesies, speaking in foreign tongues, and other forms of religious ecstasy. Many Naga Baptists saw the revival movement as a mandate from heaven. However, not all Naga Baptists agree on the indigenous origins of the revival movement. When the movement first began, many believers opposed it for its deviation from the Baptist tradition. The god of the traditional Baptists was more aloof and distant, and worship was structured, time-bound, and liturgical. The new Baptists redefined worship into something more lively, spontaneous, and creative.

In a way, the coming of revival, which marked the beginning of charismatic Christianity among the Naga Baptists, heralded a new phase in the Baptist pursuit of spirituality, which went in the direction of Pentecostalism. The Holy Spirit, it seems, had remained dormant at the time of the American Baptist missionaries, confining itself to "convicting people of their sins and saving sinners"; whereas the revival movement expanded the work of the Holy Spirit far beyond salvation and opened the floodgates to varieties of religious experience. The old Baptist faith brought by the American missionaries was otherworldly in its outlook, while the new Baptist faith spread its scope to this-worldly affairs by placing great emphasis on prosperity. Many of the Baptist faithful who embraced the revival movement saw no reason not to simultaneously embrace health and wealth while making their way to heaven.

A notable outcome in the 1970s was that religious experiences became democratised and were no longer confined to a class of "anointed" people. The revival movement made divine intervention and miracles more tangible – whether true or constructed – and the Christian deity was brought within the laity's reach. Instead of the traditional Baptist powerful god, immanent and transcendent but not easily accessible, the Lord was now made visible in daily life. American missionaries had no time for Christian oracles, healers, and self-styled prophets, whereas the revival movement of the 1970s engendered a class of the laity that was considered specially gifted and which occupied an important space in the Baptist community.

Sangkap says many self-styled prophets are misleading the congregation. There are conflicting opinions among the congregation about divine revelation, and any major disagreement can split the Baptist church. During the revival period a splinter group seceded from the Chang Baptist church and formed their own church, which today is the Nagamese Baptist church in Tuensang town. Keeping the Baptists together is not easy as the faithful can opt for other denominations and sects which are ever on the prowl in the Baptist heartland in Nagaland. So, striking a balance is what Naga Baptist leaders like Sangkap seek to do. Having completed his master's degree in psychology and counselling from Martin Luther Christian University, Shillong, Sangkap is well informed about theories and explanations on the subject. He observes that the majority of the oracles are women, as in the past. Baptist theologians like him have different psychological explanations for such phenomena; however, their "highbrow" teachings are not suited to the Sunday pulpit sermon. Moreover, some religious beliefs are intractable and explanations from a different viewpoint do not register with the seekers. The 1970s revival movement is still talked about because it sparked off mass conversions among eastern Naga tribes that had mostly remained aloof from the American Baptist mission; but the movement also became famous, or infamous, because it sowed a new strain into the Naga Baptist faith. A compelling puritanical view of the world came as part of the new movement.

According to Sangkap,

> Among the Chang Naga, the ascendancy of the Baptist faith owes to the revival movement. Christianity came much earlier but the growth was slow, but with the coming of revival the Christian population increased considerably. Today, the Chang Naga has achieved 100 per cent Christianity, the majority of whom are Baptists, although there are a few Roman Catholic families in Nokseng, who joined Catholicism to get education facilities for their children.

The Chang Naga could indeed have been one of the earliest tribes to become Baptist, since in 1892 the famed Godhula and his wife Lucy came to Nokseng village bordering the Ao Naga area.[24] In hindsight, even a highly regarded missionary figure like Godhula could not have kindled the fervent pietism that the Naga Baptist preachers managed during the revival in the 1970s. "Before the revival, the Baptist faith that first came to the Chang Naga was more liberal, as some believers were still drinking after their conversion, but during the revival period they completely gave up drinking and other old habits. People abandoned old rituals, and between 1976 and 1977 log drums were burnt in villages like Hakchang," Sangkap said.

During the revival period in the 1970s the Naga Baptist missionaries that came preaching to the eastern Nagas certainly had personality differences, as legends about these missionaries suggest, but they shared a renewed puritanical outlook which became a distinct feature of Naga Baptist culture that continues into the present. Regarding the American Baptist mission in the colonial period, Fürer-Haimendorf says: "It is a pity that the American Baptist mission had little sympathy with the aims of the Government and even less appreciation for the valuable elements of Naga culture."[25] But the change in the traditional way of life during the spiritual awakening of the 1970s was unprecedented, and the eastern Nagas were at the receiving end of this new religious tide. However, according to Alem, a Sangtam Naga who works with a university-based evangelical student ministry,

> People may rightly say that the Naga culture witnessed irreparable losses during the mass conversion movement of the 1970s, but in defence of the mission, it was only those aspects of Naga culture which had discernible connections with spirit worshipping that were denounced; otherwise the missionaries did not discourage our rich textiles, folklore, knowledge of flora and fauna, indigenous farming

[24] See Nagaland Baptist Church Council, *One New Humanity*, 70.
[25] Fürer-Haimendorf, *Return to the Naked Nagas*, 51.

techniques, and so on. The critics of the Baptist mission tend to pigeonhole Naga culture only with headhunting and exotic rituals and perishable material objects.

Alem's parents are from a remote village in Kiphire district; they embraced the Baptist faith during the spiritual awakening of the 1970s. A staunch defender of the Baptist mission, Alem added with a hint of sarcasm that "it is easy for us to look back and criticise our Baptist heritage for allegedly destroying our traditional culture, but you'll find that those Nagas who hold such views are highly educated people from premier universities, who would never have got the privilege in the first place if it weren't for the Baptist mission."

Alem found my rhetorical questions irksome, since she works in a university setting and often fences intellectually with "insincere critics" of the Baptist mission:

> No one is claiming that the Naga Baptist mission is perfect; in some instances, the American Baptist missionaries can be charged of racism, if we read into some of what they said or wrote hundred years ago. Universities in the West are even monitoring correct pronoun usages; by this yardstick, most missionary accounts would become imperialistic, sexist and racist writings. These white missionaries did not come straight from heaven; they were people of their time raised in a Western culture, which was imperfect if not sinful. It is hypocritical for outsiders to decide what is good for the Nagas; these are the same people who will live in air-conditioned rooms, drive the latest cars, have access to good healthcare, and go to the best universities, but will not even bat an eye telling natives to live as they were happy and free in their undisturbed world, at least for the sake of the environment. In the past, Nagas rarely spoke ill of the missionaries, which does not mean that they were gullible. They accepted the gospel out of their own free will.

Alem was perhaps used to debating the issue and made what appeared to me a well-rehearsed argument. An erudite and well-read person like her represents the best of the new generation of Naga Baptists who are apologists for the faith.

VI

The Sangtam Nagas lived in a hilly tract just across the Dikhu river, which acted as a natural demarcation between the British Naga Hills and the unadministered region east of the river. Nevertheless, the British government held a loose kind of authority over the eastern Naga tribes and did not permit the American Baptist mission to enter this "controlled" area. This refusal brought the mission into conflict with the colonial government. When district judges were called upon to rule on disputes that divided Christians and non-Christians in a village, "The officers sought wherever possible to rule in favour of the traditionalists, giving rise to claims that the British punished people who converted."[26]

At the close of the nineteenth century Ao Naga Baptist churches, which had grown to six in number with a total of 500 members by 1898,[27] initiated a fund to send missionaries to the trans-Dikhu tribes, known as the "border tribes" in American Baptist mission phraseology. The Sangtam Naga being the nearest trans-Dikhu tribe, they became a viable target for the Baptist mission. In 1926, which marked the fiftieth year of the American Baptist mission to the Ao Naga, Semsalepzüng of Jakpa, an Ao Baptist who had studied under the American missionaries, became the first Naga missionary sent to the unadministered region. Largely supported by the Ao Baptist churches' association, Semsalepzüng became a pastor-cum-evangelist in Tsaru village in the northern Sangtam area. A "shrewd" and tireless missionary, he would become a living legend among those who knew him, more so among the Sangtam Naga Baptists.

The long arm of Pax Britannica was a double-edged sword to the American Baptist mission. On the one hand the government's presence facilitated security for the mission; on the other the British tried to curtail its activity since they saw it as obliterating

---

[26] Jacobs, *et al., The Nagas*, 153.
[27] Philips, *The Growth of Baptist Churches in Nagaland*, 70.

the Naga traditional way of life. Within less than a century the Baptist mission had irrevocably affected Naga indigenous culture, and long after the British had gone the American Baptist faith remained a powerful legacy.

Rev. Longkumer, a retired Ao Baptist minister in his late eighties who knew the American missionaries, says:

> In those days Mokokchung had a small police outpost and the office of the SDO, and later a few small-time traders began to move into this British sub-divisional headquarters. The eastern Naga tribes like the Chang and Sangtam began to visit Mokokchung, and the British officers employed some of them as *dobashi* or interpreters. On some occasions, the eastern Nagas living beyond Dikhu river would come to Mokokchung on the summons of the British government to settle cases and pay fines for defying the authority. The British considered the eastern Nagas as unadministered tribes, but they were not totally free, since the British influence was felt as far as the Sangtam area in Kiphire district. The British administration was particularly strict when the American missionaries wanted to start a mission among the eastern Nagas, although it was considered as an unadministered area. On one occasion, when an Ao missionary sent by Impur was penalised by the SDO for preaching in the Sangtam area, Rev. J.R. Bailey, who was then a missionary in Impur, replied that the trans-Dikhu tribes "were in the unadministered region, and therefore had no owner." And so the British administration let the missionaries continue with the mission.

The Naga tribes were ambivalent about colonial rule, but, viewing American missionaries as divine ambassadors, saw their history as following a divine plan. This is best exemplified in a mission encounter story of the Sangtam Nagas. Seeing divine handiwork even in a famine, the late Lanuyanger, a prominent Sangtam Baptist leader and Bible translator, eulogised the first Sangtam Naga convert thus:

> Had there been no famine
> Sekyuling would have not been to Aonokpu

Had Sekyuling not been to Aonokpu
The Gospel would not have come to the Sangtam soil.[28]

Sekyuling of Tsaru village embraced the new faith while seeking refuge in an Ao Naga village, Aonokpu. He had left his native village, which was hit by extreme famine in 1912–16, to work in Aonokpu, though earning a livelihood in another village was considered demeaning. He was baptised by an American missionary in 1912 and later joined the WWI Labour Corps. He returned to his village on 14 June 1918, the date that the Sangtam Naga Baptists mark as the coming of the gospel to their land. Sangtam Baptists believe that Sekyuling's conversion was no ordinary affair: suffering from a chronic illness, he made a pact with a Baptist believer in Aonokpu that he would turn to the new faith if the prayers of a Christian healed him. As a devout lady's prayers worked and Sekyuling was miraculously healed, he became a Christian.

Amid great opposition, Sekyuling started a small Baptist community in his village, and the first church was established on Sangtam land on 23 August 1925 with the help of the American Baptist mission in Impur. With the coming of the Ao evangelist Semsalepzüng in 1926, the Sangtam Naga became one of the first eastern Naga tribes in the unadministered region to come under the purview of American missionaries. Unlike the tribes in the British Naga Hills, who were evangelised by white missionaries, Ao Baptist pastors and evangelists led the mission to the border tribes starting with the Sangtam Naga, making the trans-Dikhu mission a native Baptist mission enterprise. The spread of the new faith was very slow due to the colonial administration's restrictions on the free movement of missionaries. As Apise puts it, "the fear of losing their heads was not the main issue for the missionaries; the biggest challenge was the British government's restrictions, and the recalcitrance of the people."

According to their oral history, the Sangtam Nagas are said to have migrated from Myanmar via the Chin state, some settling in

---

[28] Sangtam, *The Trans-Dikhu Mission*, 65.

Kiphire district, others moving north to settle in Longkhim circle in Tuensang district. The state highway connecting the two districts is 122 km long, with the Yimchunger and Sumi Naga areas jutting in between Sangtam-inhabited areas.[29] Due to greater proximity, it was the northern Sangtam who first came in contact with the American Baptist mission in the Ao Naga country in Impur. "The Sangtam Naga occupied a long strip of mountainous land due to the migration wave, and while the northern Sangtam heard the gospel much earlier during the time of the American missionaries, the gospel reached the eastern Sangtam only in the 1960s," says Sangyu Sangtam, mission secretary of the United Sangtam Baptist Lithroti Ashimukhong (USBLA; i.e. United Sangtam Baptist churches' association). Ao Baptists in Impur supervised the Sangtam mission, but the Sangtam Nagas formed their own separate Baptist association in 1946. In fact, Sangtam believers formed the first Baptist association in Tuensang area, but since church growth was slow Ao Baptist leaders headed the association till the late 1950s. In 1959 Rev. Litsase Sangtam became the first field supervisor of the association. It was because of his initiative that Yangli was chosen as the Baptist mission centre for the Sangtam Nagas; later a sub-centre was opened in Kiphire town in 1966 to cover the eastern Sangtam, since the villages were spread out.

Yangli is a small Baptist settlement 3 km from Longkhim town in Tuensang district. Located on a lower mountain range with salubrious weather, the land for the mission centre was donated by Sangsomong and Holongba villages. Yangli has the infrastructure and facilities of an ideal Baptist centre, though sans a museum showcasing American missionary memorabilia. While it cannot measure up to old mission stations like Impur and Kohima, Yangli is modelled along the same lines with regard to its landscaping and development, and is characterised by immaculately maintained premises and well-maintained roads. A large church building stands in the middle of the mission compound. Besides an administrative building and a residential area occupied by the staff,

---

[29] Hutton, *The Angami Nagas*, 375.

the mission centre has a seminary, a common feature of all Naga Baptist mission centres, to train novices for ministry. Exceptionally, the seminary here is not named after an American missionary or pioneering native convert but is called simply Oriental Theological College; it offers bachelor degree courses in theology.

Sangyu is an enthusiastic church worker devoting most of his time to planting churches and expanding the Baptist mission outside the state; "as long as there is poverty and illiteracy, the Baptist mission will continue," he told me. Appointed the first mission secretary of the USBLA in the year 2000, Sangyu oversees a young but fervent and expanding Baptist mission venture that has entered the fray in Assam. "The government schools do not run properly, that is why our mission school has been successful in Dima Hasao, Assam. We have a total of twelve missionary-teachers working among the Dimasas. Our plan was to open up to the eighth standard, but we were stopped when the BJP [Bharatiya Janata Party] government came to power in Assam," he said. In the past, it was the need to educate their children that made Nagas more receptive to the Baptist mission; and more than a century later education remains an entry point for the Naga Baptist mission in uncharted territories.

Many middle-class Sangtam Nagas are settled in Dimapur town. The migration happened in the latter half of the twentieth century as more eastern Nagas entered the workforce outside Tuensang district. And, wherever the community went, the Baptist church followed, since it was the educated who mostly moved to this metropolitan town. Notably, it is the affluent Baptist churches in fast-developing towns like Dimapur which generate substantial revenue for the Baptist mission centres; and the best seminarians and seasoned Baptist ministers are appointed in the town churches. Apise Sangtam is one such pastor tending the flock in a Baptist church in Dimapur town, with membership comprising mostly middle-class Sangtam families. From a small and remote village in Kiphire district, Apise has risen to prominence in the Sangtam Baptist world.

Having earned his doctorate from the International Theological

Seminary in Los Angeles, California, he witnessed firsthand the complex relationship between American politics and the evangelical movement there; after his return from the States he kept track of global politics, which he largely interprets in keeping with his strongly held millenarian view. Complex geopolitics, Apise believes and teaches his large following, is not a matter of chance; behind wars, natural calamities, and even "blood moons" there is a divine hand at work, and human history will culminate in an apocalypse – an eschatological view common to a large section of Naga Baptists. He maintains complex charts and calendars and keeps track of global events and happenings, of which he informs the congregation during sermons, and shares with followers on social media.

To a Baptist preacher like Apise, disbelief in what has been foretold is part of the larger problem: "it is the Holy Spirit which reveals to his servant about things to come; divine revelation is from God and the Bible is very particular about the blaspheming of [i.e. against] the Holy Spirit," he says. There is a whole body of work to prop Christian millenarianism, full of exquisite symbols and intricate interpretations popularly held by Naga Baptists. This strand of thought also reveals the inescapability of the influence of global Christian movements from the West, especially the United States. It was the evangelical tide in North America that made the Baptist denomination a force to reckon with in Nagaland, and, ever since, periodic Christian waves from there wash the Naga faithful here.

Sangtam Baptist leaders like Apise are still wrestling with issues of tradition and cultural identity. In particular, the Baptist tenet of separation between church and state has vexed a religious community that believes in the autonomy of local churches. According to Apise, "The Baptists believe in the separation of church and state, but this does not mean that state can function independently of God. The Bible tells us that all authority in heaven and on earth belongs to Jesus, and so the conduct of the state should be according to the teachings of Christ, only then we can claim 'Nagaland for Christ', otherwise we are deluding ourselves." Likhum Pumji, the Sangtam Naga tribal front organisation which acts as a cultural custodian of the community, influences even the Baptist church on matters deemed important for ethnic identity. Among other Naga tribes, too, similar relationships exist between tribal front bodies and the Baptist church. Both are formidable forces in Naga society.

Among the Sangtam Nagas, who still strictly follow practices such as clan exogamy, tradition can impinge on religious matters, and the Baptist church is dragged into the predicament; Apise says that

> the penalty for same clan marriage is excommunication from the church, and defaulters are allowed to have membership in the church only during jubilee celebrations; even after their re-acceptance, they are not allowed to become deacons or hold any other important positions in the church . . . This is a case of intermixing church and tradition. I do not support ostracism from the church, but the Naga Baptist case is different, and such disputes and negotiations will take some time.

In the ongoing clash of Baptist faith and tradition, Baptist culture seems to be emerging victorious.

Such cultural issues vex even an influential Baptist preacher like Apise, but at least the Sangtam Naga Baptist leadership does not have to face the onerous issue of language and translation, as do other Naga groups. Though they are spread over more than 60 villages in 2 districts, Tuensang and Kiphire, with a total of 76 Baptist churches and 24,553 baptised members (2016 NBCC census), the Sangtam Nagas are blessed with the convenience of a "common" language. There are village-specific dialects, especially among the Lower Sangtam, but the implementation of a common Bible and hymnal has been successful.[30]

---

[30] The Sangtam Nagas in Tuensang and Kiphire districts are also known as Upper and Lower Sangtam, respectively. The language diversity is notable in the Lower Sangtam area. For instance, Longmatra circle in Kiphire district,

VIII

The formation of a Chakhesang Naga identity, a modern phenomenon, exemplifies the fluidity of ethnic identity in the Naga context. The ethnonym "Chakhesang" is now common currency and identified with one of the sixteen tribes of Nagaland. The Chakhesang Baptist community faces an ethnicity and language conundrum that has eaten into the heart of their church politics and spilt into their social life, putting a strain on their tactfully and delicately maintained (or constructed) ethnic identity. The beginnings of this issue go back a century and a quarter, when in 1895 in Chozuba – a Chokri-speaking village – three men, Ngakhra, Hülüyi, and Swüzümo, converted under the influence of the Kohima Baptist mission. The Chakhesang Baptist Church Council (CBCC) records these first conversions in Chozuba as the beginning of Christianity among their ethnic group. With Chozuba as the epicentre, the new faith spread to neighbouring villages under native Angami evangelists like Siliezhü Sorhie of Kohima village. In 1936, four decades after the start of the first Baptist community in Chozuba, Fürer-Haimendorf visited Chozuba's neighbouring "Eastern Angami" villages and gave one of the first ethnographic accounts of change among the Nagas with the arrival of the Baptist faith. He toured the Chokri-speaking Angami villages (then known as Eastern Angamis) in the present-day Chozuba circle in Phek district, headquarters of the Chakhesang Nagas. He saw these villages, where the new faith was poised, as an undisturbed living museum: "Only a beginner is so sentimental, but even today that first moment is unforgettable: when Naga culture, so familiar from books and ethnographical museums, appeared as a living entity."[31] Between 1931 and 1941 the Naga Christian population grew by 5.1 per cent from 22,908

---

which has eleven villages, is known for its high concentration of village-specific dialects.

[31] Fürer-Haimendorf, *Return to the Naked Nagas*, 8.

to 34,000, and exponentially over the following decades. By 1950 the Chakhesang Naga Baptist Association was formed with a total of fifty-two churches and about 3000 baptised members with the centre at Phezu, inaugurated by Rev. A.F. Merril, the first general secretary of the Council of Baptist Churches in Assam.[32] Fürer-Haimendorf's living museum was a Baptist enclave within less than two decades of his visit.

Roughly up to Indian independence, the gospel was preached to the Chakhesang (Eastern Angami) in the Angami language (spoken mainly in Kohima village): it also functioned as the mission language for neighbouring tribes like the Rengma, Southern Sumi, and Zeliang, who were evangelised from the Kohima mission station.

The process of Bible translation was as always arduous when it began. Missionaries would waylay villagers on their way to the fields and talk to them to pick up new words, usually by pointing to common objects and gesturing. The first Bible translation into the Angami language was the Gospel of Matthew. In 1890 S.W. Rivenburg, missionary to the Angami, reported: "I have received from the press an Angami primer. This, being the first book in the language, has some significance. Matthew, which I went to Calcutta to print, has gone on proverbially slow . . . I have translated four chapters of the Acts and worked some on an arithmetic for beginners."[33] In a context of village-centric dialects, Rivenburg was among the early translators whose work resulted in the formalisation of a language because of Bible translation. Subsequently the Chokri- and Khezha-speaking groups, known as the Eastern Angamis, were primarily evangelised in the Angami language – the mission translation language.

Ten years after Fürer-Haimendorf's visit, the Eastern Angamis had reconstructed themselves into a new ethnic identity. In 1946,

---

[32] See Philips, *The Growth of Baptist Churches*, 114.
[33] See Rivenburg, "The Naga Mission", *BMM*, Vol. LXX, No. 10 (October 1890), 413.

Chokri, Khezha, and Sangtam speakers – ethnocultural entities as well as linguistic groups – had formed the Chakhesang Naga.[34] The Baptist mission boosted this new identity group, starting the Chakhesang Baptist Association in 1950. With such support from a formidable religious body, the term "Chakhesang Naga" became entrenched in popular usage. To the early Baptist missionaries and church workers the Chakhesang Naga provided an opportune mission field. However, language diversity – a common Naga phenomenon inextricable from cultural identity and ethnic pride – would come back to haunt the Chakhesang Baptists in later years and override both the shared Baptist identity and the constructed group identity. Language-identity assertion became inescapable for the Chakhesang Nagas, who are otherwise a relatively homogeneous group with many cultural similarities and who reckon their constituents share a common ancestry and history.

In Phek district, which is 48 km south-east of Kohima, a Khezha-speaking Chakhesang Naga village, Khezhakenoma, is the repository of a short but widely told migration story, and one that is quoted in every book written on the Naga tribes.[35] The legend is briefly that the three major Naga tribes, Angami, Sumi, and Lotha – who are said to be brothers – migrated from Khezhakenoma.[36] Besides this legendary Naga village, there are about thirteen Khezha- (or Kuzha-) speaking villages collectively identified as a "sub-tribe" of the Chakhesang Nagas. Taken collectively, the Chokri-speaking Chakhesang Naga villages outnumber the Khezha-speaking villages by nearly a third, but the Khezha language has remained unaffected by its counterpart, as social interaction at the village level takes precedence.

[34] Rev. V.K. Nuh, a veteran Chakhesang Baptist leader, told me that the decision to form the Chakhesang Naga was taken during a consultative meet of public leaders and church leaders on 10 January 1946.
[35] See, for instance, Hutton, *The Angami Nagas*, 19; Hutton, *The Sema Nagas*, 5; Mills, *The Lhota Nagas*, 3–4.
[36] There are various versions of the story told by different Naga tribes about their migration from Khezhakenoma.

The Tenyidie Bible – introduced successfully in all Angami Baptist churches – continues to be used in all Chakhesang Naga Baptist churches, as it has been since the coming of the Baptist mission. Atole Kazhie, the women's secretary of the Chakhesang Baptist Church Council (CBCC), told me that the issue over language emerged when Bible translation was initiated in Kheza and Chokri. In 2009 the New Testament was translated into Khezha, while the New Testament in Chokri was released in 2016.

The Chakhesang Naga Baptist front body became embroiled in the issue of Bible translation, which had to do with language identity. "This issue has affected the CBCC, since some of the Khezha-speaking churches wanted to start their own Baptist association," Atole said. The issue has even caused rifts in social life; but the executive secretary of the CBCC, Rev. Dr Vezopa Tetseo, who hails from a Khezha village, expressed optimism that it will resolve itself. In his view disputes and disagreements are part and parcel of Naga Baptist churches, but believers have almost always triumphed. The continued use of Tenyidie would be the simplest solution, but a need to preserve the mother tongue is gaining momentum among the educated class, and only time will tell whether the Chakhesang Naga identity bolstered by a shared Baptist identity can withstand this surging tide.

In the context of linguistic identity, an unusual phenomenon can be observed during the Rengma Baptist worship service in churches in Dimapur and Kohima towns that have large congregations from varying villages. The congregants are all Rengma Naga, a tightly knit ethnic group who in the 1931 census in the Naga Hills numbered just 6329. However, the pastor first delivers the sermon in Nzonkhwen and then repeats it in Nthenyi, or vice versa; or a translator is employed for one of the languages. In some cases, for convenience, Nagamese is used to give information or make announcements in the church.

A retired Baptist pastor in Tseminyu – the Rengma Naga headquarters – who speaks the two Rengma languages (colloquially known as the Southern and Northern languages), as well as the neighbouring Angami language, told me it has only been over the last generation or two that the Rengma Nagas forsook the tradition of speaking both languages, Nzonkhwen and Nthenyi. "In the recent past, the Rengma people spoke both the Southern and Northern languages. Besides, many Northern Rengma people spoke both Lotha and Sumi language, while the Southern Rengma spoke Angami language," he said.

Writing in 1937, J.P. Mills, then deputy commissioner of the Naga Hills, voiced concern that "Mission influence is spreading among the Western section of the (Rengma) tribe, and it will not be long before customs and traditions of great interest are gone for ever."[37] Not surprisingly, Mills – who went on to become a Reader in the School of Oriental and African Studies after his service in the Naga Hills – did not foresee that the language issue would cause strife among Baptist followers: "The Western Rengmas are in turn divided into a Northern and a Southern section, speaking entirely different languages and differing considerably in custom. The Northern call themselves *Ntenyi* . . . The Southern section call themselves *Nzong*." Colonial administrators like Mills were concerned with cultural loss, while the Baptist mission, in promoting particular indigenous languages through their translation work, set off new identity issues.

In 1848 British expeditionary reports estimated that nearly thirty-two Rengma Naga villages with more than 650 households were scattered in the Mikir Hills (presently Karbi Anglong district, Assam). According to Mills, the Rengma Nagas who had "migrated north-west to the Mikir Hills about a hundred years ago" were the Western Rengmas.[38] Towards the middle of the nineteenth century they were reported to be abandoning, without any impetus by the American Baptist mission, "many of their tribal customs" due to cultural contact with the Assamese.[39] In 1855 Major John

---

[37] Mills, *The Rengma Nagas*, 1.
[38] Ibid., 2.
[39] Ibid.

Butler reported many of the Rengma Naga men having "married Cacharee and Assamese wives".[40]

The Rengma Nagas in the Mikir Hills also came under the influence of the American Baptist faith, but they played second fiddle to their Rengma Baptist brethren in the Naga Hills. "The Rengma Baptist churches in Nagaland are rendering help, both financially and spiritually, to the Rengma Baptist churches in Karbi Anglong, since many of the villages there are still lagging behind," says Gwanilo Khing, an erudite Rengma Naga Bible translator. Gwanilo serves as the pastor of the Rengma Baptist church in Sovima, a residential area of Dimapur. The church caters to Nzonkhwen speakers from the Southern Rengma region; the congregation does not have any Northern Rengma Nthenyi speakers, so Gwanilo is spared the inconvenience of delivering his sermon in two languages or using an interpreter.

The first conversion on Rengma Naga soil came in 1918, and the period between WWI and WWII saw an increase of converts. During these years effervescent and larger-than-life (as Naga Baptists see them) evangelists like Phenuga Semp and Viliezhü Kent played a pivotal role in converting their fellow tribesmen. Viliezhü became the first ordained Rengma Baptist minister and spearheaded Bible translation and modern education. In 1924 he translated the first Southern Rengma Naga hymnal, containing fifty songs, under the guidance of an American missionary, J.E. Tanquist. They also worked together to translate the Gospel of John. Viliezhü, who is from a large Southern Rengma village, Tseminyu, started a school there to teach the Bible.

Rengma students in the school in Tseminyu were taught in Nzonkhwen, the Southern Rengma language. "Initially the Northern Rengma students learnt and spoke the Southern language, because the only school in the whole region was in Tseminyu; and every student spoke both the languages because of close interaction. However, when a separate school was opened in the

---

[40] Butler, *Travels and Adventures in the Province of Assam*, 124.

Northern Rengma region, the language division began to emerge," Gwanilo says.

Over the years the language divide began to get sharper as more Rengma Nagas got educated, and along with modern education came the idea of the preservation of linguistic identity (which is at the heart of ethnic identity) amid the burgeoning cultural influences from without. Gwanilo, who speaks English fluently and is conversant with Greek, is the main translator of the revised edition of the Rengma Naga Bible in Nzonkhwen. "The complete Bible in Nzonkhwen was published in 1995, while the Bible in Nthenyi was released in 2002. The language issue nearly split the church in Tseminyu, but the Rengma Baptist leadership worked tirelessly and discerningly to resolve the matter," says Gwanilo, who is part of a ten-member Bible translation committee. "Our hymnal had become very thick because it contained hymns in both the languages, but the same cannot be done with the Bible," he added.

The Chakhesang Naga Baptists still use Tenyidie, a safe alternative, but the Rengma Naga Baptists, with a total of forty churches and 12,403 baptised members under the Council of Rengma Baptist Churches (CRBC), do not use this old Angami mission language, since they were among the early Naga tribes to be exposed to translated works back in the 1920s. The formalisation of the native language through the American Baptist mission's translation work consolidated the distinctiveness of the Rengma Naga identity.

Gwanilo, the moving spirit of Bible translation in the Southern Rengma language, has the gift of seeing visions and dreaming dreams (as he told me). He narrated an incident in Tseminyu town when "the Rengma Baptist leadership told a dissenting Baptist group, who wanted to start a new denomination along charismatic lines, to continue in the Baptist faith, since there is not much difference with regard to spiritual beliefs and experiences." Gwanilo said that behind the controversy over denomination lurked the irrepressible issue of language, but Rengma Baptist leaders were able to resolve the matter on the basis of shared beliefs and practices.

Another ethnic group confronting language diversity is the Pochury Naga community. With a total of 6550 baptised members distributed across thirty churches (according to the 2016 NBCC census), the Pochury Nagas are one of the smallest ethnic Baptist communities in the state. This group was formed post-independence from a congeries of ethnic communities who, over the generations, came from different directions to settle in the present Meluri circle in Phek district, arguably the most ethnically diverse region in the state. The Pochury Naga area borders the Chakhesang Naga area to the west and the Sangtam Naga area to the north and north-east; to its east are the Naga Hills of Myanmar. The term "Pochury" is said to be a combination of three ethnic group names: Sapo, Küchu, and Khwiry.[41] Thus, there exist different migration stories, as well as myths of autochthonous origin, which often vary from village to village.

One of the earliest mentions of villages that are settled by the Pochury Nagas is in J.P. Mills' monograph on the Rengma Nagas. The "Eastern Rengmas, who call themselves *Anyo* . . . have only three villages, Meluri, Sahunyu and Lephori, of which Meluri is by far the largest."[42] Meluri village, which was the centre of Baptist mission activity in this region in the initial years, would emerge as an important denominator of Pochury Naga identity formation, especially with regard to language.

The Pochury Naga cultural heritage is diverse. Akhwego village in the Apoksa area houses a legend of autochthonous origin, which says the first humans emerged from a hole in the ground. Some Pochury Nagas point to their migration route from Myanmar, while some echo the tale of the magical stone at Khezhakenoma in the Chakhesang Naga area. John Latsutho Poji, the first ordained Catholic priest from the Pochury tribe, told me that

---

[41] Kire, *Walking the Roadless Road*, 149.
[42] Mills, *The Rengma Nagas*, 2.

the word "Pochury" was coined during the British period, but "till recently, the Pochury were identified as part of the Chakhesang Naga. It was on 21 April 1991 that the Pochury Naga separated from the Chakhesang Naga and became a distinct ethnic group. In fact, some say that the Pochury people comprised the Sangtam part of the triple ethno-linguistic category: Chokri, Khezha and Sangtam."

The spread of Christianity in the Pochury area continued up to the third quarter of the twentieth century, by which time Catholicism had already spread in the region. The area has the rare phenomenon of an exclusively Catholic village, Khumiasü, in the establishment of which Poji's father played an instrumental role. Poji said

> My father came under the influence of the Catholic faith as there were priests from Chizami (a Chakhesang Naga village) who would travel to Kiphire to visit the Sangtam Catholic faithful. A Lushai police officer, a Catholic from Mizoram, lived in Meluri, and the priests would stay in his house during their journey. And this was where a Pochury man employed as a sweeper came under the influence of the Catholic faith, thus beginning the history of Catholicism among the Pochury people.

To Poji's father, Tsiviitho, the new faith came with a miraculous vision. "My father was on his sickbed, and he recovered when he dreamt of a man in a white robe pulling him out of a lake of fire." After his conversion to the new faith, Tsiviitho was told to move with his family to the outskirts of Meluri. "So in 1978, my parents along with us three siblings went to settle on a spot that used to be frequented by tigers. Today, there are eighty-seven houses, and the entire village [Khumiasü] follows the Catholic faith."

Poji, whose family hailed from Meluri village before his parents moved out to start the new Catholic settlement, said that this old and large village serves in many ways as the basis of integrating Pochury Naga identity. "The Pochury tribal frontal organisation wishes to promote a common language and traditional shawl for the entire community. There are different types of traditional shawls, specific to villages and regions, but for the identification of the Pochury tribe at large, the Meluri-based shawl is being advanced," Poji says. This Diocesan priest from Khumiasü believes that problems over language and identity among the Pochury Nagas are unavoidable as more people become educated and understand the need to preserve their indigenous language and culture.

Rhochusie Katiry, a Baptist pastor in Dimapur town, is optimistic about the future with respect to language diversity. Rhochusie belongs to Matikhru village, where the inhabitants speak at least three languages, but the Baptist church has been able to achieve uniformity by using a common Bible. "Since the gospel first came to Meluri village, and the first educated people were from the Meluri area, Bible translation was in the language spoken in Meluri and Lephori," Rhochusie told me.

The Pochury Nagas, who are spread over five regions (which are also linguistic zones) – Apoksa, Kanali, Poisha, Pokhungri, and Meluri – and speak at least seven distinct languages, have been able to transcend their prodigious diversity, at least for now, because of Baptist translation work. The concept of a common language is gaining ground because of the same Bible and hymnal. "The younger generation usually speak two languages. For instance, I speak both Meluri language and the language of my native village," Rhochusie said.

Looking at the complexities of identity formation among a diverse community like the Pochury Nagas, there is no doubt that the Baptist faith has been a game-changer in ethnic identity formation and linguistic configuration among the Nagas in modern times. The faith, which underpins Naga society, has resembled shifting tectonic plates, and the loud and messy cultural wars over religious identity pale in comparison to the subterranean influence of the Baptist faith on issues of ethnicity and language that have been silently erupting for generations.

5

Exotic Natives No More

> The Nagas are like birds and monkeys, lighting on this mountain and stopping on that, and no white man can live among them to teach them. As soon as the boys are old enough, they put into their hands the hatchet and spear, and teach them to fight and make salt. Beyond that they know nothing.
>
> – Miles Bronson, first missionary to the Nagas, 1839

> The main point of Christianity was this: that Nature is not our mother; Nature is our sister. We can be proud of her beauty, since we have the same father; but she has no authority over us; we have to admire, but not imitate.
>
> – G.K. Chesterton, *Orthodoxy*

LONGWA, STRADDLING THE Indo–Myanmar border, is a famous and much hyped Konyak Naga village in the Lower Konyak area in Mon district, drawing people from around the globe. In the past, Longwa was ruled by powerful *anghs*, village autocrats of royal bloodline whose suzerainty extended over several villages. The *anghs* ruled with a degree of impunity. There were Konyak royal chiefs who were no less illustrious than the Longwa *anghs*, but the peculiar location of Longwa – a post-colonial creation – has made a legend of this village in recent years: one half of the settlement is on the Indian side, the other in Myanmar, with the *angh's* house, which sits on a hillock along a contiguous ridge of land, strikingly straddling the international border.

The Longwa Baptist church at a lower elevation overlooked by the *angh's* house is on spacious ground and spills similarly over the international border; villagers from either side have to walk more or less equal distances to their place of worship, which has somehow democratised this once inordinately hierarchical society. Longwa boasts of having achieved a 100 per cent Baptist population within the space of a few decades. This, according to the Konyak faithful, is nothing short of a miracle, since the Longwa *anghdom*, which controlled a vast area stretching into Myanmar and Arunachal Pradesh, was notorious for autocratic rulers, famed warriors, penchant for headhunting, and exacting tributes; and most importantly, it had because of its remoteness withstood the Baptist mission long after other Konyak villages had embraced the new religion.[1]

What makes Longwa distinctive is not traditional cultural heritage, since that is visible in other Konyak villages as well, but the impact of the nation-state on this once "backward" and remote village. The Baptist church overlooks a village artificially divided between India and Myanmar, extending downhill; the village houses in Myanmar are mostly thatched and look impoverished, still lacking proper electricity, water, and roads.[2] Those in Nagaland are a contrast because the Indian state is more focused on the welfare and development of border regions. Beyond that, the Baptist mission has adroitly manoeuvred for general gain.

[1] I have used the term *anghdom*, since Konyak villages like Chui, Mon, Longwa, and Shangnyu behave like kingdoms with some degree of centralisation of power and authority, with the *anghs* of lesser villages tracing their royal bloodline to the liege village or liege *angh*. These subject villages under an *anghdom* pay tribute to the liege village and pay homage to the liege *angh*, who mandatorily has to be a *pongyin angh* (an *angh* who has performed the royal coronation ceremony).

[2] At the time of writing, there is still no electrification or water connection on the Myanmar side of the village, though development has been slowly trickling into the region since the regime change in Naypyidaw in 2012. As of 2020, the Myanmar government is slowly constructing roads, investing in schools, and bringing solar lighting to villages in the border regions.

The Baptist church in Longwa is a truly transnational institution which flouts international border protocols as far as church membership, fellowship, and mission go. The faithful living next door to each other on either side of the border may have noticeable differences in standards of living, but inside the church this distinction does not matter. With the dwindling of the *morung* (bachelor's dormitory) system that once bound the community together, the Baptist church has stepped in to reinforce common ties, fostering an identity assertion which mixes ethnicity and religiosity.

On weekends, tourists throng the large museum-cum-visitor's room set up in the *angh's* house, courtesy of the Nagaland state government. Given the curiosity of gawking tourists, the young *angh* has to stick around home much of the time. The faithful in the village go about their normal lives, attending services dressed in their Sunday best. As in all Naga villages, the Sabbath is taken seriously as the day for rest and worship. The first conversion to the Baptist faith in Longwa happened in 1978, and over the initial period converts fastidiously observed the Sabbath as a marker of their new identity. This created a furore in the village since the day of rest often clashed with event-filled days in the traditional calendar; but in less than three decades the practices of the new faith had supplanted the ancestral.

The road leading to the *angh's* house takes a sharp curve near the Baptist church and wends uphill to a scenic open space overlooking the vast expanse of Myanmar's Sagaing region; the stately new house was built at enormous cost by a state government already heavily in debt. Photographs on the wall reveal that the *angh's* earlier abode was a nondescript traditional Konyak house, its length almost four times its breadth, with abysmal ventilation, poor lighting, and inflammable thatch roofing. The newly constructed house with its high roof of hardy corrugated metal, airy compartmentalised quarters, and proper lighting resembles government-built tourist lodges and is nothing like the old structure, except for its interior where traditional embellishments overwhelm the part-wood part-concrete structure. Not surprisingly, the house has become a must-see for tourists and visitors; the aura surrounding the *angh* and his home is a reminder of what the American sociologist Dean MacCannell calls "staged authenticity".[3] Compared to other Konyak *anghs*, who are far removed from the scrutiny of outsiders, it appears that the life of the Longwa *angh* is staged, a nod to the tourist's appetite for the exotic.

Mundane life is represented by commoners who toil in *jhum* fields; run into debt sending their children to English-medium schools outside the village; spend time, energy, and resources on the village church; and once in a while earn a few hundred rupees by selling locally produced wares to tourists. Most visitors do not even peep into the church, unaware of it as the most influential institution in the village. It is the young, weaned on American pop culture, who socialise in the Baptist church and are the future of Konyak society. They contrast with the dwindling population of elders who have researchers, photographers, and tourists enthralled.

The house of the Longwa *angh* – its living members included – has been converted into a living museum, the domestic life of its inmates on view for visitors. In comparison, the houses of the once sublime, powerful, and celebrated *anghs* of Chui and Mon lie in ruins. These two villages, erstwhile *anghdoms*, have no state patronage from well-off local politicians who are now the ruling elites. But for the village's cross-border location the Longwa house could have made a trio with those in Chui and Mon since the young *angh*, who dropped out of high school, has no marketable skills or regular source of income; he would normally have been a commoner dependent on cultivation.

He and his home were saved a dire fate when a three-time Angami chief minister of Nagaland chose to adopt Longwa village under the Sansad Adarsh Gram Yojana (SAGY, the Indian parliament's "ideal village" scheme). Huge funding enabled a

---

[3] See MacCannell, "Staged Authenticity".

complete makeover of the *angh's* house.⁴ The project kicked off in 2015 and took a year; the overhauled house was inaugurated in 2016 by the governor of Nagaland, a devout Hindu Brahmin, in the presence of state dignitaries, village elders, Baptist church leaders, and hundreds of villagers. Built of quartzite-hewn blocks, the house, unlike ordinarily perishable Naga habitations, looks like it will last a century.

At the entrance of the *angh's* house it says "Sagaing and India" to advertise its transnationality. Outside, native women sell traditional novelties and trinkets. They add to the exhibition-like atmosphere, cameras clicking away. The walls of the house are panelled with massive planks hewn out of a single trunk. On them are etchings of Naga artwork and symbols; another attraction is a large, misshapen, grotesque-looking wood carving of a tiger that stands next to an impressive doorway leading to a large hall designed as a museum filled with Konyak traditional memorabilia. This includes a gigantic log drum, brass gongs of different sizes adorning the walls along with mithun (*Bos frontalis*) and ox skulls. Photos of the young *angh* with politicians and dignitaries hang alongside older ones of the late *angh*.

Following Naga custom, I took packets of powdered milk, sugar, and Assam tea – which have replaced rice beer as objects of value in Naga homes – for the *angh*. He indicated through his assistant that my gesture was welcome: most visitors come empty-handed and he has to entertain them for nothing. It appears that in spite of the grandiose home and aura surrounding him he is not all that well off since the cultural goods that raised his status in the past have become redundant in present consumerist society. Cars, electronic items, and Western clothes, which are a measure of affluence in Naga villages, have replaced the much-treasured brass gongs, wood carvings, and other traditional artefacts of high value. The Longwa *angh* could have found a use for all these once coveted

---

⁴ After a stint as a Lok Sabha MP, Nephiu Rio returned to state politics and became the chief minister of Nagaland for the fourth time.

items passed down the generations as showpieces in the museum. But in many Konyak homes the traditional paraphernalia gathers dust in unkempt storehouses or lies abandoned.

On a routine day, a bevy of enthusiastic visitors surround the *angh* for photographs while he poses poker-faced, perceptibly bored by the monotony of his condition. A few village elders, more informed than the *angh*, act as translators and answer queries. He himself has become a museum showpiece with no chance of proving himself worthy of a bloodline of illustrious predecessors; and, given the fast-changing Konyak society, he never will. Beliefs and practices that gave substance and even a small halo to the *angh* are no longer followed; and in terms of social power the traditional Konyak *anghs* have pretty much lost out to the emerging political and religious class. They may still hold some sway in their villages but play second fiddle to state legislative assembly members and bureaucrats – mostly from the educated middle class – who take all the important decisions.

The Baptist church, now entrenched in Konyak society, has helped dim the aura of *anghs*, whose repository of magic and the esoteric has been replaced by soteriology. The exploits of famed *anghs* are still bruited about, but Naga Baptist missionaries view the once-powerful *anghs* as ordinary "heathens" destined to eternal damnation unless they allow the salvation of their souls by the Saviour. Konyak *anghs* who tried clinging to the traditional faith soon came a cropper: their subjects having succumbed to the power of Jesus, most *anghs* succumbed too, if only for convenience.

The *angh* of Longwa, Tonyei, is a believer, as was his father Luhngam, who converted to the new faith late in life – the main reason for the belatedness being that Baptist missionaries arrived in Longwa long after other Konyak villages. A photograph of the late *angh* on the wall of the new building shows him in traditional headgear and was taken during his prime. *Angh* Luhngam, who passed away in 2015, was the first in a long succession of renowned Longwa *anghs* to convert to the Baptist faith. Gossip has it that he did not lead a model Baptist life and stumbled toward his own destruction via alcoholism and opium. A close aide of the late *angh* blamed visitors for the premature death of their "raja"; "unscrupulous" visitors apparently got the *angh* hooked on "rum and whisky" offered him as gifts. Also, rumour has it that the lanky, meek, and soft-spoken young *angh* of Longwa may already have taken a step forward in his father's footsteps by experimenting with opium, an addiction that has ravaged almost the entire new generation of Konyak *anghs*.

In spite of a declining *angh* system, the preference for a male heir is strong. When a son was born to Tonyei, the whole village celebrated and gunshots in the air indicated happiness; some of the Baptist faithful said God had finally answered their prayers. On my first visit, the precocious heir-apparent was a toddler turned two who was made to mingle with strangers taking photographs. Unlike his father and grandfather before him, the tyke is making an early start socialising; perhaps this will later salvage some of his family's lost glory.

The museum-cum-hall where the *angh* carries out his social duties leads through the family's living quarters to a quasi-modern kitchen at the other end of the house. The kitchen is bereft of traditional showpieces and artefacts and filled with household articles found in every Naga home: no staged authenticity here; it shows an unpretentious domestic life free of feigning and the warmth and hospitality of rural areas. Inside the kitchen, removed from the prying eyes of tourists, the *angh's* royal wife – the daughter of a Wancho Naga *angh* from Arunachal Pradesh – tends to the young heir while an older subordinate wife who is not blue blooded works in the kitchen and serves the tea. At least on the surface, the wives carry on harmoniously while the young *angh* sits like an exhibit among visitors. Interestingly, both wives take an active part in the village's Baptist church and the *angh's* polygamy is, I was told, not an issue; in the past the Konyak *anghs* had several wives and concubines, so the current incumbent has shown commendable moderation: his ancestor, Phawang, is said to have had sixty consorts.

Because the Baptist faith influences every aspect of Konyak life, rulers now are not the autocrats they were. In many instances they must toe the line of the Baptist church. In Luhwang, a vassal village of Longwa, the *angh* of Nyahnyu who is now forty-one told me in jest he would have taken many wives had it not been for the strictures of the new faith. Luhwang's coronation took place in 2013, by which time he was already a baptised member of the church, so the village's Baptist community played an important role on the occasion. Luhwang is reduced to a single wife she is from the Tizit area. He is not in a position to trifle with Baptist precepts by acquiring additional wives and concubines or getting divorced; excommunication is a real threat now, even for an *angh*.

Luhwang's liege *angh*, Tonyei, who has fallen short of the Baptist code by getting himself two wives, has faced the consequences: the church has not afforded him water baptism and his name is not among the church's membership. This has huge implications, at least symbolically. Luhwang told me that the *angh* of Longwa wishes to undergo water immersion but the church is holding its ground and flatly refusing. His father, *angh* Luhngam, who had four wives, was allowed water baptism because his conversion had, luckily for him, happened after he had married the full quartet.

II

If there were a contest for Konyak *anghs* as role models in the present, the *angh* of Wanching would be the front runner. Married for forty-eight years, this 68-year-old has an impeccable record of marital fidelity, as is expected of a practising Baptist.[5] Everyone who knows Keamang attests to a husbandly adoration bordering on the uxorious, blackened teeth and all. With an encyclopaedic memory and vast knowledge of Konyak society, Keamang is the

[5] The social class in Wanching was divided into *angh*, *longh*, and *pen*. In the past, it was usually the *angh's* wife from the *longh* class who looked after the needs of the *angh* and his "queen" (an *angh's* daughter who would give him an heir) and supervised the *angh's* concubines from the *pen* class.

go-to person when people need an *angh's* counsel. The Konyak *angh's* sway in the village remains palpable.

Keamang claims he is from the bloodline of the highly esteemed *pongyin anghs* of Chui; these were powerful enough to be regarded as next to Kahwang, the Konyak creator-god. The Konyak *anghs* of Longwa, Shangnyu, Mon, and Chui who performed the royal coronation ceremony (*pongyin*) were known for their autocratic rule and control of many villages beyond their village kingdoms. It was the *angh* of Chui, Meiwang, who sent a vassal *angh* to Wanching when its *angh*, Molem – who Keamang said was an oppressor like Saddam Hussein – was speared to death by a disgruntled commoner. For his misdeed the killer was subsequently struck dead by lightning. Keamang is seventh in line to that *angh* sent from Chui to Wanching on the request of villagers. Though it goes back generations, a simmering hostility continues between the two *angh* families; a descendant of Molem lives next door to Keamang and from time to time makes his displeasure known, claiming his royal family's rightful place was usurped by Keamang's bloodline.

In 2017, when the chief minister of Nagaland visited Wanching during an election campaign, Keamang's "rabble-rousing" neighbour created a scene, claiming he himself was the rightful ruler. As a practising Baptist, Keamang swallowed the indignity; such an act would earlier have ended with the parties coming to blows, if not spears. Keamang's toleration of the ignominy is attributable to his repute as a devout Baptist and regular churchgoer. His forbearance enhanced his reputation for fortitude within the Baptist community.

Keamang hints that curses uttered by some *anghs* still work, implying he is not to be messed with despite his newfound identity as the follower of a religion preaching egalitarianism. However, not all Konyak *anghs* possess oracular power, nor is every *angh* treated with reverence; to be royally blue blooded, as the *pongyin anghs* are said to be, the *angh* has to undergo lengthy and rigorous rites and rituals that constitute a coronation ceremony. This is much dreaded as it can be life threatening. The royal coronation ceremony is imperative before an *angh* can become a true royal blue blood, and his village (*anghdom*) elevated as a *pongyin anchen*: a village that has braved the fire of a formidable ceremony. Some initiates may die during the process, but if they emerge successful their social rank and ontological status are reckoned transformed. The Konyak Nagas, while predominantly following the Baptist faith, still believe in the legend of "were-tigers": their belief is that an *angh's* spirit becomes a were-tiger once he has undergone the royal coronation ceremony. This makes *pongyin anghs* not only enigmatic but fearsome; they therefore grow punctilious in their words and actions lest their power rub off on others. The Indian state and the Baptist church have between them levelled the field for "the *Ang* and *Bens* (chiefs and commoners)".[6] The impact of the new faith is palpable in Keamang's trajectory, domestic life, and the changing dynamics between *angh* and *ben* (or *pen*) in the village.

Phengna, the 57-year-old wife of Keamang, shows no sign of royal bearing and attempts no masquerade by playing a part. If not for the transformation in the *angh's* traditional role, her status would not have soared as the only wife of an *angh* with a pedigree traced to the Chui *anghdom*.[7] In the recent past it was the prerogative of a pure-blooded *angh's* daughter (*anghya*) to become an *angh's* wife, give him a male heir, and daughters indispensable in marriage alliances with other Konyak *anghs*.[8] Modernity has meant that the *angh's* wife is free of a queenly façade, sartorial requirements, and even the tattooing associated with the regalia of the exalted. Except for her blackened teeth and a traditional

---

[6] See Fürer-Haimendorf, *The Konyak Nagas*, esp. Chapter 2.

[7] Fürer-Haimendorf says "the paramount chiefs of Mon and Chi (Chui)" had a wide sphere of influence and had many vassal *anghs* from other villages under their jurisdiction. See ibid., 52.

[8] The Konyak Nagas settled in the Sagaing region, Myanmar, and the Nocte and Wancho inhabiting Longding and Tirap districts, Arunachal Pradesh, are all considered a part of the larger Konyak Naga group because of their shared history and cultural similarities.

bead necklace that she wears occasionally, there are no cultural carry-overs from the past indicating her status as an *angh's* wife. Like most women of her age group, Phengna had blackened her teeth alongside her friends because they, as she told me, looked "funny and out of place when rows of white teeth peeked out when they smiled". The technique involves collecting moist soot from raw burning bamboo and rubbing it continuously on the gums and teeth till they are blackened. This traditional practice, which new-generation Konyaks find outlandish, warded off gum disease and tooth infections that were rife given the abysmal oral hygiene in the older generation.

With her simple way of dressing, plain looks, short stature, and trademark suntanned skin of those used to working long hours in the sun, Phengna does not stand out in a crowd. She and her husband are seen to lead an ideal married life by a community that values the normalisation of monogamy; she has raised children, as expected of a godly woman; and despite her eldest dropping out of high school, the children are well educated with some holding government jobs. Phengna's success as practising Baptist, exemplary wife, and happy mother has trumped the earlier requirement of pedigree.

When Keamang was only a boy, his father, *angh* Aonyei, passed away, and so his uncle, Temwang, assumed the office till the heir could come of age. But before this could happen, Keamang and his siblings were ousted from their parents' home; and had it not been for his uncle's untimely death at the hands of a man from a neighbouring village – which Keamang later avenged despite his conversion to the new faith – he would not have secured the inheritance rightfully his. God is the ultimate judge, Keamang says, and as a believer he is trying to follow the teachings of Christ, which means ending blood feuds – a primary reason for headhunting. It means forgiving and forgetting, and doing unto others as you would have them do unto you.

Blood feuds ran deep in Konyak society; there was no greater shame than hesitating like Hamlet to exact vengeance on a kinsman when imperative. Konyak menfolk were required to deeply honour their dead, specially those done in by enemies. In 1983 Keamang was sent to jail in Tuensang, along with 120 men, for killing the man from the neighbouring village whom they had held responsible for the death of Keamang's uncle. Their revenge had been planned in great detail and was the last blood feud witnessed in recent years. Even though Keamang was by then a Baptist – having undergone the water immersion in 1970, as he told me – he did not want to live the rest of his life as an *angh* who had failed to avenge the murder of close kin; he had to put "a full stop to the perpetual cycle of shame". When he returned to the village along with his men after fifty-nine days in Tuensang jail, his children, Keamang says exaggeratingly, "had all grown up and the clothes I brought for them wouldn't fit." Keamang did not regret avenging his uncle, he had carried out the duty expected of a worthy successor; except now his devout Baptist beliefs make him see how they conflict with his past acts.

When Keamang became *angh* after Temwang's murder, he did not want to return to his old home – which had housed six generation of *anghs* – from where he had been wrongfully evicted.[9] He had led a difficult life as a young adult and when his usurper uncle took over the consecrated house that was once his home, he was distraught. But tradition cannot be entirely done away with, and so Keamang had to return to the place where his parents had lived. The site for constructing the *angh's* house had been chosen carefully, the oracles consulted and auguries considered, so it was auspicious, sacred, and irreplaceable. Outside Keamang's colourfully painted house there still stands a sacred tree and an upright stone where hunted human heads were laid out for ceremonial purposes before being proudly strung in the men's dormitory (*morung*). Despite being a hundred per cent Baptist, Wanching

---

[9] Keamang's renegade elder brother Wangtong relinquished his prerogative to become the *angh*; so Keamang, who was the second son, became the *angh* in his father's place.

village's menfolk still revere their sacred spaces, and so whenever wild animals are shot they are first brought to the *angh's* compound and kept beside the standing stone and sacred tree.

III

There are no traditional motifs, animal skulls, or other Konyak paraphernalia adorning the Wanching *angh's* house. The biggest room in the centre has been converted into a drawing room and is bedecked with family photographs, mostly taken during cultural programmes and church events. Only in this room does one notice some traditional knick-knacks common in most middle-class Naga homes. The decorative items speak of changes that have come about in Konyak society: they include ancient Ahom memorabilia, family portraits, Christian mementos, and portraits of Indian politicians. The modern home of the Wanching *angh* appears no different from other well-to-do family homes in the village. Living standards, including personal hygiene and sanitation, have improved tremendously, which the faithful in the village attribute to the Baptist mission.

Keamang and Phengna have raised their children in a godly environment; the family attend church services religiously and there are regular prayer meetings at home. Keamang is an avid Bible reader. He got his children going on the scriptures early and regular doses of them paid off: the seven children are believers and actively involved in the churches where they work or study. Keamang's eldest son Tonyei dropped out of high school and went "a bit wayward" during his teenage days, but now as a father of two has begun to seriously contemplate his future. Keamang is grooming his eldest son to take over after his death, and not surprisingly the heir-apparent iterates oral history and pithy sayings from the Bible, just as his father does.

Not long ago a young British documentary filmmaker visited Wanching and stayed with the *angh's* family for nearly a month to document the life of an heir-apparent and record the daily routine of a future *angh* in the making. After his departure nothing was heard of him or his film; possibly the material he gathered did not add up to an interesting film, which may be because there is nothing left of the esoteric or the uncommonly interesting in the life of the initiate *angh*. The *morung* that used to be a place of learning is no longer inhabited, making society more atomised; besides, there is no training manual that the heir-apparent can read to become an effective *angh*. There are no special skills which he can acquire to set him apart; modernity has largely democratised the learning process.

This fact does not escape Keamang and so he tries his best to groom his eldest son with the means at his disposal. But, most importantly, Keamang considers it his utmost priority to inculcate in his son "the fear of god" and make him a responsible believer. This entails some amount of chiding and pep talks; Keamang is not happy that his son skips church and plays cards with friends on Sundays, and drinks occasionally: he thinks this unbecoming of a good future *angh*. His consternation is justified because within his lifetime opium has ravaged many Konyak *anghs*, and the "evil habit" has rubbed off on Tonyei's age group.

Keamang's second son, Manshong, apparently the mother's favourite, happens to be knowledgeable, articulate, charming, and more educated than his older brother. But in a society that has upheld primogeniture, "lesser" sons have had to live in the shadow of the eldest. However, times have changed and in the new ethos upward social mobility is no longer as monopolised – other ladders exist. The second son has chosen and achieved the most coveted means to establish himself in contemporary Konyak society – a secure government job. The older brother did not marry along the Baptist ritual, whereas Manshong and his bride had a lavish white wedding that was long talked about in the village.

Marrying a girl from the neighbouring village, Wakching, was an expensive affair, this being among the few Konyak villages that still practise a form of bride price: the bridegroom's family have to gift circular brass discs to the bride's, and prestige is measured in terms of the quality and number of discs gifted. The practice is looked down upon by Baptist followers, who see it as an animistic hangover, in part because brass discs serve no purpose nor have any value while putting a financial burden on the groom's family. Keamang's family was not keen on the tradition, but in a Konyak marriage the bride's family, at least till the time of marriage, holds bargaining power. Therefore Keamang ended up gifting twelve brass discs of fine quality that had been passed down as family heirlooms. Manshong on his part believed that the practice preserved cultural tradition, and, since the number of brass discs depended on the girl's status, his wife deserved every one of them, being a graduate and a government employee. Aside from this "petty" difference of opinion, it was the grandest white wedding that the village had ever witnessed, so meticulously planned that even the sacred tree in the *angh's* compound, beneath which in former days human heads had been laid, was festooned with Chinese-made decorative lights to make it look like a sacred tree from the Hollywood sci-fi movie *Avatar* – as the bridegroom's younger sister told me.

IV

Wanching is at a distance of a few kilometres from Wakching, a Konyak Naga village made famous by Fürer-Haimendorf, who conducted his fieldwork in it in 1937–8. There is still an old British road connecting Wakching with Naginimora, a small town in the plains adjoining Assam, the name of which is testament to centuries of complex relationships that existed between Konyak Nagas and Ahom rulers long before the British appeared on the scene.[10] During the colonial period it was Wanching's neighbour,

[10] According to the legend in Wanching, a native princess went down the plains to see off her elder sister who married an Ahom prince, and while returning home missed her sister so much that she died of a broken heart. So the place was named *Naga-rani-mora* (which in Assamese means "the place where a Naga rani died"), later shortened to Naginimora.

Wakching, that became a model Konyak village for colonial administrator-ethnographers. Today, Wanching is recognised as one of the most advanced and progressive Konyak villages, by far outstripping once-powerful villages in levels of education and development. Being among the first Konyak villages to embrace the new faith, Wanching had access to the fruits of modernity, including formal education. When the Baptist mission came to the Konyak, people in smaller and subjugated villages converted to the new faith in large numbers. In the new milieu, villages that were earlier underdogs, such as Kongan and Tamlu, took precedence in the Baptist movement that soon overwhelmed the Konyak Nagas.

In Wanching the influence of the Baptist faith is visible in every aspect of social and cultural life; gone are the days when the *morung* was the most important institution; the grand Baptist church that stands literally and symbolically at the centre of the village has dislodged the *morung* as the place of learning and leisure. To the credit of the village, the *morungs* in Wanching, five in total, are among the best preserved and maintained, cleaned occasionally and colourfully painted, giving off a glossy and almost artificial appearance. On the other hand when I visited Wakching I found the Paala *morung*, which had formed the basis of Fürer-Haimendorf's study on the Konyak Naga dormitory system, abandoned and in a dilapidated state; inside the once-hallowed hall the stench of human faeces was unmistakable; a lone log drum had gathered a thick cover of dust and was a canvas for whimsical charcoal art – the handiwork of village children; the corrugated aluminium roofing was in need of repair and the walls were weatherbeaten; the whole had the appearance of a long-abandoned ramshackle wooden house.

The *morungs* of Wanching, though deafeningly empty, have maintained at least the interiors. In addition to intricate wood carvings, which the local artisans have not forgotten or outsourced to people from the plains, the natives have used acrylic colours to make designs on the main pillar, beams, and arches; along with the wooden carvings of birds, animals, and human heads are colourful paintings of these. In the Anghpan *morung* a painting of an aeroplane stands out amidst more traditional motifs. In the Panshong *morung* there is a new addition to the embellishments: the wood carving of a bespectacled man in suit and tie holding a Bible, representing perhaps the coming of the Baptist mission.

In Monyakshu, a large and powerful Konyak village in the Upper Konyak area near the Indo–Myanmar border, the *morungs* are still inhabited but not in the earlier prescribed way: now the menfolk gather in the *morung* and discuss hunting, the agricultural *jhum* cycle, and important social activities. When *morungs* were converted into voting booths in the last state legislative assembly election, it created a scene since women had to be allowed in to participate in the democratic adult franchise, much to the chagrin of the village menfolk. Ao Naga Baptist missionaries brought Christianity to Monyakshu in the 1950s; within a few decades many had embraced the new faith, and by the turn of the century Monyakshu had become predominantly Baptist. The

Ill. 7: Panshong *morung* (bachelor's dormitory) in Wanching showing a wood carving of a modern man with a Bible alongside traditional motifs. Photo by the author.

Shahkhe *morung* overlooking the Baptist church on a hill became famous for its corrugated-iron roofing (a modern innovation of great prestige), the first in the village; today, it stands as the largest and best-maintained *morung* which the locals proudly show to an annual smattering of visitors. While the wood carvings of animals, birds, and reptiles are large and richly painted, mostly in hues of red and black, what stands out is a medium-sized wood carving of the first Baptist missionary-teacher. A stark reminder of how deeply the Baptist faith has entrenched itself in Monyakshu is visible in this slow, effortless encroachment of Christian motifs on traditional artwork in the *morungs*; boards displaying pithy Bible verses put up in public spaces, along pathways, and at road junctions; not to mention the high-rise church steeple visible from every corner of the village, reminding people of the pinnacle of their social life.

In the past, the Konyak Nagas' sexual life, associated with the dormitory system, was permissive. Fürer-Haimendorf described a common nocturnal practice: "The ideal places for such

Ill. 8: A miniature *morung* with a painting of Jesus Christ stands next to an uninhabited traditional *morung* in Changway *khel*, Monyakshu village.

prolonged meetings were the sheltered verandas of the granaries on the outskirts of the village. There, couples of lovers could remain undisturbed until morning, and the owners of granaries favoured such use, which protected the stored grain from thieves, and added, in Konyak belief, to the fertility of the seed grain."[11] The Baptist faith was by contrast not much different from Victorian morality. The faithful frequently fell short of Baptist teachings and suspensions from the church became common. The new teachings on social propriety and etiquette were imbibed without resistance, but Konyak "licentiousness" perhaps reminded Baptist missionaries of Sodom and Gomorrah.

I was bemused on occasion by charcoal doodles, undoubtedly the handiwork of schoolchildren and teenagers, on the walls of the village rest house and government school toilets; some of these flummoxed the devout Baptist parents of their artist-creators and psychoanalysts could have had a field day interpreting them. In Wanching's Anghpan *morung* the local Picassos had left their creations on a weathering whitewashed wall, the misshapen charcoal artwork including a man with automatic rifles, hunters with *dao* and spears, and a lewd drawing of copulation. In former days the male sanctum sanctorum would not have been vandalised thus because of the fear of severe punishment by *morung* keepers.

Wanching has a thriving population of youth that would once have filled the men's dormitory, but there is no modern-day equivalent institution; the Baptist church is no substitute, naturally. The traditional male club disciplined its young recruits with mandatory and institutionalised practices; the rite of passage in the *morung* was gruelling and an important part of adolescent development. Yet it was also a place of camaraderie, male bonding, and entertainment. The Baptist church youth group is a voluntary association and cannot replace the *morung* as a holistic place of learning. Though people may face social disapproval if they are not involved with the church, baptised membership is not

[11] Fürer-Haimendorf, *The Konyak Nagas*, 73.

imposed on individuals by virtue of birth into that society – as in the traditional male dormitory system; and the institutions and places of learning for modern Konyak youth to be trained into becoming educated citizens have diversified.

An unusual degree of dissonance between modernity and tradition is obvious in Konyak society. Though Konyak Nagas have harmonised many aspects of their cultural life with changing times, many aspects of old tradition continue in the new worldview. The tattooing tradition, however, declined precipitately when the Konyak Nagas converted; as the sagacious *angh* of Wanching argued, tattooing had an overtly symbolic connection with headhunting. In Wanching a huge number of human skulls that had once adorned male dormitories were first buried in a mass grave in 1948–9, when the Baptist faith gained pace in the village. For the young men of a *morung*, acquiring a human head was what had entitled that age group to body tattooing; thus the end of the headhunting tradition and the mass burial of human skulls across Konyak villages heralded the death of ceremonial tattooing.

Though the end of headhunting had far-reaching effects on tattooing, it is still not unusual to see young Konyaks – the wayward ones – with atrociously done tattoos unrelated to past tradition. However these are aberrations because tattooing is frowned upon in all of Naga Baptist society. Konyak Baptist elders now display their tattoos with an element of nostalgia to fawning tourists and the curious, but their display is skin deep and unconnected with cultural significance. Among women, too, tattooing was much sought after: it was considered aesthetic and fashionable among unmarried adolescent girls in former days. But the new faith raised an eyebrow, which sufficed to dissipate the practice. A tradition once treasured is now beyond resuscitation.

Baptist culture fills the void in folk life and aesthetics through various means such as songs and literary thinking, but this cannot substitute for Konyak traditional culture. *Angh* Keamang explained it incisively:

Bringing human heads served several purposes in the community life: if there was an epidemic in the village, human blood was sprinkled for cleansing it; also, men would bring human heads as a sign of their bravery and manhood, to increase their attractiveness in the eyes of prospective brides; and when human heads were brought to the village, it was a occasion of great rejoicing as men and women would sing and dance for days beside the *morung*.

The Konyak Nagas were not homicidal; compassion and forgiveness were not alien to traditional Konyak society, says Keamang, they coexisted with the virtuous imperative of avenging one's kin. In his argument, compassion and vengeance do not cancel each other, especially when retribution is against long-standing enemies in a blood feud. Blood is thicker than water, and in Konyak society not even the Baptist ritual of water immersion necessarily washes away lingering bad blood between families.

V

In 1854 the *Baptist Missionary Magazine* reported the death of an obscure Ao Naga who had been converted in Sivasagar. The promising life of Longjanglepzuk of Merangkong was cut short during a headhunting raid and the perpetrator was none other than a Konyak Naga. A noted Baptist historian, F.S. Downs, says, "The second Naga Christian was Longjanglepzuk of Merangkong village, an Ao . . . Longjanglepzuk had taken up residence near Sibsagar . . . In the summer of 1853 he did go to his village, but only to find a wife. While there he was killed in the course of a Konyak raid."[12]

Behind the death of this second Naga Baptist convert were the long-standing intrigues of war, peacemaking, and breach of treaties between two powerful villages, Merangkong and Wanching. According to Keamang, "Wanching village felt that Merangkong had not kept their word to pay tribute [know their place];

[12] See Downs, *The Mighty Works of God*, 53–4.

meanwhile, in the other eight Konyak villages (all collaborators), there were many age-sections in the *morungs* that wanted to tattoo their body and needed human heads to complete the ceremony. Back then no one knew Longjanglepzuk was a Baptist convert, and so he was killed along with several other people during the attack."

This incident dragged Wanching into the Baptist mission story, although there was no inkling then about a new faith in Upper Assam inching inexorably towards the hills. It was nearly a century later, in 1946, that Wanching became the first Baptist mission outpost in Konyak land when the Ao Naga Baptist Churches' Association from Impur started a mission sub-centre among the Konyak Naga. In 1950 the Council of Baptist Churches in Assam (CBCA) decided on three ethnic populations – the Konyak, Abor (Adi), and Meitei – as their mission field. The Konyak Naga Baptist mission was thus supervised from the plains, although its pioneering missionary was from the Ao Naga tribe – Rev. Longri Ao, who became a household name among Naga Baptists.

The Baptist mission in the Konyak area germinated in Tamlu, a vassal village of Wanching, when a young man studying in the mission school in Impur was converted to the new faith: Longna of Tamlu was baptised by Rev. Wickstrand, an American Baptist missionary, in Impur on 11 December 1932. Unlike the first Konyak Naga converts in the nineteenth century – Hubi, Aklong, and Amlai, who played no role in the spread of the Baptist faith – Longna became a consummate evangelist who converted many in Tamlu to the Baptist faith and these formed the first Konyak Baptist community of the area. Tamlu, which is now in Longleng district and the administrative headquarters of the Phom Nagas, has Konyak and Phom *khels*, with separate Baptist churches; the Konyak Baptist church in Tamlu is the oldest in the Konyak region, having been established in 1935. Tamlu owed fealty to Wanching, since it was Wanching that had sent an *angh* to Tamlu; but when the Baptist faith began to spread from this small and subservient village, Tamlu attained a new status and its fame began to spread near and far. Since Tamlu was only a few hours' walk from Wanching and the latter was the liege village, native Baptist preachers soon reached Wanching and converted some of the villagers.

A full-fledged Baptist mission station was set up in Wakching after independence. Despite being a backward area, the village had remnants of colonialism; besides Kohima and Mokokchung, Wakching in the Lower Konyak area was one of the earliest Naga villages to have a British administrative outpost in 1913.[13] The village had long maintained relations with the Ahoms in the plains via a trade route, but it was the British who had a paved road constructed to Wakching, connecting it with the small railhead at Naginimora in the plains.

The British annexed a strategic area in Lower Konyak to curb headhunting; meanwhile, the Upper Konyak near the Indo-Burmese border remained unadministered, which meant leaving the natives to their fate. In the Upper Konyak region it was the Naga Baptist missionaries who made the initial contact with Konyak villages in the post-independence period; the growth of the Baptist faith in the post-colonial period was an exceptional success story, since infamous headhunters were in the eyes of the world domesticated. The coming of the Baptist mission rapidly changed the religious demography as well as the socio-cultural landscape. Between 1932 (the year of Longna's conversion to the new faith) and 1949, the baptised membership of the Konyak Naga increased to 1600.[14]

The township of Wakching is now recognised as an Extra Additional Commissioner headquarters with an old Indian army outpost. The township is contiguous with the old village. The mission quarters, which the CBCA built in the early 1950s (repaired several times), is still in a liveable condition and occupied by a Baptist missionary's family. The British-type quarters were home to the first residential missionary to the Konyak Naga, Longri Ao. Longri went on to head the Nagaland Baptist Church Council after proving his mettle with seventeen years as missionary to the Konyak Nagas.

[13] Elwin, *Nagaland*, 28.
[14] See Konyak, *The Konyak Naga*, 143.

Konyak Baptist numbers increased exponentially under Longri's supervision, so that a year after statehood, in 1964, there were a total of 10,733 baptised members and 52 churches. By 1967, when the leadership was handed over to a local Baptist leader and Bible translator, Chingyang Konyak, the number of Konyak Baptists had increased to 12,148 spread across 68 churches. Konyak Nagas spoke such diverse tongues that a new village-specific language or dialect could be found every few miles. Konyak Baptist workers did exceedingly well in that they made Konyaks the fifth Naga tribe – after the Ao, Angami, Sumi, and Lotha – to have, in February 1992, a complete Bible translation in the vernacular. It was the language spoken in Wakching village which was chosen for the Konyak Bible translation. This translation and hymnal gave perceptible shape to the modern Konyak ethnic identity.

VI

About fifteen years before the first Konyak Baptist mission station was begun in Wakching, Fürer-Haimendorf, who shared an affable relationship with British administrators, had already made the village familiar to European audiences. He stayed in Wakching in 1936–7, by when the Lower Konyak area had come under British control. This Austrian anthropologist not only bypassed British restrictions on other nationalities entering the Naga Hills, he also enjoyed the patronage of an influential political agent, J.P. Mills. (In 1938 Fürer-Haimendorf married the daughter of a British civil servant, which gained him even more clout with the colonial bureaucracy.)

Fürer-Haimendorf participated in a punitive expedition against Pangsha village in 1937 that ended with this powerful Khiamniungan Naga village being set on fire to teach the recalcitrant natives a lesson. He did not return empty-handed from the Pangsha expedition, having chopped down a head pole and bagged some skulls. For this he was given a hero's welcome on his return to Wakching; the Konyak menfolk, parched by the British restriction on headhunting, sang his praises for the brave act of sneaking away with some skulls.¹⁵ Fürer-Haimendorf's Wakching in old black-and-white photographs is now unrecognisable. The old images show identical low-roofed thatched houses squatting on a hillside; naked children with bulbous foreheads and rotund stomachs; minimally covered men smiling for the photograph, appearing amused by the undue attention; and bare-breasted adolescent girls gazing sombrely into the lens, not a bit discomfited by their "nakedness" – a far cry from prim-looking, well-dressed, churchgoing young girls in present-day Wakching.

In Wakching today, as elsewhere in rural Nagaland, the houses are a medley of types with no trace of traditional architecture. They reveal the modern status and wealth of their occupants. The *morungs* too have changed, their corrugated metal sheet roofing being corroded by the elements. All five *morungs* – Anghpan, Aokeang, Paala, Paalang, and Topong – still stand, but are maintained halfheartedly. They look forlorn, except for the Anghpan *morung*, which stands inconspicuously next to the most expensive, grandest, and largest building in the village, the Baptist church. The Anghpan *morung* exhibits over-the-top painting on dreary wood carvings, possibly to compensate for the disproportionate attention given to the new institution that has usurped the *morungs*.

Though the days are past when the so-called advanced Naga tribes ridiculed Konyak Naga "backwardness" and lampooned their way of life, mutual ethnic prejudices existed between neighbouring Naga communities before the American Baptists and persist as thinly veiled ethnic jibing. A Naga anthropologist from an "advanced" tribe writes in a satirical essay: "The Konyak was taught by the Ao and he has been a faithful student all the time . . . But the Konyak had a habit of having opium and has not gotten over the hang-over."¹⁶ Back in 1913, when some of my own tribesmen went on the "Chinglong expedition" to Konyak Naga country as hired hands of the Great Sahib J.H. Hutton, there, in

¹⁵ See Fürer-Haimendorf, *The Naked Nagas*, Chapter 21, "The White Head-hunter".

¹⁶ Lotha, *The Raging Mithun*, 30–1.

the words of Hutton, they "put down their loads and burst into fits of uncontrollable laughter at this sight of [Konyak] men who, though hardly more naked than they were wore no three-inch flap."[17] However, by the end of the twentieth century, these "naked Konyak Nagas" were around 99 per cent Baptist – as Chemyuh Konyak, leader of the Konyak Baptist Churches' Association, told me. Improved standards of living and better education were the accompanying consequences.

Menton Konyak, pastor of the Wakching Baptist church, claims the Baptist mission was not wholly responsible for these drastic changes in Konyak society. Menton is a man of few words, a rarity among usually gregarious Naga Baptist pastors. A native of Oting, this soft-spoken middle-aged pastor oversees more than a thousand baptised members in a village of 378 households. Not all is well with the Baptist community in Wakching; the Baptists have won the cultural war, but small battles are still being fought, and the gentlemanly pastor is in the midst of an ongoing tussle against resilient traditional practices which the church leaders see as antithetical to the Baptist faith. Menton is an outsider, and he would not have risen to his respectable position in a well-known village like Wakching had it not been for his calling as a Baptist minister; being the religious head, he seems to take the failings of his flock personally: he is critical of "unwarranted" traditional practices that refuse to go away.

Tradition is still strong in Wakching, he says, and its wholesale conversion has not meant wholesale assimilation into Baptist culture. He gave me an example: "There is this mortuary practice that is followed religiously: when a rich man dies, his coveted objects are displayed publicly and traditional attire is kept alongside the dead body; and only after this is done are the pastor and church officials called to perform the funerary rites." Menton clarified that he is not against tradition, but this kind of practice he associates with syncretism, which is not compatible with Christian belief in

[17] See Hutton, *The Sema Nagas*, 13.

the afterlife. Also, Menton says, though the church had for long asked villagers to give up the practice of bride price, it continues; he was clearly exasperated by the faithful feeling the need to straddle two traditions. However, looking at the trajectory of the Baptist faith among the Konyaks as well as Nagas more generally, practices now deemed contentious will not take long to die out.

The whitewashed church with its tall steeple in Wakching may have cost Rs 50 lakhs or more. Tourists on a visit to Fürer-Haimendorf's famous village usually spend their limited time looking for dilapidated *morungs*, rundown traditional houses, and other traces of the traditional past, which they have read about or seen in old colonial photographs. Those looking for the exotic and strange are dismayed by the rapid modernisation, the disappearing old way of life, and the pervasiveness of Western culture among the younger generation. A few remaining elderly tattooed people in Wakching – a *thenkoh* group (without face tattoos) – proudly declare themselves followers of the first-century Jewish teacher from Galilee. They call him the "son of Kahwang" – although Kahwang, the old Konyak creator-god, has been toppled from his pedestal of reverence and worship, and the name is now merely an indigenous term for "God the Father" in the Christian Trinity, or more precisely an alternative for Yahweh, the Hebrew god of the Old Testament. The tattooed elders tend to oversell past exploits and pre-Christian-era stories to enthralled outsiders, some of whom have travelled hundreds of miles to see fearsome tattooed headhunters. What makes them worth looking at are the pale-greenish etchings on their skin and their memories of a fading past; while some of these tattooed elders, as I found out, are devout Christians well versed in Baptist doctrines and teachings, having been its practitioners for decades, they are remembered by the outside world mainly for an exotic, fast-fading past.

VII

As elsewhere, the student community in Konyak villages is growing and becoming influential; the students' union is behind new voluntary associations working in the village, replacing the traditional institutions in which people were made to participate. It was Konyak villages like Tamlu, Kangching, Wakching, and Wanching which had the earliest contact with the Baptist mission and produced a new class of educated, reform-minded youth: they are now a force to reckon with. The earliest mission-school-educated young men who sought to reform social, religious, and cultural life worked at first under the aegis of the Konyak Students' Union (KSU) in 1946.[18] These student bodies now act as cultural custodians, the first of their kind in Konyak Naga society; the rise of the KSU as a modern organisation was the beginning of a new identity politics concerning modernity, tradition, ethnicity, and even nationalism. These developments were not separable from the Baptist faith, since the rise of modern institutions and voluntary associations has been largely a result of the Protestant mission. While the KSU attempted to preserve and promote traditional culture, some long-held practices came under scrutiny and a kind of moral crusade was begun against them.

The first traditional practice that the KSU protested against was the "peculiar" mortuary practice of the Konyak Naga: the disposing of dead bodies on raised platforms. This practice was not exclusive to the Konyak, it was also found among other eastern Naga tribes on both sides of the Indo–Burmese border. The exposure of dead bodies on a raised platform continued after the Baptist mission's proselytising since people were not willing to suddenly give up a practice that had been followed for generations. The KSU campaigned vehemently against this raised platform disposal of the dead, even imposing fines, and were able to stop it in the 1950s, though the majority were still with the traditional religion at the time.

[18] With the spread of education, more student unions came up and these village-based unions came together under the same umbrella, renaming the parent body Konyak Students' Conference (KSC) in January 1949, during the fourth annual session held in Wanching. Almost five decades later, the name was changed back to Konyak Students' Union.

In present-day Wakching the dead are afforded a proper Christian burial, whereas eight decades ago Fürer-Haimendorf had vividly described the problem of open burial thus: "A small boy complained to me that the smell of the corpse in their back garden was so sickening that he could hardly swallow a mouthful of rice in his parents' house."[19] A platform would be raised over six feet above ground. On this the body was placed without being embalmed so that it would desiccate quickly in the open, after which the final and most important mortuary rite might be performed: the preservation of the human skull in an earthen pot or a receptacle chiselled out of a lump of soft stone. The rest of the remains were buried. "The profusion of skulls that the British saw in Konyak villages were not all victims of headhunting; villages abounded with human skulls because the Konyak believed that the soul resides in the head and after death it stays behind with families, so skulls were preserved and not interred", *angh* Keamang explained.

In Wanching the students' union stopped the age-old practice of letting the porcine population loiter freely in the open; the student body castigated errant owners for the unhygienic rearing of pigs; while earlier, swine had served an important sanitary role in the villages – getting rid of human waste – this had become unacceptable. Pigs now live in sties and away from humans.

The student community next turned its attention to the practice of tattooing, passing a resolution against it. The Konyak tattoo tradition suffered a huge setback as a result of the combined effect of the British government's ban on headhunting, the Baptist missionaries' deterrents, and the determined reformism of educated Konyak youth. The persistence of the label "naked Nagas" long after the British left made the students' union take the initiative to persuade people in remote villages to be less parsimonious when donning apparel. All the same, though there are now no naked Konyak Nagas, the prejudicial image of them as a naked tribe has

[19] Fürer-Haimendorf, *The Naked Nagas*, 73–4.

not disappeared in the Indian mainland. The KSU also launched literacy campaigns in villages to promote modern education: this is the weapon that has made the student community a formidable force, allowing them to challenge even the once-powerful *anghs*.

VIII

On 21 December 1973 the Mon district of Nagaland, covering an area of 1786 square km, was recognised as the Konyak Naga headquarters.[20] The Konyak Nagas of this district form one of the largest Baptist communities in the state, with a total of 85,083 baptised members distributed over 199 churches (NBCC 2016 census). Besides Mon, cognate Konyak Naga groups inhabit Changlang, Longdin, and Tirap districts of Arunachal Pradesh, and Khamdi and Tanglang divisions in the Sagaing region. In this cultural zone traversing international and state boundaries, the Konyak Naga family speaks at least thirty-two different languages.[21]

Mon, on a lower mountain range, is fast becoming a cosmopolitan town of cultural import because it is in the heartland of the *pongyin anghs*. The modern administrative centre falls in the traditional jurisdiction of Chui and Mon villages, which remain important stakeholders despite the increasing influence of small-time bureaucrats and local politicians and the dwindling authority of new-generation *anghs*. The *anghs* of Mon and Chui were renowned for their "glorious" rule and imposing authority; these two rulers controlled a vast territory, and even today there exists a loosely maintained relationship between guardian and vassal villages. Modernity took a toll on their tributary system; when the Konyak Nagas became Baptists they faced the imperatives of egalitarianism and had to rethink the practice of tribute exactions.

---

[20] The district was enlarged in 1991 by transferring some villages from Tuensang district and creating new administrative circles at Tobu, Monyakshu, and Mopong in the Upper Konyak region.

[21] Konyak, *The Konyak Nagas*, 148.

But old habits die hard and some powerful villages continue the tradition.

A good number of Konyak Naga villages, especially those ruled by *pongyin anghs*, were not the village republics that most Naga villages were popularly perceived to be: there existed an idea of territorial power extending far beyond an individual village, where a *pongyin angh* exerted influence over lesser *anghs*. Konyak villages were independent with regard to socio-cultural and economic life, but political power was located in guardian villages. In the colonial records the *anghs* of Chui, Mon, and Shangnyu were said to be by far the most influential and powerful. With the transition of cultural and political power to the Baptist mission and the state bureaucracy, the glorious rule of *pongyin anghs* had by the end of the previous century waned considerably.

Wangkhao (1923–2009) of Chui, who lived into the new millennium, was arguably the most popular Konyak *angh* of modern times. Over his lifetime, politicians, government officials, and tourists alike thronged to Chui to meet *angh* Wangkhao. A bust of Wangkhao in traditional attire stands in Chui village, between the towering Baptist church and the small, unkempt concrete *morung*. Wangkhao was renowned far and wide and his legend survives. The conversion of Wangkhao to the new faith is much narrated by the Konyak Baptist faithful. These lofty words have been inscribed on a memorial stone erected in his memory:

> He is the hereditary angh believed to possess supernatural power and born with the spirit of a mysterious wild tiger/lion. He ruled over a large empire with great wisdom and dedication for a period of 49 golden years . . .
> He embraced Christianity and was remarkably the first to be baptised amongst the hard core crowned anghs (pongwen anghs) of this region. His conversion to Christianity sowed the seeds to the advancement of education, economy, politics, technology etc., to the Chi villagers in particular and the Konyaks in general.

In a twist of fate, Wanching, which was once a vassal village of Chui, has superseded Chui in all aspects of modern development;

what keeps the relationship going between the two villages is age-old tradition. Past his prime, Wangkhao saw the eventual decline of his *anghdom*; he had no true heir to continue his legacy and now modernity, not tradition, was in the driving seat. Notwithstanding, *angh* Keamang thinks his mentor Wangkhao was one of the greatest Konyak *anghs* who ever lived, and that the coming of the Baptist faith did not dent his magnificence.

Chui used to be frequented by visitors, but after Wangkhao's death the numbers have considerably decreased. Photographs of "famous" skulls kept in rows close to the *angh's* home were reproduced in coffee-table books and travel magazines, taking the story of Konyak headhunters around the globe. Such public exhibits were incompatible with the Baptist faith but past valour and exploits could only be commemorated by showing off enemy skulls, so the faith had to turn a Nelson's eye at such displays. By the 1990s the entire village had converted, and in September 1991 the skulls, more than 300, were finally interred; with the highlight of Chui given a Christian burial, visitors began to decline. About 50 metres from the Baptist church a monument marks where the skulls were once on display and are now interred. The circular memorial consists of perpendicular stones erected in place of every buried skull. Some stakeholders say the burial was a heritage loss of great significance. The locals offer a different perspective and explanation: "Outsiders will not understand why we decided to inter the skulls; it is a matter of forgive and forget. The victims could be someone's relatives or even grandparents," Wangkhao's longtime confidant, Wanghei, told me.

Wangkhao was the epitome of an autocratic royal chief; he ruled with an iron hand. In Konyak Naga tradition the *pongyin anghs* were considered extraordinary beings, but Wangkhao was in a different league. He may not have been worshipped, as the Konyak Nagas do not have a concept of deifying humans, but he was greatly revered and by legend commoners attributed magical gifts and even healing powers to his presence. With the coming of the Baptist faith to Chui – Wangkhao's seat of power – the heart of his supremacy and sacredness were struck a body blow. "How dare you say that kings (*anghs*) and commoners (*bens*) have all been created equal? I was particularly annoyed with that song," Wangkhao once fulminated against a Baptist hymn to his friend, Yamyap, the veteran Konyak Baptist minister.

Wangkhao resisted conversion to the new faith for very long; he continued to practise the ancestral faith and uphold the proud tradition of his forebears. Even when the majority had converted, he remained obdurate, though he did not castigate or persecute adherents of the new religion, very possibly because they were now the majority and he realised the new faith was unstoppable. In many Konyak Naga villages the persecution of the faithful had aided rather than prevented the new faith from spreading; "Wangkhao was a tolerant *angh* and very respectful of the Baptist mission, although he did not agree with it at first; he did not stop people in the village from practising the new faith," Wanghei, a Baptist convert himself, said amiably of the late *angh*. It was not easy for Wangkhao to give up his former glory; however, his admirers insist that even after his conversion he was no ordinary believer – the Holy Spirit guided him to perform wondrous acts.

Wangkhao's successor, incapacitated by opium eating, could not continue the legacy. The *angh's* house is now in a shambles, a far cry from the glorious days of Wangkhao. Adjacent to the quasi-traditional kitchen is a rectangle-shaped concrete house whose main entrance is ornately decorated with the horns of buffalo and mithun. Wangkhao's lifetime of possessions have been converted into museum objects and locked away in a room opened to tourists on payment of a few hundred rupees. In this dark and unventilated storage room Wangkhao's family and followers have preserved the "*angh's* court room" for visitors to see: a stout wooden chair with worn-out red cushions stands next to an unused fireplace, and behind the ceremonial chair hang oversized brass gongs, three long and curved mithun horns, weapons and agricultural implements, old family portraits, a collage of wooden plates, and various traditional trinkets.

Wangkhao's successor Chingpong, a man of few words, pointed at the late *angh's* possessions and spoke of their antiquity and significance, while Wanghei, who now advises the young *angh*, narrated most of the history and legend of the late ruler. Wanghei spoke with reverence, as if the late *angh* were listening in. "Women were not allowed to enter the court room, let alone approach the *angh*, while he was sitting there for hearings and dispensing justice," Wanghei said, pointing to the empty chair that no one has dared to sit on after Wangkhao's demise. It appears that the legend of famous *anghs* like Wangkhao has grown over the years to compensate for the rapid change that has seized hold of Konyak society in general and the *angh* tradition in particular.

IX

Along with other crops, the Konyak Nagas grew the poppy plant both for medicinal purposes and as a stimulant (*afukani*). Contrary to the belief that the British weaponised opium to subdue the Konyak, the British administration opened the first opium retail shop in Wakching in the 1920s and issued licences to the natives to curb overuse. Trade in opium with the plains and across the Indo–Myanmar border burgeoned into a thriving black market after the British left. By the time educated Konyak Nagas clamped down on the trade, opium eating and addiction among the natives had become an epidemic.

Keamang has been raising the issue of opium addiction with the church and civil society organisations; as a responsible *angh* and practising Baptist he has been fighting the social evil, but opium use is deeply rooted in Konyak society and difficult to eradicate. When the British came they found opium eating had made men lazy and unproductive, so they assumed that by limiting opium sales and discouraging its local production they would reduce addiction while earning revenue. So they brought in a much more potent variety of opium from Assam and sold it to the natives. The first British-licensed opium shop was opened in Wakching in the 1920s, which sold only to licence holders; this encouraged black marketeers who began to smuggle it and inflated the price. This then wrecked generations of Konyak men who became a burden on society. In 1959 the Konyak Student Union finally shut the British-licensed opium shop in Wakching, but the damage was done; many Konyak men could not break the habit. Also, opium cultivation had increased on the Burma side and even now feeds the addiction of many young people, including *anghs*.

Keamang's second son Manshong, who works in the Excise Department in Mon town, told me that Konyak villages near the border are the entry point for coarsely produced opium from across the border which has been flooding Mon town; it is difficult to stem the flow since opium cultivation is a source of livelihood for many impoverished families in Myanmar, and the state authority lacks the manpower to monitor the international border in remote places. For many years, opium has been serving as a medium of exchange in the remote Naga villages of Myanmar. "Taxes to the insurgents are paid in opium, since these poor villagers do not have cash. In some cases, the Baptist church pastors in remote villages in Myanmar are given salaries in opium, which the pastors out of desperation have to sell to feed their families," Manshong said despondently.

Keamang is relieved none of his sons have succumbed to the habit. "The new generation of *anghs*, most of whom are my age, got into the habit of smoking opium; some of these young *anghs* even have assistants to prepare it," Tonyei, the *angh*-apparent of Wanching told me, and added with amusement, "In the opium dens in Mon, the sellers tell a joke that their establishments are visited by people with Bible names like David, Moses, Joseph, and so on; it seems only a person with the name Jesus has not visited the dens so far."

The Baptist church has initiated a drive against the opium epidemic, but so far the success rate has been negligible. In recent years a new religious group called Yahoi has become popular among the Konyak and many Baptist faithful are defecting to this new sect, much to the consternation of the Konyak Baptist churches. The word in Konyak Baptist circles is that the reason for the popularity of the Yahoi "cult" is its success in weaning people off opium and alcohol.

The coming of the Baptist faith in Konyak land reinvented group solidarity and led to strict adherence to the new religion, but it also empowered an impoverished woman from a nondescript village to grow into an authority figure who wields power over thousands of religious seekers. The Yahoi leader is in her mid-sixties – a Baptist-seminary-trained "turncoat". The Baptists are not as invincible as their leaders earlier assumed they were; they are facing an onslaught from the new religious movement with its charismatic leader. A seasoned Konyak evangelist in Mon town expressed the view that new upcoming sects and denominations that cater to the needs of believers could overthrow Baptist hegemony in the state, if the church – bogged down in prosaic bureaucracy and unwholesome politics – remains complacent about the present state of affairs.

Rev. Chemyuh Konyak, executive secretary of the Konyak Baptist Bumeinok Bangjum (KBBB; i.e. Konyak Baptist churches association), was worried by the competition. He had drawn flak as head of the Konyak Baptist church for not being able to curb the spread of the "cult" but was also suspicious of outsiders because Konyak Baptists have been portrayed by some investigators as oppressors of the minority Yahoi. Chemyuh is an astute church administrator and adept fundraiser; over his tenure many development projects by the mission centre have flourished. An acquaintance of his told me the executive secretary also works part-time as a contractor, which his critics say is unbecoming of a Baptist minister. But such criticisms are dismissed as "negligible" since Chemyuh has steered the KBBB to heights unachieved since the mission centre was shifted to Mon in 1978. The biggest challenge in recent years has been Yahoi Walim, the woman who ingeniously deployed a popular millenarian belief among the Konyak faithful against the Konyak Baptist church.

Yahoi Walim was born sometime in the 1950s in Wangti village in the Chen area near the Indo–Myanmar border, into a family practising the traditional religion. Yahoi, the oldest child of Nyemlao Walim, converted to the Baptist faith in 1964 when the new religion reached their area. Her early education in her native village was followed by middle school in Monyakshu and theological studies in a Baptist seminary run by the Chakhesang Baptist Church Council in Pfutsero town of Phek district. After her graduation she settled in a small town, Aboi, in Mon district, to work as a teacher in a Baptist church-run school. She was actively involved in the Baptist ministry before founding her popular charismatic sect at the turn of the century. Konyak Baptist believers say she was a disgruntled church worker who went rogue after falling out with the Konyak Baptist front body.

Yahoi is a gifted orator, reputedly a medium, and a divine healer. A registered Baptist who works in the police department in Mon town, Chingshei told me with unconcealed sarcasm: "Yahoi speaks with such charisma and conviction that even staunch believers can be easily persuaded to her side; she claims to have divine gifts, but there is no doubt that being honey-tongued is one of them." Yahoi male followers are noticeable in the streets for their long flowing hair; some of the faithful tie their long tresses into a bun hidden beneath a cap, perhaps to conceal their identity in a Baptist-majority town. Of late, Yahoi followers, invariably converts from the Baptist denomination, have become more open and operate freely since their numbers have increased and the faith is becoming popular among the masses. This new sect is conspicuous by its eccentric apparel, finicky food habits, intense worship pattern, a unique chain of command, and organisational novelty; the Baptist majority find their unconventional teachings and practices bothersome.

They charge the Yahoi cult with disreputable practices and false teachings; the Yahoi deny wrongdoing, claiming to be bearers of the new truth and heirs to divinely revealed plans for the new age. They say they have superseded the Baptists – claims not very different from those made by the Baptist faith when it supplanted the traditional religion in Konyak society. The Konyak Baptist leadership and churches have denounced the group as heretics, if not religious kooks, but this has not stopped several Baptist adherents from defecting to Yahoi.

A former head of the KBBB, Rev. Yamyap Konyak, admitted that the rise of the Yahoi cult represents an existential threat to Konyak Baptist churches. Like most Naga Baptist leaders, Yamyap had not anticipated an ordinary woman from a remote village rising to lead a popular religious movement with thousands of followers: "It was during my tenure as executive secretary of the KBBB that I wrote a recommendation letter for Yahoi to study in a Baptist College in Phek district; she was then a young adult with a likeable personality, polite and soft-spoken, and very keen to join the church ministry," Yamyap told me.

Before the Baptist mission's dominance the genius of Yahoi Walim would have been snuffed out by her social status and gender – as a woman born into a commoner's family. But within the new milieu, in which a potent blend of Baptist faith and modernity has shaped the contours of Konyak society and culture, new roles and social hierarchies were created within which religious innovators like Yahoi could emerge and thrive. Modernity generated new apprehensions, aspirations, and an identity crisis that gave ample scope for these new religious leaders to feed off the neurosis in a new social world shaped largely by the American Baptist faith.

Initially, Yahoi had no intention of forming a new religious group, but some of her teachings contested mainstream Baptist teachings and doctrines and therefore became unpopular with the church; so she formed a new religious group comprising preponderantly rural followers, all former Baptists who opted out of their church.

The strain of the Baptist faith prevalent in the Konyak area is a version of twentieth-century Pentecostalism which, as noted earlier, places great emphasis on the Holy Spirit's work via miracles and divine intervention. Also, Konyak Nagas at the grassroots are still enthused with Naga ethnonationalism, largely because a good number of them live in areas adjoining Myanmar where the idea of a united Naga homeland remains alive. Yahoi's teachings appealed to a large section of Konyak Baptists; her doctrines are a blend of primal religion and Christianity with a dash of Hinduism and a topping of ethnonationalism. Yahoi adherents claim that the group is in possession of a "Naga script" which is not of this world, but from a divine source, and that someday when Nagas attain independence they will use this special script. Konyak Baptist leaders have clandestinely procured this "Naga script", of which Chemyuh gave me a photocopy.

The script appears no different from a so-called Naga script that I have come across which is publicised by the followers of Heraka, a politico-religious movement revolving around the cult of Rani Gaidinliu (1915–1993), a Rongmei Naga from Tamenglong district, Manipur. "Yahoi had been in touch with Heraka followers and came under the influence of Hinduism. The Naga script was borrowed from Heraka followers, which Yahoi brought to the Konyak soil," Chemyuh told me.

For her notion of the divine source of the Naga script Yahoi received support from the veteran Konyak ethnonationalist leader Khole Konyak: she claims that without the script Naga independence will not be realised. A Naga faction, National Socialist Council of Nagaland (Khaplang) NSCN(K), with a stronghold in the Indo–Myanmar border area, allowed Yahoi to carry out her work in the region, but the Konyak Union and the Konyak Baptist church opposed her mission. In 2010, and a second time in 2012, the Konyak Union burnt down a Yahoi prayer house in Mon, but this did not stop the group garnering devotees; Yahoi proved as resilient as pioneering Konyak Baptist converts during the initial years of the Baptist movement.

Resistance from the formidable Baptist church have failed to stop her: "Religious movements are difficult to stop once they appeal to the masses; the pressure from the Baptist church did not stop the Yahoi movement but rather encouraged its growth. A timeless saying that persecution is the seed of a religious movement can be applied here," says Chingmei, a young Konyak social worker in Mon town. Some of his relatives had become Yahoi and Chingmei declared that many beliefs and practices of the Yahoi cult are questionable, but it has catered to religious seekers; it would be better if the Baptists perform their religious duties faithfully and let the Yahoi movement die out. The Yahoi cult does not have a centralised authority and a chain of command like the Baptists; unless it copies the blueprint of the Baptist church, it will not survive for long; people's interest in this cult will wane once their religious fervour subsides.

Being the head of Konyak Baptist churches, Chemyuh was less optimistic. Conflicts, because of the entry of new denominations in the Baptist stronghold, are common among other Naga communities as well, but they have never had to contend with a denomination or sect originating as a personality cult. Chemyuh says

> Yahoi's rise to power is sensational; she now has gun-toting bodyguards keeping a constant vigil over her; this is remarkable for a woman whom nobody knew some years ago. Power and fame are alluring and contagious. The Yahoi adherents have increased in number, because they have been goaded into thinking that they are people of great significance; that they matter; this has appealed to a lot of people in the villages whose access to power and fame is limited.

He was particularly worried at her even having convinced a certain *angh* to join up by "telling the *angh* that god has chosen him, and that he will be greatest among all the Konyak *anghs*."

Chemyuh was willing to lay bare the fallibilities of the Konyak Baptist church, but believes Yahoi is distorting the scriptures and subverting church tradition. "First of all, Yahoi is not an indigenous Konyak Naga religion; I want outsiders writing on the issue to be clear on this matter," Chemyuh says as a caveat before expatiating on the doctrines of the sect:

> The Yahoi cult group have become more secretive and wiser regarding their beliefs and practices; they have got rid of some practices which the Baptists opposed as false teachings and not within the confine of mainstream Christianity. There were even reports that Yahoi followers would wallow in muddy ground during special gatherings; even today the devotees go into deep jungles on full-moon nights to

hold prayer and worship sessions. I am sure that is the video clip that you must be talking about, which was shared widely in the social media.

Chemyuh was alluding to my query on the recording of a Yahoi full-moon midnight worship service that had recently gone viral in Naga Baptist cicles. He continued:

Yahoi claims that the Old Testament name for god 'Yahweh' is in fact her name 'Yahoi'. Her followers also began to call her *sakizu*, which is a native term for 'witness', because she extrapolated from the Book of Revelation, chapter 11: she claims to be the first angel mentioned there. She claimed that god had created Adam and Eve from the soil taken from Shangnyu village [in Mon district], and that the Garden of Eden must therefore be in Shangnyu soil. They try to follow the Mosaic Laws in Old Testament, saying that the Bible must be followed in its entirety. Yahoi even makes a remarkable claim that the Bible is incomplete, and therefore one of her missions is to complete God's revelation to humanity. She claims that the Holy Bible is outdated, except for the Book of Revelation and the commandments of Moses, and so must be renewed. She has told her followers that within a hundred years she will rewrite the Bible.

"As for her followers," he continued,

they behave like the Nazirites in the Old Testament; they do not eat pork, rodents and certain fishes restricted in the Old Testament; the menfolk keep long hair and walk barefoot; the devotees build small huts outside their homes as worship places and keep their valued items there. They design and wear clothes of different colours according to the social and religious rankings – *anghs*, priests, leaders and commoners. These *anghs* are not the traditional royals, but are appointed according to the inspiration of the spirit; besides they have spirit-appointed pastors, deacons and other leaders of the group. Yahoi worshippers do not have a permanent worship place, but they keep shifting their dwelling place wherever the Holy Spirit guides them and directs them. They worship and pray in places and spots which people think are haunted by malicious spirits, such as lakes, caves, mountains and forests. Following the traditional practices, they sprinkle salt in the new settlement before making a fire; they offer a portion of food to the main post of the house in addition to other rituals performed in the traditional religion. In relation to Christianity, they use the Bible and Baptist hymnal; appoint church leaders in various capacities; collect tithes and offerings; organise prayer meetings and fasting; and believe in the power and working of the Holy Spirit. They do not use the name Jesus, but say 'lord'; otherwise their worship pattern is almost same as the Baptists.

As head of the Konyak Naga Baptist church, Chemyuh's worst fears came true when the governor of Nagaland inaugurated a new village of Yahoi settlers in December 2017. The Konyak Baptist leadership as a whole was perturbed by the fact that the state was now getting involved in religious hostilities and the possibility that the governor – not popular among Christians in the state – would side with the Yahoi group. Already wary of the Bharatiya Janata Party (BJP) – the ruling party at the centre known for its Hindu nationalist opposition to religious minorities – the church feared Hindu right-wing organisations combining with "state protectionism" to give greater leverage to the Yahoi group. "Yahoi followers are claiming the status of an indigenous group, which is fallacious, because except for our religious differences, we are all Konyak Nagas, an indigenous tribe; also Yahoi is a syncretised religion borrowing elements from various religious traditions, and it has little connection with the Konyak ancestral religion, although they have revived certain aspects of traditional beliefs," Chemyuh declared.

The issue is certainly complex. The governor of Nagaland, P.B. Acharya, started out as a student activist of the Akhil Bharatiya Vidyarthi Parishad (ABVP) and is now a political strategist for the BJP in north-east India. Any new iconoclastic religious movement that contradicts Baptist Christianity is, in the view of Baptists, grist to the BJP mill. Acharya's track record as an ardent promoter of "indigenous religions and tribal cultures" has not escaped people's notice; his detractors argue there is more to him than meets the eye: he is promoting Hinduism under the garb of preserving diverse cultures and identities.

A prominent Angami Naga Baptist leader told me, no holds barred, that the governor is "an RSS man". The Nagaland Baptist Church Council (NBCC) leaders who have done their homework say Acharya, a Hindu Brahmin from Karnataka, has long been an active promoter of the BJP in north-east India. He maintains a close relationship with the leaders of a reformed traditional religion, Heraka, found among the Zeliang Nagas of Peren district in Nagaland.

The Konyak Baptist leadership was apprehensive that the Yahoi founder had come under Heraka influence: "There is a connection between Yahoi and Heraka; Heraka is already a well-established religious group and Yahoi adherents are adopting a similar strategy", Chemyuh says. The Yahoi faith stands out as a syncretic form of Christianity in comparison to Heraka and Donyipolo, the latter a reformed traditional religion of the Tani-speaking group in Arunachal Pradesh. These two reformed religions are anti-Christian and anti-Western in their stance and hinge on their indigeneity status, whereas the Yahoi movement claims it has superseded the mainstream Christianity of Baptists and Catholics; they claim they are the new truth bearers and practitioners of the one true faith; and their claim rests on the prophesies of their leader and rarely on things of the past. In fact, Yahoi followers are infuriated by the Baptist charge that they have appropriated the traditional religion.

The Konyak Union hit out at the governor in a local daily for "meddling" in Konyak Naga customary law. The statement in the daily read:

> Asserting that only it has authority over social and cultural lives and tradition of Konyaks, Konyak Union (KU) has denounced the royal coronation ceremony (Pongyin Mozu Moyong) organised by a section of 'social renegades' and [a] cult that had deviated from the parent traditional norms near Wangti village on February 1 this year. It has

also asked Governor PB Acharya not to interfere in the traditional custom and practices of the Konyak community.[22]

Some Naga Baptist leaders have begun comparing Yahoi with the Rongmei Naga mystic and leader Gaidinliu, which does not bode well for her followers, for reasons made apparent below.

In Kohima, about 350 km from the KBBB centre in Mon town, a cultural war revolving around the cult of Gaidinliu had been simmering. Below the Nagaland secretariat, on the outskirts of the state capital, an unfinished two-storey building lies exposed to the region's unrelenting monsoon. With generous funding from the centre, the state government had initiated a project to establish a "Naga culture centre" here in memory of Gaidinliu, a legendary Naga personality born in Tamenglong, Manipur. The landowners, the Angami Naga, opposed the idea of starting a memorial for the Naga leader who, they said, was an outsider (she was from Manipur) and had made no contribution to Nagaland state; meanwhile, the Angami Christians argued that the memorial was a ploy to bring in "Hindutva ideology in the name of development". As one Angami leader in Kohima said:

> Why this surging interest in Rani Gaidinliu in Nagaland among the political elites after the BJP came to power at the centre? I was also told that the government is trying to name Dimapur airport after Rani Gaidinliu, which is preposterous; why not name the airport after Hokishe Sema, Shilu Ao, J.B. Jasokie or S.C. Jamir, even if not A.Z. Phizo, who is not acceptable to the Indian government, since these Naga leaders are responsible for founding Nagaland in 1963, I am not denouncing Rani Gaidinliu, nor discrediting her legacy, but just stating the fact that she has not contributed to the formation of Nagaland as a state under the Indian Union.

Naga tribesmen have not forgotten that in the mid-1960s this mystic Naga lady had opposed the Naga National Council

[22] "KU denounces Pongyin Mozu Moyong; hits out at Governor", *Nagaland Post*, 3 July 2018.

(NNC) movement spearheaded by the Naga nationalist leader A.Z. Phizo; besides, the Heraka movement had openly defied the Baptist mission, and Gaidinliu's successors had made great strides in their anti-Western and anti-colonial stance, charging fellow Nagas with embracing a "foreign religion". And to top it all, a gradual Hinduisation of the Heraka religious movement has made its founder, Gaidinliu, a controversial figure in the Naga Baptist world.

6

Legends, Mystics, and Converts

My great hope of evangelizing India is in pressing home upon these poor deluded natives the truths of Christianity, and I believe the cross will yet triumph over idolatry.

– E.W. Clark, missionary to the Nagas, 1869

India is a secular state. It has equal respect for all religions. Even if constitution is not secular, Hindu Dharma was never against any religion because of its all-inclusive and all-pervasive character rather it welcomed Christianity and Islam in the early days. We expect that they would also have the same attitude toward Hindu Dharma at least on the soil of India – the place of origin of Hindu Dharma.

– Rani Gaidinliu, letter to prime minister during the visit of Pope John Paul II to India, 1986

IN WHAT CAN BE called a middle-class neighbourhood of Kohima town, populated largely by state government employees, a "type-five quarters" built by the state government remains overshadowed amid multistoreyed buildings of various sizes crammed asymmetrically on a hillside. A narrow and steep alley leads to a house built in the typically drab official style that mushroomed in the capital after statehood in 1963. In recent years this unassuming house has seldom seen visitors, but not long ago top Indian government officials, political leaders, and important public figures, including the controversial, frequented it. This is where the charismatic Naga leader Gaidinliu was rehabilitated after she laid down arms in 1966 and emerged overground. Post-surrender, Gaidinliu continued to play an important role among her tribesmen, the Zeliangrong Nagas – dispersed through Assam, Manipur, and Nagaland – as she successfully amassed a large following based on her personality cult.

The neologism Zeliangrong is relatively recent and gained currency only in the mid-twentieth century.[1] In the past, the Zeme, Liangmai, and Rongmei Naga groups which formed the Zeliangrong were known to their neighbouring communities by different names: the Meitei called the Rongmei settled in Imphal valley "Kabui"; the British called the Zeme and Liangmai in Manipur "Kacha Nagas"; the Kuki collectively called the Zeme, Liangmai, and Rongmei "*milong*", or referred to the Rongmei alone as "Kabui"; the "menacing" Angami Nagas called the Zeme and Liangmai "*mezhamia*"; and after statehood the Zeme and Liangmai, who inhabit present-day Peren district, were officially named Zeliang.[2]

Gaidinliu had strategically established her stronghold along a receding range of hills in the southern part of Nagaland (now Peren district), which forms a contiguous Zeliangrong territory with the western part of Tamenlong district in Manipur, and Dima Hasao district (formerly North Cachar Hills district) in Assam. Her movement for a separate Zeliangrong homeland within the Indian union coincided with an unrelenting armed insurrection for Naga self-rule being waged by the Naga National Council (NNC) against the Indian state. Therefore the government of Nagaland, which had enough trouble on its hands in the newly created state, decided to rehabilitate Gaidinliu and her armed followers. At the peak of Gaidinliu's movement the state authorities

---

[1] The available records show that the term "Zeliangrong" was coined on 15 February 1947 in Imphal, Manipur, during a meeting of the cognate groups Zeme Liangmai, Rongmei, and Puimei. See Pamei, *The Trail from Makuilongdi*, 51; All Zeliangrong Students' Union, *A Brief Account*, 1.

[2] Peren, which was carved out from Kohima district, became the eleventh district of Nagaland in 2003.

had in fact planned a harsh step: to relocate the Zeliang Naga villages supporting Gaidinliu so as to dismantle her support base and push her out of Nagaland; this was in the hope that "she and her men would be deprived of their food and refuge and then forced to surrender." However, the government was apprehensive of trouble erupting among the Zeliangrong Nagas in neighbouring states, and as this was bound to affect Nagaland, the plan was abandoned.[3] After Gaidinliu's surrender the state government provided her with bodyguards, an official vehicle, and a house in a neighbourhood of Indian bureaucrats and state government officials; the government also provided her with monthly "bags of rice" which became irregular over time, as Gaidinliu's surviving relatives, who still live in her Kohima quarters, told me.

The recipient of a Padma Bhushan, India's third-highest civilian award, Gaidinliu also received a small stipend from the central government as an Indian freedom fighter, an endorsement from none other than Jawaharlal Nehru. It was Nehru who bestowed on Gaidinliu the title "Rani", which then became the honorific prefixed to her name. The two leaders had first met while Gaidinliu was serving life imprisonment in Shillong Jail for rebelling against the British government. The honorific, not even remotely related to traditional Naga usage, became Gaidinliu's trademark as her fame spread far beyond the landlocked hills of Tamenglong. At the time of her death in 1993 she was a national figure, with admirers and followers comparing her to the Rani of Jhansi and Veer Savarkar. However, to the Baptist mission – a force that outlived the British empire in the Naga country – Gaidinliu presented a conflicting case of ethnic self-pride and religious resilience; the faithful saw her legacy as an impediment to their evangelical worldview.

---

[3] According to S.C. Dev, the state government had sanctioned lakhs of rupees to shift five villages, namely Nsong, Njana, Ngalong, Nkio, and Lalong, to Dimapur area and keep them under surveillance. See Dev, *Nagaland*, 69–70.

Gaidinliu's journey to prominence began in 1932 when, as a young girl of sixteen, she succeeded a Rongmei mystic and millenarian leader, Jadonang (1905–1931), who had during British rule envisioned a Zeliangrong homeland. The young Jadonang, barely out of his teens, advanced the idea of a Naga Raj with himself as its messiah king. His movement came to be known variably as the "Kabui Naga movement", "Kacha Naga movement", or "*kamphai* movement" – *kamphai* being a pejorative Zeme Naga word, meaning "failed group".[4] Within his short lifespan Jadonang established himself as an enigmatic figure and trailblazer; his followers down the line imputed to him lofty roles such as cultural reformer, millenarian prophet, spiritual guide, bard, physician, seer, and hero of the Zeliangrong people – if not all Nagas. But even as he garnered admirers and supporters and inspired generations of his tribesmen, Jadonang aroused detractors and critics: the man and his movement became contested categories bewildering scholars and the laity on both sides.

Religious beliefs then, as now, were intrinsic to the Naga conception of the universe, and so Jadonang, the Rongmei Naga "seer" from Puiluan village, merged religious revivalism with the idea of an ethnic homeland – "Naga Raj".[5] It was a political masterstroke, for the revitalisation movement that Jadonang pioneered touched the very soul of an ethnic group seen as underdogs living in the midst of two dominant communities – the Kuki and the Meitei – whom Jadonang's tribesmen identified as the "other". Besides, colonial rule in combination with the new effervescent faith – censured as the white man's religion – was seen as bulldozing its way among the Kuki and Naga communities, which gave some leverage to the millenarian leader.

The obverse was an image of Jadonang as a charlatan, a troublemaker, and pernicious character – as he appeared to his many

---

[4] Zeliang, *A Brief History of Zeliangrong Heraka Movement*, 84.

[5] Puiluan is now the Rongmei village of Kambiron in Tamenglong district, Manipur.

detractors and critics. One contemporary British writer, for example, calls Jadonang and Gaidinliu an "idolatrous pair".[6] Regarding the incident which finally sent Jadonang to the gallows, another says the British authorities apprehended a "Kambiron buck" who, in a moment of drunken bravado, bragged that he had with a few companions killed four Manipuri traders. Investigating this report the British found evidence "to hang Jadonang for murder by human sacrifice, and to jail for several years the bucks who had done the butchery for him."[7] The conspiracy theory on the event is that it was a plot hatched to besmirch Jadonang's image, get rid of him, and tear down his movement. In this many see the dubious hand of the Kukis and Meiteis, not to mention the British. The argument is that Jadonang's religious reform included a ban on pointless animal sacrifices, and so human sacrifice was out of the question. After his hanging, Jadonang attained a cult following among Zeliangrong Nagas, many of whom rejected outright colonial writings and narratives critical of him.

For many a devout Naga Baptist, Jadonang's claim to messianic divine revelation from his god in Bhuban cave (in Dima Hasao district), and widespread stories of British soldiers shooting his pet pythons and ransacking his temple (mentioned in colonial reports) made him controversial and sinister. Jadonang's pet pythons had a long-term effect: up to the time of her death, Gaidinliu had to live with the rumour that she was rearing pet pythons inside a dark room, practising black magic.

Besides the British, Jadonang's movement featured the Kukis as antagonists. Jadonang castigated the British government for taxation, forced labour, and "preferential treatment" of Kukis and Meiteis over his tribesmen. Historically, the gun-wielding Kukis had the upper hand in inter-village conflicts and ethnic-based skirmishes,[8] but there were also several villages where Kukis and

---

[6] See Steyn, *Zapuphizo*, 50.
[7] Bower, *Naga Path*, 45–6.
[8] The British reported that between 1907 and 1917 as many as 1195 guns

Zeliangs coexisted and had long-standing cultural and linguistic relations.[9] However, the Kukis – an expansionist tribe with a chieftainship system – were charged with unwarranted encroachment into Zeliangrong land.[10]

The young millenarian leader was successful in rallying his people against the British, the Christian missions, and the Kukis.[11] Graham Bower observed that behind the rapid success of "the Kacha Naga movement" was pent-up animosity towards the Kukis that finally found an incendiary release: "Their programme was an attractive one, the very blue-print of a Naga heaven – the millennium was at hand, the faithful were to spend everything in one stupendous feast, massacre the Kukis and live in plenty ever after on their Gods' miraculous bounty; and cash and converts came rolling in."[12]

The Baptist mission stood out like a sore thumb, a grievance fuelling Jadonang's uprising against British "imperialists" seen as aiding and abetting missionaries to destroy the traditional way of life. Nonetheless, this did not prevent Jadonang ingeniously borrowing elements from Christianity, alongside Meitei Vaishnavism, for his religious reform movement. This legacy outlived his short-lived uprising; whether through divine inspiration or not, Jadonang had discovered the holy grail of ethnic movements of indigenous communities around the world: cultural resilience and ethnic self-pride. His able successor, Gaidinliu, would build upon his legacy in nurturing an alternative religion, Heraka, to

---

were confiscated from the Kukis. See Administrative Report of Manipur, 1918–19.

[9] In villages like Chamcha, Henima, Kholuilen, Jolpi, Tolpi, and Paona, the Kukis and Zeliangs lived in the same village, often with headmen from both the communities.

[10] The belief is that knowledge of guns gave leverage to the Kukis led by autocratic chieftains. See Nagaland State Archive, Kohima, File No. 131, "Brief Memorandum on the Naga Country by John Butler", 1873.

[11] See Yonuo, *Nagas Struggle against the British Rule*, esp. Chapter 1.

[12] Bower, *Naga Path*, 46.

withstand the Baptist juggernaut, and this religion continues to thrive.

The Heraka movement did not become popular in its place of origin in the Tamenglong Hills, but spread to the lowlands in Assam, the Imphal valley, and Nagaland. In Nagaland's Peren district, the battle lines have been drawn between Heraka followers and the Baptist faithful. The largest concentration of the Heraka faithful is in Dima Hasao district, Assam, which is contiguous with the Zeliang Naga territory in Nagaland. Though Zeliang Nagas are ardent followers of the Baptist faith, the presence of a traditional reformed religion like Heraka gives rise to a complex relationship between ethnic affiliation and religious allegiance, unlike that among other Naga groups.

II

The affable David Hanneng's wry smile betrayed a painful memory as he pointed me to a spot behind the kitchen: "This is where my family dug a pit to hide ourselves if we came under attack; almost every family in the village had dug similar pits to keep themselves out of harm's way," he said. Unlike the family of our common acquaintance Khupma in neighbouring Molvom, David's family had been spared the misery of hiding in a septic tank when miscreants torched the village late one night in 1995. Standing sombrely in the kitchen garden, David reminisced about the ethnic conflict in the 1990s that had affected his village, Maova, in Medziphema subdivision, 38 km from Dimapur town. Tall areca nut trees of at least twenty years now flourish where the pit was, but David like other inhabitants in Maova and other Kuki villages in adjoining areas has been scarred by the ethnic conflict: "The main problem suffered is not the physical harm, but the fear psychosis that is still ingrained in us." His father, fearing eviction by the dominant Naga population surrounding them, had had to sell off at throwaway prices to their Angami neighbours the many forest lands and terrace fields that he owned.

The Kukis settled in the present Athibung circle in Peren district and Medziphema subdivision in Dimapur district had long lived in proximity with the Angami and Zeliang Nagas. Interaction between these communities had been through important historical events such as the formation of the Naga Hills district in 1866, the coming of the American Baptist mission, and the First World War. The antiquity of the ethnic Kukis in the Naga Hills is debated, although some trace it to the seventeenth century.[13] However, the Kuki settlement in the lowland area of Medziphema is dated to the first quarter of the twentieth century, and the new villages here shared something in common: they were the persecuted followers of a new religion. The long arm of the American Baptist mission had reached the Kukis of the Naga Hills.

While travelling in the hills towards Piphema (on NH29, between Dimapur and Kohima), where there was once a British rest house, one gets a scenic view of a fertile valley occupied by Kukis and contiguous with the Zeliang Naga territory stretching far into the horizon; the flatland has been mostly converted into wet paddy fields, adding to the spectacular beauty of the valley, with the towering Barail range in sight. Nestled among the hills, the mist-covered valley in the morning and the green plains opening up to clear blue skies in the afternoon appear serene, almost heavenly; it is hard to believe that such a landscape has been fraught with ethnic differences, land disputes, and denominational schisms.

The Kuki–Naga conflict that was sparked off in 1992 and engulfed Manipur state spilled into the adjoining area in Nagaland, putting the minority Kukis at a disadvantage. "Many who read or hear about the conflict think that it was a Kuki and Naga conflict, but the issue had nothing to do with the Nagas of Nagaland,

---

[13] According to oral tradition (counting the generation depths), Songlhuh village adjoining Athibung township is said to have existed since the seventeenth century. Ghosh also traces the Kuki settlement in the Naga Hills to the seventeenth century: see Ghosh, *A History of Nagaland*, 54. In one of the earliest census operations during British rule, the Kuki population of the Naga Hills was estimated to be 2524 in 1869–70.

although the Angami Nagas taking advantage of the tumult bought Kuki lands at throwaway prices. More precisely the real conflict was between the Kuki and the Tangkhul Nagas supported by the NSCN(IM)." This was David's blunt view – the kind that ruffles many feathers.

David's ongoing doctoral thesis from Visva-Bharati University is on the Kukis of the Naga Hills, the first of its kind. He has sifted through the colonial archives and most of the relevant writings, but his painstaking research also seems driven by the need to prove that the Kukis of Nagaland are not outsiders or immigrants, as commonly perceived. David had this to say:

> During the colonial period the Kukis of Naga Hills were not seen as very different from their Naga neighbours; the Kukis were signatories of the Naga Club in 1918; the Kukis were among signatories who sent a memorandum to the Simon Commission in 1929; the Kukis were also part of a 16-point agreement, and joined the self-determination movement led by the NNC; in fact we have been part of all the important events in Naga history, you name it; but the Kukis have now been reduced to a state where we are struggling for survival.

Kukis are recognised as one of the sixteen tribes of Nagaland, and despite their distinguishable ethnicity have been subsumed within dominant Naga society. Like the Kukis of Manipur who speak the language of the dominant Meitei community, the Kukis of Nagaland speak Nagamese, intermarry with Naga groups, and share many cultural similarities: "We do not get along well with the Kukis of Manipur and the Mizos because of shared idiosyncrasies with the Nagas," David chuckled. As regards religious life, the Kukis became part and parcel of Baptist denominational politics in Nagaland.

Christianity in north-east India has roots in both the Welsh Presbyterian mission and the American Baptist mission, but the Baptist faith remains notable in the Kuki "traditional homeland" extending to Chin state, Myanmar, and the Chittagong Hills of Bangladesh, notwithstanding the switching of denominations that sometimes happens. David believes "The Kuki Baptists miscalculated church politics. They should have stayed with the NBCC [Nagaland Baptist Church Council] instead of shifting to KCC [Kuki Church Council]; this positioned the Kukis of Nagaland as different from the Nagas with whom they have had shared significant ties dating back to Rev. Rivenburg in Kohima." David's father had served as a Baptist pastor once, but the family "defected" to the KCC and later joined the charismatic Christian Revival Church (CRC) that superseded the KCC, the latter being no different from the Baptists in liturgy, doctrines, and practice. According to the Baptists, the formation of the KCC was propelled by ethnic self-interest, the result of a "dubious" alliance between religion and ethnic identity, while KCC adherents in Nagaland charge the Baptists with stepmotherly treatment of Kuki Baptists.

Maova with more than 130 households has four churches belonging to three denominations. Along with four other villages in Medziphema subdivision, its history is related to the American Baptist mission: all these villages began as Kuki Baptist settlements escaping mistreatment at the hands of traditional-faith adherents. Sirhima, the first Kuki village to come up in the Medziphema area, was established in 1905, although its official recognition came in 1912; the village owes its existence to a Kuki Baptist convert, Ngulhao Thomson, who was baptised while studying in a mission school in Kohima. With the help of Rev. Rivenburg, Ngulhao approached the British administration in Kohima to start a new village for followers of the new faith. Other villages in the Medziphema area (Molvom, Maova, Bungsang, and Khaibung) followed, becoming vibrant Kuki Baptist communities. Kuki Baptists say it was the famed Angami evangelists Rev. Nisier and Rev. Krunieze who planted the first Kuki Baptist church in Sirhima in 1912, and next in Chalkot village in the Athibung area in 1917.

The Kuki and Zeliang Baptist association was formed under the Kohima mission field in 1926, bringing Kuki Baptists closer into the Naga Baptist fold. Kuki and Zeliang Baptists organised joint annual conferences and outreach programmes until their separation in 1953 on account of the language issue. David said candidly: "If the majority of the Kuki were still Baptists and with the NBCC, then Kuki society would have taken a different direction." He meant to say that Kuki social and religious life would have been significantly shaped by their Naga Baptist neighbours. The Baptist faith, which was a consequential bridge between the two ethnic groups, was severed when a new church politics emerged that mixed religious affiliation with ethnic identity.

The Baptist church in Maova looked desolate by comparison with the KCC church, the biggest in the village, as well as with the small but appealing CRC church which has an immaculately maintained compound. And, not far from the Baptist church compound, the Nepali church supported by the KCC looked better maintained. "This is the usual state of Baptist churches in Kuki villages," David said. When the KCC movement had run its course among the Kuki Christians, Kuki Baptists in Nagaland had been reduced to a minority.[14]

The predominance of a denomination or sect does not guarantee its perpetuity in the context of ethnic-based religious communities, as is observed with the ethnic Baptists of Nagaland. Sooner or later the rise of a charismatic leader can change the equation if he or she is able to offer an attractive blend of ethnic identity and religious tradition. For more than half a century, the Kukis in Nagaland adhered to the Baptist denomination, adding many converts to the fold. Only after the Baptists had long overwhelmed the followers of the traditional faith did the new sect, the KCC, with an alluring message of ethnic and religious solidarity, rout the Baptist bastion. The KCC owed its success to a gifted and charismatic Kuki Baptist minister with seminary training from the United States; word in Kuki Christian circles is that this Baptist theologian-turned-"dissident" was so brilliant that he had

---

[14] The Kuki Baptist Association headquarters is in Khaibung, Medziphema, with 14 churches and 1 fellowship and a total of 3191 baptised members (NBCC 2016 census).

within a year translated the entire Bible from Greek into the Kuki language.

David and his siblings were raised as Baptists, but his parents shifted to the KCC during the height of the denominational issue that besieged Kuki Baptist churches, especially in Manipur and Nagaland, during the 1970s. "The inception of KCC was more or less a one-man show," David avowed,

> the person behind the new denomination was Rev. Tongkhojang Lunkim, who is arguably the finest Kuki theologian of his generation; Rev. Lunkim from Kangpokpi district in Manipur conceived of a new association to unite the Kukis scattered across Manipur, Assam, Nagaland, and Tripura. Initially it was envisioned as an ethnic-based organisation, but it began to take a religious turn and his vision became widely popular among the Kuki Baptists who were under the MBC [Manipur Baptist Convention] and NBCC and other church associations in their domiciled home states.

The allure of a union of Kuki Christians separated by state boundaries made many people join the new denomination. Although the KCC was like old wine in a new bottle – its beliefs and practices were no different from those of the Baptists – it consolidated Kuki identity along the lines of denominational affiliation.

Treading on sensitive ground, David was circumspect in hinting that the denominational conflict with the Baptists did not bode well for the Kukis in Nagaland, and that in hindsight the NBCC, the most influential church organisation in the state, failed the Kukis during the ethnic conflict in the 1990s. "To my knowledge, the NBCC did not carry out a mass campaign nor did any Naga Baptist leader come to assure us during the thick of conflict," he said. Being a clear minority in Nagaland, the Kukis who had settled in the Medziphema and Athibung areas suffered the brunt of the conflict: "In Athibung area, there were incidents where the NSCN(IM) militants skipped the Baptist villages while burning down villages with KCC following; there are stories that some Kuki Baptist churches were told to raise a white flag to distinguish themselves," David told me.

Instances of miscreants sparing Baptist churches in Kuki villages have drawn the Naga Baptist church into the controversy. An elderly Baptist minister and former NBCC leader from Dimapur said that

> the church was against violence and condemned perpetrators on both sides; but in those days there was no proper medium to instantly disseminate news and happenings, and moreover, even the newspaper was in the formative stages in Nagaland, and these factors added to a lack of public awareness, including among the Baptist churches. In fact, except for Dimapur and Kohima districts, Nagas from other districts remained oblivious to the conflict. Tension was running high those days and the Baptist churches should have been more vocal and proactive, but the church was caught unawares.

Though in Manipur, the epicentre of the conflict, some Baptist leaders from the warring groups carried out peace and reconciliation drives to defuse tensions and build inter-ethnic relations, they were largely overshadowed by the hideousness of the violence that captured the attention of the world. "Some Baptist leaders like my father and Rev. Kaikho Hokey, past-General Secretary of the MBC, from the Mao Naga community, went to the worst affected areas conducting church services and reconciliation meetings at the peril of their own lives, but are hardly remembered. It is rather the hardcore ethnonationalists on both sides, who still harp on the past for political gains, who are heard by many," the eldest son of Rev. Prim Vaiphei, former president of Manipur Baptist Convention, told me.

Monstrous ethnic conflict can torpedo long-held religious teachings on ethics, but such difficult and harrowing times can also produce the best form of human fortitude and civility, as evident from the life of Satpau Hangsing, the eldest son of a Kuki Baptist convert who started the Baptist church in Chalkot village in Athibung area. Satpau lost his father and nephew to the conflict. The establishment of Chalkot in 1917 had historical connections with the American Baptist mission in Kohima and Satpau's father, Douseh Hangsing, the chief of the village, had started the settlement.

On 4 March 1993 some armed men came to Chalkot and burned down the village, but not before shooting the chief and some village men in cold blood. Satpau, the chief's eldest son and heir, was in Shillong for his studies when the incident happened; "If it were not for my faith in God, I would not have survived the ordeal," Satpau said. His grim face belied his composure as he narrated the incident: "That day most people had gone to the fields, otherwise the casualties would have been more. The gunmen ordered the men in the village to lie on the ground and sprayed them with bullets; most of them died on the spot, but my nephew was found breathing." Satpau's eyes welled up with tears as he remembered the trauma his nephew went through:

> We took him immediately to the hospital and transferred him to Vellore once he was out of ICU. Since his spinal cord was severely damaged, he could not stand or walk and so he had to be taken care of; we sold off lands for his treatment and even hired a physiotherapist from Australia, but to no avail; his upper trunk was getting healthier, but from the waist below his body withered. Knowing that he would not get any better, one afternoon I brought him a wheelchair; he had not shed a tear since the day he was shot, but seeing the wheelchair broke him and he cried for the first time in months. He passed away some months later.

Pastor Satpau confessed he has forgiven the perpetrators but lives with the memory of loss.

David Hanneng said the conflict was sparked off near the Indo–Myanmar border where the two communities had lived side by side for generations. "The Nagas will have their own version," he interjected, subtly invoking his researcher self, "but the violence that continued intermittently for nearly half a decade had been festering for generations, and finally burst out. It was the worst ethnic conflict between the two communities in generations. Among several causes, the Nagas in Manipur for one thing had not forgotten the high-handedness of the Kukis under their domineering chiefs in the colonial and the pre-colonial period."

David did not fail to mention that the presence of armed militants on both sides not only escalated the conflict but also spiked the casualty list.

The American Baptist mission that found success among the Kukis and Nagas had not addressed the ethnic dissonance between the groups, so when the conflagration began the Baptist message remained ineffective. In a way, the respective ethnic groups had domesticated the Baptist message and fashioned it according to their own ethnic and cultural dispositions. They invariably bore allegiance first to their ethnicity and next to the Baptist brotherhood – a phenomenon common to ethnic groups with large Baptist followings like the Chins, Karens, and Kachins in Myanmar.

By the close of the twentieth century, the Kukis and Nagas had both converted to Christianity in large numbers, but their shared religious affiliation mattered little when it conflicted with allegiance to an ethnic identity. Unlike mainland India, where communal riots are overwhelmingly religious in character, conflicts in the north-eastern states, including Baptist enclaves like Nagaland and Manipur, are primarily motivated by ethnic allegiances. Communal violence happens in the Assam and Imphal valleys – tension simmers between the Hindu majority Meitei people and the Pangal, an ethnic Muslim community, and erupted in the 1993 communal riots – but is sporadic in comparison to regions like north India. The plains more than the hills have generally been where Islamic and Hindu civilisations have flourished and clashed. And so in Assam even tribal communities of the plains have been dragged into the communal fires. But among these ethnic communities conflict over land and resources, and the fear of loss of cultural identity and inundation by "outsiders" always underlies the problem. Communal riots of a purely religious nature are relatively recent in north-east India and not necessarily rooted either in colonial history or in the post-independence phenomenon of Partition.

North-east India was a powder keg in newly independent India when it came to ethnic conflict. Ethnic communities with differing languages and cultures were numerous and had the "minority complex" fear of their land traditional and culture being overwhelmed by surrounding dominant communities and "outsiders". They had every reason to be fearful, it must be said, since several of these groups numbered only a few thousand and yet had nourished a distinct and rich cultural heritage as well as a proud history that were all vulnerable. Even a dominant group like the Assamese were not free of such fears because densely populated Bangladesh loomed large. For native inhabitants the immigrant who might overwhelm indigeneity presented a far bigger problem than the religious Other; religious identity could and sometimes did exacerbate conflict but was not the heart of the problem. As for the Kukis and the Nagas, their longstanding ethnic disputes were mostly over land and resources, often manifest as raids and the pillaging of villages. When the British entered the scene the rift between the two ethnic groups widened. After independence, the rise of ethnonationalism was the final nail in the coffin.

Sitting by the fireplace in the family's quasi-traditional Naga kitchen, David inched closer to his father and asked in a loud voice, "Was the *kamphai* army's harassment the main reason that Kukis of Mechangbung [his father's native village] relocated from Henima [Tening] area?" Haokhojang Hanneng, who is in his mid-70s is hard of hearing. He replied: "I left the village to study before the conflict began, but the villagers did face harassment from Rani Gaidinliu's army, and it made people abandon the village." Mechangbung was a Kuki village with a Zeliang population as well, but it is now an exclusively Zeliang village. Grey-haired Haokhojang maintained his composure while rehashing a past of hardships enough to last a man several lifetimes. David told me that Kuki villages like Chamcha, Holkang Songsang, and Sailhem in the Tening area had been abandoned around the time Gaidinliu went underground for the second time in the early 1960s. "The NNC armed fighters harassing these Kuki villages to collect tax and rations is common knowledge; however, the failings and mistakes of Rani Gaidinliu are rarely highlighted by mainland historians and her followers," David says.

That afternoon, at a white wedding in the small Revival Church in Maova, an elderly man solemnly told me a Kuki legend that the world will come to an end when the Kukis once again come to power. "Thangkam, the Kuki prophet of old, had already foretold that the Nagas would ascend after a long dominance of the Kukis; the Nagas are in power now, but the Kukis will rise again, and if Thangkam's prophesy is to be believed the world will come to an end." It appears that millenarian beliefs are common to both Kuki and Zeliangrong Nagas and have shaped the social history of both.

The legend still making the rounds in Maova is that the Rongmei mystic Jadonang, and the Kuki legendary sage Thangkam, studied together in a supernatural university in Koubru – a revered mountain in Manipur. Gaidinliu, who succeeded Jadonang and continued his legacy, overshadowing him in the process, achieved nothing less than demigod status, with some diehard followers seeing her as a goddess incarnate. A journey through Jadonang and Gaidinliu's region of influence reveals several myths and legends associated with them. These survive and flourish as more interested parties, including the Hindu Right, are captivated by their political possibilities.

What escapes the notice of many is the homely and mortal side of a charismatic woman revered by thousands; a closer look at her private life reveals Gaidinliu interacting closely with her devout Baptist relatives. In her humble residence in Kohima, she plunged herself in the religious environment common within every Naga Baptist household, but the Baptist influence failed to rub off on her. Her "favourite" nephew, Gaikhanglong, who now resides in her Kohima quarters, said his aunt may well have been convinced to change her mind had it not been for the thousands following her movement.

III

The modest room where "Ranima" – as Gaidinliu is reverentially addressed – slept is pleasant and simple, measuring about 3 × 4 metres. It is devoid of traditional paraphernalia, portraits, and embellishments that might remind visitors of the iconic figure. This is quite contrary to Heraka homes that I have come across where, along with the mandatory portrait of Gaidinliu, such paraphernalia is displayed in part as strident identity assertion. Portraits of Gaidinliu and Jadonang have even made their way into the stately hall of Nagaland's Raj Bhavan, courtesy the incumbent governor. They hang impressively alongside those of Indian freedom fighters like Mahatma Gandhi, Bhagat Singh, and Subhas Chandra Bose.

In Gaidinliu's old type-five quarters the drawing room in the middle is by far the most spacious, and here the family have kept some memorabilia that were presented to Gaidinliu during her nationwide tour. A memento that catches the eye is a black bust of Birsa Munda, the legendary nineteenth-century Adivasi leader from Chotanagpur. Surprisingly, there is no portrait of Gaidinliu, nor traditional objects, except for some Rongmei and Chang Naga decorative beads, miniature Naga shawls, and old paintings. The Naga Baptists are particular about the trimming down of religious icons in their homes and churches, but their obsession for pithy Bible verses is well known and it is no surprise that the former home of the Heraka movement founder is now decorated with framed and embroidered scriptural verses.

The walls separating the rooms are part-bamboo and part-concrete, particular to government-built quarters. Gaikhanglong described how, anytime Gaidinliu was home, his own devout Baptist parents would be praying in their bedroom while Heraka followers would be singing and dancing in the adjacent drawing room, as if engaging in a spiritual duel. There was no religious rivalry between Gaidinliu and her younger brother Kuisinang; he looked after her well and respected her deeply, but their lives took very different paths after her arrest by the British in 1932. Gaidinliu found national fame, founded a popular politico-religious movement, and her name entered the hall of the great, at least for her tribesmen and among a section of the mainland Hindu population. Meanwhile Kuisinang found a calling in his

Ill. 9: Rani Gaidinliu meeting Prime Minister Indira Gandhi at her residence in New Delhi, *c.* 1983. Courtesy DIPR.

newfound faith, served the Baptist church, and after his demise vanished into obscurity.

When the British hanged Jadonang on 29 August 1931 in Imphal they thought that would be the end of the "Kabui movement", but Jadonang's closest confidante, a girl of only sixteen, took the helm and the movement gained prominence. What Jadonang and Gaidinliu had in common was a resilient spirit, a charismatic presence, and an aura of mysticism all directed towards the vision of an ethnic homeland. Gaidinliu was born in 1915 (the fifth child of eight children born to Lothonang and Karotlenliu) in Lungkao in Tamenglong district, Manipur.[15] By her followers she was said to have led quite a miraculous childhood. Stories abound of the duo's encounter with the supernatural, but the most crucial and inventive one comes from their connection with the Bhuban sacred cave in Dima Hasao at the tri-junction of Assam, Manipur, and Mizoram. Briefly, the faithful believe that

---

[15] See Yonuo, *Nagas Struggle Against British Rule*, 84.

the god Tingwang revealed the Heraka tenets to Jadonang and Gaidinliu in Bhuban cave. This concept of divine revelation puts the Heraka religion on an equal footing with the Baptist faith in its claim to be revealed by the "one true god".

The claim of divine revelation legitimated Gaidinliu as the prophetess of the one true god, Tingwang. The superlatives that describe her deeds and achievements are the stuff of legend, but it was through her immediate family in Kohima that I was allowed to see the human if not the frail side of her. From what I could make out, she was neither superhuman nor the dreaded figure that admirers and dissenters make her out to be: she was a motherly figure, and almost certainly a woman in conflict with her beliefs and convictions. Gaidinliu's surviving family in Kohima are considered a sell-out for their Baptist allegiance and have come under criticism from Heraka followers for not staying true to her legacy. Gaidinliu's kin in Kohima retort that unscrupulous individuals have misused her name for their own ends and mired her legacy in a controversy she would never have wanted.

Next to the narrow entrance of Gaidinliu's well-maintained old quarters are tombstones of Kuisinang and his wife Tongpangnaro. The epitaph reads: "Earth has two gentle souls less ... Heaven has two special angels more. Thy remembrance shall endure all generations – Psalms 102." It is not surprising that Kuisinang's life story barely registers in the fecund writings on Gaidinliu. His Baptist inclinations are tepidly normal as against her fiery and impassioned political religiosity.

According to Gaikhanglong, his father when a young boy left for the jungles with Gaidinliu when she went into hiding from the British. The authorities captured Gaidinliu in 1932 in a Zeme Naga village, Poilwa, in the southern part of the British Naga Hills. J.P. Mills, the deputy commissioner who authorised the massive womanhunt, voiced his apprehension that "one or more mediums" would take over the movement even if Gaidinliu were captured. Contrary to the image by her supporters of a regal personage arrested by the British, the colonial authority on the

Zeme Naga, Ursula Graham Bower, gives a picture of the teenage Gaidinliu as a tomcat, "screaming, scratching and kicking and inflicting the only casualty on the expedition by biting a Naik severely in the thumb." This is at odds with her as divine-like leader whose "agents" even sold miracle water drawn from a local pond named "Gaidinliu water" for Rs 10 a bottle to ward off illnesses.[16] Gaidinliu was sentenced to life imprisonment and kept at various times in colonial prisons in Aizawl, Imphal, Guwahati, Tura, and Shillong; according to legend she once escaped by changing herself into a rat. As for Kuisinang, he was rehabilitated in Mokokchung, far from his native village.

The events leading to Gaidinliu's capture would go down in infamy since some Nagas who were British subjects aided the authorities; a "detested" name among the Heraka followers that often crops up is Dr Harielungbe Haralu, a Zeme Naga from Poilwa village, who had studied in a mission school and earned repute as the first Naga doctor. To make matters worse, Dr Haralu was a Baptist convert and it was said that in providing information to the British authorities he had responded to the call of duty. This embittered Heraka followers who charged the Baptists of working hand in glove with the British. The Kuki historian David Hanneng remarked perceptively that several acts of aggression and the arrests carried out by armed Kukis were more in obedience to the ruling authority of the day and less to do with ethnic conflict. The British did indeed sow the wind, and the natives reaped the whirlwind.

At the time of Gaidinliu's capture, her adversaries included the British, the Kukis, and the Christian mission. But after independence, being given a new lease of life, Gaidinliu's movement – which harped on cultural and religious revivalism – became "infamous", at least in the eyes of her opponents, for religious conflict. Both admirers and dissenters are unanimous that Gaidinliu's Heraka movement was a reformed version of a traditional religion known as *paupaise*, which was known for extravagant

---

[16] Bower, *Naga Path*, 47–8.

sacrifices that ate into the scarce resources of its practitioners. The religious reformation was not seamless because *paupaise* adherents accused Heraka followers of deviance. Thus, in some Zeliang Naga villages, boundary lines were drawn between the two religious groups – without the Baptists in sight.

Much to the annoyance of Heraka followers, Baptists charge them with killing Baptist believers. In Tousem, a large Zeme Naga village in Tamenglong district, the villagers have raised a monolith on which are inscribed the names of those killed by the "Heraka army" in the 1960s. The monolith in Tousem has been erected to cast a poor light on the "incidents of Rani Gaidinliu movement". The words on it read: "In 1960, before the incidents of Rani Gaidinliu movement, 222 households were living together peacefully. The conflict between Heraka cult and traditional beliefs culminated in division and split the village into five hamlets. Martyrs of the incident i) Tousem – 18 ii) Namtiram Baptist church – 4." A Zeme researcher has published a "controversial" book listing the names of people belonging to both the "animistic religion" and the Baptist faith killed by "Rani Gaidinliu's army" in the 1960s.[17]

By 1960, when Gaidinliu was underground, British rule had become a memory, though traces of colonialism remained in the shape of a fractious identity crisis. To followers of the reformed traditional religion, the Baptist faith was seen as a Western religion peddling pernicious Western culture and native Christian converts were seen as fifth columnists subverting their own distinctive way of life. As a revitalisation movement Heraka thrived on its anti-colonial, anti-Western, and anti-Christian worldview, and in all this the Baptist faith was the butt of their greatest scorn.

IV

The British authorities chose to rehabilitate Kuisinang, a native of Lungkao, in Mokokchung subdivision in the far north, where the

[17] See Zeliang, *A Brief History*, 72–80.

people had no inkling of Gaidinliu or her movement. Kuisinang grew up among strangers in this mixed settlement and learnt to speak several Naga languages. Being far removed from his home and people, the young boy began to identify more as a Chang Naga – the eastern Naga tribe we have encountered earlier in Tuensang district – since he came under the care of an influential Chang *dobashi* from Yimrup village. Yimrup became Kuisinang's adoptive village, and Gaidinliu too stayed there after her release from prison in 1947 – she was purposefully kept away from her area of influence in south Nagaland. Mokokchung, located in the heart of the Ao Naga country, was only 15 km from the thriving American Baptist mission station at Impur. At the time of Kuisinang's rehabilitation, Mokokchung was witnessing an exponential growth in Baptist converts; unsurprisingly, the prevailing religious climate of the place rubbed off on the young man. The baby brother of the nativist leader whose movement had been propelled by an anti-outsider and anti-Western stance embraced a "Western" religion, becoming its champion and following it steadfastly to his last breath.

After its success in Mokokchung, the Baptist mission movement was moving towards the land of unadministered tribes in the east. Kuisinang was by then a believer and married to a Chang Naga; being a conventional Baptist and a polyglot, he became involved in the Baptist mission's spread towards the land of his adoptive tribe, the Chang Naga. "My father could speak both Ao and Chang fluently and so when the well-known Ao Baptist missionary, Onenlepden, from Changki village went to the Chang Naga area, my father went along as his interpreter," Gaikhanglong said. Kuisinang had met his wife, Tongpangnaro, while in Mokokchung and even adopted an Ao Naga name, Merang. According to her family, Tongpangnaro was a spiritually gifted woman. Gaikhanglong said:

> My mother was from Yimrup, daughter of a Chang *dobashi*, whose parents were among the earliest converts from the village; not many people know of her but she had a deep respect for Ranima and prayed

for her soul and well-being till the end . . . On her release from prison, Ranima was sent off to Tuensang district so as to prevent her from mobilising followers and resuscitating the Naga movement; she lived for some time in Yimrup and became a citizen there. Ranima later left for her native place and once again went underground to fight for her people, but my father stayed back in Tuensang. It was only after Ranima surrendered to the government of Nagaland that my father, who was then employed as a peon in the Deputy Commissioner's office in Tuensang town, left everything to take care of Ranima in Kohima.

Kuisinang raised seven children, as was worthy of a bornagain Christian; the devout Baptist upbringing stayed with the children despite their sharing a close bond with their illustrious aunt. "When my father moved to Kohima to look after Ranima, he left his entire lifework in Tuensang out of selfless devotion to her. He remained a strong believer in Christ till his last breath, but to my knowledge not even once did he speak ill of Ranima or Heraka religion; he was a devoted Baptist but also believed in equal respect for all religions," Gaikhanglong said reverentially of his late father. "In fact, he was among the founding members of the Chang Baptist church in Kohima; it was my father along with four other families who toiled very hard to build that church from scratch," he added, mentioning a medium-sized church a few blocks away from Gaidinliu's old quarters.

Apparently, of all Kuisinang's children Gaikhanglong was Gaidinliu's favourite and became her close confidant. As the eldest son, he stayed in the service of his aunt for twenty-two years, even relinquishing his government job in the Art and Culture Department: "Ranima told me that life is worth more than government service, so I left my job to look after her and my parents. Many people will not acknowledge my many years' service and devotion to Ranima since I am not a Heraka believer, but I was like her personal bodyguard, driver, and unofficial personal secretary," Gaikhanglong said. In keeping with the tradition of his family, Gaikhanglong has raised his three children as dutiful Baptists.

Khoney, his eldest son and apparent spokesperson of Gaidinliu in the making, maintains the leader's paperwork and personal records that were left at the family's disposal, and corresponds with those interested in her legacy. Like his father, Khoney addresses Gaidinliu as "Ranima", speaking fondly of her and expressing exasperation at having to defend her memory from many "criticisms and malicious rumours" in the locality and beyond. He told me: "Since her arrival in Kohima we had to dispel malicious rumours about my aunt. Rumours were widespread that Ranima was a witch; that she gorges on human blood; that she rears pythons inside a dark room. Once we even challenged neighbours to come and see for themselves that there are no pet pythons in the house."

Gaikhanglong's situation is parlous, given his combination of Baptist belief and position as confidant-nephew of a highly controversial figure for Naga Baptists. His unease was palpable when the subject of Gaidinliu's religious reforms and her role as the Heraka movement's leader came up. He tried to distance his aunt from what the Naga Baptists see as a "dubious religious movement". His pressing concern now is to distance her from Naga Baptists who associate Gaidinliu with Hindu right-wing groups and project her as "a stooge of the RSS and VHP to penetrate the Christian heartland": this sentiment has been unabashedly expressed by a well-known Baptist pastor in Jalukie town. Gaikhanglong's riposte to this is to assert that "Ranima was more of a freedom fighter than a religious leader. It was Jadonang who was responsible for starting the Heraka religion." The problem is that Gaikhanglong served for many years as deacon in his local Baptist church and has been vocally critical of the rival religion: "I once told Heraka followers that theirs is a meaningless religion and it will die out when my aunt passes away; this was in Haflong in N.C. Hills." This kind of unswerving Baptist affiliation continues to displease Heraka followers; they consider it a betrayal of their leader by her closest relatives.

In the eyes of Baptists, Gaidinliu was no different from other humans who have perished without the assurance of salvation.

This Baptist belief in salvation by faith alone (*sola fide*) has not changed since the time of the American Baptist mission and puts the Naga Baptists in a fix, especially with liberal theology gaining prominence in Christendom. For a devout Baptist like Gaikhanglong the fear is not what the outside world thinks but a far more important existential problem: the question of life after death. His "demigod" aunt cannot fall outside the boundaries of his concern for her soul.

The family did try to make a Baptist out of Rani Gaidinliu: at home she was exposed to all manner of Baptist beliefs and practices. "Whenever Ranima was home she would join us during the family prayer meetings as we prayed and sang hymns. My father was very mission-minded and was also a deacon, so believers from Tuensang settled in Kohima town would come and have prayer meetings in our home; besides my mother was a devout believer and she unceasingly prayed for Ranima's life and well-being; many times my mother fasted and prayed for Ranima's salvation," Gaikhanglong said.

He believes Hindu right-wing groups have besmirched Gaidinliu's memory, that her movement has taken an unwarranted political turn. He was quick to mention that the Zeliangrong Heraka Palace Association (ZHPA) had split from the Heraka parent body, the Zeliangrong Heraka Association (ZHA), with the ZHPA charging the ZHA of moving away from Gaidinliu's original teaching and assimilating into the Hindu fold. Gaikhanglong argues that

> Ranima's Heraka movement was never associated with Hinduism; she was a national leader and so she met with people of high level from different faiths, but she had no intention of leading her followers into the Hindu fold. Some Heraka leaders are misusing her name for their own benefit and in the process have joined hands with Hindu organisations . . . While my aunt was alive many missionaries and pastors came to talk to her; contrary to what many think, Ranima was not very interested in religion, although she believed that religious reform is the best way to preserve the cultural tradition. She stayed in the traditional religion to promote her people's identity and culture . . .

Gaidinliu died in her old faith – a matter of great pride to her followers. For her practising Baptist relatives she died "without accepting Jesus Christ as her lord and saviour". Khoney, her grand-nephew, says, "I think Ranima accepted Jesus Christ towards the end of her life, and I think that her soul was saved, although she did not tell us of her personal beliefs." This is no doubt what he wants to believe, but it cannot be doubted that Gaidinliu would have been much more widely accepted among the Nagas had she been a Baptist: "The Nagas of Nagaland will not accept Ranima because of her religion; many know of her role as a freedom fighter, but are not willing to acknowledge it because of her association with Heraka," Khoney said sombrely.

Gaidinliu's role as one of India's freedom fighters is indeed much debated in the Naga community. Kailadbou Daimai, a Liangmai Naga linguist with a doctorate from Delhi University, maintained that "In hindsight, Rani Gaidinliu would have even fought against the Indian government to achieve a 'Naga Raj'; fortuitously the British happened to be the ruling authority of the day and the political consciousness emerged with them as the primary adversary." Although Gaidinliu's followers claim she was no less a stalwart than the other great nationalists, Naga critics say the "*kamphai* movement" was narrower and more localised than it is purported to be. Kailadbou is unambiguous about this:

> Rani Gaidinliu's movement had no connection with the Indian freedom struggle; it was a localised ethnic movement against the 'others' – the others being the British, Kuki, Meitei and Christian missionaries – with distinct messianic overtones and an exceptional assertion for an ethnic homeland, which is a first of its kind in Naga history. It was only after Indian independence that Rani Gaidinliu's movement began to be identified as part of the Indian freedom struggle and she was elevated to the status of a national freedom fighter.

There is no doubt that Nehru needed a tribal icon from the north-east for his national integration project; he had inherited disparate communities, castes, ethnicities, religions, and cultural groupings. Gaidinliu had the right credentials: a tribal woman, a leader of tribal resistance against British rule, a cultural custodian, a traditional-faith reformer. She ticked too many boxes to stop being positioned in his nationalist pantheon.

What is less known is that another Naga personality to emerge from the region, A.Z. Phizo, had come into contact with Subhas Chandra Bose and given his support to the Indian National Army (INA) and the Japanese forces in a bid to drive out the British from the Naga Hills. Phizo, with his unyielding dream of a Naga nation, remained Nehru's nemesis throughout and outlasted his heir Indira Gandhi. Had Phizo not been a Naga nationalist opposed to the post-independence Indian state, would he have been afforded the status of an Indian freedom fighter – he had after all joined hands with Bose to end the British occupation of the Naga Hills. It is a question to discomfit every nationalist, so silence has been the answer. What is certain is that Phizo's devout American Baptist roots did not escape the notice of Indian political leaders, including Nehru; Phizo never faltered in using Biblical rhetoric or invoking his Baptist faith in pursuit of Naga self-rule. To this day the imagery of the Baptist faith as nonconformist and incompatible with Indian nationalism, and even more so Hindu nationalism, has persisted in the national debate, and Phizo, unlike his contemporary Gaidinliu, has remained an unpopular if not villainous figure to many in the mainland, even if he has generated a great deal of interest.

V

Jasazo, the youngest child of Phizo and Jwenle, was only two years old when Phizo left for London to internationalise the Naga issue. The first time Jasazo saw his father was in 1990, when Phizo's coffin was flown back home from London; out of nine children, the last three hardly saw their father, which was the price the family had to pay for Naga nationalism, Jasazo told me regretfully.[18] At sixty-four a grandfather himself, Jasazo remains an unwavering

---

[18] Four daughters and five sons were born to Jwenle and Phizo.

believer in his father's dream of Naga independence; but he has found a higher calling as a Baptist Revival pastor.

Phizo himself had dreamt of becoming a missionary – maybe he could have gone to China, his Baptist pastor son said, following in the footsteps of the American missionaries. In the mid-1960s, when Gaidinliu went underground to fight for a Zeliangrong homeland within the Indian union, Phizo's comrades had snaked their way to East Pakistan and China for training. Some of Phizo's close lieutenants and battle-hardened fighters were trained in the ways of Maoism, far removed from their devout American Baptist roots. The Chinese connection made the Naga movement more controversial and dragged Phizo deeper into the political quagmire, since the Nagas' "seditious" trip to China happened within a few years of the Indo–China War of 1962; in fact, Phizo himself had never reached China because he was arrested in Burma. Phizo played the China card close to his chest, divulging little regarding his personal connection and political stance; however, he did avow that "Turning to China had long been a possibility" if the West did not help.[19]

Phizo's Baptist pedigree and Chinese connection were mere cogs in the engine of his irrepressible desire for Naga self-determination, but they nevertheless had far-reaching effects. His political stance made him both a foe and a disreputable person in the corridors of power in New Delhi – the very establishment that had honoured his contemporary Gaidinliu as a national freedom fighter. If he had not followed his dream of Naga independence, Phizo's early Burma days (1934–46) would have been viewed quite differently. Phizo seems in this sense the poor man's Jinnah. Jinnah got his homeland, Phizo never did.[20]

[19] Quoted in Steyn, *Zapuphizo*, 148.
[20] It is in fact most interesting to think of both Maulana Azad and Jinnah from the Muslim world in connection with their contemporaries Gaidinliu and Phizo in the Naga world. Azad's nationalism was, like Gaidinliu's, primarily against the British and in favour of Nehruvian secularism's ethos of tolerance, so he like Gaidinliu works well as an Indian nationalist mascot of

Jasazo concurs that his father's tryst with Netaji Bose and his subsequent incarceration by the British in Insein Jail as an enemy of the Raj could have been seen as a contribution to Indian nationalism had he not doggedly followed his dream of Naga self-rule. Given the versatile nature of Naga oral tradition – demonstrable in the legend of Rani Gaidinliu – Phizo could have been stiff competition for Gaidinliu as India's chosen freedom fighter from the Naga tribes. On Phizo's connection with Netaji Bose and the Azad Hind Fauj, his Angami biographer writes:

> Phizo often visualised even during his childhood the British being driven out of the Naga country one day. He was not against the British as a nation but he despised their colonial policy of 'divide and rule', and their racist views. Thus while the Nagas at home stood by the Allies in World War II, Phizo and his brother Kevi Yallay helped the Japanese in collaboration with Netaji Subhas Chandra Bose and his Indian National Army. His main aim was liberation of Nagaland from British colonialism. At that time the question of Indian domination over Nagas was not an issue yet. Nagas took Indians as neighbours only. Phizo worked hard, hand in hand with the Japanese and the Indian National Army (INA) in Burma in 1943 and fought side by side with them till 1944, when Burma was recaptured by the Allied Forces.[21]

Phizo's grave is in the outskirts of Kohima town, the heartland of his Angami tribesmen, overlooking the massive Nagaland state secretariat. It attracts more tourists than ethnonationalists. According to Jasazo,

> not long after my father died, an old Azad Hind Fauj veteran came into contact with us in Kohima to pay homage to my father. He said that he is a Bengali settled in Tripura and that my father and

---

secular India. Jinnah as Muslim was like Phizo as Christian – both opposed the British, but both also opposed what they saw as Hindu and Indian nationalist hegemony, so both remain villains in the nationalist imaginary.

[21] Zinyü, *Phizo*, 35.

uncle, Kevi Yallay, saved his life while in a jail in Burma. During the Second World War when the British recaptured Burma my father and uncle were imprisoned along with others who had supported the Japanese during the war; along with them were many Azad Hind Fauj soldiers in Insein Jail and the elderly Bengali veteran happened to be one of them. He told us that he became stricken with cholera and was nearing death when my father and uncle came up with a Naga herbal concoction and cured him . . . I think it was an old Angami remedy of banana stem that saved the elderly Bengali man's life. He knew my father had died and came searching for my uncle who had also then recently passed away; when he reached my father's grave, the Bengali veteran walking feebly with a walking stick suddenly dropped it, stood at full attention and saluted. It was a nostalgic moment and a glimpse into a moment in my father's life that I had never known about.

When Phizo joined forces with Netaji Bose and the Japanese in 1943, Gaidinliu, who led a short rebellion against the British following the hanging of Jadonang, was still languishing in a colonial prison where she remained for nearly ten years. In 1937, when Nehru learnt of Gaidinliu's life imprisonment, he wrote of her plight to the British authorities, a communication of little consequence to them, since small uprisings were endemic through their empire.[22] "The rebellion [led by Gaidinliu] had no clear-cut political objectives, having its genesis in an age-old prophecy that a Naga king would one day arise to destroy the British," writes a British observer.[23] Up to the time that Nehru chanced upon Gaidinliu, the British thought the "*kamphai* movement" of no consequence in relation to the demand for independence in the mainland.

The actions of Phizo in the province of Burma were far more seditious than those of Gaidinliu. He had connived with a foreign power to bring down the British empire. Phizo narrowly escaped death row – an opportune incident of rioting in Insein Jail

---

[22] For Nehru's letter, see Nehru, *Unity of India*, 187–8.
[23] Steyn, *Zapuphizo*, 50.

literally saved his neck.[24] Gaidinliu's anti-British movement was a far more localised event spurred by a millenarian vision of an ethnic homeland shrouded in mysticism, while Phizo's nationalism was modern in character and impelled by anti-colonial intellectualism. Moreover, Phizo's nationalism was shaped by his village tradition, modern education, and years of interaction with other ethnicities like the Chinese, Shans, and Karens in Burma. As elsewhere in South East Asia, Phizo's movement was political and had roots in decolonisation; Gaidinliu's movement was politico-religious and, though shaped by the colonial encounter, impelled at its core by cultural revivalism and a return to native roots. Both these Naga leaders found an ally in religion for political mobilisation, but Gaidinliu was far more successful, tethering the movement to her divine-like status.

If Phizo's ethnonationalism set out an idealistic view of a homogeneous Naga nation, Gaidinliu's more pragmatic and limited idea was a Zeliangrong homeland within the Indian union (at least after independence). Phizo appealed to the Naga masses with his steely determination and superior statesmanship, while Gaidinliu's charismatic mystique was restricted to her followers. Notwithstanding his anti-colonial politics, Phizo's deportment was that of an English gentleman.[25] In all his publicised photographs he wears a three-piece suit. Gaidinliu's public appearances show, by contrast, a graceful woman in traditional Rongmei Naga garb in her trademark dark shades; she is usually accompanied by two

---

[24] According to Jasazo's account, it was his uncle Kevi Yallay who instigated the riot. His Angami biographer writes that Phizo came close to facing the firing squad, "but his impending turn to face the firing squad triggered off [a] riot by fellow war prisoners at the infamous Insein Jail." See Zinyü, *Phizo*, 36–7.

[25] When Phizo's mortal remains were flown back to India from London, there was high drama at New Delhi airport, since the Naga leader had for years held a British passport. According to Niketu Iralu, Phizo's nephew, it was Rajmohan Gandhi, then a Rajya Sabha MP, who liaised with the Indian government to allow Phizo's body to reach Nagaland.

nubile young attendants (some say she preferred that they be virgins).

Gaidinliu's dress sense was emblematic of a profound identity assertion. At the time of the "*kamphai* movement", though she may not have claimed to wear "ghost shirts" that could ward off bullets (as was claimed in the Native American Ghost Dance movement),[26] her armed followers – somewhat like the Chinese followers of the Boxer Rebellion (1899–1901) – were convinced by her that enemy bullets would melt away; weapons would appear out of thin air to help them; rice would be showered on them from the heavens.[27] Jeremiah Pame, an English Literature lecturer at Delhi University, told me that "Rani Gaidinliu hoodwinked her followers into thinking that they would get weapons and ammunitions from a magical source; that bullets would not hit them due to her anointed presence; and that there would be showers of rice from the heavens. She even told young people to keep books under their pillow while sleeping, and they would remember everything, and also many gave up their studies." A polite critic of Gaidinliu, Jeremiah, who hails from a Zeme Naga village in Tamenglong, argues that fixations with mythicised glorious cultural pasts tend to happen at the expense of material development in the present.

A notable feature distinguishing Phizo from Gaidinliu is that the Angami Naga leader had to relentlessly wrestle with detractors within the movement. The inescapably mortal side of Phizo was too fragile to keep conflicting ethnic groups together – unlike the "demigoddess" with a smaller and more compact sphere of

---

[26] The Ghost Dance movement has its origin in the Native American prophet Wovoka (also known as Jack Wilson) who prophesied the extinction of white people and a return to the pre-conquest world. This spiritual movement began among the Northern Paiute of Nevada in 1889 and spread to most parts of the country. One of the distinguishing beliefs of this millenarian movement was "Ghost shirts", believed to ward off bullets. For more details, see Mooney, *The Ghost Dance*.

[27] See Bower, *Naga Path*, 47; Zeliang, *A Brief History*, 80.

influence. Phizo settled scores with his detractors with far-reaching ramifications for his personal faith and credibility; every time his detractors were liquidated, the Baptist community held him guilty of transgressions. Unlike Phizo, Gaidinliu had the luxury of bypassing criticism from close associates and co-religionists and faced no revolt from within the ranks, she being perceived as above mere mortals.

Some of Gaidinliu's tribesmen of Baptist background are less than forgiving in often highlighting her culpability in the killing of religious dissidents. These charges were made against the backdrop of her armed movement in the 1960s for a Zeliangrong homeland, which coincided with the NNC-led armed struggle. The Christian overtones of the NNC movement clashed with Gaidinliu's, leading to skirmishes between the two on Gaidinliu's turf in present-day Peren district.

This tumultuous phase reinforced the notion that Gaidinliu was opposed to overarching Naga ethnonationalism. This then prevented Gaidinliu's image as an Indian freedom fighter being tarnished, which it would have been had she taken a hardline secessionist position like Phizo in the post-independence period. Gaidinliu's principal objective was to bring the Zeliangrong people dispersed in three states, Assam, Manipur and Nagaland, within the same fold – some say she went underground to protect her people's culture and identity – and if need be take up arms to achieve this limited objective.[28] Her concern was tabled before Prime Minister Indira Gandhi after her surrender in 1966, but the goal of a Zeliangrong homeland was never realised.

From the Baptist mission's perspective, Gaidinliu's movement was a huge blow to the Zeliang Baptist community; after independence, she stoked an impressive religious movement that laid bare Baptist vulnerabilities.[29] The religious angle of Gaidinliu's

---

[28] Dev, *Nagaland*, 69.

[29] Naga Baptists consider Heraka a religion on par with other major faiths in the region, although many Zeliang Baptist faithful equate Heraka with

Heraka movement appealed particularly to Hindu groups in the mainland. In no time she was thrust into the national limelight as she, with help from her close confidants, sought to bring the movement closer to the mainstream through the Hindu route. She participated in the second World Hindu Conference in 1979 in Allahabad, the first participation by any Naga personality in recent history, after which there was no question of entirely dissociating her religious predilections from mainstream Hinduism.

Phizo was a legend, but fraught with inconsistencies and human frailties. To this his disillusioned followers and critics often bear witness, and his personality cult was considerably diminished by his belonging to the Baptist fraternity – whereas Gaidinliu thrived on a personality cult. Their two movements divided both Naga society and Western observers. Phizo's British biographer gave a scathing critique of Gaidinliu's movement in the 1960s: "Her movement was no longer the mystic cult of Jadonang but rather a crude attempt to become embroiled in Naga politics of the day. However, she never regained her former eminence and once more subsided into obscurity."[30] This belies the facts: Gaidinliu attained a quasi-divine status that no Naga leader has ever managed.

Phizo's ethnonationalism had clear roots in the mostly middle-class educated people who rose against colonial rule – in this specific respect he parallels Gandhi, Nehru, Bose, and Ambedkar. His ideology too was based on the concept of the nation-state in the West, though in his case sustained by a healthy dose of biblical verses: his deep religious convictions kept him going even in his hardest days. One British observer notes that he "took religion very seriously," that "he was a bundle of contradictions," and paradoxically that "alongside his role as a devout Christian was

---

Hinduism. The existing literature and oral tradition show that the term Heraka began to be used in the post-independence period. Interestingly, some of Gaidinliu's closest confidants in Nagaland claim that the term was popularised only in the 1970s.

[30] Steyn, *Zapuphizo*, 50–1.

his role as a warrior leader who felt no compunction in planning the death of a political adversary."[31] This violent side of Phizo still confounds many practising Naga Baptists, but one thing is clear: Naga ethnonationalists like Phizo, though deeply religious, fashioned their faith according to their political outlook; their faith was not allowed to determine their politics.

Phizo's biggest defeat was arguably in 1975, when some of his trusted lieutenants – including his longtime aide and younger brother Kevi Yallay – signed the Shillong Accord. This in a way ceded the armed struggle to the Indian government and the controversy it generated divides the Naga political struggle to this day. This event was devastating for Phizo personally, and a contradiction of his lifelong struggle; in London he received the bewildering news stoically, and, according to his British biographer, told his eldest daughter, Adinno: "Never forget that without God man is nothing . . . his life has no significance. It is like the dust of the desert which blows without a destination."[32]

Religion for him was not a crutch but a sobering philosophical outlook that kept at bay his overconfidence, laid bare his vulnerabilities, and ruled out any desire to play demigod – notwithstanding his cult following. This quality of his was becoming of a man raised in the Baptist tradition. Phizo had attended the Baptist mission school in Kohima; here he came into contact with the celebrated missionary Rev. Sidney Rivenburg and was drawn to his personality and teachings.[33] His lifelong relationship with the American Baptist mission ran deep. He spent several hours during the Japanese takeover of Rangoon in 1942 "packing and saving the extensive Baptist library at the Judson seminary" and derived the "greatest satisfaction" in the effort.[34] He was baptised on 12 December 1922 at the age of eighteen, so that he understood the religious profundity of water immersion; he was never

[31] Quoted in ibid., 111.
[32] Ibid., 156.
[33] Ibid., 42.
[34] Ibid., 53.

once excommunicated from the church and remained its lifelong member and on his death was afforded Baptist funerary rites.[35]

If Phizo found solace and meaning in religion, Gaidinliu found solidarity and her basic identity survival through it. Intrinsic to Gaidinliu's religious consciousness is what Durkheim has argued, namely that religious belief is nothing but the worship of a collective identity, and social solidarity is the latent function of divine worship.[36] Gaidinliu founded an identity movement revolving around religion which not even the unyielding Baptists could tear asunder. Gaidinliu's human frailties and weaknesses rarely feature in her legend and the Heraka religion thrives on her enduring legacy. Gaidinliu never disavowed the sense among her adherents that she was a divine messenger. Phizo was by comparison merely a brilliant political leader and nationalist to his followers, and a secessionist to mainland Indian audiences.

VI

When the famed American televangelist Billy Graham visited the conflict-weary state of Nagaland in 1972, thousands of Naga Baptists from all walks of life thronged the capital to see a fellow Baptist preacher in action. It was the biggest gathering of Nagas in recent history and spoke volumes for the popularity of the Baptist faith in the state. Nearly 100,000 of the faithful listened enthralled as the fifty-year-old evangelist in his prime preached at a jam-packed public ground in Kohima.

Singing is indispensable in every Naga Baptist conference and the Baptist leadership chose their best choir for the occasion. N.C. Zeliang, at thirty-two the first Baptist seminary graduate from the Liangmai Naga community, assumed the coveted role of choirmaster; it was the last time that Zeliang would take part in a Naga Baptist gathering, for he would soon become the faith's most

[35] Phizo was born on 16 May 1904 to Krusietso Dolie and Lhuyietsüü. See Steyn, *Zapuphizo*, 39.
[36] Durkheim, *The Elementary Forms of Religious Life*.

formidable detractor. This gentlemanly Baptist seminarian discredited his former faith and left behind a legacy that still challenges Baptist ascendancy in his home district. In his prime, Zeliang became a proponent of the Heraka faith, rubbing shoulders with dignitaries from Hindu organisations such as the RSS, the VHP, the Ramakrishna Mission, and the Bharat Sevashram Sangh, etc.

The most striking feature, especially to an initiated Baptist, of Zeliang's elaborately built tombstone is the absence of a crucifix or any invocation of the Christian message. On the four-sided gravestone of polished black marble are inscriptions of accolades and achievements, etched pithily and paradoxically (all in upper case):

> HE WAS THE FIRST THEOLOGIAN FROM NTUMA VILLAGE AND AMONG THE ZELIANG COMMUNITY . . . CHOIR LEADER DURING BILLY GRAHAM CRUSADE AT KOHIMA IN 1972 . . . FOUNDER PRESIDENT ZELIANGRONG HERAKA ASSOCIATION ASSAM, MANIPUR & NAGALAND FROM 5TH JANUARY 74 TILL DEATH . . . VICE-PRESIDENT RAM KRISHNA SOCIETY, DIMAPUR 1991 . . . FIRST NAGA TO RECEIVE VIVKANANDA [SIC] SEVA SAMMAN AWARD FROM BADA BAZAR KUMAR SABHA PUSTAKALAY, KOLKATA FOR SELFLESS SERVICE TO SOCIETY . . .

These convey Zeliang's prodigious talent as a non-controversial change-maker – a fact that surviving members of his family downplay: they see him as a god-fearing man, a relentless social activist, a simple son of the soil, a selfless leader.

N.C. Zeliang was arguably the most eminent personality to emerge from the Zeliang Naga. This polymath, who could have been a great asset to the Baptist church, became the greatest champion of the Heraka faith. It appears that Zeliang's turning of his back on the Baptist community was a reaction to inordinate religious pietism.

Religious fundamentalism can have serious repercussions, not always helpful to the community of the faith concerned. In this case, a promising member fell victim to the excessive pietism of the day – as a close family member related to me in hushed tones.

Apparently, Zeliang was excommunicated from his local Baptist church for smoking a cigarette, which meant he lost face as his community's leader. "Following his excommunication," Zeliang's genial daughter told me, "Ranima told him to join her movement if the Baptists had rusticated him; even before that fateful incident my father-in-law was very close to Ranima, but he never joined her movement since he was the first [Baptist] theologian from the community. Although he never did confide in us, it is probable that the excommunication made him change his mind."

Zeliang went on to become founder-president of the Zeliangrong Heraka Association (ZHA). He formalised the Heraka faith, composed the Heraka hymnal and liturgy, developed the Heraka "pastoral" handbook, compiled the religious text, and wrote religious tracts. More importantly, Zeliang promoted Gaidinliu at the national level through his writings and facilitated the link between Hindu organisations and the Heraka movement. Henry, Zeliang's eldest son, stated categorically: "If my father had not been the founding-president of Zeliangrong Heraka Association, the Heraka movement would have waned and would not be where it is now; also Rani Gaidinliu would not have attained the heights if not for my father's acumen and ingenuity in promoting her at the national level."

For Gaidinliu to have had Zeliang as a close confidant and tireless advocate of the movement paid rich dividends. Henry, who deeply reveres Gaidinliu, did not invalidate her legacy but highlighted his father's contribution in the making of Rani Gaidinliu as a national brand. Gaidinliu as tribal icon was ripe for the taking, but Zeliang made her something of a national icon. "Two people in particular, Professor Gangmumei from Imphal and my father, worked very hard to promote Ranima at the national level.[37] After my father joined the Heraka movement in 1969, he started documenting the life of Ranima; before that stories

---

[37] The late Gangmumei Kamei was a renowned Rongmei Naga historian and a close confidant of Gaidinliu. He played an instrumental role in forming

about her movement and struggle against the British rule existed mostly in oral form, but my father put them on paper," Henry said.

It is clear from his writings that Zeliang was influenced by the idea of religious pluralism. "My father used to say that one can be a good Christian, a good Heraka or a good Hindu since they all lead to the same god," said Henry, a practising Baptist, outlining his father's philosophy of life. Coining the term Heraka from the Zeme root words *Hera* – god, and *ka* – pure, owed, he said, a great deal to his father's contribution.

> When Ranima went underground in the 1960s the Indian government was willing to supply her with 3000 rifles, since her army was at loggerheads with the NNC. My father advised her not to take up arms as it would result in more bloodshed; he made a resolve not to join her movement if it became an armed struggle. People rarely talk about it but my father played a pivotal role behind the scenes in Ranima coming overground and surrendering to the government. As far as I know Ranima's movement till then was known as the *kamphai* movement, but the term Heraka came only after she came into contact with my father. It was my father who suggested that she steer her movement along the lines of cultural revivalism and identity preservation.

Zeliang reached out to Kalyan Ashram, a Hindu mission organisation involved in educational programmes and social work, to open schools in remote villages in Peren district. The list of Zeliang's "social activities" with Hindu organisations, as inscribed on his tombstone, includes:

> 1968 LEADER NAGALAND CULTURAL TROUPE TO KOLKATA AT NORTH-EAST STATE CULTURAL MEET . . . GAVE SPEECH AT KALAMANDIR ON FREEDOM MOVEMENT IN THE COUNTRY . . . 1981 CHIEF GUEST ALL INDIA WORKERS' CONFERENCE BHARATIYA VANVASI KALYAN ASH-

---

the Tingkao Raguang Chapriak (TRC), a variant of the Heraka faith among the Rongmei in the Imphal valley.

LEGENDS, MYSTICS, AND CONVERTS 297

RAM, NEW DELHI . . . 1987 PARTICIPATED AT KOLKATA CULTURAL
TROUPE PROGRAMME ORGANIZED BY BHARAT SEVASHRAM SANGH AS
LEADER . . .

Zeliang's social activism translated into a political career. He became the first Congress-I MLA from his constituency, then changed sides to become founder-president of the BJP in Nagaland and a member of the national executive committee of the party. Henry said:

> During those days there were only regional parties in Nagaland and so for the first time my father brought the Congress party to the state and was its first President. He got dragged into a bitter political difference with his party colleague, S.C. Jamir, who later became the Chief Minister of Nagaland; they went to court and Ram Jethmalani, the famous Indian lawyer, represented my father. Unhappy with the party infighting, my father went on to start the BJP in Nagaland along with Dr Rhetso and our present Governor, P.B. Acharya, who has been in Northeast India as a party worker since the 1960s. L.K. Advani wrote a statement certifying that the success of the BJP in Nagaland owes to the hard work of leaders like my father and Dr Rhetso.

Hindu organisation workers occasionally visit Zeliang's grave in Jalukie to pay their respects. This politically loaded gesture does not escape the notice of Baptists, given Zeliang's status in this small town.

> When my father started the cultural revival in the 1970s, the Baptists used to pray that he may fail in his plan. My "old man" used to retort that they [the Baptists] are driven by emotions and not true spirituality; he used to say that Baptist believers are very difficult to negotiate with. At one point he was even threatened by the Naga underground for his social work . . . the main factor that led my father to spearhead the Heraka movement was his concern for our tradition and identity; my father was a straightforward man; he harboured no ill will towards any denomination or religion. When Zeliang people converted to the Baptist faith they left behind their cultural tradition; there were some cases in the Liangmai Baptist

churches where converts were excommunicated for participating in traditional festivals. These things have changed for the better, but such were the circumstances when my father devoted his life to the uplift of the Zeliang people.

In retrospect it was dereliction of duty on the part of the Baptist mission – whose efficacy in the Naga-inhabited areas had been in the spheres of medical work and education – that led to Hindu organisations making inroads in the Baptist heartland. The intervention of Hindu mission societies such as the Kalyan Ashram in promoting education and poverty-alleviation programmes paved the way for their access to Zeliang Naga areas. Within no time the Heraka leader-icon Gaidinliu was being felicitated by various Hindu organisations around the country.

The pastor of the oldest Baptist church in Jalukie town remarked that their unreflective fixation on traditional culture would be the downfall of the Zeliang community, which is now watched hawk-eyed by Hindu mission organisations. In fact the American Baptist faith no longer enjoys monopoly among Nagas today, though it remains a force to reckon with. These words etched on Zeliang's tombstone show that the Naga Baptists are being given a run for their money by traditional faiths, and that such faiths are now sought to be appropriated by Hinduism:

> HE WAS ONE OF THE ARCHITECTS OF INDIA TRIBAL CULTURAL FORUM AND ESTABLISHED COHESION BETWEEN ZELIANGRONG HERAKA ASSOCIATION OF NAGALAND, ASSAM & MANIPUR, SENG KHASI OF MEGHALAYA, DONYIPOLO OF ARUNACHAL PRADESH, BATHOU FOLLOWERS OF BODOS SAMAJ, JAPFUPHIKIKRUNA NAGALAND, CHAKHESANG LHIKIRI LENYU KEZUMI MAPAO NAGALAND, FOCHURI LANO NALE KAVERI NAGALAND, TINGKAO RAGUANG CHAP-RIAK MANIPUR, INDIGENOUS FAITH AND CULTURAL SOCIETY OF ARUNACHAL PRADESH.

In an interesting turn of events, Naga Baptists are beginning to seriously discuss the "dangers" of Hindutva as they slowly but inevitably become part of larger Indian society. Hindu mission organisations have replicated Christian mission strategies and decoded the two-millennia-old forte of Christianity: social welfare as religious duty. Among Zeme, the young and erudite pastor of the Local Baptist Church in Jalukie argued that the entry of right-wing Hindu forces into Zeliang Naga areas will not be overt but through a subtle and insidious stoking of tensions between Christianity and traditional culture. Pastor Among pointed out the irony of traditional culture continuing under threat:

> The Zeliang Baptists do not have a problem with Hinduism, but there is a legitimate fear that our traditional past will be swallowed up by Hinduism. The Hindu right-wing groups are pushing an agenda that Christianity is a foreign religion, and the Heraka adherents have picked up this narrative. Heraka followers claim that the Zeliang Christians are a sellout for adopting a Western religion, while not being aware that the Hindutva forces have hoodwinked them.

VII

Established in 1967, the first Baptist church in Jalukie town is as old as the settlement itself. Indubitably the biggest in Jalukie valley, the Local Baptist Church brings together the majority Zeme and Liangmai Naga (who speak different languages) within the same fold. Zeliang Baptists cannot outdo their Christian Revival Church counterparts when it comes to their mode of worship, which is too ecstatic for the Baptists, but they are convivial and not averse to experimentation, which separates them from the solemn and ceremonious Zeliang Catholics who also operate in Jalukie town.

The Naga Baptist churches are skilled fundraisers, feeding off the religiosity and generous nature of their faithful, but the scenario outside Jalukie's Local Baptist Church, apparently a regular Sunday affair, is a sight to behold: a deacon hawking livestock and agricultural products as tithes. No wonder the Baptist church coffers never run a deficit: they have put a premium on an important Baptist practice – tithing. The dividends are diverted towards mission and evangelism. As long as Naga Baptist churches thrive, there will be no end to missions in the country and beyond, a fact that has not escaped critics and detractors of the Naga Baptists.

In its religious composition Jalukie is a predominantly Baptist town, but also home to several other Christian denominations and religions. The landowners were Zeme Naga, but this valley-town became a model settlement attracting Zeme, Liangmai, and Rongmei Nagas scattered across Assam, Manipur, and Nagaland. The town's moderate climate, fertile plains, and thick-forested hills made it grow in size within a short span of time. It became an ethnic melting pot attracting migrants even from the mainland, but it also became contested ground between ethnic Baptists and followers of Heraka. No Naga Baptist community in the state faced a battle as uphill against a "rival" religious group as the Zeliang Baptists. The conflict persists and the population of Jalukie is getting more polarised. Willing Dailam, the youthful pastor of the Liangmai Baptist Church, said towards the end of 2018: "recently the Heraka association sent a notification to the district administration, the village councils and to the churches that evangelists should stop coming to Heraka homes to preach the gospel. They warned that if young hotheaded Heraka followers manhandle anyone coming to preach Christianity, they will not be held responsible. This has affected the mission effort in the villages with Heraka population, but the churches are not giving up; they have set aside every Wednesday to pray for the Heraka believers."

Pastor Among of the Local Baptist Church submitted that Baptists need to seriously rethink their mission strategy. "The ultimatum that was issued to the churches is not from the Heraka believers. This strategy indicates the involvement of the Hindu right-wing groups; there is no doubt that the Heraka leaders are consulting with the RSS leadership to counter the Christian mission in the region," he said. "No Baptist missionaries believe in forced conversion or material enticement as the RSS are accusing Christian missionaries of, but the gospel must be preached, since mission is the heartbeat of the Baptist faith."

The Zeliang Naga Baptists have celebrated a hundred years of Christianity in the land but still confront the charge from their fellow tribesmen that they are the recipients of a foreign religion. "Heraka followers are claiming that our traditional culture is under threat because of Christians, and that they are the champions of Zeliang culture and identity. They have conflated Christianity with Westernisation. Ironically, Heraka followers are getting Hinduised by the day," Pastor Among argued.

The Baptists are clear winners in Naga-inhabited areas, but small battles are still being fought over culture and identity. Naga Baptists are renowned for their incorrigible piety and punctiliousness in religious transactions; during the beginnings of the Baptist community they were noted for their strict adherence to protocol and for ignoring the cultural challenges of the day. In meeting the challenge posed by traditional Naga culture, there were strong differences even among the larger-than-life American missionaries.[38] This identity consciousness had a long-lasting impact on the Baptist faith even as it opened a Pandora's box of cultural wars. In some cases, what was once a distinguishing feature of Baptist culture has become its Achilles heel. For instance, their teetotalitarianism has impeded mission efforts. In Jalukie, Heraka followers accuse Baptists of double standards. "The Heraka followers now see themselves as morally superior to the Baptists and they hold Christianity responsible for the ills of society. They have even developed a defence mechanism against the mission effort, accusing missionaries of trying to convert them while children from Baptist homes come and empty their vessels [drink their traditional rice brew]," said Pastor Among with some exasperation.

Divisions within the Baptist church, too, have not helped its cause, and the Zeme, Liangmai, and Rongmei have all formed their separate Baptist associations. "The Zeliangrong Baptists," Pastor Among said, "are a house divided. The Zeme have two separate Baptist associations in Nsong and Peren; while the

[38] See McFayden, *Travelling in Time*, 56.

Liangmai have their association in Tening and the Rongmei in Jalukie. The associations in themselves are not a problem but they are not immune to infighting, which sends a negative message to the Heraka, since for the Heraka the unifying principle is their religious identity."

The trump card of Heraka adherents is their assimilation into the Indian mainstream, which is part of a larger Hinduisation process; and this assimilation process inculcates the idea of nationalism and patriotism, tempting Heraka followers away from an enduring idea of Naga ethnonationalism. As regards the Naga Baptists, their views are seen as tendentious given the complex history of the Naga political movement. This has not only strengthened the hands of Hindu right-wing groups, it has also drawn suspicion more generally from the Indian political spectrum. Post-independence, many among the Naga educated middle-class who happened to be Baptists found ultimate identity expression in Naga nationalism, much to the bewilderment of the Indian political class. This complex relationship between religion, ethnic identity, and nationalism remains a vexing issue for the Naga Baptist community in an increasingly interconnected world.

7

The Baptist Intellectuals

> The highest position in the country is open to every Naga: in the parliament, in the central cabinet and in the various services, military and civil.
>
> – Sarvepalli Radhakrishnan, president of India, 1 December 1963

> Democracy in its purest form exists among the Nagas.
>
> – T. Sakhrie

TO COMMEMORATE THE hundredth anniversary of the Naga Labour Corps that sailed to France during World War I, the chief minister of Nagaland unveiled a monolith at a busy Kohima junction on 21 April 2017. The brief ceremony was attended by state dignitaries dressed smartly in mostly dark suits, and a swarm of onlookers. The crowd that sunny afternoon was a far cry from those in old black-and-white photographs of the Naga Labour Corps that I had stumbled upon in the archives, mostly half-clad, squatting in large groups looking into the camera. The record showed that around 2000 Nagas were recruited as the 35th, 36th, 37th, and 38th [Naga] Labour Companies. Of these, the 35th Company left the Naga Hills as part of the Labour Corps on 21 April 1917 and sailed for France on 26 April.

At the time that the Naga Labour Corps crossed the great waters, the American Baptist mission in the region was about four decades old with 3308 native converts, or 2.2 per cent of the total population (according to the 1911 census). Those in the Naga

Labour Corps were preponderantly animists. On a personal note, my maternal great-grandfather, a Labour Corps veteran, returned home in 1918 and died in the old faith. In a folk song about my tribesmen's expedition to France is manifest the quintessence of traditional Naga society:

> O you young bloods go and search for Shiyihe, mine elder brother, and you colleens for darling Losheli his sweetheart. Tell (her) what he went forth to do; tell [her] that he went forth to pluck a flower, flower of the Germans he went to pluck, went forth to pluck and take. In going, in going, fare thee well.[1]

Around the time of the Great War, many natives were still singing the praises of the most respected white man in their world, the British political officer; however, a few white preachers from across the great waters would soon tilt the scales. The Naga paean to J.H. Hutton was among the last of its kind before "upstart" American missionaries took over.

> O Hutton Sahib, young man of foreign race,
>
> What is that letter which has come from you from abroad?
> O Hutton Sahib, young man of foreign race,
> The letter you got so quickly
> Is it to call us to go to the German War?
> Look how in every village
> The bucks plan each with his friend to go . . .[2]

Among the majority animists were some in the Naga Labour Corps who had come under the influence of the Baptist mission. "Gwizao is also back," writes Rev. Rivenburg about one of his flock who had returned from France, "and preached the morning sermon. I was much pleased." The Kohima missionary also reported another convert: "Budanuo returned as a non-commissioned officer."[3] The Labour Corps' trip to Europe was a watershed

---

[1] Hutton records that the folk song was "composed in France by the Sema labourers": Hutton, *The Sema Nagas*, 369.

[2] Mills, *The Lhota Nagas*, 205.

[3] Rivenburg, ed., *The Star of Naga Hills*, 132–3.

moment in modern Naga history: it contributed to the notion of a pan-Naga identity and arguably a flickering sense of ethnonationalism. These new emotions were channelised in forming the first modern Naga organisation, the Naga Club, whose members were mainly Naga Labour Corps veterans back from France. Men like Khosa and Neikhriehu had broadened their outlook and took an active part in the Club on their return.

Before the entry of personalities like Aliba Imti, Phizo, Kevichusa, Sakhrie, Khelhoshe, Longri, Mhondamo, and Jasokie into the Naga political arena, there was already a generation of mission-school-educated natives who had made their presence felt in the emerging modern society of the Nagas. These were the new elites comprising clerks, schoolteachers, and interpreters who had moved away from the traditional occupation, farming. A well-known Naga Labour Corps recruit to Europe was Rev. Rivenburg's most promising student Khosa Angami, possibly the most qualified native to sail to France. Khosa had studied in the Kohima mission school under Rivenburg and was later sent by the missionary to study medicine in Berry White Medical School in Dibrugarh, from where he graduated in 1916. "When the Labour Corps duties were over, his comrades returned home [in 1918] but he was sent to England for further studies by the DC [deputy commissioner] and he came back home only in 1920," becoming Assistant Surgeon, the highest medical position of the time.[4] Khosa became an important member of the Naga Club, and his son J.B. Jasokie would later be one of the architects of the Naga National Council. Jasokie, a one-time lieutenant of A.Z. Phizo, was the face of "moderate" Nagas – whose political stance differed from that of Naga "extremists" – and he would rise to become chief minister of Nagaland.

II

The Naga Club formed in 1918 comprised small-time colonial employees. The hub of the Naga Club was Kohima but they had a

---

[4] Chasie, *The Naga Memorandum*, 54.

Mokokchung chapter. Some say that the formation of this native club happened in response to the exclusive British club meant for evening carousals. This modern Naga organisation, the first of its kind, was bound to make an impact since people cutting across tribal lines came together for a common goal. "The combination was far-reaching as Naga society, mostly in their Village Republics, had never witnessed such a combined phalanx! So, the then Naga Club became the centre of Naga intellectual, political and economic discussions – it became, in effect, the Naga Think-Tank!"[5]

The high point of the Naga Club came in the form of a memorandum submitted to the Simon Commission on 10 January 1929. In the history of Naga nationalism, this political document is unanimously considered the forerunner of the demand for self-determination. Although interpreted differently by contending parties, a Naga political writer observed that "The resultant memorandum was on behalf of the whole of the Nagas and has become one of the first and foremost historical documents of eternal value and significance."[6] The historic five-paragraph memorandum developed into a rallying point for the Naga ethnonationalist claim that their movement was never secessionist since their desire for self-determination pre-dated the formation of the new Indian state. The meticulously worded memorandum dramatically ends: "If the British Government, however, wants to throw us away, we pray that we should not be thrust to the mercy of the people who could never subjugate us, but to leave us alone to determine for ourselves as in ancient times." The catch phrase "leave us . . . as in ancient times" would resonate in the minds of average Nagas down the years.

Of the seven statutory members of the Simon Commission, it was the future British prime minister Clement Attlee (then a Labour Party junior minister and secretary of the Commission), and Edward Cadogan (a Conservative Party member) who met

[5] Ibid., 44–5.
[6] Lhousa, *Strange Country*, 25.

the Naga Club members in Kohima in January 1929. Drawing attention to this first modern Naga organisation, Elwin remarked: "The Nagas recognised very early that India would inevitably gain her independence and it is remarkable how very seriously they prepared for the changes which they knew were on the way."[7] In May 1935, over the deliberations on the Government of India Bill in the House of Commons, Cadogan recalled his meeting with the Naga Club representatives in Kohima: "These little head-hunters met us and had a palaver ... I am telling this to the Committee in order to prove that these little tribesmen are more sophisticated in their own particular way than perhaps the Committee may imagine. They have a very shrewd suspicion that something is being done to take away from them their immemorial rights and customs."[8]

Cadogan's little head-hunters who initiated a palaver were mission-school-educated natives instrumental in framing Naga political aspirations. At the start of the Great War there were more than 14 schools in the Naga Hills, which in 1931 had increased to 52, with 42 in Kohima and Mokokchung.[9] These two British administrative headquarters were the Baptist mission's mainstay. "The spread of education aroused a political consciousness among the Nagas and crystallised into a concrete aspiration for a free and self rule."[10] A glimpse into the Impur mission school curriculum of 1905 reveals the extent of native exposure to liberal education:

> They study arithmetic, writing, spelling, physiology, hygiene, geography, and history; at the same time special attention is given to the study of the Scriptures and practical Christian work. The brighter pupils are taught English as soon as they can read their own language, and thus is opened to them the way for more advanced work in secular subjects as well as for the study of the entire Bible.[11]

---

[7] Elwin, *Nagaland*, 49.
[8] Ibid., 7.
[9] Atsongchanger, *Christian Education*, 12.
[10] Atsongchanger, *Unforgettable Memories*, 9.
[11] *BMM*, Vol. LXXXV, No. 1 (January 1905), 19.

Out of twenty signatories of the memorandum to the Simon Commission belonging to five Naga tribes and the Kuki, a good number had either studied in mission schools or had some degree of exposure to the American Baptist mission. Some went on to become notable missionaries while a few became actively involved in the Baptist ministry. Special mention may be made of a Labour Corps veteran Naga doctor, Khosa; the famous Angami Naga evangelist, Nisier; the headmaster who drafted the memorandum, Rüzhükhrie; the founder president of the Naga Club, Nisalie; and the educator and translator, Zapuzhülie. Some of the offspring of these Naga leaders became the next generation of native intellectuals, shaping the political contours of the region.

In 1929 the Nagas could "boast of two or three graduates of an Indian University"; this was the first generation of mission-school students pursuing higher studies in the mainland. The Naga Club signatories of 1929 had in fact two highly educated natives of the day, Rüzhükhrie and Khosa, within their ranks. Rüzhükhrie (b. 1901) was a protégé of Rev. Rivenburg. Hailing from Kohima village, he was the first student to come to the Baptist mission school, surprising the American missionary "who was restlessly walking up and down the corridor not expecting anyone to come to school."[12] Rev. Rivenburg arranged for Rüzhükhrie to be paid a monthly stipend of 5 rupees, and the latter passed Class 6 from the mission school. After high school in Shillong he passed his Intermediate Arts from Calcutta and returned to Kohima to become a teacher at his alma mater. Rüzhükhrie became a member of the Naga Club and, being highly qualified, was assigned to draft the most consequential political document submitted by the Nagas to the British.

A devout Baptist, Rüzhükhrie believed it was the hand of God that guided him in his work on the memorandum.[13] He went on to serve on the Angami Literature Committee, founded by Rev.

[12] Chasie, *The Naga Memorandum*, 57.
[13] Lhousa, *Strange Country*, 18.

Tanquist in 1939, till his death in 1985. Following in the footsteps of the Kohima missionaries, Rüzhükhrie wrote many books in the Angami vernacular, promoting the native language. Though he did not enter the hall of fame of Naga nationalism, serving virtually unnoticed as a schoolmaster till his retirement, he was one of these earliest educated natives to do some of the foundational work for Naga identity and self-determination.

Two of Rüzhükhrie's Naga Club compatriots and mission school alumni, Nisale and Zapuzhülie, also contributed to the educational and literary tradition. Nisale Angami, then employed as a *peshkar* in the deputy commissioner's office, served as the first founder-president of the Naga Club.[14] His Angami translation of Aesop's Fables was read widely, and he was a champion of school education in Kohima district.[15] Zapuzhülie was already a missionary – inducted by the American Baptist mission in 1928 – when he became a Naga Club signatory. His growing years were with American missionaries who had educated him. He translated John Bunyan's classic, *The Pilgrim's Progress* (*Rüvemia Rüvedze*), a favourite among the Naga Baptists, into Angami. He became a well-known Baptist preacher and educationist. Rüzhükhrie and Zapuzhülie were lauded by an American missionary for their contribution to Christian education:

> Mr Tanquist, aided by Zaphüzhilie, a gifted linguist, translated the New Testament into the Angami language and also assisted in similar work for Rengmas, Lothas, and Semas . . . Mr Rhuzhukhrie and others are also at work on the Angami translation. The copies of the Scriptures are of great importance not only as devotional reading but also as textbooks in the schools.[16]

Arguably the most prominent Baptist convert among the Naga Club members was Nisier Angami, the first convert from the

---

[14] A *peshkar* was a high-ranked native government employee who worked closely with the deputy commissioner.
[15] Chasie, *The Naga Memorandum*, 51.
[16] Walling, ed., *Down the Memory Lane*, 57.

exemplary Baptist village of Khonoma. His first job after finishing mission school was as a constable, but when a prisoner escaped under his watch and he was sacked, he became involved in spreading the new faith to neighbouring Naga groups. In 1919, a year after the formation of the Naga Club, he was an ordained missionary – the first Baptist preacher to become a member of the Naga Club. Nisier also served as a schoolteacher and was a signatory of the memorandum to the Simon Commission. His son Kevichusa became a key player in modern Naga society, and his grandson Sakhrie, who had a short but meteoric spell in Naga politics, was a prominent intellectual of his time.

III

Students' organisations remain noteworthy in the lives of NNC leaders. Pioneering educated Nagas like Longri, Mayangnokcha, Kevichusa, and Sakhrie were all at some point involved in students' unions. The first NNC president, T. Aliba Imti, and other like-minded Naga students had formed the first Naga students' organisation in Shillong in 1939, the city being a primary educational hub for students from various hill tribes in Assam in those days.[17] It was in their college days that Nagas like Sakhrie and Aliba Imti honed their intellectual acumen, broadening their horizons, building networks, and learning the basics of statecraft – though this last was condescendingly dismissed as unbecoming of a race only recently educated.

Longri Ao, an illustrious Baptist leader in the making, dabbled in the Indian National Congress movement while a Bible College student in Jorhat and was watched as a suspect by the authorities in the Naga Hills. Another educated native, Imkongmeren, had refused to join government service and begun running a small business; and Aliba Imti, a schoolteacher's son in a Baptist mission school (supported by the British government), defied

[17] Imti, *Reminiscence*, 9.

the authorities in matters of dress and hairstyle. Meanwhile, an Angami intellectual, Phizo, had proved a nuisance to the British, and was during WWII charged with high treason for conniving with the enemy to drive out the British from the Naga Hills. One British intelligence report called Phizo a "thoroughly nasty piece of work if ever there was one".[18]

Occasionally, Naga student leaders like Aliba Imti had the opportunity to meet Indian leaders like Jawaharlal Nehru and Subhas Chandra Bose on their visits to Shillong, the picturesque hill-station capital of British Assam. Aliba Imti recalled that the British authorities had threatened to remove his father, a schoolteacher, from service since Aliba Imti was associating with a "troublemaker", Subhas Chandra Bose.

> In 1938, the first ever visit to Shillong by a top leader of the Congress was Subhas Chandra Bose. He was then President of the Congress party. He stayed at a modest hotel, Earle Sanatorium, near the Ward's lake and addressed two or three public meetings, giving reasons why the British would leave India. More out of curiosity, eight or nine of us Naga boys went to his lodging to meet him and he welcomed us warmly and spent about 15 minutes talking to us. In sparkling white Dhoti and shirt and with a fitting Gandhi cap he struck me as one of the handsomest men I had ever met. A Naga sword was presented to him which he accepted joyfully. I was amongst the juniors in the group so I cannot recall the exact gist of the talk. But one sentence of his still remains clearly in my mind, he laughingly said, "You Naga people are very brave and so you must join us in the struggle for independence of India."[19]

Naga students in places like Calcutta and Shillong had begun asserting their common ethnic identity and culture. During Nehru's visit to Shillong in 1945, Naga students went to meet him and Aliba Imti gives an account of their meeting:

[18] Quoted in Ramunny, *The World of Nagas*, 32.
[19] Imti, *Reminiscence*, 10.

Approaching the venue, four Naga boys dressed splendidly in native costume saluted Panditji. He got down from the car and shook hands with all four of them and proceeded to the platform which was just a short distance away. The dais itself was encircled by more tribal boys in full costume. It was a very impressive meeting. The ground was packed with people. There were also many Indian and foreign correspondents covering the event. I was surprised when Panditji opened his speech by mentioning the Naga boys and Naga people. I felt a bit awkward in front of my friends from other tribal areas and Assamese and Bengalis. But he continued in this vein for a good five minutes and said that if he were to give a collective name to the Nagas, he would give the name "Bahadur".[20]

Eight years later some of these Naga students clashed with Nehru, now the prime minister of independent India. Over Nehru's first visit to the Naga Hills district in 1953, the NNC, of which Aliba Imti was the first president (1947–8), staged a public walkout during the Indian premier's speech in Kohima. To add insult to injury, Nehru's close friend U Nu, the Burmese premier, was present on the occasion. The incident became an unforgettable mark of protest from an ethnic community for whom Nehru had special regard. The complex Naga political issue bewildered even Nehru, a great advocate of Indian tribals.

As elsewhere in the country, the Naga class that had been the primary beneficiary of modern education formed the vanguard against colonialism. Having been exposed to statecraft, bureaucracy, and the legal system, Naga intellectuals worked within the same paradigm while developing new narratives of history and identity to assert their "rights and freedom".

Contrary to popular perception, the mission-school-educated Naga elites were ahead of their time. Their skirmishes with the ruling authority of the day started with the British. According to Aliba Imti,

> In the Naga Hills there was a regulation . . . "no student to dress in the western way and to have his hair cut in the western mode." They

[20] Ibid., 18.

were to dress in loincloth, as that was the dress of the tribals, and to have their hair cut in the tribal way, round the head and any one not found in this tribal attire and haircut was to be fined a sum of Rs 2/-, a big sum in those days. In this regard, I told the Mokokchung High School boys that this was nonsense and a stupid order which should be challenged. "I am the owner of my head," I said.[21]

As a student Phizo, the longest-serving NNC president, would put on a necktie daily in an act of defiance, since this "unusual flap" hanging from the neck separated the white man from the native.[22] Meanwhile, a noteworthy architect of the NNC, Angami Kevichusa, son of the first Baptist convert from Khonoma and a close friend of Phizo (they played music together, and Phizo was best man at Kevichusa's wedding), was spelling out the idea of self-determination: "Self-government should mean a government of the Nagas, for the Nagas, by the Nagas. Nothing else means anything to the Nagas."[23] Sensing trouble in the British-administered Naga Hills, the administrator-ethnographer J.P. Mills, in a letter to a fellow administrator, castigated the NNC for its political aspirations and questioned its legitimacy, although he took no action, knowing that British rule in India was coming to an end.

In the initial years of independence the Indian political class underestimated the Naga educated class, over-stressing the role of American missionaries in the political dispute while patronising natives who were on the fast track toward the modernisation that the Baptist mission and British rule had kick-started. The Nagas accused the chief minister of Assam, Bishnuram Medhi, under whom political turmoil had escalated, of mocking their political aspirations.[24] Educated Nagas perceived his attitude as being the result of "a feudalistic mindset, a casteist attitude". The Naga peace activist Niketu Iralu said, "Bishnuram Medhi was very unpopular among the Nagas for his stance in the Naga political issue. Many

---

[21] Ibid., 35.
[22] Steyn, *Zapuphizo*, 45.
[23] "Freedom", *The Naga Nation*, October 1946, 3.
[24] See Swu, Introduction, in *Hails and Blames*, xxii.

Indian political leaders including Medhi thought that the missionaries were instigating the Nagas to rebel against the Indian state. It was an insult to the Naga intelligence that some white man had to come and teach them about nationalism."

Gone were the days of empires, when American Baptist missionaries with evangelical single-mindedness spoke out against "Oriental despots".[25] The post-colonial period had brought a new dispensation with checks and balances as never before. Missionaries had to be extra cautious with the new authorities in the emerging political reality; in places like the Naga Hills, where political aspiration among the natives was strengthening, foreign missionaries were in a precarious position. They had first taught the natives to read and write – a dangerous weapon; educated Nagas were now putting their ideas and aspirations on paper and corresponding with leading British politicians like Churchill and Attlee. On 28 March 1947 Sakhrie, the finest Naga political propagandist of his time, wrote, with no help from the American missionaries, to Churchill: "To [the] British, we the Nagas never said 'Quit'. But when time has decreed that British should quit, we must say – Quit honourably."[26]

IV

What these Nagas had in common was a religious faith; the roots of Naga intellectualism lay in the encounter with the American Baptist mission. We have seen that the formation of Baptist associations along ethnic lines, going beyond the palisades of "village republics", began in the early days of the mission. At the start of the twentieth century, Baptist associations in Kohima and Impur included various tribes, e.g. the association under the Kohima mission comprised tribes like the Angami, Sumi, Zeliang, and Kuki.

[25] Wittfogel coined the term "Oriental despotism" in the context of empires and monarchs in the East. See Wittfogel, *Oriental Despotism*.

[26] T. Sakhrie's letter to Winston Churchill, 1947. Apparently, Churchill did not reply to the young Naga intellectual – unlike Nehru who responded to Sakhrie's letter on 1 August 1946.

THE BAPTIST INTELLECTUALS 315

These Baptist associations, formed purely for mission strategy and budgetary convenience, were those from which the Nagas had the first inklings of centralised authority and identity mobilisation. "The first rally of the churches was held at Molung in 1897."[27] The idea of a modern and voluntary association was beginning to take shape; the Baptist association was starting to meticulously record minutes of meetings, elect native members to the body, raise budgetary concerns, and debate doctrinal issues. The first Baptist association meeting, organised by E.W. Clark, saw an assembling of the faithful from mission stations under the British subdivisional headquarters, Mokokchung. The Perrines of Impur station, accompanied by "preachers, helpers, and load-carriers", walked for three days with their four-month-old baby to reach the venue; while the Haggards "having entered upon the work in the Lhota tribe, a long way removed, were unable to be present".

The topics discussed during this first meeting at Molung in 1897 included "evangelization, the Holy Spirit, Christian benevolence, should the Nagas bury their dead? Should all Christians learn to read? By what changes in food, houses, sanitation, and clothing shall Christians better their mode of living?"[28] Also, "It was decided to hold these associational meetings annually, and the Yazang church extended a very cordial invitation for the next year."[29]

While the in-house missionary in Kohima, Rivenburg, was mulling over the need for an association, a native evangelist "did not quite see how it could be financed". However, in 1912 the Angami evangelist Nisier suggested a meeting of Baptist converts from various villages under the Kohima mission. At the gathering Rev. Rivenburg lauded the mission effort: "In my address of welcome I gave a summary of the history of the mission since 1887 . . . I told them how I had asked God to let me have one hundred members in this church in Kohima . . . Nisier came out

[27] Clark, *A Corner in India*, 142.
[28] Ibid., 143.
[29] Ibid., 144.

Ill. 10: Rev. J. Tanquist, a gifted translator (front, right), and Rev. G.W. Supplee, considered the most musically gifted missionary (back, left), with Angami evangelists and converts at the Kohima mission station, c. 1930. Courtesy NBCC.

in a fine confession of faith, and then one, and then another came, till one hundred and thirty-four were added."[30] Nisier, who was instrumental in forming the Baptist association in 1912, played an important role in Naga politics. Six years later he became a member of the Naga Club whose notable members included other Rivenburg aides. The formation of Naga Baptist associations thus preceded the first Naga modern organisation, the Naga Club. In fact, it was mission-school alumni who comprised the active members of the Club; there can be little doubt that Baptist associations were the forerunners of modern Naga organisations.

The first two tribal councils – Lotha and Ao – were formed in 1923 and 1928, respectively. These first pan-tribal organisations also emerged from the hotspots of Baptist mission activity; the American Baptists had opened a mission station in Ao Naga country in 1876, and in Lotha Naga country in 1885; here, education was a common feature. At the start of the twentieth century Nagas were holding annual Baptist meetings with well-defined

[30] Rivenburg, ed., *The Star of Naga Hills*, 126.

associations in place. At these, Nagas had a platform to speak of their knowledge and experience of the outside world; an elderly Sumi convert told me that he first heard the "story of Socrates" from Hokishe Sema – later chief minister – and infamously Indira Gandhi's man in Nagaland – during an annual Baptist conference. The associations sought to evangelise and strengthen but also inform and mobilise people, and spread social interaction beyond traditional boundaries. The process brought former feuding villages and strangers under the same umbrella; a new community beyond the fortified village walls was beginning to take shape.

The rise of the mission-school educated coincided with the early years of India's struggle for independence. Not all educated Nagas of the period became architects and champions of ethnonationalism. Their attitudes towards the idea of a nation-state, independence, and self-rule were of various shades, although those propounding ethnonationalism gained much prominence and attention. In towns and cities to which Naga students went for higher studies, the struggle for independence was gaining mass popularity; naturally, some of these young and idealistic students studying in the plains were influenced by the larger anti-colonial narrative of the Indian National Congress.

The most prominent Naga leader in recorded history to be influenced by the Indian freedom struggle was Longritangchetba, popularly known as Rev. Longri Ao. "On receipt of a report from the SDO, Mokokchung, he was banned from entering the Naga Hills due to his political leaning" – so outlines the NBCC's eulogy of Longri.[31] The ban came when the British administration in the Naga Hills came to know of Longri's connection with the Congress. While in Upper Assam, he was said to have "visited the villages and tea gardens around Jorhat on his bicycle, holding meetings and talking to the people about the Indian freedom movement."[32] He had earlier come to the notice of the British authorities for his involvement with student activism, which had

---

[31] See Nagaland Baptist Church Council, *One New Humanity*, 177.
[32] Rao, *Longri Ao*, 25.

begun taking root among the Nagas. His fellow Baptist Indian biographer says Longri's "fiery speeches in the [Ao Naga students'] Conference against the established British order (which was against any change) and of the need to bring a new social order among his people had already drawn the suspicion of the administration. When his reported association with some of the Congress leaders and their activities surfaced in 1933, he immediately fell into disfavour with the British Sub-Divisional Officer of Mokokchung."[33]

Born in 1906 in Changki village to a practising animist family, Longri had parents who had come under the influence of the new faith when Western medicine cured their sick daughter. They were baptised by Rev. James Riley Bailey, and this changed the mind of an adamant father who had not wanted to send his son to a mission school for fear that "he would incur the wrath of the irate spirits".[34] The Impur mission school and later the Jorhat Bible School prepared Longri for his role as negotiator on behalf of the Baptists when Naga leaders battled for Naga self-determination in jungle hideouts, small towns, and villages. He fell afoul of some Baptists because of his involvement in Naga political issues; a prominent Assamese Baptist leader in Jorhat, Comfort Goldsmith, severely criticised Longri's involvement in politics, saying that as a churchman he had blemished the Baptist tenet of separation between church and state. In response to Goldsmith's letter – which was even translated into regional languages and widely circulated by Longri's detractors – Longri issued a circular on 29 June 1963 "To My own People" from his NBCC office in Kohima: "I am not a politician, nor would I enter into the controversy as to which side is responsible for all the sufferings and miseries that have been brought upon our people in the villages. But I, an ordinary man, am looking into the darkness which surrounds us today."

Dubbed "a man of peace", he would become the face of the influential Naga Baptist church in tortuous political negotiations. Before his entry into the political drama as church representative,

[33] Ibid., 11.
[34] Ibid., 2–3.

Longri was already a well-known figure as a Bible teacher and preacher in Baptist circles in north-east India – a legend of sorts when he went as the first native missionary to the Konyak Naga. It was the Council of Baptist Churches in Assam that sent Longri to Wakching, a village that Fürer-Haimendorf wrote about in great detail. After serving in the "Konyak mission field" for seventeen years (1950–67), Longri was called to head the largest religious organisation in the state; he took office as executive secretary of the NBCC in April 1967, serving till 1979.

Longri's tenure as leader of the Naga Baptist church was not easy, since it was a time of political upheaval and violence. For common people caught between state repression and the obstinacy of Naga insurgents, life was hard; Baptist leaders like Longri, Kenneth Kerhuo, Kijungluba Ao, and Toniho Chishi, who were the face of the Baptist church during the much-publicised Peace Mission in the mid-1960s, were a breath of fresh air. The Peace Mission was manned by three renowned personalities: Jayaprakash Narayan, the socialist activist turned Gandhian social worker; Rev. Michael Scott, an Anglican priest and anti-apartheid activist; and Bimala Prasad Chaliha, the third chief minister of Assam who was genuinely liked by Nagas across the political spectrum. The Peace Mission's triumvirate were all grassroots leaders: Scott had worked in apartheid South Africa, Jayaprakash Narayan with the agrarian movement, and Chaliha with the Quit India movement; but for average Naga believers it was co-religionist leaders like Longri who spoke the Baptist language of faith, hope, and suffering that made most sense. One of Longri's reports from the field states:

> In Mokokchung, we found one hundred and twenty men, women and children locked up by the Indian army. I went to the jail to speak with the prisoners and the local Central Intelligence Department official came along. He demanded that I should speak in English or Assamese; but I refused saying, "How can they understand me?" We sang together the hymn "In the Cross" and all said the Lord's prayer. I read to them from Matthew 6, "God clothes the lilies and feeds the birds. Do not be anxious."[35]

[35] Longri's NBCC meeting report at Wokha, quoted in ibid., 80.

Longri eclipsed many hardline Ao Naga ethnonationalists, being seen as a Naga leader willing to settle amicably with the Indian government; what he wanted for the Nagas was "a place within [the] Indian Union with a high political status."[36] Writing to the governor of Assam, Jairamdas Daulatram, in 1953 from the Konyak Baptist mission field, Longri echoed what Nehru had envisaged before independence when trouble started brewing in the Naga Hills. His political stance was not popular among underground leaders, but it resonated with faceless commoners.

Contrary to popular belief, the Ao Nagas were no less ethnonationalist than the other major Naga tribes. Many of their educated joined the political movement and the underground government; the most prominent among them was a successful small-town businessman – his property was confiscated – Imkongmeren, vice president of the NNC, who remained a steadfast comrade and supporter of Phizo till his death. Imkongmeren was a member of the Naga Club, which had a division in Mokokchung; he had served as president of the Ao tribal council during WWII, and after the war played an active role in the formation of the NNC. He began his public career as a student leader, and successfully organised the first Ao Naga students' conference in his native village, Longkhum, along with other student leaders (a team that included Longri).

Born in 1900, Imkongmeren is said to have converted to the new faith while still in a bachelor's dormitory (*morung*) as a teenager. He studied at Baptist mission schools in Impur and Jorhat before starting a "general shop" in the British administration town of Mokokchung. With his education Imkongmeren could have joined government service but chose to start a business to retain some sort of independence from the ruling authorities.[37] Besides the British restrictions on Naga dress and hairstyle, the patronising interest of the colonials in preserving the old way of life did not go down well with educated Nagas. The first NNC president, Aliba

---

[36] Ibid., 75.
[37] Atsongchanger, *Unforgettable Memories*, 138.

Imti, recalled a time when his elder brother, Stephen (named so by his devout Baptist parents), was denied a scholarship of a few rupees because "he had a Christian name".[38]

Among the topnotch Naga guerrilla commanders to make a mark in the Naga armed uprising in the early days (1950s and '60s) was "General" Merentoba, a soft-spoken man from Mopungchuket raised in a devout Baptist family. Larger-than-life guerrilla commanders like Kaito Sukhai and Mowu Angami overshadowed tenacious Ao guerrilla commanders like Maken, Merentoba, and Panger Walling, though Ao Naga guerrillas fought with resilience as well. Their actions brought untold misery to their tribesmen in the shape of counterinsurgency measures by the Indian army. This foremost of educated Naga communities (courtesy the Baptist mission) became stereotyped as comprising "Naga moderates". This was because its finest mission-school products, such as the first Ao Naga graduate Mayangnokcha, the pioneering Ao Naga doctor Imkongliba, and the former NNC president Aliba Imti, all advocated an amicable settlement within the Indian union. Besides, educated men like Dr Talimeren Ao, the son of a Baptist minister who captained the Indian football team in the 1948 London Olympics, faithfully served the state as model citizens. It was for his moderate political stance that Dr Imkongliba, whose surgical instruments are now displayed in the state museum in Kohima, was assassinated by guerrillas in his hometown in 1961. The respected Naga doctor's transgression was that he had led a group of so-called Naga moderates, which included some former NNC leaders, and convened the first Naga People's Convention (NPC) meet in 1957, an organisation instrumental in the founding of the state of Nagaland in 1963.

The trajectory of the NPC was not without controversy. One of its key members, Kevichusa, the first Naga graduate and Indian bureaucrat, who was mistrusted by underground leaders as a government official and regarded as a troublemaker by Indian

---

[38] Imti, *Reminiscence*, 36.

Ill. 11: Sarvepalli Radhakrishnan, president of India, arrives in Kohima on 1 December 1963 to inaugurate the state of Nagaland. He is flanked by Vishnu Sahay, first governor, and P. Shilu Ao, first chief minister of Nagaland. Courtesy DIPR.

intelligence, walked out of the Convention as he felt that the exclusion of Naga hardliners could not end well. Meanwhile the Indian government, advised by a shrewd intelligence chief, S.M. Dutt, took advantage of the deepening rift among Naga intellectuals on matters of their community's political destiny. Another veteran intelligence chief, B.N. Mullik, who proved his mettle in the Naga theatre, saw the sly hand of the Indian intelligence bureau and "a band of dedicated officers" serving in the Naga areas behind the formation of the NPC "as a rival to the Naga National Council".[39] Mullik dubbed Kevichusa "the evil genius of Nagaland" but claimed that this Naga intellectual was no match for "a brilliant Intelligence Officer" like Dutt.[40] In this context, a Kuki friend from the Indian Revenue Service, who is a strident critic of ethnonationalism in north-east India, made the cutting observation that "while the Kukis and Nagas just came out of

[39] Mullik, *My Years with Nehru*, 319–20.
[40] Ibid., 318.

the jungles, their Chinese and Indian opponents were mastering Sun Tzu's *The Art of War* and Kautilya's *Arthashastra* for at least a thousand years."

The former joint secretary of the NPC, Dr S.C. Jamir, a veteran Naga politician and five-time chief minister of the state, maintained, fifty-eight years after the signing of the 16-point Agreement in 1960, that the Convention was

> the only way forward for a lasting peace and amicable political solution since ordinary villagers were suffering the most in the armed conflict... The choice was between survival and annihilation. The choice was between getting submerged in Assamese culture and asserting the Naga identity, between enjoying freedom to exercise traditional rights and being respected as a people and getting trampled under the weight of mightier neighbours.[41]

This grand old Congressman of Naga politics recalled harrowing days when a section of Naga intellectuals craved a solution to end the widespread suffering:

> Repression by the Indian Army was marked by acts of cruelty which touched a new bottom in Free Nagaland. Battalions moving to villages and remote areas spread terror, intimidating the simple highlanders. Village folk were hanged upside down, bayoneted, burnt alive, raped and were subjected to all kinds of torture.[42] ... During these eventful days 1735 representatives of the 16 Tribes of the Naga Hills and Tuensang Frontier Agency met at Kohima "to discuss, deliberate and explore all possible means for the early and lasting restoration of peace, unity and harmony in the beleaguered Naga lands."[43]

A lifelong practising Baptist, Dr Jamir honed his oratory and leadership skills as a leader of Christian Endeavour, a Baptist youth evangelical outreach wing with roots in the American Baptist mission, before going on to pursue a law degree from Nehru's city, Allahabad. Like most educated Nagas of his time, Jamir was

[41] Jamir, *Nagaland*, 31–2.
[42] Ibid., 26–7.
[43] Ibid., 37.

involved with NNC activities before the organisation was outlawed. When in 1951 the NNC under Phizo's leadership conducted a plebiscite, Jamir was a young student leader involved in mobilising villagers for the signature campaign in Mokokchung district. Undoubtedly the most successful Naga politician to make a mark in the mainland, Dr Jamir, whom I met at his farmhouse in Chumukedima in Dimapur in 2018, was 87 but still religiously following his routine of reading, writing, and speaking engagements. Seated on an imposing chair behind a large mahogany desk and surrounded by books, this recently retired governor of Odisha narrated his political journey starting from a small village, Ungma, which had come under the influence of the American Baptist mission. Having survived three assassination attempts by Naga insurgents, he said his life had been preserved by the "sheer grace" of God. He is among the last of his generation to have seen the American Baptist mission's halcyon days, the departure of the British, the beginnings of the Naga national movement, the Nehru era, the rise of the Gandhi dynasty in the Congress Party, and the Naga political movement through various shades – and through it all what remains for him is his "faith and personal relationship with Jesus Christ". An old-school Baptist, he laments the culture of "prayer houses" mushrooming everywhere in his hometown in Dimapur district, and the widespread belief in self-styled prophets among modern Naga Baptists. "Politics devoid of moral responsibility is harmful," he says, speaking like a true Baptist of the "woeful" political climate in the state.

The Ao Naga educated class that produced a relatively large number of leaders on the moderate end of the political spectrum could not all the same rescue ordinary villagers when the time of reckoning came. When the army operation started, the Ao region went up in flames; in a bid to flush out insurgents holed up in the jungles, the Indian army razed *jhum* fields, torched villages, and herded people into "concentration camps".[44] The

---

[44] See Atsongchanger, *Unforgettable Memories*, esp. Chapter 3.

idea of Naga independence that was in the air in Ao villages was stamped into the ground by military operations which brought unimaginable suffering to this ethnic group who had been the first to encounter the Baptist mission. This retired schoolteacher from Ungma spoke poignantly of how "in the years after Indian independence the villagers would come rushing from their *jhum* fields and cluster around the lone radio to hear news about the elusive Naga independence." The idea of nationalism was not confined to the educated class, it had percolated to the poorest. "The optimism of the villagers was high those days; it was as if Naga independence was only a day or week away. How innocent and simple-minded we were," he added.

The idea of a separate state had spread to the remotest villages, and ordinary village farmers eking out a livelihood revelled in the idea of a Naga nation cutting across village and ethnic boundaries. Naga intellectuals had achieved the remarkable feat of spreading the idea of self-rule to virtually every Naga, but the idea had germinated at great cost to dignity and livelihood. And from there it led to a lifetime of trauma and fear for Dr Jamir's generation and beyond.

Never very far from the prying eyes of the state machinery in the administrative headquarters, NNC volunteers had travelled from village to village spreading their message and recruiting people to their fold. Yehozhe, a former Baptist missionary and chief of Ngozubomi – a frontier Sumi Naga village in the erstwhile NEFA – said that in the early 1950s his late father donated cows and money to the "Naga cause" so that his children might get privileges when "freedom dawns in Nagaland". Around the same time, as narrated by Baptist theologian Ezamo Murry, the Lotha Nagas were singing a revolutionary song that went, "If we persist there will be bags of gold . . ." When the army operation began, and with it the suffering, they had in a sense to change their tune. The faithful turned to religion for solace, as is clear in the poignant Sumi Naga song from the NEFA region in the 1950s at the start of the counterinsurgency operation.

Tizu-Tsutha kuma dolo kuami
Kuxu ju aye
Mulo kepu likhi

Anu mighimi akilo sasumono itsuche ketoyi
Suphahemino akilo sasumono ghasu ghave qholo itsuche

Aghalono anga sasu muloqa
Kimiye no tsughu tsu kevilo
Impeu Jehovah

Asu atu qholo chepimu-chepimu
Nono sachelo
Iza no he . . .

Which is, roughly translated:

Natives between [the rivers] Tizu and Tsutha
How heart-wrenching, if we ponder our lot

Like wandering orphans without a home
Chased out of homes by the armies, we wander in the jungle

Deep in the jungle with children we shed tears
Have mercy on us; please don't let it rain
Our lord, Jehovah

Though we hide beneath trees and rocks
Lead us O lord
O dear mother . . .

V

When the most powerful man in the land, Deputy Commissioner Charles Pawsey, assembled disparate tribal councils to form the Naga Hills District Tribal Council (NHDTC) in 1945, the Baptist faithful already had religious associations in place. Under the watchful eyes of American missionaries, these associations did not get involved in political protest or civil disobedience against the British, maintaining the Christian injunction to render both unto Caesar and to God.

THE BAPTIST INTELLECTUALS 327

The NHDTC was Pawsey's brainchild, but he had educated natives working with him – emerging leaders like Mayangnokcha, Kevichusa, and Sakhrie. The wartime administrator had initiated the NHDTC to alleviate the aftermath of WWII and create a platform for Naga tribes to collectively address their grievances. Many saw the NHDTC as a post-war relief body. Modernity was creeping into the region despite the authorities trying their best to keep the natives "uncontaminated" from the ways of the world; the cash economy had taken root and the lure of harvesting all that was not Caesar's or God's was increasing unabated; the noble savages of the Rousseauean imagination were in India's tribal north-east no longer all that noble. Upset at the way many falsely sought post-war reparations, Pawsey is said to have remarked: "The first Naga casualty of the war was their honesty."[45]

Pawsey had formed the NHDTC altruistically, but it metamorphosed into an exacting political organisation under his watch. By the time of his departure, as the British were relinquishing their eight-decade-old strongholds in the Naga Hills, the organisation he had initiated had reconstituted itself and grown more vociferous in its political demands. It had been taken over by a new educated class, superseding the elders of the traditional set-up, the "noble savages" Pawsey had wanted to retain as the mainstay of Naga customary practices. The NHDTC changed its name to Naga National Council (NNC) during a conference at Wokha in March 1946.[46] And soon enough Pawsey began to lose control over the new Naga organisation. The Naga leaders in their new setting did still want to guard their so-called traditional way of life and customs, but they were more politically ambitious and modern in their outlook, and with the decline of British rule the strong whiff of nationalism had seeped into the Naga regions as well.

Pawsey was well liked by the natives and he liked them in return – perhaps too well. Though he respected the convention common

---

[45] Quoted in Government of Nagaland, *Heralding Hope*, 81.
[46] Elwin, *Nagaland*, 51.

among British political officials which said "over-familiarity bred impertinence", he was said to have had a secret passion for a Naga woman. Unlike the sociable American missionaries, British administrators were expected to stay aloof in their interactions with the people they administered – their monographs on the Naga tribes suggest this too. Pawsey did not produce enthralling academic tomes for European audiences but was arguably the most admired of all deputy commissioners stationed in Kohima; stories of his reign attest to this. He was a wartime hero and earned the respect of his Naga subjects as he refused to leave them to their fate. As deputy commissioner he literally dug in and held out against the severe bombing and waves of Japanese kamikaze. On occasion he joined villagers in their work in squelchy terraced fields.

At the time of the Japanese invasion of 1944, Pawsey's worries multiplied as waves of refugees fleeing Burma descended on Kohima. Pawsey set himself to work. "He had . . . refugees to deal with, labour to find for airfields and roads in the slippery terrain of landslides . . . He found time too to go all over his part of the Naga Hills."[47] He was later awarded the Military Cross and subsequently knighted for his exemplary service to the Crown, but meanwhile in the short post-war period he was vexed by the new political awakening.

The authorities in general saw the winds of change in the Naga Hills. They tried to remain indifferent, if not wash their hands of the new political ferment. Writing to W.G. Archer, Sub-Divisional Officer, Mokokchung (1947–8), J.P. Mills, formerly Deputy Commissioner, Kohima (1935–7), highlighted the emerging ethnonationalism among the Naga educated class even as he shrugged it off: "There is [a] somewhat nebulous body in existence (more or less self-created) called 'The Naga National Council'. It is not 'National' at all, of course, though it may be nationalistic."[48] Mills seems to have been suggesting that supercilious indifference was

---

[47] Mason, *The Men Who Ruled India*, 327.
[48] Quoted in Thomas, *Evangelising the Nation*, 102.

the way to deal with Nagas who lacked the good sense to remain the merry tribal headhunters of yore.

A day after independence Archer's wife Mildred – later recognised in the British academic world as a significant art historian – gave an account of natives giving Pawsey the cold shoulder as he hoisted the tricolour on 15 August 1947, marking the end of British rule; apparently no Naga had been seen in the great parade ground, there having been only a few plainsmen.[49] Resistance was simmering. Only the day before, on 14 August 1947, the "Khonoma group" had taken to subversion, "declaring the independence of the Naga Hills"; they had drafted "twelve copies to be sent to the leading newspapers" which Pawsey had seized when the postmaster alerted him to them.[50]

Who were these Khonoma renegades? The ringleaders were all former students of the Baptist mission school in Kohima; they included an emerging key player in Naga politics, Angami Zapu Phizo, who had recently returned to the Naga Hills from Burma after having done time in Insein Jail on sedition charges. Many who knew Phizo say that this high-school-educated native did not join the colonial service because he disliked the authorities. Losing his father, a peripatetic trader, at an early age, he had grown up under the guidance of Rev. Rivenburg, whom the Angami Nagas affectionately called *chahaketsau* (the old boss). It was from American missionaries that schoolchildren had learnt a great deal about the new faith, the mannerisms, the eccentricities, and the outlook of the white man, since the *borchaha* (the big boss), i.e. the deputy commissioner, was too far removed from children: Phizo's tribesmen had a saying – "the big boss is next to earth and sky".[51]

Administrators had, however, to often descend from their empyrean to quell rebellious natives: the Nagas were many things but not submissive. As a boy Phizo had witnessed an incident

[49] Quoted in Lhousa, *Strange Country*, 60.
[50] See Thomas, *Evangelising the Nation*, 108.
[51] Zinyü, *Phizo*, 22.

in which a certain Naga Labour Corps recruit in a mass parade had, on being reprimanded for "filthy cooking pots", hit the big boss, Deputy Commissioner Hutton, "with a piece of firewood".[52] Hutton also recalled an incident of a mischievous native sending him a message with chillies, challenging him to a duel.

Years later the two personalities – Hutton, then a retired professor, and Phizo, then the NNC president – got into an altercation in London over the Naga question. This happened on 21 July 1966, at the release of a book by Rev. Michael Scott. The ageing former big boss raged to the effect that the Nagas had received more than their due, and that the Indian government had best put a bounty on the heads of troublemakers. The brouhaha showed that Naga society had changed, and that the former British rulers were now irrelevant and out of touch with the change. Their last deputy commissioner, Pawsey, inadvertently provided further evidence that the Nagas were very much their own masters and their former rulers old fogeys. When Pawsey revisited Nagaland in 1965 – said his interpreter Kawoto Sukhalu to me – the administrator who had once commanded such esteem was denied entry into the Sumi Naga area by the renegade guerrilla commander Kaito Sukhai. Negotiations had to be conducted to avoid embarrassment. Ironically, Kaito's own father Kuhoto, a Sumi chieftain, had served as Pawsey's head *dobashi* in Kohima. In the new milieu, men like Phizo and Kaito held sway, and those who debated their legitimacy were merely evidence of colonialism being passé.

Phizo's position on that day, as earlier, was that the British administrators had had their day and had long needed to step aside. He criticised other educated natives, especially NNC members, for continuing to let the political officer have the final say on important matters. One of the first things that Naga intellectuals like Phizo did was challenge the status quo: he, in particular, was known for rebellious nonconformism. Hutton, an authority on the Nagas in Western academic circles, still claimed ownership of

---

[52] Steyn, *Zapuphizo*, 41.

a sort over the people that he had written so much about. This former William Wyse Professor of Cambridge University was now anachronistically fulminating that, "if left to themselves", Nagas would revert to "the state of savagery in which the British had found them".[53] It was the old condescending colonial narrative of the White Sahib directed by the heavens to shoulder the burden of benighted natives who were believed incapable of managing themselves. The irate professor's outburst against the temerity of Phizo and his Nagas taking on a government that the British had bequeathed them served only to show the senility of antiquated colonials. Way back in 1921, Hutton had been all praise for the "Khonoma Angami group" – though in the racially loaded context of grading the intellect and physical attributes of the natives on whom he had cast his post-phrenological gaze.[54] The American missionaries too had indulged in this supposedly serious pastime: Rivenburg said the Angami are "a taller, handsomer race than [are] the Ao Nagas".[55] Angami men, who wore a knee-length garment fastened around the waist, belonged in the white man's view to a higher culture than other Naga groups who used a "flimsy" covering.

The Angami Nagas had in fact picked fights with the British more than other Naga groups; they were in the forefront against British expansionism. Khonoma stood out in particular for a number of skirmishes with the British, and between 1844 and 1879 the British had torched the village four times. And the Angami did have an edge over neighbouring tribes, not necessarily intellectually, but in innovations like their farming methods, which were based in an indigenous knowledge system. They practised an advanced method of rice cultivation in water-fed permanent terraces which enabled a settled lifestyle and larger settlements. Their terraces, fed by alluvial slush from alder plantations uphill,

[53] Ibid., 142.
[54] See Hutton, *The Angami Nagas*.
[55] Rivenburg, ed., *The Star of Naga Hills*, 73–4.

increased soil fertility and enabled a surplus; this food surplus gave them extra time to raid, trade, and travel. Some Khonoma men travelled far and wide; Phizo's father Krusietso was one of them. He went as far as Calcutta and Burma to trade items in great demand, like fabrics, beads, and semi-precious stones. As early as 1915, Rev. Rivenburg reported that a Baptist convert from Khonoma had died while returning from a trading expedition to Burma, his body having been sent to the village.[56] The dead man is very likely to have been Phizo's father.

Phizo's great-uncle Pelhu, a famed warrior, was one of the Khonoma leaders who made a deal with the British after being defeated by them in 1879. Stories of valour – with a sense of triumphalism despite eventual defeat – were retold time and again in the *thehu*, a meeting place for males. These tales were bound to have left a deep impression on adolescent boys. Young men like Phizo, inheriting the proud tradition of their forebears, revamped their heritage with the new attitudes of modernity. This generation of educated men found an outlet for their pride and patriotism in the new-found ethnonationalism, which they subsequently pursued with fervour.

The rise of nationalism among Nagas, though a modern phenomenon tied up with British colonialism, Indian nationalism, and American Christianity, had its wellspring in ethnic pride. Khonoma intellectuals like Phizo, Kevichusa, Jasokie, and Sakhrie pursued their political consciousness with flair and inventiveness; their propaganda appealed to a populace that had for generations lived in tribe-based villages.

VI

Before independence the only NNC leader to have done jail time for political reasons was Phizo. If some accounts are to be believed, he had narrowly escaped a firing squad while in Insein

---

[56] Ibid., 129. Krusietso Dolie died on 7 January 1915 when Phizo was eleven years old.

Jail. Post-independence, he was jailed twice, once in Burma again, and once in Calcutta. Jail time hardened his resolve to be a practical doer, not an armchair ideologue. He grew into a man of action, maybe even, as some critics say, an impetuously active man. His interest in concrete action and measurable outcomes led him to differ with his NNC colleagues, including his close confidants, with far-reaching consequences.

Unlike his contemporaries who vied for top positions in the NNC, Phizo had no college degree. His education in the Kohima mission school had been minimal; after passing Class 6 he had gone to Government High School in Shillong. In this hilly capital where the British rode horses, sipped afternoon tea served by natives, and waltzed the evenings away over jolly parties, Phizo was silent witness to the unmentionable class and racial divide. He dropped out of high school after failing the matriculation examination. He returned to his alma mater in Kohima, wanting to be a schoolteacher, but the headmaster Rev. Supplee thought otherwise. Education was now a springboard for upward mobility, a change from earlier days: Phizo's brother-in-law Seville Iralu, the third Naga to study medicine, had only been sent to school because "he had suffered from poliomyelitis attack on the right foot and was not fit for other important work except school" – as Seville's surviving son, Niketu, said to me. Attitudes had changed; the educated were now at the helm of affairs.

Niketu Iralu was about eleven when his uncle returned from Burma with his family in June 1946 and stayed for a time in his parents' home. Phizo was by then a man on a mission, always at his typewriter churning out pages of political prose. To the government this was subversion against the state and, as Niketu remembers it, one day the Assam police arrived and confiscated Phizo's typewriter and papers, the only property he owned. This was around the time the American missionaries had started running into trouble with the authorities. The house where Phizo was staying was in the mission compound.

For a man who had not passed the school-leaving exam, Phizo

wrote a lot. He was also an avid reader on a wide variety of topics, with biographies of famous people inspiring him most. It was the only leisure activity in a mind forever planning and plotting. "My father used to tell him to relax sometimes but he was always in a hurry," Niketu said of his eccentric uncle. Equipped with a small briefcase and piles of paper, Phizo would visit villages in the Mokokchung area, a political missionary spreading his ideology. His clothes were always washed and neatly folded, his papers stacked, his briefcase ever ready to move; his restiveness and ability to be continuously on his toes were part of his personality and well suited to a driven man constantly pursued.

Phizo was a maverick intellectual; a self-taught propagandist, a bohemian ideologue drawing inspiration from the rustic appeal of ordinary people. Politically he was a zealous nonconformist who romanticised the greatness of his "people" while showing an almost morbid mistrust of the mainstream, which he saw as corrupting and denuding "the simplicity and innocence" of Naga society and culture. "Our apparent backwardness is an asset to us. We start our new life on virgin soil with modern plans," he wrote to the governor of West Bengal, C. Rajagopalachari. The words were part of a 41-page letter written while he was "penned" in Calcutta in 1948.[57]

But Phizo was never tied down by the dictates of the state; he was the inveterate rebel. He staunchly – and bafflingly – took the position that there had always been a Naga nation; that Nagas were not asking for sovereignty from India, or, before that, from the British; that the world community must recognise the "inalienable rights" and already existing sovereignty of the Nagas. To Phizo, Naga sovereignty had been relinquished "unjustly" by the British to a neighbouring country, India. He denounced both the British and Indian governments till his last breath, labelling them "occupation forces".

Whatever their attitude towards the state, Phizo's contem-

---

[57] The opening paragraph of the letter starts "I, A.Z. Phizo, Naga, Your State Prisoner, address this letter to you as one of the spokesmen of the Naga people." See Lasuh, ed., *The Naga Chronicle*, 53–65.

poraries Kevichusa, Mayangnokcha, Aliba Imti, and Jasokie all occupied important positions in the state machinery, and were thus viewed as having joined hands with the "occupation forces". Mayangnokcha, a noted educationist, was later awarded the Padma Shri for his service to the Indian state. Phizo's former NNC colleague Jasokie faced an assassination attempt by armed insurgents; Phizo even began to distrust his clansmen and bosom friend Kevichusa, who was a government official – and therefore viewed as sitting on the fence. After his retirement Kevichusa would form a regional political party, the United Democratic Front, and be elected to parliament. While government employees and Naga intellectuals like Kevichusa and Mayangnokcha had

Ill. 12: T. Aliba Imti, the first NNC president, 1947–8.
Courtesy DIPR.

worked with the authorities to revamp the NHDTC into the more politically active NNC in 1946, within a few years Phizo took over the organisation completely, becoming its de facto president for forty years.

One of the popularly held views is that the NNC began as a moderate organisation and that Phizo steered it towards a hardline position. However, its trajectory, like that of the man who became synonymous with it, is intricate. It is replete with instances of friends turning foes, the clash of ideologies, charges of betrayal, and high-profile assassinations. Narrowly defeating a politically "moderate" fellow tribesman, Visar, Phizo became the fourth NNC president on 9 December 1950, after a stint as president of the Kohima Central Council of the NNC. Behind his rise was the support of Khonoma compatriots, including the charismatic T. Sakhrie, secretary of the NNC (1946–55). The Khonoma elites pursued their new-found ethnonationalism with great zeal and a tinge of romanticism. In particular Jasokie and Sakhrie, both young, musically gifted, educated, and handsome ("ladies' men"), would often be seen sitting over tankards of *zu* and breaking into song – in particular one popular patriotic song composed by Kevichusa's son Diethozor, another bright, educated native of Khonoma.

> The dawn is breaking,
> The time is coming
> To Nagaland, all hail!
> For her we'll never fail . . .

Several of these educated Nagas found themselves in the cross-hairs of armed insurgents who were remorseless in "taking out dissidents" and political opponents. Government officials became easy targets, but as the armed struggle spread across the region, ordinary villagers bore the brunt. Some NNC members had been against the armed option, fearing it would go out of control. In September 1955 a strong contingent of NNC members issued a public statement declaring their ideological stance and charting

Ill. 13: A.Z. Phizo, the fourth NNC president, 1950–90.
Courtesy DIPR.

out a road map for the organisation amid rising tension and dissension within. No doubt the notice was a result of their differences with the incumbent president, Phizo. While it strongly denounced "the use of military by Government in Naga Hills", it also stated that "There is the other policy, the moral policy of non-violence which NNC has as its declared policy. Every individual Naga must accept this moral policy of non-violence as an article of faith."[58]

In 1953, when the state's armed police had poured into the region, the NNC had called for an abandonment of the non-

[58] The "public statement" was dated 26 September 1955 and issued under the names of Silie Haralu, K. Chiiselie, T. Sakhrie, Thinuoneiu, Ngurohiezao, Jasokiazinyü, Kehozhol, I. Chubatemsu Ao, Neilalie and Krutsulie Phewauo – all former colleagues of Phizo. See Ramunny, *The World of Nagas*, 78–9.

cooperation strategy and the adoption of "an alternative policy, a constructive and positive policy". As a preliminary, the state had slapped the Assam Maintenance of Public Order (Autonomous District) Acts 1953, soon to be followed by the Assam Areas Disturbed Act 1955, and the Armed Forces Special Powers Act 1958. The Nagas, labelled a martial race, did not at first pick up guns in their political struggle; they tried the Gandhian method of civil disobedience initiated by the educated class. The civil disobedience method failed: it was never a sustained effort and lacked an icon – such as Gandhi or Aung San – to tether the movement. Public servants and *gaonburas* withdrew voluntarily from the state machinery; however, critics accused the NNC of using coercive tactics to force them to resign.

With the military crackdown, the NNC was tested as never before. Gone were the days of dialogue and memorandum writing, now they faced assault by an army. It was an existential crisis for the NNC; many core members maintained that defeat was inevitable and therefore taking up arms counterproductive. The armed insurrection proved costly for the organisation; many leaders resigned. Phizo, however, fastened himself to the rudder.

His position had always been that talks alone would not solve the Naga political issue as the other side was insincere in its dealings. He had fumed against the ebbing of British rule in Assam and at the colonials conveniently passing the buck to the new Indian government. He denounced the approach of his colleagues as half-hearted, saying the NNC was lacking in spirit and confidence and sitting indecisively on the fence. A few months before Indian independence he even unsuccessfully launched a radical new party, the Independent League or Independent Party, as an alternative to the NNC.[59] The new party was formed with an uncompromising view on self-determination and a hardline stance. The NNC was, however, an unassailable organisation with

[59] Ramunny records that Deputy Commissioner Pawsey knew of a new political party being floated as the "Naga Independence Group": Ramunny, *The World of Nagas*, 42–3; according to Yonuo, Phizo formed a new party

a popular mandate. The new organisation did not pick up pace, so Phizo returned to the NNC fold, biding his time.

When he entered the Naga political arena in 1946, Phizo was already a tough man who wore his failure and hardships, his run-ins with the authorities, and jail time in Burma like a badge of honour. Unlike every other Naga intellectual, he was cut from a different cloth. He quickly eclipsed his peers through sheer hard work and incredible determination. Soon after he was elected the fourth NNC president, a party session held in Kohima on 11 December 1950 passed a resolution to conduct at the earliest a plebiscite on the issue of "Naga independence". The plebiscite was conducted under Phizo's presidency and cemented his status as unrivalled leader of the Naga political movement.

For their plebiscite argument the Naga leaders had adeptly availed themselves of a provision in Indian electoral politics. Earlier, in 1946, the NNC had demanded a separate electorate for the Naga tribes, and five years on it swiftly executed its plebiscite campaign to boycott the 1951–2 general elections. This contrasted with the position of ethnic groups like the Mizo, Meitei, and Khasi, who turned out to exercise their democratic rights in those first general elections; and in neighbouring Burma, ethnic minorities like the Chins, Kachins, and Shans had signed the Panglong Agreement in 1947 to accede to the new Burmese union (with full autonomy in internal administration for the frontier areas).

This act in favour of a plebiscite, carried out by a bunch of Naga leaders, was a small setback in what was otherwise the biggest democratic exercise in the new independent nation, with *circa* 176 million adults going to the polls. In April 1950, Nehru had introduced the Representation of People Act which was passed in parliament; he had hoped that elections would be held around the same month in 1951. Behind this first massive democratic

---

named People's Independent League on 5 May 1947: Yonuo, *The Rising Nagas*, 200–1; meanwhile, Zinyü writes that Phizo had the "temerity" to launch the "Naga Independence League": Zinyü, *Phizo*, 48.

exercise were some of India's finest civil servants. Meanwhile, in the remote Naga Hills district of Assam, with a few lakh voters, a different kind of exercise was taking place to circumvent the first universal adult franchise of democratic India, and the man behind it was Phizo.

The thumb-impression campaign that the NNC carried out was not sophisticated but it was high on rhetoric. The NNC general secretary Sakhrie was actively involved in the process; he had made arrangements for the printing of plebiscite papers. It was in the early part of 1951 that the papers were printed in Imphal and "transported to Khonoma in a truck"; then the papers were sealed inside bamboo cylinders and dispatched to various tribal regions under the NNC fold.[60] In a letter circulated on 30 April 1951, NNC president Phizo addressed all "the Presidents of Tribal Councils":

> It is already known to everyone that the plebiscite will be started on the 16th May, 1951 . . . We are to see that the plebiscite is conducted in a normal way. There should be no agitation nor demonstration. Every person must feel perfectly free to say and record what he or she likes. We are fighting for independence for a fuller freedom, for a separate sovereign state of Nagaland. But for those people if there is any wish to say that Nagaland must be within the Indian Union they must have the full freedom to express their views without fear. I hope everyone will have the courage to say exactly what he or she wants to say.[61]

The Phizo-led Naga plebiscite was a wake-up call for the Assam Pradesh Congress Committee: a small tribal group had come out and flatly rejected the new Indian state's democratic process. Phizo had proved his prowess as a grassroots leader and made known his resolution. However, given the minuscule size of the Naga population, this refusal of participation remained inconspicuous

[60] Sakhrie, *The Vision of T. Sakhrie*, 11.
[61] Ramunny, *The World of Nagas*, 57–8.

among the larger troubles of a huge country. Phizo was astute in his political approach and planning; to gain the support of the global community he had to legitimise the political struggle, and the best way was to invoke the idea of democratic participation and not coercion. He pushed the narrative that "Nobody need worry or fear for his and her safety in expressing oneself freely. All will be put on the record in the form of fingerprint. We are making three separate copies for historical document and one copy shall be presented to the Republic of India."[62]

The claim that the NNC plebiscite campaign had gained a thumping success of 99.99 per cent was dismissed by the chief minister of Assam. In the state assembly he stated that the government "cannot allow them [NNC] under the cloak of non-violence to resort to the murders and various crimes. The anti-Indian activity of the N.N.C. must be curbed to some extent."[63]

The NNC did not immediately take up arms or resort to violence to make their demands known. They employed every method of modern political negotiation at their disposal: civil disobedience, plebiscite, boycotts, mass protest, disseminating political propaganda, and so on. From their perspective this was a successful experiment with modernity; they had recognised that their traditional customs in dealing with conflict management and political negotiation were not workable for a project as enormous as the demand for a Naga nation-state. The Naga protests against the new state were reminiscent of Gandhi's non-cooperation movement: village *gaonburas* (elders) returned their red woollen blankets to the government; state employees relinquished their jobs; parents removed their children from government schools; and students boycotted the classes and the Independence Day function. When the government shut down schools to deter student protests, educated Nagas opened alternative schools in Kohima and Mokokchung.

[62] Lasuh, ed., *The Naga Chronicle*, 138.
[63] See Alemchiba, *A Brief Historical Account*, 176.

VII

Phizo was unsparing with his political opponents, revealing a stoniness of heart that made him a formidable foe.[64] Some NNC core members went into hiding after denouncing the Phizo-led NNC for "extreme views". On 27 April 1955 Phizo convened a meeting in Lakhuti and issued a decree, especially targeting dissenting native intellectuals. The decree empowered the NNC to indict any Naga for harbouring or espousing an "anti-national agenda" and included this: "Any person or persons in order to destroy or undermine the integrity and the well-being of Nagaland, and who for this purpose act, abet or set up organizations against or oppose the political, administrative, and traditional institutions of the Nation, or attempt to do so, whether with or without the aid of another country or countries, shall be deemed to have committed treason."[65]

The resolution put some former colleagues of Phizo into a difficult situation, including leaders like Sakhrie, Jasokie, and Silie Haralu. Silie's eldest daughter, Miyano, spoke to me of a time when his family lived under police protection: "I still remember as a child playing with the security guards in the kitchen." Silie, Miyano remembers, was ever vigilant, fearing the worst; he rarely slept at the same place over consecutive nights. He was a contemporary of Sakhrie, both two decades younger than Phizo. Silie's father, Dr Harielungbe Haralu, was a pioneering Zeliang Naga Baptist convert and celebrated as the first Naga doctor. It took the brutal killing of this elderly retired doctor to make the world outside become aware of the armed violence in the Naga Hills. Dr Haralu was beaten severely and shot point blank by Indian soldiers on duty, and many unnamed civilians later met the same fate during the Naga armed uprising.

The fear of the fallout of an armed struggle that led Silie to forsake the NNC became his own private tragedy. He had

[64] Steyn, *Zapuphizo*, 111.
[65] Quoted in Zinyü, *Phizo*, 120.

THE BAPTIST INTELLECTUALS   343

studied in a mission school in Kohima and, like most students from the emerging middle class, had completed his Intermediate Science in Calcutta. He had joined the NNC in his prime and had for years devoted time and energy to the organisation before a disagreement arose on ideological grounds. Silie was among the core NNC Naga leaders designated "moderate". The tag "moderate" or "liberal" came at a cost: in the eyes of an irredentist as hard-hearted as Phizo, moderation was akin to heresy. It was at best an abdication and at worst a betrayal of responsibility in the struggle for Naga self-rule.

A good number of Phizo's former colleagues and detractors went on to successful political careers within the Indian union. Jasokie became chief minister of Nagaland; Kheloshe was elected a deputy minister in Assam; the second NNC president Mhondamo Kithan became a cabinet minister in the state government; Silie Haralu contested elections, though his political career yielded little fruit; Kevichusa founded a regional political party and was elected to parliament after his retirement as an Indian bureaucrat; and the first NNC president T. Aliba Imti joined the Indian Frontier Administrative Service and later became a member of parliament. Sakhrie did not live to achieve any such exalted post.

His resignation as general secretary of the NNC due to ideological differences and the impending new path of the organisation did not bode well for him. Not long before his death, leading Khonoma leaders had held a secret meeting up in a cave at some distance from the village. A well-respected Khonoma elder told me, "Phizo pointed to Sakhrie and is supposed to have said, 'Such men do not deserve to live', as the two leading men sparred with each other."[66]

The young Sakhrie, who had a college degree, was known for his eloquence as a speaker and for a fine command over words; as an architect of the NNC, he was a worthy competitor to Phizo and had more support in the intellectual wing of the NNC. Phizo

[66] See also Hazarika, *Strangers of the Mist*, 99.

had, unfortunately, suffered facial paralysis while in Burma. This disadvantaged him when it came to oratorical prowess. Sakhrie suffered no outward physical infirmity, but he was prone to sickness and lacked the energy and bodily sturdiness with which Phizo was richly endowed. Sakhrie's other weakness was alcohol. Niketu said Sakhrie's drink problem probably worsened after his fallout with Phizo. Rice liquor was synonymous with traditional culture, but the educated middle class had begun acquiring a taste for stronger spirits. The last time Sakhrie was seen alive was in a booze joint in the northern Angami village of Chiechama. There, danger to his life was imminent, so his friends and relatives had advised him to stay for a time in Shillong, his wife's parental home. Sakhrie did not heed them. On 18 January 1956 he was abducted and killed. His murder was the final nail in the coffin: Sakhrie's "moderate" colleagues ended their relations with the NNC.

What gave Phizo the edge over his political opponents was his firm grasp of the grassroots. The NNC's main support base was in the villages, and Phizo had literally and metaphorically walked every extra mile to garner their support. Thus, it was in remote places that trouble – armed skirmishes – began; this was where the propaganda seeds Phizo sowed started to sprout.

In the early 1950s Langshie, then a young man, first saw Phizo in his native village, Lengnyu. This was then a "backward" Khiamniungan Naga village that not even the Baptist missionaries had yet visited; and there was not much state interference, so headhunting had not ended here. Such was the milieu when Phizo came with a Chang Naga interpreter from Chingmei to talk, as Langshie remembers, about Naga self-determination and to build a support base. According to Langshie, Phizo had toured the Sangtam Naga villages before setting foot in Lengnyu, and he then went further to Wui in the Saramati foothills.

Had Phizo confined his activities to the educated class in the two small towns of Kohima and Mokokchung, he would never have made it to the top, and his armed struggle would not have gained much momentum. Of course, the big guerrilla commanders like Kaito, Mowu, Merentoba, Thinuoselie, Yambamo, and Zuheto had been to school at some point, but most of the Naga insurgents were village-bred men who formed tight-knit groups under charismatic guerrilla leaders. One of Phizo's greatest guerrilla commanders, Kaito, led his tribesmen fighters by the sheer force of his cult-like personality.

Phizo's zenith of achievement was arguably 22 March 1957, when the NNC established the underground government by hoisting a flag in the Rengma Naga region. With the formation of the Federal Government of Nagaland (FGN), Phizo was now the clear and unopposed leader of the NNC, which in turn was now the political shape of the "outlawed" underground government. It was from this point on that a kind of official mobilisation of a guerrilla force (military wing) began to take concrete shape along modern lines, making Phizo a man to be feared.[67]

A new generation of Naga intellectuals spearheaded the NNC, and especially the underground FGN. Chief among them were Scato Swu, the first Sumi Naga graduate; Whenha Rengma, a Kohima mission-school alumnus and first prime minister of the FGN; Mhiasiu, a Baptist minister; Isak Chishi Swu, son of an itinerant Baptist preacher; Yongkong, a young and promising Ao Naga graduate from Shillong; Zashei Huire, a Kohima mission-school product and former WWII recruit of the Indian Air Force from the Chakhesang tribe; Mowu Angami, an alumnus of the coveted St Joseph's School, Darjeeling; and the brothers Kughato and Kaito from a prominent Sumi Naga chieftain family. There was hardly a Naga group on the Indian side of the border among which Phizo had not spread his propaganda. Besides men like Noksen, Khodao Yanthan, and Imkongmeren from the so-called advanced Naga tribes who became his indispensable allies in the NNC political wing, there were those like Hopong from

[67] An obvious South Asian parallel of Phizo closer to our own time is the Tamil Tiger leader V. Prabhakaran (1954–2009) of Sri Lanka, a separatist renowned for his ruthlessness with moderate colleagues.

the Yimchunger tribe and Thungti from the Chang tribe in the Tuensang frontier area.

The rhetoric and language of ethnonationalism and patriotism remained unchanged from the early days of political awakening, but Naga ideologues like Khodao and Scato wrote a great deal of propaganda in their own capacities and commanded a large following, at least within their ethnic groups. Khodao hailed from Lakhuti, a pioneering Lotha Naga village in the field of education; he was born on 25 August 1923, the same year as Sakhrie, and studied in a mission school. He worked with the Allied forces in Burma during WWII and was awarded the "Burma Star" for his services as a quartermaster in the Naga Labour Corps, having engaged in road-clearing and construction efforts. After the war he finished his Intermediate Arts and worked as a schoolteacher before joining the Naga movement. Scato also followed the same route of studying in a mission school, graduating from Shillong, and working for a while as a headmaster before leaving for the jungles.

What all these Naga ethnonationalists shared despite their ideological differences was their cognisance of the importance of modern education: their training in classrooms was truly tested in the Naga theatre. A potent arsenal in the hands of educated Nagas was the print culture that was part of their American Baptist mission training. In Burma too, the anti-colonial campaign and demands for nationalism had been widely disseminated to a large extent via print; the American missionaries had pioneered the region's print media and democratised literary culture by emancipating it from the elites, mostly of the Buddhist religious order.

As we saw earlier, the journal *Orunodoi* started by the American Baptist missionaries in the Assam valley had not only rescued the Assamese language from being swamped by Bengali, it had also played a role in initiating Assamese nationalism down the years.[68] In the case of the Nagas, a local publication, *The Naga Nation*,

[68] See Mahanta, *Confronting State*, 4–5.

became a mouthpiece of the NNC and was predictably shut down by the government. Unlike *Orunodoi*, which the native Assamese continued well after the American missionaries, *The Naga Nation* came into circulation in 1946 independently of the American Baptist mission. In a first of its kind, its contents were no longer Baptist mission reports or colonial documentation but articles on Naga political issues and aspirations. *The Naga Nation* was the first politically informed journal of the Naga educated class in an otherwise religion-oriented print culture. Not surprisingly, educated NNC members like Sakhrie and Aliba Imti assumed responsibility for the publication. This short-lived journal contributed considerably to shaping Naga political consciousness.

Thus, when the Naga educated middle class began its quest for self-determination, it had in place all the prerequisites of a modern political movement: an ideological base, a literate class, print culture, purposeful and impassioned grassroots activists, and a steady political organisation. In hindsight, it was the ideological differences that dealt the first blow to the movement rather than the ethnic differences and "tribalism" that had loomed large from the start. As elsewhere in modern India, the clash of ideologies was an exigency of modernity, and in this respect the Nagas were no exception.

8

Pragmatists and Idealists

> As whetstone our opponents sharpen us.
>
> – A.Z. Phizo's epitaph, Kohima

TOUCHING NINETY, but still enthused by mission and evangelism, Rev. Theruja tottered toward a glass-fronted steel cupboard to draw out documents from stacks of old files relating to his Baptist ministry. He wanted to show me the names of Naga Baptists who had worked closely with the American missionaries, starting from Rev. Rivenburg, to the last missionary in Kohima station, Rev. Supplee. Rev. Theruja's hearing has gone completely, but he spends most daylight hours writing Christian tracts which he generously distributes to his now rare visitors, and on Sundays to the congregation in his local Baptist church. His 85-year-old wife Khrieleno, a well-known educationist and the first Naga woman to hold a bachelor of divinity degree (some say the first woman in the country), nudged him on the knee not to digress; she herself couldn't help sharing with me that the smell of fresh loaves from the oven still reminds her of the American missionaries who first gave her a taste for bread. She wrote on a yellow sticky note in neat cursive script, "He wants you to recollect whatever you know of T. Sakhrie?" The retired Baptist minister stopped his talk midway, "Oh, about Theyiu . . . T. Sakhrie!" Admiration for the man was visible in the elderly Reverend's eyes: "He was my schoolteacher in Khonoma," he recalled.

The British government gave aid to the primary school in Khonoma, but its manpower comprised mostly Baptist mission-school-educated natives. Rev. Theruja was one of the beneficiaries of this arrangement. By the time he joined the mission school in the nearby town, Kohima, fellow Naga teachers were taking up the coveted profession there as well. "T. Sakhrie was my relative; we both belong to the Lievüse clan. He was a brilliant man and very talented as a teacher, but most importantly he was a gifted musician. His favourite instrument was the banjo, which he carried with him. He would play it beautifully and add impromptu singing," Rev. Theruja fondly said of the most artistic and distinguished person from his clan.

It was mostly from the recollections of ageing people like Rev. Theruja that I saw a different side of a man whose brief political career researchers have covered extensively in writing the modern Naga story. The Naga intellectual T. Sakhrie, who came from a devout Baptist family, was far more than the "controversial" political figure he was reduced into after his death. A respected Naga intellectual – and Rev. Theruja's brother-in-law – Niketu Iralu, had directed me to this elderly Baptist minister from Sakhrie's clan. A well-known Naga peace activist in his own right, but better known in many circles as A.Z. Phizo's nephew, Niketu too had met Sakhrie in his prime. While Niketu is careful with his words – though generous when describing the contentious life of his uncle – his account of his fellow clansman Sakhrie is nothing less than admiring.

In his words, "T. Sakhrie was slim and handsome with a prominent forehead, clear and searching eyes, effervescent in his conversation, and very candid in his facial expressions." It was in 1954 that Niketu, who had cleared the eleventh class in Barapani, Meghalaya, decided to seek counsel from the man of the hour, T. Sakhrie, in Kohima, then a sparsely populated capital town. Niketu was "captivated by Theyiu's intelligence and amiable personality." He had much to add: "He lived a simple life and was very friendly. I still remember he was in a simple *lungi* and wooden slippers and welcomed me into his small kitchen. He told me that every college student should read Greek classics, and that he read a lot of Greek philosophers and learnt a lot from them. Sakhrie was a voracious reader, and he read widely on different subjects. Those days there was no bookshop in Kohima but the educated ones were getting bulky hardbacks from outside." It was the first and last time Niketu met the Naga intellectual famous for his stint as NNC general secretary, and for writing some "timeless" treatises on the Naga nation and nationalism. Niketu heard of Sakhrie's death while he was away at college.

A skilled writer and orator, Sakhrie was the chief architect of the "Memorandum of the Case of the Naga People for Self-determination" published on 20 February 1947. With this political strategist and intellectual at its helm, the NNC was becoming the de facto mouthpiece of an entire ethnic group despite the number of communities with cultural and language differences. The idea of a pan-Naga identity was ripe for the taking, and Sakhrie rose to the occasion. A segment of the memorandum reads:

> The Naga Tribes are not a single tribe, but a whole group of them, Angami, Rengma, Sema, Tankhul, Mao, Bhums, Konyak, Lothas, Sangtam, Chang, Zemis, Kabui, etc. each different from the others in custom and dialect, but all clearly related with the others in forming a distinct block. They have a distinct culture and their custom and ways of living are widely different from those of the plains people of Assam or others of India.[1]

When Sakhrie drafted the memorandum, the new nation-state was only six months away. Less than a decade later, in 1955, the American missionaries were evicted from the Naga Hills, and a year after this Sakhrie himself fell victim to the Naga quest for self-determination as the political deadlock took a turn for the worse. It was downhill all the way from there. At the time of

[1] T. Sakhrie, Memorandum of the Case of the Naga People for Self-determination and an Appeal to H.M.G [His Majesty's Government] and the Government of India. See Appendix 1 in Sakhrie, *The Visions of T. Sakhrie*.

Sakhrie's death, Naga Christians numbered 93,423, about 45.7 per cent of the total Naga population (according to the 1951 census). The overwhelmingly Baptist believers were headed for a gruelling test of faith in the emerging political reality. Sakhrie's death, in a way, presaged a harsh and remorseless Naga society in the post-independence period.

Niketu's eldest brother, Vichazelhu Iralu, and T. Sakhrie were contemporaries and close friends. Vichazelhu would go on to become the first Naga to earn a PhD in microbiology from the University of North Carolina at Chapel Hill, after which he led a successful life as an academic and researcher in the US. The story faithfully told in the Iralu family is that it was a young Vichazelhu who, after an emergency meeting of some Naga leaders, pedalled hastily on a bicycle to the post office in Kohima on 14 August 1947, carrying Rs 300 for postal charges, and sent a message to the UNO and to the new Indian government "declaring Naga independence". In 1960 it was also Vichazelhu, then settled in the US, who liaised with Rev. Michael Scott to allow his uncle Phizo entry into Britain.

Sakhrie did not have high academic accomplishments, but he had established himself as an intellectual powerhouse among those who knew him, and many considered him more eloquent, engrossing, and charismatic than his relative A.Z. Phizo. Kolezo Chase, an educationist from Phizo's clan whose father was a close friend of Sakhrie, recalled that "T. Sakhrie was a progressive and easygoing man; he was one of the first men in Kohima town to roam hand-in-hand with his girlfriend." It was a rare sight those days, and in a context where the new faith was inculcating sobriety in conduct between the sexes, many may have looked askance at Sakhrie. But modernity was creeping into the sleepy little town of Kohima, and young men like Sakhrie were its embodiments. "For the first time young people like Sakhrie behaved like foreigners (white people) and copied their lifestyle," Kolezo said with a smile, implying what we both understood.

Theyieuchüthie Sakhrie, popularly T. Sakhrie, and fondly

Ill. 14: T. Sakhrie, the first NNC secretary, 1946–55.
Photo courtesy Khilhu Sakhrie.

called Theyiu by family and friends, was one of the finest Naga intellectuals to emerge from the American Baptist missions. Born in 1923 to church-worker parents – his father was a Baptist minister – Sakhrie was weaned on a culture of Sunday school, Bible stories, choral singing, and prayer meetings. One of his gifts was delivering vivid and moving sermons, a talent that could have garnered him thousands of followers. He could have been in the Baptist hall of fame, but he chose the path that ended in his death.

His family belonged to the Merhema *khel* of Khonoma village. The *khel* was famous for producing Naga nationalists, including Phizo and the guerrilla commander Mowu Angami. Sakhrie's maternal grandfather, Nisier, was the first convert from the village, baptised by Sidney Rivenburg, who was vital in shaping Nisier as well as Sakhrie's father Kekhulhu for the Baptist ministry. The missionary emphasis on English education, Western music, and the Western canon – which included Bible-inspired works like *The Pilgrim's Progress* – was conducive to an evangelical worldview. It impelled men like Nisier and Kekhulhu to become missionaries spreading the new religion to neighbouring tribes. Sakhrie's mother Pfheno was among the first native women church workers, and she inculcated Christian values in her two children. Sakhrie's sister Sokhrieno would go on to become the first Naga woman graduate.

Sakhrie's father Kekhulhu was the first Baptist ordained minister from the Angami Naga tribe.[2] Rev. Kekhulhu Sakhrie raised his son as a devout Christian and Theyiu was afforded the best English education that a respected Baptist minister could arrange. Like his fellow Naga nationalist Phizo, Sakhrie had also grown up in an environment deeply influenced by British colonialism. Their village Khonoma stood directly on the route of British expansion in the second half of the nineteenth century; and when the British annexed the Angami Naga country and established an administrative headquarters in Kohima, the American Baptist missionaries, as earlier noted, began to evangelise the proud and hardy natives of Khonoma village about 20 km from the Kohima Baptist mission station. As elsewhere, the first Baptist converts' children went to mission schools and joined the native educated class of the day. And this class provided the leaders of the Naga National Council (NNC), the formidable modern Naga organisation which spearheaded the demand for self-determination. When the NNC was formed in 1946, Sakhrie became one of its leading intellectual and political propagandists.

Since Sakhrie's parents worked in the Kohima Baptist mission field, his early life was spent amid church and evangelical activity. He was also part of the first generation of mission-school students to learn Western classical music and, being naturally gifted, played

---

[2] See Zinyü, *Phizo*, 126.

and sang with finesse, which gained him many admirers as an adult. During the colonial period the Supplees – regarded by the Angami Nagas as a most musically gifted missionary couple and who had a huge impact on the church music tradition – started a High School Brass Band with an assortment of Western instruments that included the "clarinet, saxophone, French horn, flute, trumpet, baritone [sic], bass horn, bass violin, and trombone"; a good number of the young band members were from Sakhrie's village.[3] George Washington Supplee had also composed the Kohima anthem that would be sung widely by students from various Naga communities in the Kohima mission school.

Kohima will shine tonight
Kohima will shine
When the sun goes down
And the moon comes up
Kohima will shine

There is no place in this world
Half as fair as Kohima
They talk about Niagara
With its waterfalls so high
But here in Kohima
Water falls from the sky
Beautiful for situation
It's the acme of creation
That is Kohima

In Switzerland the snow-clad Alps
Majestically rise
They talk about the Rockies of America,
And Everest too with its lofty head
Pierces the very sky
But the half has not been told
About Kohima.

---

[3] The High School Brass Band had fourteen members and Sakhrie's elder sister Sokhrieno played the double bass. See Government of Nagaland, *Heralding Hope*, 96.

In the spring of 1943, with the Japanese invasion looming large, Sakhrie was to be seen with his banjo serenading "the British soldiers camped in preparation for the defence of Kohima". And Sakhrie's cousin, Nitomeü, *née* Kevichusa, reminisced on his talents:

> I recall a variety show. It was staged in the Mission Chapel just before the war, round about the end of 1943: A makeshift stage of lined-up planks hosts the most talented artistes – Yao (Thepfoorya Haralu), Sokhrieno (Mrs Rosaline Sokhrieno Lungalang), Neichülieü (Neichülieü Nicky Haralu) and Theyieu.
>
> Theyieu stilettos onto the stage wearing an ankle-length black dress; scarf on head, twirling a parasol, singing:
>
> Aye! Aye! Aye!
> They call her Minnie from Trinidad . . .
>
> in a Freddy Mercurian voice. The smooth act is jarred ever so slightly when his stiletto gets lodged in between the planks and breaks.
>
> Theyieu would often sing to us a song from the Wizard of Oz:
>
> Somewhere over the rainbow
> Skies are blue
> And the dreams that you dare to dream
> Really do come true.[4]

The mission school quite clearly played a significant role in shaping the minds of students like Sakhrie; the modern education it imparted changed the attitudes and outlook of these young Nagas, making them markedly different people from those of their parents' generation, and perhaps unrecognisably different from those of their grandparents and great-grandparents. The exposure now was to modern philosophies and ideas of the West, to concepts such as identity consciousness, nationalism, and self-determination. Students from middle-class homes went off for higher studies to Shillong or Calcutta, sometimes to cities further away.

[4] Ibid., 104.

Sakhrie finished his Intermediate Arts from St Paul's College, Calcutta; while in the British Indian metropolis, which attracted students from as far as Burma, he became actively involved in college politics, interacting with tribal students from the different parts of north-east India. His short spell in the Naga political theatre was nothing less than stellar; he was a skilful ideologue, a pragmatist, a singer, a sharp-witted writer. His political outlook suggests he was possibly a closet Gandhian: it was certainly a political stance that cost him dearly. If the Mahatma showed traits traceable to Ruskin and Tolstoy and Christian morality, the rich colours of Sakhrie's mind show traces of Gandhi and, most strongly, Baptist Christianity.

II

Besides cutting short an interesting life, Sakhrie's killing heralded the demise of one stream within Naga ideology. Sakhrie as NNC secretary was among the Naga leaders to have met Gandhi in New Delhi on 19 July 1947. These leaders had made known their desire for self-determination. Gandhi, whom the Naga leaders met only once, would become their most loved and respected Indian. Nehru they did not see with the same eyes since military intervention against the Nagas began during his leadership. Sakhrie, having been raised on Bible stories and able to quote scripture verses at the drop of a hat, could not fail to observe the influence of the Sermon on the Mount on Gandhi's life and teachings. Soon enough he befriended a young Gandhian and confidant of Nehru, Trilokinath Purwar.

Purwar was a young Congressman and social activist from Allahabad. Born in Garhwal, he had proved his mettle during the Indian freedom struggle and was one of the first activists from the mainland to step into the Naga turmoil. Here he witnessed first-hand the political dilemma that confounded and wearied many people in positions of power. With tensions flaring in the Naga Hills, some Naga leaders, among them Rano Shaiza and

J.B. Jasokie, had met Purwar in Shillong in 1953 and were impressed by his political outlook. Purwar made a low-key official visit to Kohima to meet some NNC leaders but was denied entry at the foothills. The Indian nationalist staged a lone satyagraha at the checkpoint in Nichuguard on the outskirts of Dimapur and was arrested on charges of violating the Inner Line Permit – a colonial mechanism in place since 1873 to forestall the politically undesirable. Purwar lay flat on the ground, making a huge scene, but without raising his voice. The police removed him, but not before his non-violent protest had made an impression.[5] Apparently Jasokie, then the NNC's information and publicity secretary, paid a fine and secured Purwar's release. The two had met in Shillong in 1953 when Purwar was carrying out a study of the Indian tribes. Purwar understood the Naga mindset and showed genuine respect for Naga leaders; years after Sakhrie's death he said, "One of the finest and most intelligent men I have ever come across was Sakhrie."[6]

In the winter of 1953, when political uncertainty was hanging like a dark mist in the Naga Hills, Sakhrie met this Allahabad Congressman and social activist. The two struck up a friendship and their admiration was mutual. Being a leading member of the NNC, Sakhrie knew that the axe might drop on him any moment. His Khonoma compatriot Phizo, who was at the helm of affairs from 1950 as the fourth NNC president, had plans up his sleeve to escalate the struggle. Sakhrie's own sense was that the Nagas might have bitten off more than they could chew. Back in 1946, writing in the *The Naga Nation*, he had spelt out the need for connection with soon-to-be-independent India: "Our country is connected with India in many ways. We should continue that connection. I do not mind whether the future India is a Congress government or a League government. But as a distinct community, as I stated before, we must also develop according to our genius and taste.

[5] See Stracey, *Nagaland Nightmare*, 77–8.
[6] See Nibedon, *Nagaland*, 71, footnote.

We shall enjoy home rule in our country, but on broader issues be connected with India."[7]

This was pragmatic; Sakhrie did not relinquish the idea of Naga nationhood but recognised that the nascent Naga society might take a while before it could stand on its own feet. In the interim, a relationship with a neighbouring nation as large and imminently powerful as India would be to the advantage of Nagas. Nehru, in a letter to Sakhrie on 1 August 1946, did not agree with Sakhrie's idea of a Naga nation, but concurred that

> the Naga territory in eastern Assam is much too small to stand by itself, politically or economically. It lies between two huge countries, India and China, and part of it consists of rather backward people who require considerable help. When India is independent, as it is bound to be soon, it would not be possible for the British Government to hold on to the Naga Territory or any part of it. They would be isolated there between India and China. Inevitably, therefore, this Naga territory must be part of India and Assam with which it has developed much closer association.[8]

Among the saddest things in modern Naga history is Sakhrie not being allowed to live long enough to fence intellectually with Nehru. Sakhrie's incorrigible colleague Phizo, however, remained at loggerheads with the Cambridge-educated prime minister until Nehru's death in 1964. Phizo, himself an avid reader and prolific writer, did not possess Sakhrie's flair, charismatic personality, and writing ability. Sakhrie's writing was known for its evocative and poetic phrasings: "If I were to choose a country, it would be Nagaland, my fair Nagaland." Phizo's by contrast is no-nonsense and bluntly rhetorical. In 1952 he wrote to "the President, Republic of India . . . [I believe] it will be a dastardly act of aggression on the part of India to gratify her inordinate desire for territorial expansion, if Free Nagaland should be ravished."[9]

[7] *The Naga Nation*, Vol. 1, No. 5 (Kohima, 1946), 5–6.
[8] Jawaharlal Nehru's letter to T. Sakhrie, Secretary, Naga National Council, dated 1 August 1946. See Lhousa, *Strange Country*, 29–30.
[9] See Lasuh, ed., *The Naga Chronicle*, 99.

On several occasions Phizo invoked his meeting with Mahatma Gandhi in 1947, along with Sakhrie and other Naga leaders, to charge the Indian government with not honouring Gandhi's "promise to the Nagas". In 1977, during a highly charged tête-à-tête with the Indian prime minister Morarji Desai at India House (the offices of the Indian diplomatic mission in London), which lasted less than thirty minutes, Phizo again pulled out the Gandhi card. According to the version that was widely circulated in Naga areas – courtesy of Phizo – Desai flippantly shot down Phizo: "Why have you brought up Gandhi's name? I know him better than you. I will not follow him. I will do everything that I consider to be right." Desai threatened to "exterminate all the Naga rebels. There will be no mercy."[10]

By the time Phizo met this Gujarat-born Janata Party leader in London, Gandhian principles had in any case been shelved on both sides within the Naga theatre. Nagaland had already waded deep into the waters of armed insurgency and counter-operations, which led some observers to label the state as "India's little Vietnam". Desai's predecessor Indira Gandhi had stealthily air-bombed Naga guerrilla jungle hideouts near the Indo–Myanmar border. Various stakeholders, including the Naga Baptist church, had worked for a peaceful solution during the course of the protracted armed struggle, but matters had spiralled out of control in a way that would have mortified the Mahatma had he been alive. As for the Nagas, the end of a Baptist intellectual like Sakhrie was an irreparable loss for the effort to find a non-violent solution.

Phizo too was in some ways an admirer of Gandhi, or so his writings suggest, but the concept of passive political resistance did not gel with his intransigent personality and ideology and therefore did not feature in his arsenal of political methods. In his career as a Naga nationalist and statesman lasting almost five decades, he seldom adopted satyagraha as a political tool; by contrast Sakhrie, whose career in the NNC lasted barely a decade,

[10] Transcript of the Desai and Phizo talk, London, 14 June 1977. See Naga National Council, *The Naga National Rights and Movements*, 187–93.

considered non-violent political protest the better option. Later generations of experts and the laity were of the opinion that the colossal Indian state took notice of the Naga movement only because of its guerrillas, but this observation needs to be inflected with a sounder appreciation of Sakhrie's contribution.[11] In the Naga political drama, it was not that the Gandhian principle was tried and found wanting, but that passive political resistance could not, despite Sakhrie's effort and because of his early elimination, send down deep roots.

As I see it, Gandhian values floundered in the Naga areas because both the warring sides found them irrelevant in the remorseless jungle warfare and counterinsurgency measures that became the order of the day. For Naga insurgents Gandhian teachings were unromantic, impractical, and protracted. On the Indian side, non-violence was believed toothless against the ruthless. Sakhrie, an astute political thinker, foresaw a chaotic political future for his people. Ten months before his killing he wrote a private letter to "a certain non-Naga gentleman interested in Naga affairs":

> The situation is getting out of control. I do not know if India Government had wanted these developments to take place. I like to think they hate it as much as we do. After the first strike, it will not stop until it exhausts itself. We must therefore prevent the first strike from being ever struck. This must be attempted by peaceful methods. There is a lull now, a terrifying calmness. Do you know what that means? The God who had so far saved Nagas and India from resorting to the most undesirable method of settling their differences can still deliver us from evil and shame.[12]

[11] An Angami critic of Sakhrie and former high-ranked FGN leader writes, "Some top leaders including Mr Sakhrie . . . lost courage and became pro-India . . . they broke away from the NNC and formed a parallel party called the Co-operation Party and tried to mislead people.' See Keyho, *My Journey*, 17.

[12] Towards Peace in Nagaland (speech delivered by A. Kevichusa on 6 September 1964). I found this quote in A. Kevichusa's unpublished speech, delivered in Kohima in 1964. The speech is not an archive, I found it in the

At the time, the Indian army was trickling into Naga areas. Sakhrie had experienced the force of the state when in 1953 the Assam police raided his residence in Khonoma and confiscated his writings and documents – they were never seen again.[13] He belonged to an emerging class of native intellectuals in South and South East Asia who were charting nationalism along ethnic lines, which distinguished them from Congress mainstream movement. This distinctive ethnic nationalism went on to take root in upland Burma and in India's north-east. Sakhrie envisioned a Naga homeland sandwiched between the Chindwin and Brahmaputra rivers. He quoted a well-known British administrator in the Naga Hills: "Mr Mills in his monograph on the Lotha Nagas defines the area inhabited by the Naga tribes as bounded by the Hukawng Valley in the North east, the plains in the Brahmaputra Valley to the North West of Cachar of the South West of the Chindwin to the east."[14] This idea of a Naga traditional homeland hinged on a romantic vision of the past, the triumphalism of tribal identity, and a more or less homogeneous cultural tradition: "Truly we are a peculiar people. We are all equals. Men and women have equal social status. We have no caste distinctions; no high or low class people."[15]

In his writings and speeches Sakhrie emphasised the need for education and development but he was simultaneously a traditionalist at heart. The essence of Naga society did not for him lie in the allure of progress and modernity but in the simplicity and old-world values of its forebears. His imagery of Naga uniqueness was an idealisation of the past, as every such idealisation is bound

---

private possession of Kevichusa's grandson Kethoser Kevichusa, who has kept the letters, documents, and unpublished speeches of his grandfather. See also Sakhrie, *The Visions of T. Sakhrie*, 13–14.

[13] See Sakhrie, *The Visions of T. Sakhrie*, 2.

[14] T. Sakhrie, Memorandum of the Case of the Naga People for Self-determination. See Sakhrie, Appendix 1 in *The Visions of T. Sakhrie*.

[15] Quoted in ibid., 6.

to be, but the point of such nostalgia lies less in its lack of absolute historical accuracy than in showing up contemporary failure when modernity sweeps aside some essential elements of value in earlier ways of being and living. What outsiders considered provincial and backward, the mission-school-educated Sakhrie valorised: "We talk freely and often fight freely too. We have no inhibition of any kind. Wild? Yes. But free. There is order in this chaos, law in this freedom."[16]

What brought together Purwar, a devout Hindu, and Sakhrie a practising Baptist, was a shared vision of dialogue and non-violence as the way forward.[17] Purwar, though an unwavering Indian nationalist, was never dismissive of the Naga desire for self-determination. He was both Gandhian and Nehruvian in agreeing that the Nagas comprised an important social fabric of their own, and so their rights and way of life must be protected from the hegemonic cultural assimilation of the plains. Nehru's argument was merely that the Naga demand for self-rule was ill-advised and that the Nagas could enjoy autonomy within the ambit of the Indian constitution. This was in fact the core dilemma that divided generations of Naga intellectuals and leaders. Phizo maintained up to the time of his death that Naga destiny lay outside the framework of the Indian constitution.

Purwar felt in addition that Indian observers had in general given too much importance to Naga Christianity when thrashing out the reasons for their "uprising", though he did recognise that the roots of modern Naga ratiocination and intellectual life lay in the Christian mission. "The Assam authorities just could not comprehend the role of Christianity in the Naga Hills. Who were the leaders of the revolt? They were all Christians. To brand them

---

[16] Ibid., 7. Quoted in Sakhrie, *The Visions of T. Sakhrie*, 7.

[17] It is said that Purwar was a devout Hindu with a penchant for praying and chanting loudly in the mornings, which his Naga friends found amusing. But the Naga leaders found an ally in the Allahabad native, whose religious zeal matched that of the Nagas, and yet, in the Gandhian tradition, found room for dialogue and mutual respect.

as agents of the foreign missionaries showed a lot of prejudice." With time, Purwar became cognisant of the fact that the Naga issue was more than a fear of "Assamization" – in other words, the key lay in their misgivings that their "tribal way of life" would be inundated. He saw that it was more than fear of the outsider that had led ethnic nationalism to take root. What distinguised Purwar's perspective, and which made it Gandhian, was his refusal to blame foreign missionaries for fomenting "anti-nationalism"; he saw Christianity as having a liberating influence on the "tribal mind", which had then translated tendentiously into political aspiration. As Purwar put it, "What happened when pagan Europe turned Christian? So much of energy was released that the converts ran over two-thirds of Europe . . . When the narrowness of tribal minds was broken by Christianity, a lot of latent energy was released. It channelized into an insurrection." For him the freeing of "tribal minds" by the Protestant brand of Christianity was the reason "why just some five lakh tribals fought with 500 million people on terms of equality, and they are still fighting."[18]

In recalling the size of the Naga population standing up to an insurmountable adversary, Purwar was sympathising with the idealism of the Naga intellectuals of his day. His Naga confidant Sakhrie saw even more clearly the impracticability of armed struggle against invincible odds. This, I would argue, made Sakhrie a pragmatic Gandhian rather than an idealistic one. In his foremost propaganda piece, he outlined the staggering size of the "other": "Thrown among forty crores of Indians, the one million Nagas with their unique custom of life will be wiped out of existence. Hence this earnest plea of the Nagas for a separate form of Interim Government to enable them to grow to a fuller stature."[19]

---

[18] Quoted in Nibedon, *Nagaland*, 55–6.

[19] T. Sakhrie, Memorandum of the Case of the Naga People for Self-determination. See Appendix 1 in Sakhrie, *The Visions of T. Sakhrie*.

Purwar's detractor Bishnuram Medhi, then chief minister of Assam, saw Naga political aspiration as too lofty an idea for the hill tribes to have come up with themselves; certain educated natives were being used nefariously by "a few handful of leaders, mostly Christians". In this proto-Hindutva view, by contrast with the Gandhian, there was an "unholy alliance" between Christian missions and the Naga demand for sovereignty merely because it was clear as daylight that the top Naga leaders, including the unyielding NNC leader Phizo, were Baptist Christians; ergo, the Naga demand "was raised by interested foreign missionaries to keep them isolated from the rest of India."[20] Medhi disliked Purwar and, much to Nehru's annoyance, tried to cut off the latter's "dalliance" with the Naga leaders. The Nagas were united in their disavowal of Medhi who, it was apparent, had a patronising attitude towards the hill people. A seasoned Indian civil servant who served as the deputy commissioner in Kohima observed that "there was no person so much disliked by the Nagas as Medhi", and that in one instance the natives had even damaged a bridge "before the Chief Minister arrived".[21]

Medhi was the essence of the bureaucratically blinkered and intellectually limited Indian politician who saw the Naga issue as one of law and order; in this conception, patronage and the occasional handout to key leaders interspersed with more generalised doles by the welfare state would solve the problem. In 1954 Medhi declared in the Assam assembly that "the people of Naga Hills want jobs, school, dispensaries, new roads, and as a matter of fact, we have undertaken schemes for affording better educational, medical and other facilities. We want to impress these people by undertaking welfare activities for all-round development of Naga Hills. Is this not [a] human approach?"[22] The recalcitrance of the Naga intellectuals was from this perspective a perverse aberration

---

[20] Quoted in Alemchiba, *A Brief Historical Account*, 175.
[21] See Ramunny, *The World of Nagas*, 56.
[22] Alemchiba, *A Brief Historical Account*, 175.

fostered by foreign Christians. Niketu Iralu recalled that "with regard to ethnonationalism the Nagas were much ahead while other north-east communities like the Mizos, Khasis and Meiteis were still to make political demands." It was a context that made the chief minister of Assam express plain bewilderment:

> The Nagas in Burma have accepted the constitution of Burma Government, the Nagas in the Mikir Hills, North Cachar Hills, etc., do not want independence, the Nagas in the NEFA also do not want independence. Why this handful of persons want independent Nagaland? The Nagas, as I have stated are the citizens of the Indian Republic and enjoy equal rights as any citizen. They have much more independence than ourselves in some matters.[23]

Shillong was the nearest important educational hub where many tribals from the hill districts pursued their studies and gained exposure to Indian politics: among such were Aliba Imti, Sakhrie, Jasokie, and Phizo. It was also where the first "hill leaders union" was formed in 1945 and various leaders like "Captain Lyngdo, Rai Bahadur Ropmei, Mr McDonald and Rev. Nichols Roy, Jobang Marak and others" from the Naga Hills, Lushai Hills, and Khasi Hills had started talking about forming separate hill states.[24]

As a state, Assam had a peculiar history, geography, and ethnic diversity. The hill tribals were a minority in it but nonetheless indispensable for Nehru's idea of a many-splendoured Indian republic. It was part of the Congress heartland, but the Muslim League had its sphere of influence in the towns bordering East Bengal with substantial Muslim populations. The NNC president Aliba Imti, as a member of the advisory committee deliberating the fate of hill people, had a run-in with irate Muslim League protesters in Karimganj who were chanting pro-Pakistan slogans. His young assistant had even swished a Naga *dao* to extricate them.[25] The Naga leaders were not blind to the political uncertainties,

[23] Ibid., 176.
[24] Imti, *Reminiscence*, 12.
[25] Ibid., 51.

Ill. 15: J.B. Jasokie, chief minister of Nagaland, welcoming L.P. Singh, governor of the state. Jasokie, former information secretary of the NNC, parted ways with the Phizo-led NNC and went on to become chief minister. Courtesy DIPR.

they simply found they were being pushed headlong as part of the mishmash of communities, languages, and cultures that was Assam. Among the Nagas this was bound to create a sense of foreboding that had little to do with their Baptist Christian roots. Post-Partition, "the central government suggested that lakhs of refugees be rehabilitated in the small foothill town of Dimapur, which the NNC leaders vehemently opposed," the former NNC activist and chief minister S.C. Jamir told me. Nehru had asked the first chief minister of Assam, Gopinath Bordoloi, to share the refugee burden; Assam was threatened with a steep cut in federal funding if it failed to rehabilitate Bengali Hindu refugees from East Pakistan.[26] There were already nearly 200,000 landless Assamese peasants – about the size of the population of the Naga Hills district in 1951 (205,950) – waiting to be settled on reclaimable land. By 1961 the Congress government in Assam had been coerced to absorb at least 600,000 refugees.

[26] Bhaumik, *Troubled Periphery*, 115.

Against this backdrop of national upheaval, the Naga problem paled in comparison. In August 1946 Nehru had written a pragmatic letter to Sakhrie, the NNC secretary, outlining the need for the Nagas to remain with Assam and the Indian mainland once India become independent. With independence and Partition the following year, his plate was full, so Naga politics was now second fiddle and left in the hands of the Assam government. The Indian premier relied on the Assam CM's advice on matters pertaining to the hill tribes, and when Medhi was in office the Naga political issue took a difficult turn – by then the NNC was adamant about Naga independence.

After the disastrous public reception of Nehru's first visit to the Naga Hills district in 1953, the prime minister reprimanded the Assam authorities for the fiasco. The political reality in the Naga Hills district was different from what he had anticipated. Heads had to roll, and the deputy commissioner who had managed the show in Kohima during Nehru's visit was sacked. A veteran Indian journalist, Harish Chandola, told me in an interview that a group of Nagas, dressed in traditional finery to receive Nehru and U Nu (who were coming from Imphal to Kohima), were lathi-charged and dispersed by the Assam police near the border between Nagaland and Manipur.[27] This was for the Nagas the ultimate disrespect – to be chased away from their own space. In defence of the authorities it can be said they feared the NNC would use the opportunity to slip a memorandum to Nehru. In 1956 Nehru wrote to Medhi: "Your Government may not be responsible for this and the mere fact that you have to deal with them led to this situation. But the fact remains that they are very dissatisfied with the present position."[28]

Not every Assamese politician was disliked. In fact the Congress leader Bimala Prasad Chaliha, Medhi's successor as chief minister of Assam, was well liked and respected by the Nagas. Chaliha

[27] See also Chandola, *The Naga Story*.
[28] Bishnuram Medhi Papers, NMML, New Delhi.

Ill. 16: The Naga political drama witnessed the involvement of some illustrious personalities attempting a peaceful solution: (Left) Rev. Michael Scott, A. Kevichusa, and B.P. Chaliha; (Right) B.P. Chaliha, Rev. Michael Scott, and J.P. (Jayaprakash Narayan). Courtesy NBCC.

had the good sense to see dissenting Naga leaders as equals, not as tribals to be patronised. Khrieleno Theruja, the first Naga woman to earn a bachelor's degree in divinity, who had acted as an interpreter between the government and the underground leaders in the 1960s, spoke highly of Chaliha: he "was tall with a big forehead, calm and composed and very approachable." Nagas of every stripe, including their underground leaders, liked this chief minister from Sivasagar, a town with an established American Baptist mission legacy. Chaliha won the hearts of tribal Nagas with his congenial personality and modesty. Khrieleno said Chaliha would walk into the underground camp and sit by the fire and eat their food. Niketu Iralu said Chaliha appealed to Naga intellectuals and leaders "because he did not have the patronising attitude that was common to most political leaders from the plains." Chandola says a certain Indian official is said to have commented, "These people have just come down from the trees and want air-conditioning!" Apparently this was when Chandola requested better accommodation for an ailing Naga underground leader, Kughato Sukhai, during talks between the Naga underground leaders and Indira Gandhi in New Delhi.[29] Given this long history of patronising sarcasm, verging on contempt,

[29] Chandola, *At Large in the World*, 160.

Ill. 17: Rajiv Gandhi on a visit to Nagaland, October 1987.
He inherited the vexing Naga political problem from his grandfather
Jawaharlal Nehru and mother Indira Gandhi.
Courtesy DIPR.

Chaliha was an unusual politician. He knew the region and responded well to its people; he was also a Gandhian who had been jailed in Jorhat in 1942 for participating in the Quit India movement. As an INC freedom fighter Chaliha was an Indian nationalist to the core, but he believed only non-violence and dialogue could provide a lasting solution. His leadership gave the troubled hills a respite but not, unfortunately, permanent peace.

III

The story of the Naga nationalists is incomplete without a reference to the role played by women leaders, as well as Naga women in villages that bore the brunt of terrible suffering. In 1952, when the Nagas resorted to civil disobedience, they boycotted government schools. Sano Vamuzo, founding president of the Naga

Mothers' Association, recalls that she was a student in Middle English School in Kohima when the government issued a notification saying all students must compulsorily don a "Gandhi cap". This order came in the midst of the NNC's non-cooperation movement; the regulation was passed by the state authorities as a rebuff to dissenters. The immediate reaction in Kohima was that protesters started an alternative school called National High School, independent of government, and parents began to withdraw their children from the government-run school. This had parallels with the Indian freedom movement, when Congress leaders like Annie Besant and Gandhi started national schools and national colleges in several cities that were in opposition to and independent of schools and colleges funded and run by the British Raj. The opening of National High School was a testament to Naga nationalism being a mass phenomenon, and at an all-time high. In the old British subdivisional headquarters, Mokokchung, which had once been the hub of American Baptist mission activity, educated natives like Mayangnokcha, Kiremwati, Noksen, and Yongkong led the new enterprise. In Kohima, Angami leaders like Jasokie and Vizol (both later chief ministers of Nagaland) joined the National High School as teachers. The school ran on a shoestring budget, teachers were unpaid, and the staff faced many difficulties, but the Naga educated class seemed to have sent a strong message to the government.

Joining their ranks was a young Angami woman, Rano, the third daughter of an Angami doctor, Sevilie Iralu, who had married Phizo's older sister, Vituno. Rano was among the class of educated native women who were breaking the mould of tradition. A distinguishing feature of the new political consciousness was that it transcended the traditional notion of status and gender. Education was a great leveller: Naga women were beginning to get a voice in the male-dominated society, and spirited women like Rano were finding a niche. The American missionary schools in the Naga country had placed emphasis on educating the girl child as well. Stories are still told in Molungyimsen of Mary Clark giving young girls beads, threads, and plastic necklaces to entice them to attend school. Early on, the students were mostly boys, but the girls trickled in and their numbers grew with the new generation of mission-school-educated parents.

Vituno did not attend school but taught herself how to read and write in the Angami vernacular. A self-taught diarist, her first exposure to reading and writing was at a village school that she did not even step into. As a child she would take her younger sister to school and wait outside as the children learnt numbers and the alphabet. "My mother would sit outside and watch the children learning, but nobody asked her to come in," Vituno's daughter, Sano Vamuzo, told me. A lot of parents cared little for education, placing a far higher value on the age-old occupation, farming. However, the mission-school culture rubbed off on Vituno; in time she began reading the available Christian literature in her mother tongue and fastidiously maintained a personal dairy. "My mother's favourite book was *Pilgrim's Progress* which she read several times," Sano said. Translated by the Angami educationist Zapuzhülie, *The Pilgrim's Progress* became, as earlier noted, the first work of literature to be translated by the Angami Nagas, even before their full version of the New Testament.

As I see it, the most awful aspect of the Naga political movement was the trauma and hardship inflicted on women. They had, as it is, suffered hardships under the Indian state, perhaps more than during colonial rule and the Japanese invasion – when the British had resorted to a scorched-earth policy and the Japanese to forced labour. Sexual violence had been the "collateral damage" of counterinsurgency measures, as in all jungle warfare in the Indo–Myanmar uplands. Accustomed to a history of harrowing times, some Naga women rose to the occasion, Vituno being one who, more informed and literate than many, became a representative voice. According to her son Niketu:

> In 1954 while I was in college, I accompanied my mother as her translator to meet the chief minister, Bishnuram Medhi. She had come to Shillong along with some Angami women representatives

to apprise him of the Assam police excesses in the villages. When my mother stated the grievances of women folk, the chief minister paid no attention and chuckled dismissively. Visibly irked, my mother reprimanded him in Angami: 'don't laugh, Medhi!' The chief minister turned to me and asked what my mother had said; I told him the same in English. Quite taken aback, he giggled again.

Rano Shaizo was another. She had her first run-in with the authorities as a student activist. The school headmaster, Rev. Supplee, had instituted compulsory social work, against which the students had protested. "While in Kohima government high school, I remember seeing Rano, the only girl student, on a podium with male students that included leaders like Jasokie and

Ill. 18: Rano Shaiza, the first Naga woman to be elected Member of Parliament. Courtesy DIPR.

PRAGMATISTS AND IDEALISTS 373

Ill. 19: Khrieleno Theruja, a noted Baptist educationist and the first Naga woman to hold a bachelor's degree in divinity. Courtesy NBCC.

the star footballer Kughato Sukhai; even then she was known for her fiery speeches," Niketu recalled of his sister. The fifth child of a hard-working government doctor, Rano grew up in a family of fifteen that was always on the move since her father was posted to a variety of places in the interior. Born in 1928 at the height of British rule, she grew up in a time when the new political consciousness was developing among educated Nagas. "In the 1950s and '60s every Naga was gripped by the idea of nationalism, and my mother was one of them," Rano's surviving son, Azeibu Shaiza, told me. She had pluck and a knack for politics. She wanted to pursue a career in medicine and went off to do her Intermediate

Science from Guwahati, but had to give up the idea as the family could not afford it: "My mother used to tell us that one chicken was not enough for the whole family of fifteen, and her portion would always be the neck, and that is where she learnt to be thrifty – a habit that remained over her whole life," Azeibu said.

Rano was in the eleven-member Naga Goodwill Mission that went on a tour of Assam for sixteen days from 30 November to 15 December 1953 to "secure understanding, friendship and peace, and the goodwill of the people of Assam, to eradicate suspicion, misunderstanding and exclude falsehood, conflict and bloodshed." This was before the NNC opted for armed insurrection against the Indian state. The Naga Goodwill Mission included some of the leading intellectuals of the day, and Rano as the Naga Women's Federation (NWF) president was a prominent face in the team.[30] It was during this political trip to Assam as an NNC worker that she met Trilokinath Purwar in Shillong, striking up a lifelong friendship with him.

The Goodwill Mission was confident and clear in its approach: they were wholeheartedly in favour of Naga self-rule. According to the Mission's report: "Besides other suburbs, institutions, establishments and colonies we [the Naga leaders] visited – Guwahati, Tezpur, Golghat, Sualkuchi, Dekargaon, Jorhat, Shillong, Bindukari, Sibsagar, Nowgong, Bokahat, Tinsukia and Dibrugarh." The response they received from the Assam authorities and people generally was mixed; as expected, the Naga team had generous words for the Congress chief B.P. Chaliha, blaming their troubles on the use of armed force by the chief minister, Bishnuram Medhi. The NNC representatives said one of their objectives in visiting their "neighbours" was to dispel the wrong notions there on the Nagas and their movement. Naturally, the Baptist mission's role was questioned and they rebutted the ridiculous charge of foreign missionary interference in internal politics: they happened to

---

[30] Ngutono Chase, a member of the Naga Women's Association, was another woman who participated in the Goodwill Mission.

be mostly Baptist, just as Congressmen happened to be mostly Hindu, and they declared:

> The Mission takes this opportunity to suggest and recommend that some Bhoodan workers and Ashramites should be invited to come and live among the Nagas and find out for themselves and for the people of India how far, if any, the Foreign Missions wield their influence upon the Naga National Movement. They would be afforded the same facilities and scope for work as are given the foreign missionaries.

A former NNC worker and retired Baptist pastor gave it as his view that the Goodwill Mission's invitation was largely rhetorical, for the Naga leaders knew no religious, social, or political activists would climb up to their remote hills: "Aside from the adventurous American missionaries no Hindu sanyasis, Buddhist monks or Muslim mullahs were ready to trek up the Naga Hills along the Indo-Burma border." This erudite preacher voiced simple common sense when pointing out that "the Nagas could have easily been influenced by other major religions whether it be Islam, Hinduism or Buddhism, but it was the Christian missionaries who beat them to it."

The NNC movement had started women and youth wings to strengthen its base: for the first time now, a Naga institution had moved beyond male-dominated tribal councils. Rano became the first president (1953–7) of the NWF. This short and petite woman with thick-rimmed glasses and an imposing personality relished every challenge. She had, at the start of conflict in 1953, acted as interpreter to the president of the Assam Pradesh Congress Committee, Chaliha, when he visited the Naga areas, earning high praise from him.[31]

Rano led an active political life, albeit a distressing one, because it included her being arrested, having to witness the killing of several colleagues, and living through a merciless war with the Indian state, which India saw as an insurgency. It was a time

---

[31] See Ramunny, *The World of Nagas*, 66.

when women's voices were muffled and the men hogged the limelight, of mutual suspicion and propaganda on both sides. It took a woman like Rano to bring to light the predicament of Naga women trapped in the conflict zone. Though a strident ethnonationalist, she was sobered by the relentless violence ruining everyday happiness. As Azeibu said with hindsight: "It was one of the reasons why she decided to stand for election as a member of parliament." The pinnacle of her political career came when, in 1977, she became the first Naga woman to be elected to the Lok Sabha. She had contested against the former chief minister of Nagaland, Hokishe Sema, a strong candidate who had the support of New Delhi. At the time of writing, Rano is still the only Naga woman to have been elected to parliament. "My mother was the most impoverished politician of her time, acquiring nothing while in office. The Indian army burned down our house with all the possessions inside and she also had to serve jail time for her political activism, but her greatest loss came when my father got killed; they were very close to each other," Azeibu said. Tragedy had struck in 1990, when Naga insurgents shot her husband point blank during an election campaign. It was a high-profile assassination which, for a time, was much covered by the press.

Rano was widowed towards the latter part of her life; countless and nameless young wives and mothers around her had lost their husbands and sons to the brutality. Among university-educated Naga women late in the twentieth century, these experiences inspired work in the fine arts, literature, and music. Rano had forged their path. She retired to lead a quiet life, spending most of her time reading the Bible for comfort, and to find answers; the markings and scribbles on her Bible show the importance of Christian solace to her, a truth her son confirms.

Rano's political outlook shows that though she remained a lifelong admirer of her uncle, Phizo, under whom she took charge as the first NWF president in 1953, she was deeply affected in ways that Phizo, more the cold-blooded male, was not. "As a woman and mother, she saw the Naga political issue in a different light than her male counterparts; my mother began to get actively involved in peace-making and took the position that armed struggle would only lead to more destruction," Azeibu said.

A decorated IFAS (Indian Frontier Administrative Services) officer, S.C. Dev, who was instrumental in rehabilitating Rani Gaidinliu, narrates a procedural counterinsurgency measure involving the wife of a guerrilla commander. Not knowing the whereabouts of the commander, who had laid an ambush in which jawans had been killed, "they dragged his young wife to the camp, and gripping her by her hair they rubbed her face and mouth on the gaping wounds on the corpses." The young wife's ordeal was minor by comparison with other stories of atrocities undocumented and unreported.[32] Khrieleno, Rano's younger sister,

Ill. 20: Naga women taking out a peace procession in Kohima organised by the NBCC in February 1996, a year before the ceasefire agreement between the Naga political groups and the Government of India. Courtesy NBCC.

[32] See Dev, *Nagaland*, 62.

told me that, once, when interpreting for the Peace Mission trio of Chaliha, JP, and Rev. Scott during the peace talks with underground leaders in the mid-1960s, "the women representatives meeting the dignitaries wanted me to tell them that the Indian armies are coming not only with guns but with their 'penis' as well... I was there as interpreter because no man would do the job since it was risky on both sides, but to translate what those women said in front of important people, I had a difficult time," the octogenarian Khrieleno added with a laugh.

As NWF president Rano wrote a scathing letter to the Congress president, U.N. Dhebar, on his visit to the region on 26 November 1955:

> Beating thousands of women at home, at field and at work, raping, squeezing breasts, biting lips and mouths and inserting fingers in women's private parts are the kind of insults and tortures that we are made to face under the present Authorities... All men who raped and molested our women also came out of a woman's womb just as any other creature. We carry them for ten months and care for them for years till they grow to manhood... If it is the desire of the Indian Government and a programme to carry out – shoot us directly and bayonet us but do not molest our chastity.[33]

This searing expression of rage from an educated woman contrasts with the pamphleteering and propaganda that are the usual stuff of politics. The plight of women caught between insurgents and counterinsurgents is routinely either trivialised or deployed for propaganda: the Indian machinery airbrushes their violence against women under a political carpet decorated with the euphemism "collateral damage", while the suffering of ordinary Nagas is used by ethnonationalists to bolster their cause.

This propaganda war ended even the work of the great peace activist Rev. Michael Scott, who apparently crossed a line in documenting the atrocities of the armed forces. This, compounded with other charges, resulted in Scott being expelled from the

---

[33] See Yanthan, *Wounded Tiger*, 69.

Naga theatre in 1966.[34] The documentation and statements on the military operations from the opposing sides appear as if from two different realities. In 1957 the Federal Government of Nagaland (FGN) publicised a 32-episode serialised account of the "atrocities of Indian armies" titled *Harrowing Tales of the Nagas*. An extract from it reads:

> The ladies [*sic*] are very often intended [i.e. selected, with the intent of – in the grotesque jargon perpetuated by the Indian state – "outraging their modesty"] from all Naga villages. The elders of the villages are shot to death when refused to supply them with intended ladies. For instance, intended from Huker, Sukomi, Imlomi, Yeshultomi, etc, etc, villages . . . Whenever the mighty forces of India have gone they raped the Naga women, even the mad and paralysed women. For example, a mad woman Khoholi of Ratomi, aged 40 years, was raped on November 9, 1956 led by Commandant Mickey in the 9th Garowali Regiment.[35]

The Naga underground government publicity wing was extremely active. It highlighted civilian deaths as gross human rights violations, showing up the brutality of the Indian state. In a draft note to Rev. Michael Scott, invited as a British observer, the FGN said, "The Naga people adopted no belligerent attitude towards India . . . But, the Government of India, armed to the teeth with all modern scientific weapons, have persistently seeking to crush the Nagas with every possible pressure regardless of right or wrong."[36] Meanwhile across the great waters, in Bromley, Kent, on the outskirts of London, Phizo had begun waging a "writing" war against the Indian state. He adapted to a suburban middle-class life in exile and resembled a retired academic, spending most of his time reading and writing. Despite the distance, his

---

[34] In 1960 Scott had helped settle Phizo in London, and as a Christian his sympathies were assumed to be with the Nagas, so he was always something of a suspect from the Indian point of view.
[35] See Lasuh, ed., *The Naga Chronicle*, 187–91.
[36] Ibid., 242.

eye was focused on the armed conflict in his homeland. He was meticulous in maintaining a record of names, places, and dates, and used the data to garner sympathy for the Naga cause in the world community. On several occasions he piqued the interest of Western observers and embarrassed the Indian authorities. In July 1960 he released a paper, "The Fate of Naga People: An Appeal to the World", which provided an account of Indian depredations in the Naga areas, including victims' names, and the dates and places of "atrocities carried out by the military personnel".

Elwin, by contrast, writing on the same issue over the same time, was an apologist arguing the "moderation" of the armed forces: "Army personnel too, who undertook their distasteful task [counterinsurgency measures] with great reluctance, have done much to create a climate of friendliness by their genuine sympathy and many acts of kindness. It is now being more and more recognized that the Army went to the Naga Hills not to harass the people but, on the contrary, to protect them from harassment."[37] Elwin's biographer says: "When in 1960 New Delhi began negotiating with such [Naga] rebels as were willing to talk, the Western press, and in particular *The Observer* of London, carried a series of reports on 'atrocities' by the Indian army. The government turned to the most fluent and the most credible writer in its ranks, asking him [Elwin] to write a book presenting India's case abroad."[38] Nehru told his parliament that the military was exercising the greatest restraint. In their defence, it may be said Nehru and Elwin were not making these statements glibly, they were merely oblivious of the immense toll of remorseless jungle warfare on village inhabitants.

Rano's educationist son Azeibu says Elwin's widely read work, *Nagaland*, is a "highbrow" policy-maker's rather than a researcher's book. The Angami historian Visier Sanyu is even stronger in his dismissal of Elwin: he repudiates Elwin's account as state propaganda and says – "One should not forget that he was

---

[37] Elwin, *Nagaland*, 61.
[38] Guha, *Savaging the Civilized*, esp. Chapter XIII.

Nehru's tribal adviser and right-hand [man]." Visier should know; he lived through the military operation in 1956 and the fallout when Naga insurgents tried to overrun Kohima. He continues to write and give talks on the Naga political issue and the Indian state's oppressive military operations.[39] As a native intellectual who grew up in a zone of barbaric conflict, his credibility in showing up repression and atrocities is high and his critique of distantly located policy mandarins is cogent. Nehru and Elwin are much read: their prose is powerful and their liberal worldviews are attractive. A lineage of intellectuals from Gramsci to Fanon to Said to Ranajit Guha have shown how the voices of "subalterns" who have been in the thick of suffering – such as Visier's – are implicitly or explicitly marginalised by the powerful, and how necessary it is to hear them for a proper understanding of the nature of oppression. Visier has put down his experiences and those of his close-knit community in the form of a memoir; records of lived victimhood such as his are persuasive, deserve to be heard, and placed alongside those by the exalted.[40]

IV

A mainland observer of the Naga movement, writing during the thick of the armed insurrection in 1968–72, contends that "The fault of the missionaries was to have educated the tribals and converted them. In their zeal to proselytize little did they know that religion would be an excellent therapy for the Naga tribes to galvanize their state of mind into political channels."[41] If the American missionaries sowed the seeds of ethnonationalism, then they scuttled their own ship, and to ask why would they have done that is to show up the illiteracy of the argument. First,

---

[39] The situation in contemporary Kashmir might strike many readers as an analogy of the post-1947 Naga struggle, the crucial difference being that whereas Pakistan has always fomented trouble in Kashmir, neither China nor Myanmar nor Bangladesh has played any significant role in the mostly autonomous upheavals of Nagaland.

[40] Sanyü with Broome, *A Naga Odyssey*, 61–2.

[41] Nibedon, *Nagaland*, 56.

the political uprising ended the most thriving American Baptist mission overseas; second, some of the Naga leaders, who were practising Baptists, experimented with communism – a dreaded philosophy considered an enemy of the Baptist faith; third, and most important, many exceptional Naga intellectuals, most of them products of Baptist mission schools, suffered terribly at the hands of their fellow Nagas, all for the sake of ethnonationalism. This ethnonationalism, which the American missionaries are accused of fomenting and inculcating in the minds of supposedly innocent natives – along with the counterinsurgency measures that followed – cut short the lives of Naga personalities in their prime: Dr Imkongliba, Dr Haralu, "General" Kaito, Rev. Pelesato, and Sakhrie, among many. Dissidents such as the firebrand Naga guerrilla leader Kaito were purged for "anti-national" activities by their own compatriots. Devout Baptist leaders like Dr Haralu and Rev. Pelesato met horrifying ends at the hands of the Indian military.

Inhumanity breeds inhumanity: if the Indian army was unspeakably inhuman, the Naga guerrillas were no less ruthless in eliminating dissidents, suspected fifth columnists, and political opponents; guerrillas with a Baptist background did not hesitate to execute and bomb innocent civilians. The struggle against all the odds and the reality of an unwinnable war made them savage in their warfare.

One of their options was to seek help from China. However, the rank and file of Naga fighters did not seek out Chinese communists, even if this cannot be said of some of the Naga leaders. The delicate balance that Chinese-trained Naga "rebels" struck between their Baptist faith and Maoism continues to baffle. No detailed study has been attempted and the information – barring cursory remarks and the intelligence collected from stray imprisoned China-trained rebels – is limited. Given the lack of written documents, "memory ethnography" is arguably the most useful way forward, and the next chapter is an attempt to describe the interface between the Naga Baptist faith and the communist ideology in the context of the region's guerrilla warfare.

9

Guns, the Bible, and the Little Red Book

> The end of their wars is near, the spears are being beaten into pruning hooks, and we are looking forward to a reign of peace.
>
> – Mary Mead Clark, missionary to the Nagas, 1907

> Some trust in chariots and some in horses, but we trust in the name of the Lord our God.
>
> – Psalms 20: 7

AN OLD BLACK-AND-WHITE photograph of a China-trained Naga "rebel" in her early twenties evokes a surreal memory of the infamous Red Guards. Dressed in loose Chinese military fatigues with the unmistakable cap barely concealing her innocently braided hair, she could easily pass off as one of those idealistic Chinese youths who were fodder for Mao Zedong's cultural revolution. But the photograph of this fresh-faced girl, taken somewhere in Yunnan, south-western China, is that of a Bible school dropout from a small Sumi Naga village about a day's march from Kohima. Once a highly motivated student at a vernacular Bible school run by a Baptist mission, Avuli Chishi went on to become an "elite" member of the *alee* (foreign) command, leaving behind a promising future in the Christian ministry.[1] She had earned repute by twice trekking to China (1974–5 and 1976–7) to train and procure weapons. Fer-

---

[1] *Alee* is a Pochury Naga term meaning "foreign" that the Naga army used

vent ethnonationalism had driven many idealistic young Nagas into jungle hideouts from where they waged guerrilla warfare against the Indian state, whose remorseless counterinsurgency also pushed some educated Nagas in promising careers to join the underground movement.

Born on 27 August 1954, roughly two years before the formation of the Federal Government of Nagaland (FGN) – the "outlawed" Naga government that ran parallel to the Indian state – Avuli's early years coincided with burgeoning ethnonationalism and army-combing operations in the Naga region. In 1963 Naga guerrillas ambushed an army convoy not far from her native village, Shesulimi; as in many reprisals, the entire village was rounded up and the army's anger and frustration vented upon the villagers. Among the many menfolk who were roughed up that day was Khakhu, whose nine-year-old daughter watched in horror as "gun butts" and kicks rained down on him. This scarred the young girl indelibly. In 1972 she joined a Bible school at Pughoboto, a small town in Zunheboto district, only to leave in 1974 to take up arms for the Naga cause.

A prominent Naga nationalist from Avuli's ethnic group, who too had joined the underground movement as a fallout of the military operations, was Scato Swu, former headmaster of Government Middle English School in Satakha (formerly Atuküzu) in Zunheboto district. In 1936, at the age of twelve, he had gone to study at the American Baptist mission school in Kohima but had had to leave during WWII because of the Japanese advance. After the war he returned to Kohima and finished his matriculation. He went on to earn a bachelor's degree from St Edmund's College, Shillong. Scato was believed to be the first graduate among his tribesmen; he was preparing to pursue higher studies in law, but, in 1954, as he told me, Sumi Naga chiefs from thirty-three villages in the Satakha range requested him to become headmaster of the only school in the region. And so this headmaster of a remote school

---

for those of their members who were sent abroad to train and procure arms and ammunition.

was soon catapulted to national "infamy": on 19 March 1956 he shut the school and left for the jungles, taking along with him many promising students. In 1959 he would become president of the FGN. Scato told me his destiny as an underground leader was sealed by the "military highhandedness" which did not spare even ordinary villagers. He was propelled into the Naga armed struggle during the initial military intervention of the1950s.

It was the gentlemanly Scato Swu, a lifelong practising Baptist, who during his term as FGN president wrote an official letter to the People's Republic of China, seeking their help; this came to be known as the "Chinese connection" in the corridors of power in New Delhi. On 5 May 1967, seven years after the NNC president A.Z. Phizo reached London to garner international support, Scato petitioned the "President of the People's Republic of China" from Oking, the elusive underground Naga headquarters.

> For the friendly and sympathetic consideration of your Government and your people, I am sending a few persons with Mr Th. Muivah, Plenipotentiary and Brigadier Thinoselie Keyho from our Government to your Excellency with the hope that your Excellency will seriously look into our present difficulties. That, as a small nation, it was never our intention to do anything which will offend our great neighbours. That is why in spite of being suppressed to the extreme, we have been trying to persuade the Government of India to recognise our right to regain our sovereignty but till today it has not been given to reason, and as it has become impossible for us to resist unaided the military might of Indian Armed Forces we have to look to your Government and your people for any possible assistance in any form so that we may properly safeguard our sovereignty through the liberal hand of your people. That our Government feel the paramount necessity of your kind recognition of the existence of the Naga nation and the legality of the Federal Government of Nagaland ... So, I and my people are anxiously waiting to get some encouraging news from your great and strong country, in the near future, and my people as a small nation will always remain grateful to your people.[2]

---

[2] A document reproduced in Keyho, *My Journey*, 66–7.

Scato's letter to the Chinese authorities was carefully free of even the slightest religious allusion, very unlike the normal correspondence among leaders of the underground which made generous use of Bible quotations and religious rhetoric. Scato's personal inspiration was the Book of Psalms, he said to me. Having been raised in a Baptist home and educated in mission school he could quote the scriptures at will, which came in handy during his stint as president of the underground government. While overground, he was a model Baptist believer who could deliver insightful sermons. Being the most educated person among the Sumi Nagas, he often addressed church congregations.

Scato's faith did not waver through his tempestuous stint as leader of the Naga underground government. During the Indo–China War of 1962, with fear of the Chinese invasion looming large, Scato as FGN president issued a public statement to allay the fears of Nagas. He assured them that China would recognise the Naga independence movement not because "the Nagas are Communist, but because the Nagas have the right to be free." Strikingly, he also wrote that "God has duly caused Communist China to bring pestilence to India as retribution to her that India may fear the name of Almighty God."[3] Five years later, when critics attacked him and the underground government – which was manned overwhelmingly by the Baptist faithful – for their Chinese connection, Scato tried to distance the movement from a communist connection that was unequivocally anathema to the Baptist faith. In the Naga society of the day, religion and politics often meshed to influence lives, but when news of Naga underground leaders "experimenting" with communism entered public discourse the Baptist church came out strongly against them.

The possibility of China indoctrinating the hill peoples of north-east India could hardly go unnoticed by the Indian authorities. Even before independence, in 1946, as we have seen, Nehru

---

[3] The public statement was issued under the heading "Public information on the unfounded fear of China", dated 26 October 1962, Oking.

had penned a letter to Sakhrie cautioning that the Naga territory was "much too small to stand by itself, politically or economically", lying "between two huge countries, India and China".[4] But the tiny "Naga nation" could, as Naga nationalists saw it, benefit from the patronage of the People's Republic of China. And for its part China was ready to spread its revolutionary ideals beyond its shores. According to the accounts of China-returned Naga fighters, the People's Liberation Army (PLA) did try indoctrinating the Nagas into the ways of Maoism, but their attitude and strategy towards their protégés, who were overwhelmingly Baptist, was comparatively innocuous and lax. On their part the Nagas, who were taught guerrilla warfare and attended months of political training, maintained their distance from Maoist doctrine. At least among the rank and file of the China-trained "Naga Army", their faith was unsullied and Maoist ideas remained skin-deep. In this respect the Naga encounter with Chinese revolutionary ambitions was different from that of ethnic groups in Myanmar – such as the Burmans (the majority ethnic group), Kachins, Shans, and Was. But though the communist ideology never really struck root in the Baptist heartland in Nagaland, it did create a furore in Naga society.

Mission-school-educated natives had long been exposed to world history and political philosophies in places of learning. As a student in the Impur mission school in the 1930s, T. Aliba Imti, the first NNC president, recalled that students had discussions on "the burning questions of the time", e.g. "the Spanish civil war, Germany's re-armament, and the industrialization of Japan".[5] Educated Nagas were exposed to the ideas of capitalism and socialism too, but they were not affected by the bloc mentality in the aftermath of WWII, when the Cold War tended to solidify every nation into camps supporting one and opposing the other. Naga intellectuals, by contrast, underscored the roots of their

---

[4] Lhousa, *Strange Country*, 29.
[5] Imti, *Reminiscence*, 6.

nationalism and nationhood as lying in timeless tradition and ethnicity, with the caveat that though the Word of the Lord had come in from the world beyond, it had only served to strengthen traditional bonds. With China entering this picture, it was not long before the word according to Mao arrived as well, generating debates on communism among the Nagas.

In the ensuing polemics among the educated class, not even the architect of Naga nationalism, A.Z. Phizo, was spared. In a memorable episode, he took a traditional oath denying all charges that he had supported communism.[6] He publicly stated that as a Baptist he had in no way connived with communist forces while in Burma, nor ever harboured the communist ideology in his pursuit of Naga interests. This charge of communism against Phizo was not mere theatre: in 1946 he had returned from Burma, where communism had been gaining a foothold, with many educated natives seeing communism as the antidote to Western imperialism and thus relevant to their anti-colonial struggle. The communist doctrine of social justice appealed to the colonised, fuelling ideas of nationalism, especially in South East Asia. Over Phizo's Burma stint (1934–46) the Communist Party of Burma, the Burma National Army, and the People's Revolutionary Party (later Socialist Party) had in 1945 banded to form the Anti-Fascist People's Freedom League (AFPFL). In parts of the Indo–China region, the Marxist-Leninist strand of communism had gained pace with the formation of the Viet Minh in 1941 under nationalist leaders, Ho Chi Minh being the most prominent. These developments in proximate regions did not escape the notice of the Naga nationalists, making some of their Baptist intellectuals apprehensive about the coming communist wave. Their antipathy for communism and Maoism was neither ideological nor because "political power grows out of the barrel of a gun", but because communism's atheism and rejection of religion as the opiate of the masses was everything that Naga Baptists could never accept.

[6] Steyn, *Zapuphizo*, 76.

The American missionaries, while still stationed in the Naga Hills, were not fearful of native converts embracing the communist teachings, though after WWII B.I. Anderson of the Kohima station had remarked on "invidious" communist pamphlets circulating among students.[7] Whiffs of communism had reached the hills but were not a scent heady enough to persuade Nagas against the Christianity embedded deep in their collective psyche. The communist wave spreading through South East Asia was conspicuous in not affecting this Baptist enclave that would soon be a hotbed of ethnonationalism.

Anderson, a polymath missionary, had initiated the conversion movement among Scato's Sumi Naga tribesmen in the late 1930s and '40s. And Scato knew the American missionaries well since he had studied under them in Kohima; he remained a lifelong supporter of the American mission, though as a Naga nationalist he staunchly opposed British rule. Naga nationalists had never considered the Baptist mission an imposition; they had amalgamated their ethnicity and culture with this "foreign" religion and no one saw it as external or as an intrusion. Though missionary influence over converts and mission matters naturally declined when the Americans were evicted, the strength of Christianity was in no sense weakened – quite the contrary.

Two years before Scato as FGN president wrote to the Chinese government, Rev. Anderson preached in a large Baptist church in Worland, Wyoming, on "Christians in India and the Communist Challenge".[8] This veteran missionary had worked in the Naga areas nearly twenty years and been in the audience on 30 March 1953 when Nehru visited Kohima – when about 3500 Nagas who had "filled the football field in anticipation of his [Nehru's] speech" had staged their walkout. "We were seated close to the platform and did not know what was taking place until we saw the Nagas

---

[7] Walling, ed., *Down the Memory Lane*, 86.

[8] According to B.I. Anderson's "unpublished sermon notes", the sermon was delivered on 5 August 1965.

turn their backs on Nehru," Anderson wrote. Nehru "had not expected this insulting response" and "in his speech, he made no secret of his suspicions and declared the incident to be irrefutable evidence of the sinister influence of foreigners, whose presence in the Naga Hills would in a short time be terminated. Since we were the only foreigners there we knew what to expect in the future."[9]

The troubles of the American missionaries soon escalated. On Easter morning in 1955 the armed police raided Anderson's home in the Kohima mission station, rummaging for documents or evidence that might indict the missionary for anti-state activities. He was charged by Indian intelligence with possessing a roll of copper wire and some empty cartridge shells – which Anderson said had been in his bungalow before his arrival – and dragged him into taxing litigation. According to Anderson, "The Press of India made these insignificant findings mount up to become an arsenal for fifth column activity and the wires to be part of the government telegraph communications with Burma."[10] Anderson was acquitted, but the foreign missionaries were told to pack their bags and leave.

The American Baptist mission was not immune to a changing political landscape. The final defeat of the Kuomintang Nationalists by the Communist Party of China in 1949 had huge implications for Christian missions in the Orient. Baptist foreign mission periodicals began carrying articles on the communist movement in their various regions. American missionaries did not campaign against communism in the Naga areas, but Naga Baptists had under seminary-trained leaders imbibed a suspicion and distaste for the communist movement. This had an effect on the Naga political movement.

The Naga Baptist church's crusade against communism came against the backdrop of the armed insurrection, when Naga underground leaders drew the ire of the Baptist church for their Chinese

---

[9] Walling, ed., *Down the Memory Lane*, pp. 94–5.
[10] Ibid., 95.

connection. Had the same aid and support to Naga insurgents come from Western nations – NNC leaders abroad had tried to get some without success – it would have been less controversial in the Naga Baptist world. This is clear from an incidental fact: when Naga guerrillas crossed into East Pakistan (now Bangladesh) and returned with arms and ammunition, as well as expertise in handling explosives (much to the terror of train passengers in the Assam plains), the Baptist church spoke out against violence targeting innocent civilians but not against the Islamic ideology of Pakistan. Since independence, India's closest neighbour and arch-rival had had its eye on the densely populated districts of Assam bordering East Pakistan, but Pakistan's ambition was less of a threat than the Chinese. When the Naga political movement came under the purview of China's foreign policy in the mid-1960s, communism became a household word – an odious one – in Naga Baptist circles.

II

On 12 September 1962 *The Times* of London carried an unusual snippet with the heading "Home Office frees Naga tribesmen" along with a photograph of four smartly dressed men in suits and neckties. The press release said "Four persons describing themselves as Nagas" had been detained at London airport "because the documents on which they were travelling did not satisfy immigration officers as to their identity and their nationality." The four men, calling themselves leaders of the Naga National Movement – as their colleague and NNC president A.Z. Phizo testified to the office of the British home secretary – had flown into London from Pakistan. *The Times* revealed the names of these "Naga tribesmen" as General Kaito Sukhai, Major-General Mowu, Mr Khodao, and Mr Yong Kong. In the press statement Khodao said 153 Naga soldiers had trekked for four months through Indian lines, amid tight security, twice running into an ambush to reach East Pakistan; from there they had been taken to Karachi, where they boarded a London-bound flight.

The Naga leaders had the support of Ursula Graham Bower (later Ursula Graham Betts), author of *The Naga Path*. Commissioned as a captain during WWII, Graham Bower had formed a local defence and intelligence organisation named "Watch and Ward" with the encouragement of General Slim, most notably saving RAF pilots who had crashed in the hilly Naga terrain during the war with the Japanese.[11] Graham Bower hosted the Naga leaders, who were on a mission to meet Phizo in London.

In 2012 I met Graham Bower's daughter, Catriona Child, at a function in St Stephen's College, Delhi. Catriona recounted

Ill. 21: From left to right: Mowu Gwizan, Khodao Yanthan, Kaito Sukhai, Yongkong, Ursula Graham Betts, 1962. The four Naga leaders were detained at London airport and later released by the Home Office. Courtesy DIPR.

[11] Glancey, *Nagaland*, 146–7. General William Slim was, in the Indian context, best known as the military leader whose troops had stopped the Japanese advance into India by defeating them at the Battle of Kohima in mid 1944.

her mother's meeting with the Naga leaders in 1963: her mother was impressed with the battle plans and guerrilla warfare strategy of General Kaito Sukhai, then commander-in-chief of the Naga Army, who had set up a jungle base in Myanmar.[12] Kaito, then thirty years old, was a natural guerrilla commander and military strategist who had formed a well-organised fighting force when the Nagas began their armed conflict with the Indian state. What lent potency to the Naga underground government, FGN, was its armed wing called the Naga Army, which employed guerrilla tactics against a well-armed, larger, and far superior military force. The guerrilla machinery became an important bargaining chip for the FGN, although it brought untold suffering on villagers during army counter-operations.

The Naga National Council (NNC) leaders were all political activists and community leaders, not military theorists. Many top NNC leaders had successful political careers when the state of Nagaland was created in 1963. Phizo was no military strategist, but he recognised the potential of guerrilla warfare and used it to his advantage. However, Naga nationalists maintained that they had resorted to warfare because political negotiations had failed and their armed struggle was not hostility but legitimate defence against an invading force. The Naga armed uprising became synonymous with jungle warfare, reinforcing the idea of Nagas as a martial race. The Indo–Myanmar jungle upland was naturally suited to guerrilla warfare; local fighters knew the terrain and used it to their advantage.

Counterinsurgency measures on both sides of the Indo–Myanmar border were similar: the "four-cuts" strategy of General Ne Win's Tatmadaw in the Myanmar uplands matched the Indian government's "village grouping" method, where the main objective was to isolate rebels by putting pressure on the civilian population in the sparsely populated Naga areas. The army strategy of

---

[12] Kaito had set up a camp named Kuhubo at Shera in Layshi township in the Sagaing region.

getting to the guerrillas through civilians or settling scores against villagers for supporting guerrillas was the worst fallout of the war. Scato said his family's suffering increased when he joined the movement: "My family was constantly harassed by the [Indian] army. Our home was burnt to the ground twice, and my wife and three children had to seek refuge in a Chakhesang Naga village." Visakhonü Hibo, an Angami Naga sociologist, told me from her own experiences growing up during those tumultuous years that "many Naga fighters could not continue fighting, not due to lack of courage, but they could no longer endure the sufferings of womenfolk and children during the prolonged conflict."

Civilian "collateral damage" remains a blot on any nation professing to be democratic. The terrain advantage for guerrillas was countered by state savagery against civilians, but, given the modern state's acquisition of drone and satellite technology, the Indian state may find it less easy to justify collateral damage as a counterinsurgency strategy. On the other side, self-trained guerrilla commanders like Kaito Sukhai and Mowu Angami, who spearheaded the pitiless and enervating jungle warfare, are likely to be replaced by war technicians in any resumption of warfare – which, luckily, does not seem likely for the moment.

Kaito Sukhai and Thungti Chang were the first guerrilla commanders to lead ill-equipped men in the armed uprising when the NNC decided to shift gear in their political pursuit. The armed wing, though crude and unorganised, took shape in 1954 when Phizo formed the underground government, the "Free Naga Government", in the Chang Naga region, in the eastern frontier in Tuensang.[13] Thungti, a young Chang Naga, was made commander of the armed wing known as the Naga Home Guards. In 1955 another armed group called the Naga Safe Guards cropped up in the eastern Sumi Naga region of the Tuensang Frontier Division,

---

[13] The letterhead of the new underground government that Phizo had masterminded bore the name "Government of People's Sovereign Republic of Free Nagaland". See also Lhousa, *Strange Country*, 121–2.

NEFA, led by Kaito Sukhai, a former high-school student in Shillong and NNC youth activist. The Naga Safe Guards, roughly patterned along the lines of the British Army, was comprised of Sumi and Yimchunger Naga tribesmen.[14] The Naga Home Guards and the Naga Safe Guards were the forerunners of the "Naga Army", the outlawed underground government's (FGN's) well-organised guerrilla machinery. These first Naga fighters were a ragtag lot armed with *daos* and spears, country-made muzzle loaders, and rusty rifles left over from WWII.

The Nagas took to the jungles for various reasons. At the start of the trouble the Indian authorities, who were trying to quell an uprising in uncharted territory, adopted tactics that proved counterproductive. To instil fear, they publicly displayed the dead bodies of slain Naga "fighters" – the Nagas claim they were civilians – in Kohima, which had angered and alienated the populace.[15] Harsh counterinsurgency measures and high casualties were known to have been sanitised by the propaganda wing of the Indian army. During his clandestine trip to the Naga areas in 1961, Gavin Young of *The Observer* wrote of a young Naga fighter who had left school and joined the movement after "his father had been bayoneted to death by Assamese riflemen of the Indian Army in 1956, and his mother gaoled."[16] Fighting a guerrilla force meant government troops shelving the conventions of war.[17]

The methods of recruiting guerrillas were controversial too, though many young men volunteered. Among my Sumi Naga tribesmen, who formed a large chunk of the fighting force, are accounts of how men arrived at villages to forcibly recruit young

---

[14] Allied forces had been posted near Kaito's native village, Ghukhuyi, during WWII.

[15] Apparently, the dead bodies of two men, Thepfuvicha and Lhoupizhü, of Mima village were displayed in Kohima town on 27 February 1957.

[16] See Naga National Council, *The Naga National Rights*, 71.

[17] I have a friend whose pregnant mother was bayoneted to death while working in a *jhum* field by government troops during a military operation.

boys and school students for the jungles; some parents paid cash to avoid their sons being taken. The guerrillas were mostly sons of ordinary villagers who fought hard under harsh conditions. The sacrifices of these recruits barely registered in the memory of people outside their grieving families.

The Naga political movement was susceptible to personality cults, putting it on a slippery road toward tribalism and leadership crises. Not even Phizo was above ethnic politics; his detractors, including colleagues from other Naga groups, accused him of favouritism with his own politically powerful Angami tribesmen. The shared Baptist affiliation was sidelined in favour of tribal difference when it came to internecine disputes, and group loyalty was manifest down to clan level. These quarrels were primarily responsible for the unmaking of the Naga political movement. Ironically, in this respect the Naga Christians proved themselves as bickeringly clannish as the disputatious Hindu castes of the plains. The Indian intelligence machinery grasped this reality and milked it to the hilt.[18]

Though the Naga fighters' loyalty to their commanders made them effective, in-group loyalty also often trumped the evasive ideals of nationhood and a generic Naga identity – the twin concepts which had precariously knitted various ethnic groups. And within particular ethnic groups, loyalties could be subdivided along village, *khel*, and clan ties. For instance, in the oft-quoted Angami Naga village Khonoma, a rift developed between the two *khels* of Phizo and the former NNC stalwart Jasokie. Jasokie's Semoma *khel* began to be identified as "pro-Indian", creating a huge rift with the Thevoma and Merhema *khels*, especially the latter, to which Phizo belonged.[19] The Naga armed movement was, even when effective, riven by such clashes of personality and ever brewing as an incendiary concoction of factionalism and split loyalty.

---

[18] The document "Secret Joint Directive for Counter Insurgency Operation in Nagaland", brought out at the peak of the conflict, included a strategy to exploit the rivalries between the underground leaders.

[19] See also Sanyü with Broome, *A Naga Odyssey*, 47.

The consequences of factionalism were soon apparent. Men under an able commander fought as a tight unit and remained loyal to the chain of command, but over-reliance on specific guerrilla chiefs also meant the dismantling or weakening of the war's machinery if they happened to be displaced or liquidated. The rise and fall of General Kaito is a case in point. Kaito Sukhai had amassed a large following, mainly of his tribesmen, as a result of his charisma and prowess in guerrilla warfare. But his bid for political power led to his undoing.[20] Similarly, in the Kachin insurgency theatre of Burma in 1975, the purge of the powerful brother duo Zau Tu and Zau Seng of the Kachin Independence Army (KIA) witnessed the end of the KIA's movement opposing the Communist Party of Burma (CPB). The two KIA commanders had been apprehensive of Chinese-exported communist revolutionaries taking over the ethnic uprisings in upland Burma.[21] Like their co-religionists the Kachins, the Naga rebels' relationship with communism remained complex, the reason being their Baptist faith.

Another weakness of the Naga insurgency was a power tussle between leaders of the political wing and the armed wing. It has been noted that when a strong military leader or political authoritarian steers an ethnic armed uprising, the uprising does not last long: the end is either a factional clash or a purging of the top leadership. The FGN had adopted a loose parliamentary system of government – its critics say it was not democratic and a sham – with a president, prime minister, cabinet ministers, and

---

[20] Against the wishes and reproval of his elder brother Kughato Sukhai, then FGN prime minister, and brother-in-law Scato Swu, then FGN president, Kaito declared the Army Government on 17 June 1967. Behind Kaito's bold move lay his meeting with General Ayub Khan, then minister of defence, whom Kaito met in Karachi. See also Swu, *Hails and Blames*, 148. The Chinese handlers also knew of Kaito's exploits: they had expected him to lead the *alee* command to China. The trajectory of the Naga armed struggle, had Kaito made it to China and come under the influence of Maoist doctrines, must remain a matter for speculation.

[21] Lintner, *Great Game East*, 247–8.

regional governors; the armed wing, the Naga Army, was headed by a general as commander-in-chief, with the rank and file modelled on the British and Indian armies.

The armed wing, the most operationally active part of the underground government, was the quintessence of the Naga political movement. It was what the Indian authorities were wary of as it took a toll on the state by fighting a faceless war. In the eyes of the Naga fighters, it was they who brought the authorities to the negotiating table. This fact did not elude the influential guerrilla commander Kaito, who felt that while foot soldiers risked or gave up their lives for the cause, the political wing's control diminished the armed wing. Because he was vociferous in voicing his discontent, it proved his undoing.[22] Demoted from the position of C-in-C of the Naga Army in 1963, an order he took to heart, Kaito, who was then the defence minister, drafted a letter dated Oking, 4 June 1964, to "the chief of Naga Army Staff" to ready men for action:

> The duty of the army is to fight for the defence of our country, therefore, he is not an army he who does not fight. Any command or any Naga Armed Personnel who does not stand to fight our enemies and remains passive should understand by himself whether he is or is not Army personnel.
>
> The Indian Army is heavily concentrated in the borders. Therefore, more vigorous fighting should take place in those outposts of Indian Army violating the terms of the cease-fire agreement.

Kaito was a man of action who believed in armed insurrection as against "unproductive" peace talks, which he saw as making his soldiers apathetic and complacent even as the enemy used the interval to its advantage. His diehard approach was thought impractical by some, since there was no denying he was up against an insurmountable foe, but militarily he was a guerrilla genius.

[22] Kaito's brother Kuhoi, an academic, told me that the guerrilla chief would often complain about fighters being "sidelined" and "neglected" by the political wing.

Ironically, his assassination on 3 August 1968 was during a cease-fire and in broad daylight, not behind the cloak of the jungles to which he had adapted so well.

The fact was that the Naga issue was political in nature, and even when the Nagas decided to resort to armed insurrection it was the political wing of the movement that had precedence over the armed wing. Naga nationalists steering the political movement had imbibed ideas of statecraft and modern governance from Western societies, therefore the possibility of guerrilla commanders taking over the movement was slight. Early on, Nehru's intelligence chief B.N. Mullik had come to the conclusion that the Naga insurgency required a political rather than military solution. He noted that "the Nagas fought on with great determination. There were many ugly incidents; serious casualties were inflicted on both sides; no quarter was given or asked for. The security forces exerted the maximum of pressure, but this was not enough to force the rebel Nagas into surrender."[23] The Indian state had the upper hand but had not managed to cripple the movement; an amicable political solution, though elusive, was in his view the way forward.

III

The Naga guerrillas began with ambushes on army convoys and surprise attacks on military outposts, their idea being to stock up on arms and ammunition. According to Scato, Kaito's "strategy [was] to fight the enemy with the enemy's weapons, and this method worked very well."[24]

In the early years the guerrillas followed a code of conduct. An officer with the Corps of Engineers of the Indian Army, posted in Nagaland during the conflict years, observed that Naga fighters rarely ambushed vehicles carrying women or infrastructure workers; they also usually did not fight on the Sabbath and important

[23] Mullik, *My Years with Nehru*, 312–13.
[24] See also Swu, *Hails and Blames*, 212.

Christian holidays.[25] This compartmentalising of their Christian faith from political violence was a curious, or perhaps remarkable, affirmation of their need to render unto Jesus even as they spat fire against their would-be Caesar. The post-independence Naga upsurge negated all that the American Baptists believed their mission had achieved – a new era of peace and prosperity free of violence. To salvage some of the Christianity they seemed to have jettisoned by warring against India, the Nagas were keen to indicate that their faith was a private matter whereas fighting the enemy and carrying out orders was a political necessity for their identity survival. Within this mix, there can be no doubt that it was the practice of violence rather than Christianity that was paramount. The nearly seven decades of struggle are riddled with incidents of Nagas purging political dissidents, shooting informers and spies, bombing civilians, and even exterminating suspect groupings. Bertil Lintner, a Swedish journalist and expert on ethnic insurgencies in the Indo–Myanmar uplands, argues that the Naga armed struggle in the 1950s, based on the idea of defending the Naga "homeland" from invasion, had by the late 1970s transformed into a quasi-Maoist-inspired revolutionary movement with a topping of "fanatic syncretised Christianity".[26]

Before their training in Pakistan and China, Naga guerrilla operations were limited to "taking out" dissidents, damaging bridges, and generally attacking the Indian army; civilians were not in their sights. This changed. Once they had gained knowhow in the use of explosives in East Pakistan, their bombs in mail trains killed innocent civilians.[27] Their Pakistani handlers may not have trained them in political propaganda as had the Chinese, but they had taught them to extend the scale of the war. This dismayed

[25] Anand, *Conflict in Nagaland*.

[26] See Lintner, *Land of Jade*, Chapter 5; and Linter, *Great Game East*, 92.

[27] In one instance, on 17 February 1967, a powerful bomb ripped through a "third-class" compartment of the Assam Mail in Tinsukia, killing 37 and injuring 52.

Naga Baptist church leaders, who did not approve of violence against civilians.

Kikhehe, a Sumi Naga fighter who was in the second batch of Naga Army personnel sent to East Pakistan in 1965 led by General Zuheto Swu (General-Officer-Commanding of Central Command), told me their Pakistani handlers treated them well and saw to their comfort. "We were being trained in weapon handling and hand-to-hand combat and these tall Pakistani instructors would kick us while we lay on the ground taking positions. We did not like it and told our superiors that Nagas are never treated that way, that we are not Pakistani soldiers. The treatment was different after the complaint was made."

According to Subir Bhaumik, an expert on insurgency in north-east India, a veteran Pakistani Special Service Group (SSG) officer who had trained both the Nagas and "Kashmir *mujahids*", told him "The Nagas were far better fighters than the Kashmir *mujahids*. They were disciplined and dedicated and quickly picked up tactics and weapons skills. They clearly had a cause. The *mujahids* from Azad Kashmir were unruly. It was clear they had more interest in the women and loot waiting for them in the Srinagar valley."[28]

The travails of terrain apart, bypassing the long arm of India's intelligence made Naga trips to East Pakistan arduous. In their first expedition in 1962, Kaito took 150 men "through Tamenglong Sub-Division of Manipur and then through North-Cachar Hill into Khowai Sub-Division of Khasi Hills District to Sylhet District of East Pakistan."[29] Deprecatingly termed "gangs", or more commonly "Naga hostiles", they were dismissed by the Indian authorities who said they "got some arms but not enough to make any impression on the Indian Security Forces."[30] But insurrections have a way of leaving unanticipated impressions, and in this case

---

[28] Bhaumik, *Troubled Periphery*, 158.
[29] Mullik, *My Years with Nehru*, 332.
[30] Ibid., 332–3.

the example of a small group of Naga rebels seeking help from India's rivals did impress the Mizos, the Meiteis, and the Assamese. The fact that the Indian government did not declare the Naga armed insurrection "terrorism" spoke volumes of the historical complexity of the ethnic Naga movement. The same historical and political complexity, with its roots in colonialism, is, as noted earlier, observable in the ethnic-based insurgencies among the Karen, Kachin, Mon, and Was in Myanmar's horseshoe-like uplands.

The Nagas who trekked out of their landlocked hills had their notion of ethnicity expanded. China-bound leaders like Thinuoselie, Thuingaleng Muivah, Mowu Angami, and Isak Chishi Swu connected with other ethnic groups. Swu writes that the Nagas are, in the story of their migration to their current habitation, "the older brother and the Kachin the younger brother."[31] The American Baptists had alluded to a heritage common to Chins, Kachins, and Nagas. Swu, a China veteran and devout Baptist, was struck by the idea of Naga identity as the outcome of migrations from China via Burma, and this became the basis of his writings on ethnonationalism rather than any Maoist propaganda. He argued for a connection via the meaning of the word "Naga" in the Burmese language: "*Na* – ear and *Ka* – perforation (people with pierced ear)."[32] This in his view linked Nagas with the larger Tibeto–Burman language group.

Nagas on their precarious journey to East Pakistan saw similarities in cultural traits among ethnic Chins in the jungle-matted Chin Hills, reinforcing the notion of a traditional homeland disrupted by modern national boundaries. The rank and file of the Naga Army, venturing out of its confined world for the first time, was exposed to the diversity of ethnic groups in the Indo–Myanmar frontier. A former guerrilla who went to East Pakistan told me he was surprised to see natives with tattoos still living in a very "primitive" condition:

[31] Swu, *From Generation to Generation*, 17.
[32] Ibid., 18.

these people were unkempt and flimsily covered and their homes were dirty and in shabby condition. They practised slash-and-burn cultivation and still followed their traditional religion. They would cook from a single pot and the entire family would dig in. We took shelter in the village but our commanding officers forbade us to eat with the villagers; one of our men could not tolerate his hunger and ate a morsel from a family's pot. The commander knew about it and he was punished for disobeying orders.

The year was 1965 and the Naga fighters had discovered an ethnic community they deemed primitive – the Chins – who later converted to the Baptist faith in large numbers.

Militarily, their foreign connection boosted the Naga Army's armoury and fine-tuned their guerrilla tactics, enabling them to ramp up their enterprise and pose a greater threat. In the Indian mainland their jungle war was portrayed as waged by fringe "hostiles" against the wishes of their own people who wanted peace and prosperity. This portrayal by state propaganda was rather far from the truth. The Naga movement could not have persisted without the widespread support of the common people. This inconvenient fact becomes easier to downplay by the propaganda war of the hegemonic state which ultimately prevails against those resisting it. The messaging of the victor is always louder – except that it runs contrary to the experience of the defeated, whose narrative of subalternity continues to confound the "truth" broadcast by the oppressor.

In the end it was war fatigue that eroded the armed uprisings. The relentlessness of the counterinsurgency was harsher than is known in the world outside. The huddling of villagers like cattle into cramped camps; the scorched-earth policy; the beatings and rough interrogations; the sexual violence; the custodial deaths and "accidental" killings of civilians – all of which is the stuff of counterinsurgency operations – breaks the toughest aspiration. It was no different for the Nagas: perhaps their small consolation lay in knowing Rome had done much the same to Jesus.

The Naga Baptist church also bore the brunt of the military operations; it lost some of its workers. Cases of pastors and evangelists being beaten and harassed were common, not because of their faith but as the ever-spreading collateral damage of military operations. When government troops torched villages, churches built in the midst of settlements were burnt down. For believers this was a sacrilege never to be forgotten. Naga Baptists say that the 1960s and 1970s were also the time when a great revival took place, with thousands converting to the new faith without the involvement of foreign missionaries.

The hardships of the church became an obvious and emotive propaganda weapon for the Naga underground. When the Anglican priest and human rights activist Rev. Michael Scott arrived in Nagaland as part of a peace mission, underground leaders raised the issue of "church persecution" with him: "It is a matter of great importance to note that most of the Nagas are Christians who are generally the worst victims . . . for instance, Mr Pelesato, the Field Director of Chakhesang Mission Field, was arrested and burnt alive on April 15, 1956. Free preaching of Christian doctrine is restricted up to date."[33] A veteran Chakhesang Baptist leader, Rev. Vezopa Tetseo, told me that Rev. Pelesato from Khonoma was arrested in April 1956 from the mission centre and tortured to death. The faithful still narrate the harassment of church workers and the killings of well-known Baptist ministers like Pelesato.

A feather in the Naga cap as seen in the Christian mission world at large was that the Naga Baptists were, in relation to percentage of population, reputed to have the largest number of lay pastors and evangelists anywhere.[34] Not everyone was a licensed church worker, but there were many unpaid or self-funded who had joined the underground movement as chaplains. The *alee* command was never complete without a chaplain in the group. Bible school-trained chaplains had joined rebels in the jungles. Naturally, many Baptist ministers had by contrast eschewed armed struggle

[33] Welcome Address to Rev. Michael Scott, Nagaland Peace Mission on Occasion of First Meeting with Kedahge and Other Federal Leaders. See Lasuh, ed., *The Naga Chronicle*, 244.

[34] Chute, et al., *The Baptist Story*.

Ill. 22: Rev. Yankey Patton, the first chaplain in the NNC–Federal government. Courtesy NBCC.

as incompatible with the Christian faith, and their ministrations continued apace simultaneously, bolstering the region's repute as a fierce stronghold of the Christian faith. The political ideology of the Baptist pastors who joined the Naga movement had no resemblance to liberation theology – the synthesis of Christian theology and Marxism directed towards the emancipation of the oppressed that was popular in the 1950s and '60s in Latin America among the Roman Catholic majority. The Naga Baptist exposure to the outside world was more limited. What came in handy for preachers in their pursuit of ethnonationalism was the Exodus model in the Old Testament – the oppressed Israelites up against mighty Egypt. It was a literal interpretation of the scriptures, but one that spoke to the hearts of people in their fight against a formidable opponent.

The former man of the cloth and tribal expert Elwin captured the efficacy of Biblical rhetoric that "hostile pastors" employed in their propaganda when denigrating political opponents seeking a solution within the Indian union: "While Moses (symbolising the rebel leaders) was away in the mountains receiving the Ten Commandments at the hands of the Lord, the Israelites, weary of the privations of the wilderness, went astray and created and worshipped the Golden Calf (of a State within the Indian Union)."[35] In a region where Bible knowledge and literacy were expanding, the Naga ethnonationalists used both to their advantage – and as they, rather than Elwin, thought best for their enterprise.

The Naga underground government had some well-known Baptist ministers. Young men trained in Bible colleges, such as Yankey Patton, V.K. Nuh, and Mhiasiu Chase, became household names in the armed struggle and its aftermath.[36] A former Baptist minister who served as pastor of Khonoma Baptist Church, Rev. Mhiasiu rose to become president of the FGN. The Naga Baptist church also produced at this time influential leaders like Longri Ao, Kenneth Kerhüo, Toniho Chishi, and Kijungluba Ao, who remained neutral churchmen: these Naga Baptist church leaders represented the voices of many of the faithful weary of the violence. Contrary points of view within the church were inevitable – a fallout of prolonged conflict. Much to the suspicion of the underground leaders, the Baptist church's own fatigue was clear in its urging a peaceful settlement at any cost.

The protracted conflict naturally took a heavy toll on ordinary Nagas. Starting in the late 1960s, many fighters laid down arms. Some political functionaries of the underground government were

[35] Elwin, *Nagaland*, 67.

[36] Rev. Yankey Patton from the Lotha Naga tribe became a prominent Baptist minister, while Rev. V.K. Nuh became a popular Naga Baptist church leader and writer. Both never gave up the idea of a Naga nation, despite advancing age.

either jailed or appeared overground and many battle-hardened guerrillas were either dead or caught or had surrendered to the Indian government. India had thinned the herd. With the agreement signed between a section of Naga underground leaders and the Indian government on 11 November 1975 – which came to be known as the Shillong Accord – the Naga armed struggle that had started in the mid-1950s appeared to be over. This inaugurated a new phase in the Naga political movement, and a tumultuous phase for Nagas on the other side of the Indo–Myanmar border. The grand old man of the Naga national movement, Phizo, receded into the background, and though other Naga leaders could not hold a flame to his legend, the baton had been passed on. It was Chinese-trained Naga rebels holed out in north-western Myanmar who would come into the limelight in the 1980s.

Among the signatories of the Shillong Accord was Phizo's younger brother Kevi Yallay, whose attendance placed Phizo in a most awkward position. Kevi Yallay had been Phizo's closest confidant since his Burma days. Settled in a London suburb, Phizo, though far removed from the reality of his native land, was hit hard by the news; his only audience that gloomy midday in November was his eldest daughter, Addino. His British biographer says the leader of the Naga independence movement, now in his sixties, was laconic that day: perhaps a thousand emotions were going through his mind, but hearing the news he calmly went back into his study.[37] As in most ethnic-based armed insurgencies, ideological differences, tribalism, and power tussles had derailed the Naga political movement.

By the mid-1970s, thus, the movement appeared to have run out of steam. Armed fighters had been the raison d'être of the political wing, and Naga nationalists willing to continue the fight knew that dismantling the guerrilla machinery would mean the final demise of the movement: the two China veterans Thuingaleng Muivah and Isak Chishi Swu reasoned so. When the Shillong Accord was signed in 1975, the writing was on the wall: the

[37] Steyn, *Zapuphizo*, 156.

guerrilla machinery was at its lowest ebb. Kaito Sukhai had been liquidated; the first guerrilla commander to lead the Naga fighters to China, Thinuoselie, along with another *alee* command veteran, Brigadier Neideilie, had been captured in Dhaka when the Indian forces liberated East Pakistan in 1971; Phizo's close relative, and C-in-C of the Naga Army, Mowu Angami, had been seized and handed over to the Indian authorities in 1969 by a breakaway group, the Revolutionary Government of Nagaland (RGN); and Phizo's decorated General Zuheto Swu had surrendered and joined the Indian Border Security Force. In 1961 the British journalist Gavin Young had praised the Naga rebels for organisational skill and dexterity; now, writing from a Naga rebel hideout in north-western Myanmar in 1985, Lintner felt the Naga guerrillas had lost their edge and fighting prowess.

A third batch of Naga Army personnel who had gone to China were undergoing training in the Kutumkai camp in Yunnan when a radio broadcast dropped the bombshell that the Naga underground leaders had signed the Shillong Accord with the Indian government and laid down arms. "The training was in full swing when one afternoon our Chinese instructors informed us about the signing of [the] Shillong Accord. They told us that the movement was in jeopardy, and therefore we should go back to our homeland and defend the cause," Avuli recalled. Was the movement over?

The Chinese knew that without guerrillas the Naga armed struggle was a dead end, that their investment in this small region of India was over. Contrary to expectations, though, the Chinese investment did yield a small dividend: in the 1980s the Naga armed struggle gained a second lease of life in the Burma jungles. The Naga armed movement spearheaded by the China-trained leaders became infamous, as Lintner observed, for "assassinations of Naga and non-Naga opponents, bank robberies and kidnappings for ransom."[38] In hindsight, the Chinese connection had

---

[38] Lintner, *Great Game East*, 92.

salvaged something of the Naga armed movement by infusing it with new revolutionary ideals.

IV

When 128 Nagas arrived at the Tengchong training camp in western Yunnan near the Burma border in January 1967, China was in the midst of the Cultural Revolution. In 1966, after a massive failure of its Great Leap Forward (1958–62), Mao Zedong had another plan up his sleeve for the "common good" of the Chinese people and decided to shift his attention to culture. Inherent in the new cultural policy was weeding out the "Four Olds": old customs, old cultures, old habits, old ideas. This did not bode well for religious faiths, including Christianity, a religion foreign to the Chinese. Thus began the attack on churches and crackdown on Christian missions: native Christians went into hiding. The Red Guards, comprising mostly unruly youths, went on the rampage to bring in line those deemed a threat to the Communist Party. One of the popular Red Guard slogans went:

Beating down foreign religion
Beating down Jesus following
Beating down counter-revolutionists

While the Red Guards went about attacking Chinese Christians, jailing thousands of clergymen and burning down churches, the People's Liberation Army (PLA) set up a camp at Tengchong for Naga rebels, most of them Baptists, who had trekked all the way from the Indian north-east. Keen to export the revolution abroad, the Chinese did not mind making a concession for Naga Christians. When the first batch of Naga fighters reached Yunnan in 1967, the Chinese revolutionary export was already making a mark in northern Myanmar, a strategic region for the Naga mission to China. The Kachins of this region were warring fiercely against the Communist Party of Burma (CPB) rebels. In fact, the Myanmar government under the de facto ruler General

Ne Win was mired in a communist armed insurrection led by the formidable CPB. In June 1967 an anti-Chinese riot erupted in the Chinese settlement in Rangoon, and the Red Guards were considered responsible for spreading the Chinese Cultural Revolution into the Burmese heartland.

Back in the state of Nagaland, the Naga underground leadership would soon face criticism and suspicion from the Naga Baptist church as news of their "Communist China" connection got out. The church was dismayed because the Naga rebels charged with training in the ways of Maoism were overwhelmingly of the Baptist persuasion. What the Naga Baptist church failed to comprehend then was that though the Chinese were good at training Nagas in guerrilla warfare, at politico-religious indoctrination they were not. The Baptist faith of the Nagas proved a hard nut to crack; the Chinese recognised it made more sense for them to focus on realpolitik.

Ill. 23: NSCN(IM) leaders Thuingaleng Muivah and Isak Chishi Swu. The two Chinese-trained Naga leaders gave a second lease of life to the Naga armed struggle from the Myanmar jungles in the late 1970s and early 1980s. Courtesy DIPR.

In February 1968 the second batch of Nagas led by the C-in-C of the Naga Army, Mowu Angami, and the president's special envoy, Isak Chishi Swu, were put up in the Luichang training camp, Yunnan. The squad of 354 fighters that left from Nagaland in November 1967 had reached Yunnan after nearly three months' walk. Their main man in China, Thuingaleng Muivah, had stayed back in China after the first batch of 1967 had left the country, and he was supposed to join them in Kutumkai. The rank and file of the Naga Army, like Captain Sanguto Chase – an Angami Naga fighter from Khonoma who had left for the jungle when still a student in Class 8 – were not privy to the interactions between the Naga leaders and the Chinese authorities, but they heard that political-wing leaders like Muivah and Swu, and guerrilla commanders like Thinuoselie and Mowu, were taken to meet some of the top leaders of the CPC and the PLA. The NNC general secretary Muivah was given special treatment by the Chinese authorities and made to see first-hand the "glory" of the police state.[39] At his Kohima residence in 2018, General Thinuoselie told me his most important meeting with the Chinese authorities was with the PLA's second-in-command.

The former China veteran Sanguto told me that political classes and weapons training began in earnest once the Naga trainees had settled in. Most of them were adherents of a Protestant faith, yet treated with care and respect. The Nagas were drilled in Maoist revolutionary ideals but remained oblivious of the state repression and indoctrination of citizens taking place across China. Unlike in their native Nagaland, where early risers were greeted by the crowing of roosters, here Maoist propaganda blared from loudspeakers that woke them every morning. Captain Sanguto, as he is formally addressed, still remembers the Chinese national anthem during the Cultural Revolution and sang it on record as I interviewed him in Kohima town in 2019: "The east is red, the sun is rising. From China appears Mao Zedong." He remembered most of the

[39] Ibid., 41–2.

Chinese revolutionary songs and the sayings of Chairman Mao that he had learnt at the training camp. Apparently, the trainees were all presented with English-language editions of the "Little Red Book" and the "Selected Works of Mao Tse-Tung".

The PLA instructors enforced a strict routine which the Naga trainees followed religiously: "The Chinese are sticklers for time and we learnt the value of punctuality from them; they would tell us that Mao Zedong never wastes time. Everything was about Mao Zedong, he was the respected figure that all Chinese people try to emulate," Sanguto told me. The first ritual the trainees followed every morning was to salute a large portrait of Mao, which hung on the dormitory wall, and shout in unison "Long live Mao Zedong", and sing the anthem, "The east is red". For their entire time in China, they followed this ritual. Sanguto recalled their timetable at the Luichang training camp:

5:30 a.m. Rise up and wash up
6:00 a.m. Breakfast
7–11 a.m. Political class
11 a.m. Lunch
12–1 p.m. Break
1–2 p.m. Compulsory afternoon nap
2–3 p.m. Discussion class
3–6 p.m. Games and sports
6 p.m. Dinner
8 p.m. Lights off

The charisma of Naga guerrilla commanders was, it seems, no match for Mao's: Lieutenant Yekhalu said the Chinese regarded him as God, more or less. This battle-hardened Naga fighter said even mundane preferences such as an afternoon siesta had to be modelled along Mao's – "The Chinese instructors would tell us that Mao Zedong's productivity is always at an optimum because he takes a daily afternoon nap, and that we must imitate his habit." The Chinese authorities allowed the Naga Baptists Sunday services, but it seems that over their China days the Nagas learnt more about Mao than they had in all their Nagaland years about Jesus.

Naga Army officers were taken on a tour of the Chinese mainland, the objective being to show them the prowess of the People's Republic of China. They were taken to communes, factories, and historical sites, and entertained in the theatre on the Chinese revolution and the life of the almighty Chairman. Ferried in a plane, they visited cities like Kunming, Nanchang, and Peking. They were put up in comfortable hotels and guesthouses. Sanguto said with a chuckle: "While up in the air the Chinese air hostesses would even dance and sing for us . . . we were taken to Mao Zedong's place of birth in Shaoshan; the officials gave us a tour of the place and showed us a thatch house with a small room that Mao Zedong had slept in as a boy." They were taken to the 196th PLA Division headquarters on the outskirts of Peking to see the latest Chinese weapons. "The PLA instructors taught us the handling of their latest weapons and made us shoot targets; for the first time we learnt how to fire the 4-inch mortar that we picked up quickly. The instructors told us that our weapons handling was good, so we must focus on the political training," Sanguto said.

Yekhalu was selected as the Group 1 Command Sergeant Major during the Naga Army trip to China in 1967. On his return in 1969 he was arrested along with others and sent to prison for seven years. Like most of his compatriots, Yekhalu retired to a life of obscurity after his release under an amnesty in 1976. While narrating his China trip Yekhalu observed that

> the Chinese compared Mao Zedong to Jesus; just like Jesus came from a small village in Nazareth, Mao Zedong also came from a remote village in Shaoshan and went on to become the leader of the nation . . . The Chinese are very polite people. When we were taken to the Great Wall of China, our guide told us that the Great Wall covers only nine provinces – talking modestly, but boasting about their civilisation.

A short and nimble man, Yekhalu demonstrated the Chinese technique of bayoneting enemies, comparing it with the Indian army technique: "The Chinese technique is to pierce the body multiple times; they are very quick and agile." He was all praise for the PLA soldiers, relishing putting down his Indian opponents despite the passage of years: "The Indian soldiers especially the Bihari and Gurkha regiments are very noisy and they can be easily identified in the jungle." It was their Chinese instructors who pointed out that since the Nagas could never match the Indian army in weapons and manpower, they had best stick to guerrilla warfare: "According to Mao Zedong's guerrilla warfare strategy, a small group of men fighting persistently will wear down the enemy and win the war."

According to Sanguto, the Chinese authorities made separate arrangements for the two leaders of the 1968 China mission: "We were told that Isak Chishi and General Mowu were taken to meet the top Chinese leadership including Lin Piao." He recalled that "Muivah came to meet us at Kutumkai training camp, and I remember him lecturing us on communism and capitalism. He gave an example that in a communist economy they would make a pen for 1 rupee and sell it at a reasonable price, while in a capitalist economy a pen costing the same would be sold for 10 rupees." According to Yekhalu, Muivah rhetorically asked Naga trainees during a political class: "If a dragon decides to ferry you on his back to cross the ocean, will you agree or not?" Muivah, a canny and skilled theoretician, had put the crux of the China mission in words that ordinary fighters could grasp. Yekhalu understood that this was Muivah's way of telling them that the Nagas must accept every help offered to achieve their objective: even practising Baptists needed to absorb Maoist revolutionary ideas. Sanguto could quote by heart the Maoist guerrilla code: "The enemy advances, we retreat; the enemy camps, we harass; the enemy tires, we attack; the enemy retreats, we pursue."

Sanguto's religious faith never wavered even during his training in China, and his testimony exemplifies a general feeling. He told me he had shed tears when, on turning on the radio, he heard a Christmas song on Christmas Eve while en route to China. Sanguto was the first convert from his family; his father, a captain in the Naga Army, was a practising animist who had been sent to East Pakistan in 1962. Sanguto said: "I was a good Christian; I did not smoke or drink or visit cinema halls, unlike my cousin who was a cinema addict. I was in the eighth class when I decided to leave my studies and join the movement. My father asked me who would look after the family as I was the eldest son, and both of us were in the jungle, but he allowed me to stay." The Chinese seemed to have shrewdly seen that it would be counterproductive to alienate their Naga protégés by suggesting they switch their allegiance from Jesus to Mao.

Atsi Dolie, a relative of Mowu Angami and an Angami Baptist leader, claimed that "God rescued the Nagas on several occasions when they ran into ambushes or came under heavy firing." Atsi is a mainstream Baptist minister with a PhD and not your average Pentecostal preacher, but he firmly believed their protection was God's handiwork: "I'm not implying that the Naga fighters depended on a supernatural power out of fear, but for individuals going through an ordeal, which is a matter of life and death, religious belief came as a solace. For such people turning their back on faith and becoming communists was not possible."

Each Naga foreign mission included a chaplain; the tradition had started since the first trip of the Naga fighters to East Pakistan in 1962. The fighters had at the time comprised both Baptists and animists, but the majority were Christian. Guerrilla commanders like Kaito and Thinuoselie depended more on stealth and cover than on the power of prayers, but having a spiritual guide was therapeutic all the same. "Vitoshe Sema was the chaplain during our trip to China in 1967, and even during our training in Luichang we were allowed to have prayer meetings," Sanguto said. Avuli, a third-batch trainee in 1975, said "the Chinese authorities gave us a cinema hall to be used as a church."

V

While these Nagas were training in Yunnan and forming a favourable view of China, their kin back in Nagaland were alarmed and scandalised by the China connection. The Naga Baptist frontal body, the Nagaland Baptist Church Council, viewed the development with trepidation. Memories of the powerful Chinese force overrunning Indian defences and nearly taking over Upper Assam in 1962 were still fresh in their minds. The American missionaries had long warned against communism. It was natural for the Indian authorities to see the potential in allying with the Naga church against communist China. The church started a crusade against communism; in May 1968 Rev. Longri, head of the NBCC, sent out a twelve-point circular to the field directors of the ethnic Naga Baptist mission centres warning them of the repression of Christians in "Communist countries".[40] From the Indian side, for a time even the brutal counterinsurgency measures were paused in order to allow Naga Baptists to reprimand and bring around their "lost sheep". The GOC of the Eastern Command, speaking at a jubilee gathering of Chakhesang Baptists, declared "he had read the diary of Muiva [sic] and asked how Nagaland, where the majority were Christians, could seek help from an atheistic country like China?"[41] The irony was that the GOC was speaking to an ethnic Baptist community that, only some years earlier, had witnessed the torture and killing of the first field director of the Baptist mission centre, Pelesato Chase, during an Indian army operation.

The opposition of the Naga Baptist church to communism did not go down well in one section of the political spectrum in the mainland: the Indian communist party asked the government to look into the funding sources of the Naga Baptist church.[42] The American embassy in New Delhi issued a statement saying they were in no way involved in the Naga political issue.

The dilemma over the communist connection was not merely playing out between underground and overground Nagas, but

[40] See Rao, *Longri Ao: A Biography*, 88–9.
[41] Ibid., 88.
[42] Thomas, *Evangelising the Nation*, 152.

also among warring Naga underground groups in the years after the Shillong Accord of 1975 – with deadly ramifications. The China-returned were accused of communist sympathies and polluting the Naga political movement with the Maoist ideology; the China-returned leaders Isak and Muivah denied any association with communism and accused the Baptist church, especially the Naga Baptist church peace commission, of siding with the Indian authorities and supporting other Naga factional groups.

A political firebrand Naga leader in the making, Thuingaleng Muivah (b. 1934) – a Tangkhul Naga from Somdal village in Ukhrul district, Manipur – had joined the Naga political movement in 1964 and been selected as the NNC general secretary. When he joined the movement he had a master's degree in political science and a sound understanding of political philosophies. He would go on to become a shrewd politician and ideologue, giving Phizo a run for his money. When the Shillong Accord was signed, Muivah and Isak Swu, who were at the time in China, rejected the agreement and denounced their former colleagues as traitors. This did not bode well for "dissidents": they were now up against China-trained opponents drilled in the need for ruthlessness against all forms of opposition. Niketu Iralu, a well-known Naga peace activist, said that "no Naga leader had come under the influence of Maoist teaching as much as Muivah. He took the Maoist ideology to its logical conclusion: that power flows out of the barrel of a gun." Niketu meant that, for Muivah, eliminating "dissidents" and political opponents became necessary for the movement to continue.

Muivah's rise to the top is mired in controversy, but this competent China-trained Naga nationalist emerged as the new leader of the Naga underground. He discredited Phizo for not denouncing the Shillong Accord outright, which he saw as surrendering the Naga right to self-determination. The rhetoric came in handy as Muivah and Swu revamped the underground government and rebuilt the guerrilla machinery into a well-oiled fighting force. What made Muivah a canny politician was that he knew his way around the enduring religious beliefs of the Nagas. Swu's wife, Eustar, who is also a China veteran, admitted Muivah was not very forthcoming with her husband's preaching tour among the "Burmese Nagas". However, she added that "Muivah used to be a chain smoker and was not a truly committed believer, but it was in Burma that he truly committed himself to Christ." It appears that for Muivah politics came before faith, which distinguished him from Swu, for whom personal faith was primary. Muivah was irrepressibly pragmatic while Swu was led by an almost dogmatic belief in the primacy of religion for Naga ethnonationalism.

The "Naga way to socialism" under the National Socialist Council of Nagaland (NSCN), a Naga nationalist group formed on 31 January 1980, was a curious admixture of past tradition, evangelical Christianity, and socialist doctrine. Khevihe Swu, a high-ranking NSCN(IM) functionary and a close relative of Isak Chishi Swu, explained:

> Our socialism is different; there is nothing new in it that we had not practised for ages. Look into our traditional landholding system; we never had beggars or starving people, in case a family faced problems the whole community or village came to their aid. This is the kind of socialism that we [NSCN(IM)] are advancing that people are suspicious of: it is nothing but the idea of equality, compassion and brotherhood that had been practised for generations by our Naga ancestors.[43]

When I met him at his Dimapur residence in 2018, the NSCN(IM) had commemorated the second death anniversary of its first chairman Isak Chishi Swu, whose legacy and teachings are being carried on through ethnonationalists like Khevihe. Isak Swu had baffled many with his religiosity and politics: he died a devout Baptist, but in his lifetime he earned (dis)repute among admirers and dissenters for his brand of ethnonationalism, which leant in the direction of a theocratic state.

---

[43] Presently, the NSCN is splintered into several factions, the two main being IM (after Isak and Muivah) and K (after S.S. Khaplang).

VI

In the history of the Naga political movement no leader was as adept at melding ethnonationalism with evangelical Christianity as Isak Chishi Swu. This Naga nationalist from an ancient Sumi village, Chishilimi, had joined the underground FGN as foreign secretary in 1961, when Phizo was at the height of his popularity, and breathed his last in 2016 as chairman of the NSCN(IM), having parted ways with Phizo in the mid-1970s. Swu propagated a mystical form of Christianity with an inordinate emphasis on "tangible" supernatural interventions; this strain of Protestantism was not different from Charismatic Christianity that had spread quickly in the Naga areas from the late 1960s.

Swu's religious pedigree was no ordinary one: for his whole life he had to live up to the legacy of his illustrious father, Kushe – a peripatetic evangelist, mystic, prophet, and first Baptist convert from the village. Kushe is considered a legend in Sumi Naga Baptist circles, and his miraculous claims and feats are accepted in the mainstream Naga Baptist church. This is what an NBCC publication had to say about Kushe, who had converted in the first quarter of the twentieth century: "In his unconscious state his soul was taken up to Heaven and in his dream, he was shown the heavenly realm . . . After this he was taught some Scripture verses and was brought back to earth where he regained consciousness."[44] Swu's initiation into the Baptist faith through his "prophet" father gave his religious outlook a distinctively evangelistic and pietistic slant. His idea of ethnonationalism was rooted more in tradition than in the old-school intellectualism, common among Naga nationalists, that had been shaped by the exigencies of colonialism and modernity.

The village where Swu grew up still has a bucolic air about it, with a close-knit community that follows age-old farming practices. The footpaths are cobbled and well trodden, revealing

---

[44] Nagaland Baptist Church Council, *One New Humanity*, 201.

Ill. 24: Kushe, an itinerant preacher and prophet whose son, Isak Chishi Swu, followed in his footsteps, mixing evangelism with ethnonationalism. Courtesy NBCC.

a long-inhabited village. A large Baptist church building stands in the spot where Kushe's house once stood. The faithful in the village are all Baptists, but of the charismatic variety which puts a great deal of emphasis on the work of the Holy Spirit. The village chief, a man in his forties, took me to the community ground and said with a hint of sadness: "This is the spot where the villagers were made to gather while the village and paddy fields were set on fire by the Indian armies."

Of Kushe's four sons, Isak Chishi Swu, the eldest, joined the Naga movement last. His three younger brothers had joined the movement in response to a "clarion call" for Sumi Naga tribesmen to fight for independence. Swu was no stranger to military operations as the armed conflict that engulfed the region reached his village as well. Jacob, one of Swu's younger brothers, said Swu witnessed the army sending off villagers to internment camps, which affected him deeply. Born in 1929, he had spent his student years away from his village, but like most Nagas had maintained a close relationship with the village community.

Niketu, Swu's classmate and roommate at Union Christian College in Barapani, said Swu was a good footballer and had represented Assam as an athlete. A devout Christian and the first man to earn a bachelor's degree (in political science and economics) from his village Chishilimi, Swu would have been in the church ministry had he not joined the Naga movement. Yeshito, a former underground worker and Swu's brother, told me, "Isak was supposed to go for his Bible study in America, but he told a friend from a neighbouring village to go in his place. Sometimes I wonder how his life would have turned out had he left for a Baptist seminary abroad instead of joining the Naga political movement." Eustar, Swu's wife, said what really prompted her husband to go underground was the highhandedness of the Indian army, but the trajectory of Swu's life appears more complex. Modernity struck the Nagas as a deluge in the post-independence period, shaping the lives of the educated along new trajectories. In connection with Swu's political career, Niketu put it well: "How societies react to change decides not only the fate of a nation and its people, but also the individuals."

The zeal for mission and evangelism never left Swu; like any practising Naga Baptist he held distinctive views on personal evangelism. He looked up to his towering missionary father and so entered the mission with great enthusiasm, much to the bewilderment of many. Critics of the Baptist faith jeered, and those unaccustomed to the complexity of ethnicity, religion, and politics in the region raised an eyebrow at Swu's involvement in the mission. His strident views on ethnonationalism and unapologetic religious belief made him in their eyes a "Christian fundamentalist", a controversial figure in Naga society and beyond.

One of Swu's legacies which has outlived him is the Council of the Nagalim Churches (CNC), the religious wing of the underground government – Government of the Peoples' Republic of Nagalim (GPRN). Swu was the founding president of the CNC and held the position till his death, after which his wife Eustar took over as president in 2017. Swu had started the CNC as a non-denominational organisation to bring all the churches in Naga-inhabited areas under a single body (after independence); even the confident and self-assertive Naga Baptist church had not thought of a project as ambitious: it was Swu who envisioned the overarching role of religion in building the ideal Naga nation. For him, politics and nationhood remained inseparable from religious belief, and his career was spent propagating the idea. Unlike other Naga nationalist leaders, religiosity informed his political ideology and nationalism to the extent of bordering on an advocacy of Christian supremacy within a theocratic Naga state. His eldest son Ikato Chishi Swu, who studied in a seminary abroad and now serves as general secretary of the CNC, agreed that according to Swu the idea of the Naga nation is where God's will and rule are held supreme: "The ideal nation is where belief in God should inform every aspect of our life; this is a kind of theocracy in a broad sense which is also found among the Israelites in the Bible," Ikato said.

When I met his family, it was more than a year after Swu had passed away; Eustar as president of the CNC was actively involved in organising prayer meetings and spiritual outreach to churches in the Naga-inhabited areas. The NSCN(IM) chairman's house in Hebron camp on the outskirts of Dimapur town was still with Eustar. It was a large single-storey house with four spacious rooms adjacent to an even larger and grander house of the NSCN(IM) general secretary, Muivah. The rooms were well furnished and fitted with airconditioners, a far cry from the harsh jungle life of a Naga warrior. A small room connected to the drawing room by a door appears like a shrine to the late Naga leader: a Nagalim flag with the Star of David and rainbow stands next to a large mahogany desk, and the wall exhibits a collage of photographs of Swu, many taken in foreign countries.

Swu did not of course achieve the elusive Naga self-rule for which he had struggled from the 1960s. The Naga political movement has not yet run its course and Naga society remains fraught with suspicion and conflict. An ethnonationalist to the core, Swu did not allow any of his children to seek employment with the Indian government; and as for Eustar, she still strongly believes in the dream of Naga independence, seeing it as a kind of directive from heaven. She appears now more a stay-at-home mother than a China-trained veteran who survived jungle warfare. Her life has changed tremendously; whenever there happens to be an important function in the Hebron camp, young girls dressed in army-green fatigues walk beside her holding an umbrella to protect her from the sunlight – this for a woman who faced starvation and disease for years in the Burma jungles.

Eustar might not be an astute politician or a theoretician, but her career, spanning almost four decades, followed the trajectory of the Naga movement. She saw the grim side of the armed conflict, but the harshness of it does not seem to have broken her. Faith can work wonders for fortitude and resilience, and Eustar still believes in the divine destiny of the Nagas.

The religiosity driving Naga ethnonationalism can be differentiated from the mainstream Naga Baptist faith. Elitist Baptist leaders with degrees from coveted seminaries abroad and in the Indian mainland lead the NBCC, while the CNC has no "highbrow" Baptist theologians: it is led by "anointed" prophets and "divinely inspired" leaders. Belief in divine intervention and supernatural claims is intrinsic to the contemporary Naga political movement, as is demonstrable in the foremost Naga political group, the NSCN(IM).

Writing of the Naga armed movement from north-western Myanmar, Lintner observed that among the Naga rebels "The old

Naga animism began seeping back again, now expressed in a newly adopted Christianity terminology."[45] He found religious practice in the Naga underground camp uncanny; apparently he was made privy to divine revelations, including this: "God told us to make three flags like this. One to be kept here [in the camp], another to be sent to Indira Gandhi and the third to General Ne Win."[46] Meanwhile, among the believers in Nagaland, by the 1970s and '80s a mystical form of Christianity marked by the proliferation of self-proclaimed spiritual leaders known for prophesies, glossolalia, and interpretation of dreams had overtaken traditional American Baptist teaching. During my visit to prayer houses in Dimapur and to some other districts in 2018, I witnessed self-styled prophets who have amassed large followings by making miraculous claims, exorcising evil spirits, enabling divinely inspired matrimonial matches, and practising healing; in one case a certain faith healer sliced off a patient's suspected tumour without anaesthesia, leading, not surprisingly, to the patient's death. Though large numbers of Naga Baptists now are driven by a belief that the divine interacts with them tangibly and experientially, others disagree. The old-school faith still survives and flourishes in the Baptist heartland.

[45] Lintner, *Land of Jade*, 124.
[46] Ibid., 122–3.

Conclusion

Naga Baptists 2.0

> If the Germans have lost Jesus, that is their problem. We have not lost him. We know him. We love him.
>
> – Kenyan seminary student[1]

PETER JAMIR IS AN old-school Baptist – at least doctrinally – from Longsa, an ancient Ao Naga village in Mokukchung district, Nagaland. This 60-year-old Indian Christian church worker is among the best in his profession. He is the pastor of Carey Baptist Church in Kolkata, the oldest Baptist church in India – the erstwhile "Lal Bazaar Chapel". The famed nineteenth-century missionary William Carey inaugurated this chapel in Bow Bazaar on 1 January 1809 for the benefit of native converts and European believers. Two centuries ago, the Baptist missionaries of colonial days such as the British trio of Carey, Marshman, and Ward – who are revered via histories of the Christian missions by Protestants and Catholics alike – could not have envisaged a Baptist descendant from an obscure hill tribe in the Indian northeastern frontier tending the flock in Lal Bazaar Chapel.

The legend in Baptist circles goes that Carey started a chapel in Bow Bazaar (now B.B. Ganguly Street) to evangelise British soldiers who frequented the brothels in the area: the red-light district still exists. On 16 September 1812 the first American overseas missionaries, Adoniram and Ann Judson, were (as noted

---

[1] Quoted in Wright, *The Challenge of Jesus*, 13.

at the start of this book) baptised at Lal Bazaar Chapel. This was the start of the American Baptist mission in the East. Looked at from the grand scheme of things, Pastor Jamir and his Naga tribesmen's journey to the Baptist faith began with this low-key water immersion at Lal Bazaar Chapel in the first quarter of the nineteenth century. The American missionaries eventually reached Assam via Burma, and so began the story of the conversion of the region's hill tribes, including the Nagas.

Inside Carey Baptist Church, the baptistery where Ward immersed the American missionaries (the Judsons as well as Luther Rice), also still stands, now covered by marble stone slabs. For the Baptist faithful this is an important part of their heritage in the heart of Kolkata: Rev. Jamir enthusiastically points out the baptistery to those visiting the historic church. The pastor himself occupies the old house in which William Carey once lived. The old structure has been preserved for sentimental reasons, though frequent repairs have changed aspects of it. A 200-year-old rotting wooden beam from Carey's time, removed from the old structure, lay in the premises. I suggested that this wooden relic be converted into crucifixes and donated to Baptist museums in Nagaland.

On my first visit to this historic Christian location in 2018, Rev. Jamir led me to the terrace from where a better view of the church premises can be had. The terrace floor was covered in thick concrete, plastered several times over to protect the original structure, but now weighing it down. Rev. Jamir was overseeing renovation work to slough out the old concrete.

The interior of Carey's home has retained its original design – this I could make out from old drawings in the Baptist mission archives. Along with other memorabilia in Pastor Jamir's residence is an old lifelike portrait of Carey with his "Sanskrit translation helper", a Hindu pandit with the typical *choti* (pleated tuft) and clad in a robe. Pastor Jamir could not help interpreting the gaze of the "Brahmin helper" fixed on the Baptist missionary as an expression of awe and admiration. He said Carey's first wife, Dorothy, who had lived in this same house, had gone mad living in India. Even as Carey worked on Bible translations in his study, she groaned and screamed in pain in the adjoining room. As a native Baptist weaned on stories of the devoted work of Baptist missionaries like Carey, Adoniram Judson, and Miles Bronson, I was cut to the quick by this image of spousal misery. It seemed to me an important additional fact long hidden from general view. I was seeing in real life what Charlotte Bronte's *Jane Eyre* and Jean Rhys' *Wide Sargasso Sea* have poignantly revealed to us in their powerful fictions: that heroic stories of colonial male achievement often carefully hide away the intense loneliness and suffering of the "mad woman in the attic".

Presently, back in Carey's country of origin, the Baptists are in a minority, though they are more evangelical and, by comparison with an enervated Anglican majority, maintain the autonomy of the local church. The latter denomination is way past its prime: believers are leaving this state-propped church in their droves. In fact, Christianity in Western Europe could be heaving its last sigh – at least as Eastern Christians like myself see it. In Carey's old Indian city of Calcutta the Baptist faith did not become popular, nor witnessed any substantial increase in adherents. Yet the underdogs – the American Baptist missionaries of the nineteenth century – greatly surpassed their counterparts, the English Baptist missionaries, when it came to spreading the faith in the Indian subcontinent, specially in the north-east. Now, in Carey's old chapel in Kolkata, Pastor Jamir ministers to a few Bengali believers, some of whom trace their Baptist pedigree to the time of the Raj, and to a medley of Indian Baptists from other parts of the country.

Meanwhile, not far off in the north-east, the Baptist faith of the American variety thrives and extends itself into areas of the subcontinent receptive to its message. There is an appreciable increase in Christian numbers in states like Andhra Pradesh, Telangana, and Tamil Nadu, even as the old centre of English Baptist activity, Calcutta, appears nearly derelict in this respect. The success of the Baptist faith in regions such as the north-east reinforces an old belief here: that Christianity in India is for the tribals and the lower castes who have nothing to lose by converting to a supposedly foreign religion.

Contrary to popular belief, Indian Christians like Peter Jamir – from a tribal community considered primitive in the past – represent the best of the educated Indian middle class, and as model citizens are among the finest faces of democratic and secular India, an aspect of the country that is currently in disrepair and which, if the current trend persists, will fast vanish. Many Naga Baptists like Pastor Jamir and myself consider ourselves "constitutional Indians" who, despite our distinct history and culture, which is quite different from that of the Indian mainland, share and participate in the idea of a modern India that is supposed to guarantee equal rights irrespective of ethnicity, religion, class, and gender. It is not far-fetched to claim that to the Naga Baptists – a putatively renegade ethnic community of faith from the periphery – the idea of India hangs precariously in the balance, supported by a piece of paper, the Indian constitution.

When I met Pastor Jamir in Kolkata he was delivering – traditionalist Baptist that he is – a series of sermons on the Gospel of John. As I found out, the Baptist believers in Carey's old church are not free of squabbles and differences of opinion – this is true of most Baptist churches – but the seasoned Baptist minister has brought some semblance of order and conformity to the tenets of faith among them. A worshipper from the colonial period would not have felt out of place had she heard Pastor Jamir's sermon to contemporary believers: the doctrines and teachings have not changed much, except for modern illustrations that the pastor interjects to drive home the point. Meanwhile, in his home state many Baptist churches are a far cry from those in the time of the American Baptist mission, though some have discernibly retained the old-school faith. In Dimapur town, the commercial hub of Nagaland that houses the richest and most populous churches, Naga Baptists preaching health and wealth are thriving in the marketplace of churches.

In 2019 I attended an upscale interdenominational charismatic church in Dimapur where a smartly dressed preacher exhorted the faithful to have faith worthy of "the sons and daughters of the king of kings" and therefore pray for a "Mercedes, not Maruti 800".[2] The old-school Naga Baptists have to contend with the high-spirited led by suave and charismatic preachers, most of whom are young, well educated, and equipped with church business models that rival the best from business management schools. This is one reason why traditional Baptist churches have seen a dropping out of town-bred Naga Christians from their pews.

The Naga preoccupation with wealth and status is not new but modern consumerism has reinforced it. Gone are the days when Naga status goods were limited to exotically showy cultural objects – including human heads – whose past symbolic value is comparable to the Dimapur preacher's Mercedes now. Cultural goods that are now common throughout the globe – large televisions, expensive cars, phones that are less phone and more camera – are also the new status-enhancing goods for Nagas, so church strategy and pulpit messages must be ingeniously manoeuvred to suit the changing times. Contrary to the view of sceptics, religion will not exit soon among the Nagas: the need for solace now and salvation in the hereafter is pretty much universal; the gods and their godmen may come in different shapes and sizes everywhere, but come they still do, and moreover flourish. Churches too have adapted and continue to sustain themselves by tapping into human angst, anxieties, and desires.

Kohima, capital of Nagaland, has somewhat retained its colonial history and architecture; there are state-owned archives and museums, village community museums, privately owned galleries, World War II memorials, and named landmarks. The expanding town is home to different faiths and various Christian denominations. In it the American Baptist mission's legacy is still discernible, giving a colour faintly visible to the distinct history and culture

---

[2] "Mercedes" needs no gloss; "Maruti 800" was a popular small car first made for India by Japan's Suzuki car manufacturer. The model is now obsolete, a reminder of the days when Indians were happy to own a well-functioning small car.

of this hilly capital. Meanwhile, Dimapur town, known as the gateway of Nagaland, is the region's melting pot – a mishmash of different religions, ethnicities, languages, cultures. It is growing and developing like other Indian cities, bustling with business activity, crowded and polluted, and with the country's trademark sweltering summers. It has no important landmark or monument recalling the "glorious" rule of the British here; the only remnants of a colonial past are a railhead, a few dilapidated metal bridges, and an old British road, now called National Highway 29, running through the heart of town to connect Kohima with Imphal.

But, in fact, Dimapur is several centuries older than Kohima (which became an important centre only towards the end of the nineteenth century). Dimapur was the seat of the old Kachari kingdom (c. 835–1838).[3] The Dimasa Kachari kings ruled from here. Their capital was overrun by the Ahoms in the second quarter of the sixteenth century, and the Kachari rulers retreated to the south.

Dimapur is a fine example of the transience of earthly kingdoms and empires. It reinforces the pervasive belief among the Baptist faithful that only God's kingdom can last forever. The only remains of the Dimasa Kachari kingdom are medieval ruins on the banks of the Dhansiri River, overshadowed by the nearby noisy and crowded bazaar where tourists and visitors to Dimapur ooh and aah, expressing amazement or disgust at the exotic meat, "weird foodstuff", and wild vegetables on sale.

The builders of these Dimapur ruins were Tibeto-Burman speakers of Mongoloid stock whose rule had once extended from the plains of Assam, touching the foothills of the Himalaya, and almost reaching the Burma frontier. Today, their descendants, who are identified as one of the indigenous tribes of Nagaland, are a disadvantaged minority settled in some pockets of Dimapur district.[4]

---

[3] The Kacharis comprise people of the Boro, Dimasa, Mech, Lalung, Rabha, Sonowal, and Thengal tribes.

Unlike their Naga neighbours, the Kacharis followed a traditional religion that showed the early influence of Hinduism, though their pantheon included a multitude of "nefarious" spirits – as in the Naga primeval religion – in addition to primary deities.[5] Not surprisingly, the Kacharis of Nagaland are coming under the influence of the Baptist faith. I write this while living in a Kachari-populated locality a few minutes' walk from a thriving Boro Kachari Baptist church, and despite native missionaries telling me the Kacharis are resilient and difficult to convert. Nevertheless, compared to ethnic Kacharis domiciled in other states, the Kacharis of Dimapur show a higher percentage of Baptist converts, and given the evangelical fervour among Kachari Baptists here, adherents among them are expected to grow.

The Christians of Dimapur are a microcosm of Christendom, comprising Catholics, Protestants, and Orthodox Christians. But the Baptists rule the roost in this fast-growing city. Interestingly, other communities settled in Dimapur are also experiencing the "Baptist touch"; thus we have small but evangelical Baptist churches like the Bengali Baptist church, the Bihari Baptist church, the Gorkha Baptist church, the Meitei Baptist church, the Nepali Baptist church, and so on. This development has raised eyebrows in the Indian mainland and the suspicion that Christian missions are clandestinely converting people of other faiths and communities in a cosmopolitan Naga town.

As I see it, the future of Dimapur – which is the face of modern Nagaland – depends as a multicultural, multi-ethnic, and multi-religious city on the majority Naga Baptist community here. The new generation of Naga Baptists must perform the difficult task of harmonising their faith with new emerging realities in an increasingly plural world, even while maintaining their denominational and doctrinal distinctiveness. And for the present, as I see it, this is how the world here is taking shape.

[4] According to the 2011 census there are ten Dimasa Kachari villages and five Boro-Mech Kachari villages in Dimapur, Nagaland.

[5] For more details, see Endle, *The Kacharis*.

Bibliography

Archival Sources

Administrative Report of Manipur, 1918–19.
B.I. Anderson, "Sermon Notes", SBAK Aizuto Mission Centre.
Bishnuram Medhi Papers, Nehru Memorial Museum and Library, New Delhi.
Elwin Papers, Nehru Memorial Museum and Library, New Delhi.
Nagaland State Archives, Kohima, File No. 131, "Brief Memorandum on the Naga Country by John Butler", 1873.

Census Reports

Bureau of the Census, 1955.
Census of India, 1911–2011.
Nagaland Baptist Church Council Census, 2016.

Secondary Sources

Books and Articles

Alemchiba, M., *A Brief Historical Account of Nagaland* (Kohima: Naga Institute of Culture, 1970).
All Zeliangrong Students' Union, *A Brief Account of Zeliangrong Nagas* (Guwahati: AZSU, 2009).
Anand, V.K., *Conflict in Nagaland: A Study of Insurgency and Counter-insurgency* (New Delhi: Chanakya Publications, 1980).
Ao, Bendangyaba A., *History of Christianity in Nagaland: A Source Material* (Mokokchung: Shalom Ministry, 1998).
Atsongchanger, Mar, *Unforgettable Memories from Nagaland* (Mokukchung: Tribal Communications & Research Centre, 1994).
———, *Christian Education and Social Change* (Guwahati: Christian Literature Centre, 1995).

Barpujari, H.K., *The American Missionaries and North-East India (1836–1900): A Documentary Study* (Guwahati: Spectrum Publications).

Barua, Rai Sahib Golap Chandra, *Ahom Buranji: From the Earliest Time to the End of Ahom Rule* (rpntd, Guwahati: Spectrum Publications, 1985).

Baruah, Swarna Lata, *A Comprehensive History of Assam* (New Delhi: Munshiram Manoharlal, 1995).

Beach, Harlan P., *A Geography and Atlas of Protestant Missions, Vol. 2: Statistics and Atlas* (New York: Student Volunteer Movement for Foreign Missions, 1903).

Béteille, André, "The Idea of Indigenous People", *Current Anthropology*, 39(2), 1998.

Bhaumik, Subir, *Troubled Periphery: Crisis of India's North East* (New Delhi: Sage Publications, 2009).

Bower, Ursula Graham, *Naga Path* (London: John Murray, 1950).

Bowers, Alva C., *Under Headhunters' Eyes* (Philadelphia: Judson Press, 1929).

Brown, Elizabeth W., *The Whole World Kin: A Pioneer Experience Among Remote Tribes, and Other Labors of Nathan Brown* (Philadelphia: Hubbard Brothers Publishers, 1890).

Brown, Robert, "Narrative Report of the Progress of the Survey Party, Naga Hills, Season 1874", in Verrier Elwin, ed., *The Nagas in the Nineteenth Century* (Bombay: Oxford University Press, 1969).

Butler, John Major, *A Sketch of Assam: With Some Account of Hill Tribes. By an Officer in the Hon. East India Company's Bengal Native Infantry in Civil Employ* (London: Smith, Elder and Co., 1847).

———, *Travels and Adventures in the Province of Assam, During a Residence of Fourteen Years* (London: Smith, Elder, and Co., 1855).

———, *Travels in Assam: During a Residence of Fourteen Years* (New Delhi: Manas Publications, 2004).

Chandola, Harish, *At Large in the World* (Noida: HarperCollins, 2014).

———, *The Naga Story: First Armed Struggle in India* (New Delhi: Bibliophile South Asia, 2012).

Chaplin, Ada C., *Our Gold-Mine: The Story of the American Baptist Missions in India* (Boston: W.G. Corthell, 1879).

Chasie, Charles, *The Naga Imbroglio* (Kohima: Standard Printers and Publishers, 2005).

———, *The Naga Memorandum to the Simon Commission* (Kohima: Standard Printers & Publishers, 2017).

Chophy, G. Kanato, *Constructing the Divine: Religion and Worldview of a Naga Tribe in North-East India* (New Delhi: Manohar, 2019).

Chute, Anthony L., Nathan A. Finn, and Michael A.G. Haykin, *The Baptist Story: From English Sect to Global Movement* (Nashville, Tennessee: B&H Publishing Group, 2015).

Clark, Mary Mead, *A Corner in India* (Philadelphia: American Baptist Publication Society, 1907).

Cockett, Richard, *Blood, Dreams and Gold, The Changing Face of Burma* (New Haven and London: Yale University Press, 2015).

Dev, S.C., *Nagaland, The Untold Story* (Calcutta: Gouri Dev, 1988).

Dhar, Maloy Krishna, *Open Secrets: India's Intelligence Unveiled* (New Delhi: Manas Publications, 2005).

Downs, Frederick S., *The Mighty Works of God: A Brief History of the Council of Baptist Churches in North East India: The Mission Period 1836–1950* (Guwahati: Christian Literature Centre, 1971).

Durkheim, Emile, *The Elementary Forms of Religious Life*, translated by Karen. E. Fields (New York: The Free Press, [1912] 1995).

Eaton, Richard M. "Conversion to Christianity among the Nagas", *Indian Economic & Social History Review*, 21(1), 1984.

Elwin, Verrier, *A Philosophy for NEFA* (Shillong: North-East Frontier Agency, 1959),

———, *Nagaland* (Shillong: Research Dept. Adviser's Secretariat, 1961).

———, ed., *The Nagas in the Nineteenth Century* (Bombay: Oxford University Press, 1969).

Endle, Sidney, *The Kacharis* (New Delhi: Cosmo Publications, 1975).

Enriquez, Colin Metcalf Dallas, *The Races of Burma* (New Delhi: Government of India, Manager of Publications, 1933).

Fairbank, John K., Edwin O. Reischauer, and Albert M. Craig, *East Asia: Tradition and Transformation* (revised edn, Delhi: World View Publications, 1998).

Ferguson, Niall, *Empire: How Britain Made the Modern World* (London: Penguin, 2004).

Frykenberg, Robert Eric, "Christian Missions and the Raj", in Norman Etherington, ed., *Missions and Empire* (New York: Oxford University Press, 2005).

———, *Christianity in India, From Beginnings to the Present* (New York: Oxford University Press, 2008).

Fürer-Haimendorf, Christoph von, *The Naked Nagas: Head-hunters of Assam in Peace and War* (London: Methuen and Co. Ltd, 1939).

———, *The Konyak Nagas: An Indian Frontier Tribe* (New York: Holt, Rinehart and Winston, 1969).

———, *Return to the Naked Nagas* (London: John Murray, 1976).

Gait, E.A., *A History of Assam* (Calcutta: Thacker, Spink & Co., 1906).

Gammell, William A.M., *A History of American Baptist Missions in Asia, Africa, Europe and North America* (Boston: Gould Kendall and Lincoln, 1849).

Ganguli, Milada, *A Pilgrimage to the Nagas* (New Delhi: Oxford & IBH, 1984).

Gellner, Ernest, "Tribalism and the State in the Middle East", in Philip Khoury and Joseph Kostiner, eds, *Tribes and State Formation in the Middle East* (Berkeley: University of California Press, 1990).

Ghosh, B.B., *A History of Nagaland* (New Delhi: S. Chand and Co., 1982).

Glancey, Jonathan, *Nagaland: A Journey to India's Forgotten Frontier* (London: Faber and Faber, 2011).

Goswami, Priyam, *The History of Assam from Yandabo to Partition 1826–1947* (New Delhi: Orient Blackswan, 2012).

Government of Nagaland, *Heralding Hope: Kohima 125* (Kohima: Govt of Nagaland, 2004).

Grare, Frédéric, *India Turns East: International Engagement and US–China Rivalry* (Gurgaon: Viking, 2017).

Guha, Ramachandra, *Savaging the Civilized: Verrier Elwin, His Tribals and India* (New Delhi: Oxford University Press, 1999).

———, *Patriots and Partisans* (New Delhi: Allen Lane, 2012).

———, ed., *Makers of Modern Asia* (Cambridge, MA: The Belknap Press of Harvard University Press, 2014).

Haokip, D. Michael Lunminthang, "The Chins in Manipur", in K. Robin, ed., *Chin: History, Culture, Identity* (New Delhi: Dominant Publishers, 2009).

Hazarika, Sanjoy, *Strangers of the Mist: Tales of War and Peace from India's Northeast* (New Delhi: Penguin Books, 1995).

Headrick, Daniel R., *The Tools of Empire: Technology and European Imperialism in the Nineteenth Century* (New York: Oxford University Press, 1981).

Howard, Randolph L., *Baptists in Burma* (King of Prussia, PA: Judson Press, 1931).

Hutton, J.H. *The Angami Nagas* (London: Macmillan & Co., 1921).
———, *The Sema Nagas* (London: Macmillan & Co., 1921).
Imti, T. Aliba, *Reminiscence: Impur to Naga National Council* (Mokokchung: Author, 1988).
Jacobs, J., A. Macfarlane, S. Harrison, and A. Herle, *The Nagas: Hill Peoples of North East India: Society, Culture and the Colonial Encounter* (London: Thames & Hudson, 1990).
Jamir, S.C., *Nagaland, 50 Years and Beyond* (Bhubaneswar: Pioneer Printing Solutions Pvt. Ltd).
Jenkins, Philip, *The Next Christendom: The Coming of Global Christianity* (New York: Oxford University Press, 2002).
———, *The New Faces of Christianity* (New York: Oxford University Press, 2008).
Johnstone, J., "My Experiences in Manipur and the Naga Hills, 1896", in Verrier Elwin, ed., *The Nagas in the Nineteenth Century* (Bombay: Oxford University Press, 1969).
Kanwal, Gurmeet, "A Strategic Perspective on India–Myanmar Relations", in Lex Rieffel, ed., *Myanmar/Burma: Inside Challenges, Outside Interests* (Washington, DC: Brookings Institution Press, 2010).
Keyho, Biseto Medom, *My Journey in the Nagaland Freedom Movement* (Kohima: Author, 2000).
Khosla, Madhav, ed., *Letters for a Nation from Jawaharlal Nehru to His Chief Ministers 1947–1963* (New Delhi: Penguin Books India, 2014).
Kire, Easterine, *A Village Remembered* (Kohima: Barkweaver Publications, 2016).
———, *Walking the Roadless Road: Exploring the Tribes of Nagaland* (New Delhi: Aleph, 2019).
Konyak, Phejin, and Peter Bos, *The Konyaks: Last of the Tattooed Headhunters* (New Delhi: Roli Books, 2017).
Konyak, Y. Chingyang, *The Konyak Naga, Yesterday and Today* (Dimapur: Author, 2008).
Lasuh, Wetshokhrolo, ed., *The Naga Chronicle*, compiled by V.K. Nuh (2nd revised edn, New Delhi: Regency Publications, 2016).
Lhousa, Zapuvisie, *Strange Country: My Experience in Naga Nationalism* (Kohima: Author, 2015).
Lintner, Bertil, *Land of Jade: A Journey from India through Northern Burma to China* (Bangkok: White Lotus Press, 1990).

———, *Great Game East: India, China and the Struggle for Asia's Most Volatile Frontier* (New Delhi: HarperCollins, 2012).
———, "A Question of Race in Myanmar", *Asia Times*, 3 June 2017.
Lotha, Abraham, *The Raging Mithun: Challenges of Naga Nationalism* (Kohima: Barkweaver Publications, 2013).
Luen, M.I., *The Fire of Revival* (Secunderabad: Authentic Books, 2009).
MacCannell, Dean, "Staged Authenticity: Arrangements of Social Space in Tourist Settings", *The American Journal of Sociology*, 79(3), 1973.
Mackenzie, Alexander, *The North-East Frontier of India* (New Delhi: Mittal Publications, 2016 [1884]).
Maclay, Robert, *Life Among the Chinese* (New York: Calton and Porter, 1923).
Mahanta, Nani Gopal, *Confronting State: ULFA's Quest for Sovereignty* (New Delhi: Sage Publications, 2013).
Marshall, Harry Ignatius, *The Karen People of Burma: A Study in Anthropology and Ethnology* (New York: AMS Press, 1980).
Mason, Philip, *The Men Who Ruled India* (New Delhi: Rupa Publications, 1985).
McFayden, Narola Ao, *Traveling in Time with Pioneers of our Faith: Edward Winter Clark and Mary Mead Clark* (Kohima: Knowledge Foundation, 2016).
Merriam, Edmund Franklin, *A History of American Baptist Missions* (Philadelphia: American Baptist Publication Society, 1900).
Mills, J.P., *The Lhota Nagas* (London: Macmillan & Co., 1922).
———, *The Ao Nagas* (London: Macmillan and Co., 1926).
———, *The Rengma Nagas* (London: Macmillan and Co., 1937).
Mooney, James, *The Ghost Dance* (North Dighton, Ma.: JG Press, Inc., 1996).
Mullik, B.N., *My Years with Nehru* (New Delhi: Allied Publishers, 1971).
Nagaland Baptist Church Council, *One New Humanity: Nagaland Baptist Church Council Platinum Jubilee 1937–2012* (Kohima: Nagaland Baptist Church Council, 2012).
Naga National Council, *The Naga National Rights and Movement* (Kohima: Publicity and Information Dept., 1993).
Nehru, Jawaharlal, *The Unity of India: Collected Writings, 1937–1940* (New York: The John Day Company, Inc., 1942).
Neill, Stephen, *A History of Christian Missions* (rpntd, London: Penguin Books, 1990).

Nibedon, Nirmal, *North-East India: The Ethnic Explosion* (New Delhi: Lancer Publishers, 1981).

Nuh, V.K., *165 Years History of Naga Baptist Churches* (Kohima: Council of Naga Baptist Churches, 2006).

Orwell, George, *Burmese Days* (New York: Harcourt Brace Jovanovich, 1974).

Pachuau, Joy L.K., *Being Mizo: Identity and Belonging in Northeast India* (New Delhi: Oxford University Press, 2014).

Pamei, Namthiubuiyang, *The Trail from Makuilongdi: The Continuing Saga of the Zeliangrong People* (Shillong: Gironta Charitable Foundation, 2001).

Puthenpurakal, Joseph, *Baptist Missions in Nagaland* (Shillong: Vendrame Missiological Institute, 1984).

Philip, Puthuvail Thomas, *The Growth of Baptist Churches in Nagaland* (Guwahati: Christian Literature Centre, 1976).

Ramunny, Murkot, *The World of the Nagas* (New Delhi: Northern Book Centre, 1988).

Rao, O.M., *Longri Ao: A Biography* (Guwahati: Christian Literature Centre, 1986).

Rivenburg, Narola, ed., *The Star of Naga Hills: Letters from Rev. Sidney and Hattie Rivenburg, Pioneer Missionaries in Assam, 1883–1923* (Philadelphia: The American Baptist Publication Society, 1941).

Rivenburg, S.V., "The Naga Mission", *BMM*, Vol. LXXI, No. 10 (October 1891).

Sakhrie, Ahu, *The Vision of T. Sakhrie for a Naga Nation* (Kohima: Dr Kepelhsie Terhüja, 2006).

Sangtam, Lanuyanger, *The Trans-Dikhu Mission: A History of Sangtam Baptist Church* (Dimapur: Mapula & Children, 2007).

Sanyü, Visier Meyasetsu, with Richard Broome, *A Naga Odyssey* (Clayton, Victoria: Monash University Publishing, 2017).

Schendel, Willem van, "The Invention of the 'Jummas': State Formation and Ethnicity in Southeastern Bangladesh", *Modern Asian Studies*, 26, 1992.

———, "Geographies of Knowing, Geographies of Ignorance: Jumping Scale in Southeast Asia", *Environment and Planning*, 20(6), 2002.

Scott, James C., *The Art of Not Being Governed: An Anarchist History of Upland Southeast Asia* (New Haven and London: Yale University Press, 2009).

Sema, Hokishe, *Emergence of Nagaland: Socio-economic and Political Transformation and the Future* (New Delhi: Vikas Publishing House, 1986).

Sema, Piketo, *British Policy and Administration in Nagaland 1881–1947* (New Delhi: Scholar Publishing House, 1992).

Shakespear, L.W., *History of Upper Assam, Upper Burmah, and North Eastern Frontier* (London: Macmillan & Co., 1914).

Sharma, Jayeeta, "Missionaries and Print Culture in Nineteenth-Century Assam: The Orunodoi Periodical of the American Baptist Mission, 1846–1882", in Marina Ngursangzeli and Michael Biehl, eds, *Witnessing to Christ in North-East India* (Oxford, UK: Regnum Books, 2016).

Smith, W.C., *The Ao Naga Tribe of Assam* (New Delhi: Mittal Publications, 2009).

Stark, Rodney, *For the Glory of God: How Monotheism Led to Reformations, Science, Witch-hunts, and the End of Slavery* (Princeton, NJ: Princeton University Press, 2003).

Stracey, P.D., *Nagaland Nightmare* (New Delhi: Allied Publishers, 1968).

Steinberg, David I., *Burma/Myanmar* (New York: Oxford University Press, 2010).

Steyn, Pieter, *Zapuphizo: Voice of the Nagas* (London: Kegan Paul, 2002).

Swu, Isak Chishi, *From Generation to Generation: Stories of Origin and Migration of the Nagas* (Dimapur: Kushe Foundation Society, 2003).

Swu, Scato, *Hails and Blames: A Brief Account of Naga Independence Struggle* (Dimapur: Heritage Publishing House, 2013).

Thakur, Amrendra Kr, "The Institution of Slavery in the Chin Society: A Study", in K. Robin, ed., *Chin: History, Culture, Identity* (New Delhi: Dominant Publishers and Distributors, 2009).

Thomas, John, *Evangelising the Nation: Religion and the Formation of Naga Political Identity* (New Delhi: Routledge, 2016).

Thomson, R.C. Muirhead, *Assam Valley: Beliefs and Customs of the Assamese Hindus* (London: Luzac & Company Ltd., 1948).

Tocqueville, Alexis de, *Democracy in America, Vol. 2* (New York: Vintage, [1835–1839] 1956).

Tucker, Shelby, *Burma, The Curse of Independence* (London: Pluto Press, 2001).

Walling, C. Walu, ed., *Down the Memory Lane: Mission to the Nagas, Vol. I* (Dimapur: Heritage Publishing House, 2008).

Webb, Willis S., *Incidents and Trials in the Life of Rev. Eugenio Kincaid, D.D., The 'Hero' Missionary to Burma 1830–1865* (Fort Scott, Kansas: Monitor Publishing House and Book Bindery, 1890).
Witter, W.E., "The Naga Mission", *BMM*, Vol. LXVII, No. 1 (January 1887).
Wittfogel, Karl A., *Oriental Despotism* (New York: Vintage Books, [1957] 1981).
Woodberry, Robert D., "The Missionary Roots of Liberal Democracy", *American Political Science Review*, 106, 2007.
Wright, N.T., *The Challenge of Jesus: Rediscovering Who Jesus Was and Is* (Downer Grove, Illinois: InterVarsity Press, 1999).
Wright, Robert, *The Evolution of God* (New York: Little, Brown and Company, 2009).
Yanthan, Khodao, *Wounded Tiger, The Papers of Khodao Yanthan*, Introduction and Epilogue by Abraham Lotha (Dimapur: Heritage Publishing House, 2017).
Yonuo, Asoso, *The Rising Nagas: A Historical and Political Study* (Delhi: Vikas Publishing House, 1974).
———, *Nagas Struggle against the British Rule under Jadonang and Rani Gaidinliu, 1925–1947* (Kohima: Leno Printing Press, 1982).
Zeliang, Haireiwangbe, *A Brief History of Zeliangrong Heraka Movement and Its Impact in North East India* (Dimapur: Zeme Council of North East India, 2015).
Zinyü, Mhiesizhokho, *Phizo and the Naga Problem* (revised edn, Kohima: privately published, 2014).

Newspapers and Periodicals

Asia Times, 2017
Baptist Missionary Magazine (BMM), 1857–1922.
Nagaland Post, 2018.
The Naga Nation, 1946.
Times of London, 1962.

Index

Act East policy 84, 113
Adi-dharam 14
administrator-ethnographers 48, 149, 227
aesthetics 15, 231
agriculture 115, 130
Ahom(s) 29, 51, 54, 61, 68, 105, 147, 224, 226, 234, 430
  empire 57
  race 61
  rulers 55, 57, 62, 147, 226
Aizuto
  mission centre 144
  Sumi mission centre 141
Akhil Bharatiya Vidyarthi Parishad (ABVP) 253
alcohol/alcoholism 20, 126, 218, 246, 344
alee command 397, 404, 408
Aliba Imti, T. 305, 310–12, 320–1, 335, 343, 347, 365
All Zeliangrong Students' Union 258
America 22, 28, 32, 39, 43, 74, 108, 137, 200, 354, 405, 421; *see also* United States (US)
American
  missionary 29, 36, 56, 122, 133–4, 139, 141, 147, 150, 197–9, 207, 308–9, 370
  pop culture 215
  Roman Catholic 4
American Baptist
  heritage 17, 74, 123
  mission 7, 10–11, 18, 24, 26–8, 31, 34–6, 46, 48, 50–1, 56, 60–1, 72, 74–6, 80, 90, 110, 118–20, 127, 132–4, 138–9, 144, 146, 149, 157, 161, 167–71, 184, 192–3, 195, 197–8, 206, 208, 264–6, 269, 271, 279, 282, 292, 303, 308–9, 314, 323–4, 346–7, 368, 370, 382, 384, 390, 426, 428–9
  missionaries 6, 23–4, 31–2, 39, 44, 47, 56–9, 63, 74–6, 78–80, 90–1, 93, 101, 111, 136, 141, 150, 155, 167, 190–1, 194, 314, 346, 353, 427
  Missionary Union (ABMU) 28–9, 33–4, 67
American Baptist Magazine 50
American Missionaries, The 30, 53, 57–8, 60, 62–3, 66, 119, 122
Anderson, Bengt Ivar 23, 146, 389, 390

441

Angami
  Baptist Church Council
    (ABCC) 128, 157, 160, 164,
    174
  Kevichusa 10, 313
  Nagas 3–4, 9–11, 20–1, 26, 43,
    71, 90, 92, 96, 98, 100, 103,
    117–18, 120, 127–9, 131,
    139, 141, 146–9, 153–6,
    158, 160–1, 164, 168–9,
    171, 174, 198, 202–6, 208,
    215, 235, 254–5, 258,
    263–6, 286–9, 305, 308–9,
    311, 313–16, 321, 329, 331,
    344–5, 350, 352–4, 360,
    370–2, 380, 394, 396, 402,
    408, 411, 415
  women 371
Angami Nagas, The 71, 161, 171,
    198, 204, 331
angh(s) 78, 174, 212–16, 231,
    233, 240–6, 251–2
  exploits of 217
  liege 213, 219
  Longwa 215–16
  Wancho Naga 218
anghdom 213, 215, 221, 243
Anglican
  church 24
  mission 141, 184
Antichrist 3, 4
Anti-Fascist People's Freedom
  League (AFPFL) 388
Ao, Longri 310, 317–20, 416
Ao Nagas 4, 11, 18–19, 26, 43,
    68, 75–6, 91, 120–2, 127,
    132–4, 136, 138–42, 146,
    148–9, 153, 167–70, 174–8,
    183, 186–7, 189–90, 193,
    195–8, 228, 232–6, 255,
    279, 310, 316–22, 324–5,
    331, 337, 345, 406, 416,
    425
Ao Nagas, The 169
Ao Naga Tribe of Assam, The 121
architecture 3, 163, 236, 429
  Naga style 3
armed
  conflict 9, 323, 380, 393, 421,
    423
  insurgency 104, 359
  insurrection 106, 258, 338,
    374, 381, 390, 398–9, 402,
    410
  struggle 73, 86, 88, 95, 97, 114,
    165, 290, 292, 296, 336,
    342, 344, 359, 363, 377,
    385, 393, 397, 400, 404,
    406–8, 410
  uprising 19, 101, 321, 342,
    393–4, 397
Armed Force Special Powers Act
    (AFSPA) 98, 338
Arthashastra 323
Art of Not Being Governed,
    The 106, 115, 116
Art of War, The 323
Arunachal Pradesh 14, 25–6, 39,
    73, 76, 79, 93, 108, 119–20,
    138, 143, 152, 213, 218,
    221, 241, 254, 298
Assam 1, 25, 28–43, 45–8, 50–70,
    72, 74, 83, 87, 91, 96, 106,
    108, 110, 114, 118–23,
    134, 136–8, 140–1, 143–4,
    146–9, 151–2, 156, 161–2,
    166, 168, 170, 199, 203,
    206–7, 216, 226, 233, 245,
    258, 263, 268, 271, 275,
    290, 294, 298, 300, 310–11,

313, 317, 319–20, 333, 338, 340–1, 343, 346, 350, 358, 361–2, 364–7, 372, 374–5, 391, 400, 416, 421, 426, 430
  mission 32–5, 47, 50, 56, 66–7
  opium habit in 57
Assam Areas Disturbed Act 1955 338
Assam Maintenance of Public Order (Autonomous District) Acts 1953 338
Assemblies of God 141, 150
atrocities 377–81
Aung San 85–6, 338
autonomy 5, 85–6, 105, 124, 164, 183, 187, 200, 339, 362, 427
  Baptist principle 187
  church 124
  internal administration 85, 339
Azad Kashmir 401

backwardness 18, 171, 236, 334
Bangladesh 73, 90, 116, 265, 272, 381, 391
baptism 4–6, 123, 175, 187, 219
Baptist(s)
  autonomy of local churches 5, 124, 200
  Burma missionaries 29, 32, 48, 64, 140
  charismatic 144–5
  Christianity 95, 107, 137, 253, 356
  churches 6, 11, 34, 110, 112, 124, 139, 142–4, 146, 148, 150–1, 177–8, 180, 182, 184–5, 187–9, 195, 198–9, 201, 205, 207, 233, 246–7,

249, 251, 267–9, 299, 428–9, 431
  conservative 144–5
  converts 9, 15, 19, 85, 103, 121, 172, 250, 279, 315, 353, 431
  culture 26, 127, 164, 193, 201, 231, 237, 301
  denominational politics 265
  English 37, 49
  ethnic 73, 75, 80–1, 90, 97, 111, 124, 267, 300
  faith 8, 11, 14–15, 18–19, 21, 25, 27, 64, 72, 74, 76, 80, 100, 102, 104–5, 107, 109, 111–12, 122, 125, 128, 143–4, 147, 149, 151, 162, 164, 169, 171, 173, 178–80, 182–6, 189–94, 196, 201–2, 207–8, 211, 214, 217, 219, 221, 227, 229–31, 233–4, 237–9, 243, 247–9, 263, 265, 267, 276, 278, 284, 293, 297–8, 300–1, 382, 386, 397, 403, 410, 419, 421, 423, 426–7, 431; *see also* Baptist faith and Maoism 382
  fundamentalist 3, 4
  heritage 17, 74, 123, 140, 151, 194
  highland 27, 71–4, 78–80, 82, 85–92, 95, 97–8, 104–6, 108–9, 111, 113–16
  identity 25, 106, 124, 185, 204–5
  missionaries 6, 23–4, 31–2, 35, 37–40, 44, 46–8, 51, 56–9, 63–4, 68, 70, 74–6, 78–80, 82, 90–1, 93, 101, 108, 111,

121–2, 136, 141, 146, 150, 155, 167, 171–2, 175–6, 181, 183–4, 190–1, 193–4, 204, 217, 228, 230, 234, 240, 300, 314, 344, 346, 353, 425, 427
  Mission Press 11, 60
  Northern 33
  Revival 285
  Revival churches 128
  Southern 29
  traditional 191
  "Western" religion 279
Baptist Missionary Magazine (BMM) 30, 35, 37, 41–3, 50, 53–4, 56, 61, 66–7, 203, 307
Baptist Missions in Nagaland, 4, 47, 133, 149; *see* Puthenpurakal
Battle of Khonoma 161
Battle of Kohima 3, 392
Being Mizo 79
beliefs
  dogmatic 418
  eschatological 3
  folk 111
  indigenous 15
  legalistic 6
  millenarian 247, 273
  religious 8, 16, 19, 23, 40, 106, 118, 145, 192, 260, 293, 415, 418, 422
  traditional 253, 278
Bharatiya Janata Party (BJP) 199, 253–5, 297
Bharat Sevashram Sangh 294, 297
Bhutan 6, 139, 152
Bible, the 5, 8, 11, 21, 38–9, 42, 59, 90, 139, 146, 148, 168, 172, 175–7, 179, 187, 196, 200–1, 203, 205, 207–8, 211, 224, 228–9, 235, 246, 252–3, 268, 274, 307, 310, 318–19, 352, 353, 356, 376, 383–4, 386, 404, 406, 421–2, 427
  translation 38, 90, 203, 205, 207–8, 211, 235
Board of Missions 33–4, 39
born again (Christian) 5, 22, 142, 144, 148, 164
Boro 430–1
Bose, Subhas Chandra 274, 284, 286, 311
Brahmaputra valley 28, 32, 35, 37–8, 46–7, 51, 53–5, 57–58, 62–3, 66–7, 69, 72, 83, 134, 169, 361
British
  Assam 39, 311
  colonialism 17, 27, 78, 80, 93, 111, 117, 122, 149, 286, 332, 353
  expansionism 331
  missionary 49
  political agents 24, 48–9, 93, 148–9, 169
  Raj 2, 16, 26, 167, 370
British Policy and Administration 98
Bronson, Miles 30, 33–4, 39, 47, 53, 56–60, 63, 67, 119–23, 132, 138
Brown, Nathan 32, 34, 38, 45, 47, 54, 58–9, 61, 123
Buddhism 37, 53, 59, 64, 76, 78, 87–8, 105, 110–11, 147, 375
  Theravada 59, 64, 76

Buranjis 62
Burma 29–30, 32, 34–6, 38–41, 43, 45–8, 50, 54, 56, 58–9, 64–3, 76, 80–3, 85–9, 91, 93–5, 97–100, 108, 110–11, 116, 140, 171, 180–4, 246, 285–8, 328–9, 332–3, 339, 344, 346, 356, 361, 365, 375, 388, 390, 397, 402, 407–9, 418, 423, 426, 430; see also Myanmar
  Baptists missionaries 29, 32, 48, 64, 140
  spirit worship 59
Burmanisation 73, 86–7, 89, 94
Burmans 38, 64–5, 79, 83, 85, 95, 99, 105, 110–11, 387

Cambodia 6, 74, 115, 139
Carey, William 11, 49–50, 425–8
caste(s) 51, 54, 56–8, 63, 66, 87, 283, 361, 396, 428
  barriers 63
  beliefs and practices 58
  lower 428
  system 57–8
  upper 56
Catholicism 3–4, 128, 141, 150, 177, 192, 210
Catholic(s) 3–4, 104, 128, 131, 137, 163, 164, 254, 299, 425, 431
  faith 210
  heretics 4
  missionaries 23
  missions 22
  settlement 210; see also Pochury Naga Catholics
ceasefire agreement 377
central India 14

Chakhesang
  Baptist Association 204
  Baptists 204, 416
  Nagas 20, 131, 202–5, 208–10, 394
Chaliha, B.P. 319, 367, 368, 374, 375, 378
Chang 19, 26, 140, 167, 184–8, 192–3, 196, 274, 279–80, 344, 346, 350, 394; see Chang Nagas
China, 6, 35–8, 46, 59, 64, 73, 79–82, 108–9, 112–13, 116, 139–40, 152, 285, 358, 381–3, 385–8, 390–1, 397, 400, 402, 407–18, 423
  Yunnan province 79, 108
Chin(s) 68, 71–3, 75–6, 79–80, 92, 94–5, 98–9, 106, 109–10, 271, 339, 402–3
  Hills 76, 402
  State 79, 91, 98, 105, 112, 197, 265
Christianity 3, 8, 10–11, 16, 18, 21, 23, 25, 35, 41, 43, 53–4, 65–8, 72–6, 79, 82, 87, 89–90, 95, 100, 102–12, 117, 121, 127, 129–30, 132, 134, 137, 144, 146, 151, 167, 170, 175–6, 183, 187, 190–2, 202, 210, 212, 228, 242, 250–1, 253–4, 257, 262, 265, 271, 299–301, 332, 356, 362–3, 389, 400, 409, 418–19, 424, 427
  ecumenical approach 11
  evangelical 10, 418–19
  martial 105

Protestant 25
spread of 18, 21, 76, 79, 190, 210
Christianity in India 89, 427
Christian(s) 1–4, 10–11, 19–20, 40, 75, 81–2, 101, 103–5, 108, 111, 126, 136, 183, 185, 187, 190, 195, 238, 253, 255, 267–8, 299, 301, 315, 351, 362, 364–5, 389, 396, 404, 409, 416, 427–9, 431
belief 43, 237
faith 3, 105, 162, 400, 405
Indian 10, 428
Kuki 267–8
literature 371
millenarianism 200
missionaries 283, 300, 375
missions 6, 22, 24, 26–7, 36, 74, 79, 81–2, 89, 93, 104, 110, 119, 158, 262, 364, 390, 409, 425, 431
movements 8, 200
Revival Church (CRC) 142, 150, 163, 175, 266–7, 299
reformations 23
supremacy 422
Chui 213, 215, 220–1, 241–3; *see also* Chi village
church(es) 2, 5–6, 9–11, 16–17, 20–2, 24, 32, 34, 39, 44, 46, 65–6, 91, 101–2, 105, 107–10, 112, 114, 117, 120, 123–8, 133–4, 138–40, 142–6, 148–53, 162–4, 166, 171, 173, 175–8, 180–5, 187–90, 192, 195, 197–205, 207–9, 211, 213–19, 221, 224–5, 227, 229–30, 233, 235–8, 241–3, 245–51, 253, 266–9, 274–5, 278, 280–1, 293–5, 298–301, 315, 318–19, 348, 352–4, 359, 386, 389–91, 401, 403–4, 406, 409–10, 415–17, 419–22, 425–9, 431
Anglican 24
conventional 22
evangelical 16
local 5, 124, 187, 200
traditional 9, 150
civilisation(s) 2, 32, 37, 40–1, 54, 75, 78, 81, 166, 169, 271, 413
clash of 2
Hindu 37, 54, 271
Indic 32
Islamic 271
Clapham Sect 24, 39, 49
Clark, E.W. 23, 66–7, 131–41, 147, 153, 158, 188, 315
Clark, Mary Mead 132, 169, 370
colonialism 17, 27, 48, 78, 80, 93, 106, 111–12, 117, 122, 149, 171, 234, 278, 286, 312, 330, 332, 353, 402, 419
British 17, 27, 78, 80, 93, 111, 117, 122, 149, 286, 332, 353
communal violence 271
communism 382, 386, 388–91, 397, 414, 416–17
Communist Party of Burma (CPB) 388, 397, 409
conflict(s) 4, 9–10, 18–19, 30, 55, 62, 87, 145, 150, 171, 174, 185, 188, 195, 223, 251, 261, 263–5, 268–72, 276–8, 293, 300, 323, 341, 374–6, 380–1, 393–4, 396, 399, 406, 421, 423

civil 87
denominational 150, 268
ethnic 18–19, 185, 263, 268–71, 277
inter-village 261
Kuki–Naga 264
political 10
religious 277
sectarian 4
Sumi Baptist 145
zone 376
conversion(s) 15, 20–1, 28, 65, 68, 70, 110, 120, 128, 150, 152, 154, 158, 165, 168, 171, 174, 178, 182, 189, 192–3, 197, 202, 207, 210, 214, 219, 222, 234, 237, 242, 244, 300, 389, 426
    forced 300
    mass 21, 165, 168, 182, 189, 192–3
    movement 165, 168, 193, 389
    religious 20
converts 9, 11, 15, 19–20, 34, 36, 38, 42, 54, 57, 59, 64–6, 68, 81, 85, 103, 107, 120–3, 128, 132–4, 139, 152, 158, 164, 167–8, 170, 172, 176, 184, 186, 188, 207, 214, 233, 248, 250, 262, 267, 278–9, 298, 303, 315–16, 353, 363, 389, 425, 431; *see also* native Christian converts
Corner in India, A 138, 158, 169, 315
"constitutional Indians" 428
Council of the Nagalim Churches (CNC) 422–3

counter-cultural movement 189
counter-insurgency measures 84, 95, 99, 102
cultivation 115, 119, 143, 215, 246, 331, 403
cultural
    chauvinism 175
    contact 25, 152, 206
    custodian 201, 239, 284
    dominance 108
    encroachment 81
    heritage 81, 137, 160, 209, 213, 272
    identity 120, 200, 204, 271
    loss 174, 206
    revivalism 277, 288, 296
    tradition 20, 226, 282, 297, 361
    war 211, 237, 255, 301
    wasteland 170
    zone 115, 241
culture(s) 8, 15, 17, 24–7, 29, 32, 34, 48, 50, 58–60, 73, 78, 81–2, 88, 90, 105–6, 110–11, 114, 116, 121, 124–7, 129, 137, 164, 169, 173–6, 179, 193–4, 196, 201–2, 211, 215, 231, 237–9, 249, 253–5, 272, 278, 280, 282, 290, 298–9, 301, 311, 323–4, 331, 334, 344, 346–7, 350, 352, 366, 371, 389, 409, 428–30
    clash of 27
    indigenous 17, 24, 196
    literary 81, 90, 346
    oral 81
    pop 215

traditional 17, 121, 137, 169, 175, 194, 231, 239, 298–9, 301, 344
tribal 48, 121, 253

decolonisation 82, 94–6, 288
democracy 17, 43, 73, 82, 85, 126, 303
  liberal 17
  stable 82
Desai, Morarji 97, 359
development
  economic 112
  political 27, 168, 179
  social 27
Dimapur 5, 15, 20–1, 117, 142, 153, 162, 199, 205, 207, 211, 255, 259, 263–4, 269, 294, 324, 357, 366, 418, 422, 424, 428–31
  Kachari kingdom 430–1
  the gateway of Nagaland 430
Dimasa 430–1
disputes 106, 124, 145, 155–6, 158, 171, 185, 195, 201, 205, 264, 272, 313, 396
  ethnic 124, 272
diversity 25–6, 37–8, 58, 72–3, 82, 85, 105, 122, 126, 140, 184–5, 201, 204, 209, 211, 365, 402
  cultural 72
  ethnic 58, 105, 365
  language 73, 201, 204, 209, 211
  linguistic 38, 58
  religious 37
dobashi 196, 279, 330

Donyipolo 14, 254, 298
Durkheim 14, 293

East India Company 29–30, 35, 39, 51, 54, 140
East Pakistan 73, 285, 366, 391, 400–2, 408, 415
economic
  development 112
  livelihood 115
  prosperity 43
  resources 85
economy 43–4, 48, 73, 157, 242, 327, 414
ecumenism 11
education 18–19, 32, 60–1, 81, 90–2, 101, 103, 110–11, 131, 139, 143, 148, 150, 166, 179, 181–2, 192, 199, 207–8, 227, 237, 239, 241–2, 247, 288, 298, 307, 309, 312, 316, 320, 333, 346, 353, 355, 361, 370–1
  Baptist 101
  Christian 143, 309
  English 91, 139, 353
  formal 111, 131, 227
  liberal 307
  modern 91, 131, 150, 207–8, 241, 288, 312, 346, 355
  Western 81, 110
egalitarianism 220, 241
Elementary Forms of Religious Life, The 14, 293
Elwin, Verrier 8–9, 88, 101, 307, 380–1
Emergence of Nagaland 71
England 8, 22, 40, 305

INDEX 449

English
  Baptist mission 48–50
  Baptist missionary 11, 49
  Separatist movement 5
ethnic
  communities 71, 78, 83, 88, 97, 107, 209, 271
  groups, 19, 24, 38, 48, 58, 64, 73–4, 76, 78–9, 81–3, 85–90, 92–3, 95, 106, 110–11, 115–16, 120, 153, 178–9, 202, 205, 209–10, 260, 267, 271–2, 289, 325, 339, 346, 350, 384, 387, 396, 402
  identities 14, 25, 71, 78, 83, 95, 106–7, 120, 179–80, 185, 187, 201–3, 208, 211, 235, 266–7, 271, 302, 311
  Karens 36, 70, 80, 111
  minorities 80, 85–8, 91, 93–4, 339
  movement 283
  Nagas 8, 24, 26–7, 70, 76, 86, 122
  self-pride 259, 262
  uprisings 106, 397
ethnicity(ies) 1, 86–7, 106–7, 114, 174, 187, 202, 211, 214, 239, 265, 271, 283, 288, 388–9, 402, 421, 428, 430
ethnonationalism 16, 19, 71, 73–4, 86–7, 95, 99, 101, 103, 105, 107, 109, 111, 125, 172, 183, 249, 250, 272, 288, 290–1, 302, 305, 317, 322, 328, 332, 336, 346, 365, 381–2, 384, 389, 402, 405, 418–21, 423

Evangelicalism 8, 24, 129, 144
evangelism 6, 15, 34, 40, 48, 54, 57, 90, 107–8, 122, 131, 174, 299, 348, 420–1

faith(s)
  ancestral 14, 129, 244
  Catholic 210
  rabble-rousing 104
  uber-Pentecostal 6
Federal Government of Nagaland (FGN) 163, 345, 379, 384–5
Ferguson 24, 39
First Anglo-Burmese War 29
freedom 19, 44, 64, 86–7, 97, 174, 178, 189, 259, 274, 281, 283–6, 290, 296, 312, 317, 323, 325, 340, 356, 362, 369–70
  desire for 19
  movement 296, 317, 370
fundamentalism 5, 294
Fürer-Haimendorf, Christoph von 15, 83, 90, 169, 189, 193, 202–3, 226–30, 235–6, 240

Gaidinliu, Rani 250, 255–62, 272–91, 293, 295, 298, 377
  movement 283, 296
Gandhi, Indira 284, 290, 368–9, 424
Gandhi, Mahatma 274, 291, 338, 341, 356, 359, 370
gaon buras 338, 341
Ghost Dance movement 289
Godhula 57, 63, 132–5, 193
Government of India 307, 350, 377, 379, 385

Government of the Peoples' Republic of Nagalim (GPRN) 422
Great
　Awakening 22–3, 39–40, 43
　Britain 22, 35, 44, 95
　Commission 4
　Revival 39
Guwahati mission station 51, 53

Harrowing Tales of the Nagas 379
head-hunting 1, 84, 91, 98, 136, 161, 167, 169, 171, 185–6, 194, 213, 222, 231–2, 234–5, 240, 344
Heraka 250, 254, 256, 260, 262–3, 274, 276–78, 280–3, 290–1, 293–302
　movement 250, 256, 263, 274, 277, 281–2, 291, 295, 297
Hinduism 8, 37, 53, 62, 78, 82, 147, 250, 254, 282, 291, 298–9, 375, 431
Hindu(s) 8, 26, 28, 37, 53–4, 62–5, 82, 85, 101, 103–6, 109, 126, 129, 135, 147, 216, 253–4, 257, 271, 273–4, 281–2, 284, 286, 291, 294–300, 302, 362, 366, 375, 396, 426
　dharma 257
　missions 26
　mission organisations 296, 298
　nationalist organisations 8
　orthodox 62
　right-wing groups 104, 281–2, 299–300, 302
　right-wing organisations, 129, 253

Hindutva, 8, 126, 255, 298–9, 364
hippie counter-cultural movement 189
History of American Baptist Missions, A 35, 37–8, 44, 46, 50, 64
History of Christianity in Nagaland 43, 132
Hubi 123, 233
human rights 17, 98, 379, 404

identity(ies) 14, 16, 25, 59, 71, 78, 83, 87, 89, 92, 95, 105–7, 110, 114, 120, 124, 128–9, 131, 156, 179–80, 185, 187, 200–6, 208–11, 214, 220, 235, 239, 248–9, 254, 266–8, 271–2, 274, 278, 282, 289–90, 293, 296–7, 301–2, 305, 309, 311–12, 315, 323, 350, 355, 361, 391, 396, 400, 402
　assertion 110, 204, 214, 274, 289
　Burman 87
　consciousness 301, 355
　crisis 249, 278
　formation 71, 209, 211
　mobilisation 71, 315
　movement 293
　Naga 71, 156, 202, 205, 208–10, 305, 309, 323, 350, 396, 402
　national 92
　pan-Naga 305, 350
　politics 106, 239
　struggle 106–7
　survival 293, 400
Imkongmeren 310, 320, 345
imperialism 16, 24, 111, 388

INDEX 451

Impur mission school 307
Independent League 338–9
India
  mainland 16, 271
  mainstream 104
  national integration 104, 168, 283
India Independence Act 1947 96
Indian
  army 100, 117, 163, 234, 319, 321, 324, 361, 376, 380, 382, 395, 400, 413–14, 416, 421
  Christians 10, 428
  freedom movement 317, 370
  freedom struggle 283, 317, 356
  political class 101, 302, 313
  state 9, 19–20, 88, 93, 100, 102, 104–5, 109, 162–3, 168, 170, 172, 213, 221, 258, 284, 306, 314, 335, 340, 360, 371, 374–5, 379, 381, 384, 393–4, 399
India's Look East (now Act East) policy 112
Indigenous Faith and Cultural Society of Arunachal Pradesh 298
Indo–Myanmar 15, 70–4, 76, 81, 84, 92, 105–6, 112–15, 178, 180, 183–4, 212, 228, 245, 247, 250, 270, 359, 371, 393, 400, 407
  border 15, 70, 72, 84, 178, 180, 183, 212, 228, 245, 247, 250, 270, 359, 393, 407
  frontier 72, 74, 76, 84, 92, 106, 112–13, 115, 184
  relations 114

uplands 71, 72, 73, 81, 105, 371, 393, 400
insurgency 19, 84, 86, 95, 99, 102, 104, 106, 359, 375, 397, 399, 401
  Naga 19, 86, 397, 399
Iralu, Niketu 155, 313, 333, 344, 349–50, 365, 368, 371, 373, 417, 421
Isak Chishi Swu 104, 345, 407–25
Islam 37, 104, 257, 375

Jadonang 260–2, 274–6, 281, 287
Jamir, S.C. 255, 297, 323–5, 366
Japan 81–2, 387, 429
Jasokie, J.B. 255, 305, 332, 335–6, 342–3, 357, 365, 370, 396
Jenkins, Francis 30, 47–8, 118–19
jhum 115, 143, 215, 228, 324, 325, 395
Judson, Adoniram 29, 45, 46, 49, 110, 425

Kabui 258, 260, 275, 350
Kacha Naga movement 260, 262
Kachari(s) 26, 30, 51, 430–1
Kachin(s) 68, 71–3, 75–6, 79–80, 83, 85, 87, 90–2, 94–5, 97–9, 105–6, 109–11, 271, 339, 387, 397, 402, 409
  state 76, 79–80, 98
Kalyan Ashram 296, 298
Kamakhya temple 51, 62, 63
Kamphai movement 260, 272, 283, 287, 289, 296
Karens 36, 64–8, 70–1, 79–80, 95, 110–11, 271, 288
  ethnic 36, 70, 80, 111

Kashmir 98, 381, 401
kemovo 130
khel(s) 161, 164, 229, 233, 352, 396
Khiamniungan 15, 19, 26, 84, 98, 114, 140, 167, 177–84, 235, 344
Khonoma 10, 103, 155–6, 160–4, 310, 313, 329, 331–2, 336, 340, 343, 348–9, 352–3, 357, 361, 396, 404, 406, 411
Khrieleno 348, 368, 377
King, C.D. 23, 153–6, 158
Kiphire 18, 176, 184, 194, 196, 198–9, 201, 210
Kohima 1–3, 9, 14–15, 20–1, 42–3, 90, 92, 103, 117, 123, 127–8, 131, 138–9, 144, 147, 154, 156–9, 167, 170, 198, 202–5, 234, 255, 257–9, 262, 264, 266, 269, 273, 276, 280–2, 286, 292–4, 303–5, 307–9, 312, 314–16, 318, 321–3, 328–30, 333, 336, 339, 341, 343–45, 348–51, 353–5, 357–8, 360, 364, 367, 370, 372, 377, 381, 383–4, 389–90, 392, 395, 411, 429–30
  anthem 354
  Cathedral 3
  War Cemetery 2
Konyak 14–18, 26, 78, 90–2, 98, 120, 123, 140–1, 167, 169–70, 173–4, 179–80, 189, 212–51, 253–5, 319–20, 350
  Baptist churches 246–7, 249, 251
  Nagas 15, 91, 120, 141, 179–80, 221, 226–7, 229–32, 234–5, 237, 240–1, 243, 245, 249, 253
  Students' Union (KSU) 239, 241
  Union (KU) 250, 254
Kruna 127, 128, 129, 130, 131
Kuki(s) 26, 67–8, 72, 89, 94, 106, 124, 127, 258, 260–73, 277, 283, 308, 314, 322
  Baptists 266–8
  Christians 267–8
  Church Council (KCC) 266–8
Kuki-Chins 72, 106
Kyong 75, 146

labour/labourer 56, 66, 94, 99, 105, 156, 261, 304, 328, 371
  corvée 56
  forced 99, 105, 261, 371
  market 94
language(s) 17, 24, 37–8, 45, 57, 59–60, 67, 73, 78, 81, 89–94, 103, 110–11, 114–15, 121–2, 124, 139, 143, 147, 149, 176–7, 179, 182, 187, 201–11, 235, 241, 265, 267–8, 272, 279, 299, 307, 309, 318–19, 346, 350, 366, 402, 412, 430
  Angami 90, 203, 206, 309
  Assamese 57, 59, 122, 346
  Austro-Asiatic 37
  Burmese 45, 92, 111, 402
  English 17, 81, 91, 93, 110, 139, 182, 208, 353, 412
  indigenous 143, 211
  Indo-Aryan 37, 93, 122
  Kachin 110

Nagamese 2, 16, 93, 122, 124, 187, 192, 205, 265
Sumi 143, 206
Tibeto–Burman 37, 67, 90, 122, 402, 430
Lhota Nagas, The 146–8, 204, 304
Liangmai 258, 283, 293, 297, 299–302
Baptist 297, 300
Longleng 18, 136, 184, 233
Longri Ao 317–20, 416
Lotha Nagas 4, 21, 26, 75, 96, 127, 138, 141, 146–52, 169, 204, 206, 235–6, 316, 325, 346, 361, 406

Manipur 25–6, 43, 72–3, 79, 83, 106, 108, 112, 118, 122, 128, 156–8, 162, 250, 255, 258, 260, 262, 264–5, 268–71, 273, 275, 290, 294, 298, 300, 367, 401, 417
Maoism 285, 382, 387–8, 410
Mao Zedong 383, 409, 411–14
  guerrilla warfare strategy 414
Marshman, Joshua 50, 425
martial race 338, 393
Mary Help of Christians Cathedral 3
Massachusetts Baptist Missionary Magazine 50
mass conversion movement 165, 168, 193
Mech 430, 431
Medhi, Bishnuram 313, 364, 367, 371, 374
Meghalaya 93, 298, 349
Meitei(s) 91, 105, 233, 258,
260–2, 265, 271, 283, 339, 365, 402, 431
Mighty Works of God, The 32, 38, 45, 93, 123, 140, 232
Mikir Hills 206–7, 365
missionary/missionaries
  British 49
  Catholic 23
  efforts 22, 46
  foreign 35, 74, 76, 81, 101, 108, 168, 314, 363–4, 375, 390, 404
  zeal 1, 29, 74
mission centres 24, 75, 138–41, 144–6, 151, 175, 180, 182, 187, 198–9, 247, 404, 416
Mizoram 79, 91, 93, 98, 150, 210, 275
Mizos 79, 89, 265, 365, 402
modernity 18–19, 26, 60, 121, 221, 225, 227, 231, 239, 241, 243, 249, 327, 332, 341, 347, 351, 361–2, 419, 421
Mokokchung 11, 21, 132, 138–9, 167, 170–1, 175, 189, 196, 234, 277–9, 306–7, 313, 315, 317–20, 324, 328, 334, 341, 344, 370
Molungyimsen 131–4, 136–8, 188, 370
Mon 18, 80, 184, 212–13, 215, 220–1, 241–2, 246–8, 250, 252, 255, 402
morung(s) 189, 214, 223, 225, 227–33, 236, 238, 242, 320
Mowu 321, 345, 352, 391, 394, 402, 408, 411, 414–15

Muivah, Thuingaleng 402, 407, 410–14, 417–18, 422
mujahids 401
Munda, Birsa 274
Murry, Ezamo 149-50, 325
Muslim 63, 271, 285–6, 365, 375
  League 365
Myanmar 6, 15, 18, 25–6, 70–4, 76, 78–86, 89–95, 98–9, 105–6, 108–9, 111–15, 120, 139, 152, 177–81, 183–4, 197, 209, 212–14, 221, 228, 245–7, 249–50, 265, 270–1, 359, 371, 381, 387, 393, 400, 402, 407–10, 423; *see also* Burma
My Years with Nehru 98, 322, 399, 401

Naga Chronicle, The 334, 341, 358, 379, 404
Naga(s)
  armed uprising 321, 342, 393
  Club 103, 265, 305–10, 316, 320
  Goodwill Mission 374
  Hills 6, 10, 21, 42, 72, 74, 76, 79, 83, 86, 90–1, 93, 96, 98–9, 101, 117–18, 122, 124, 128, 138–9, 146–7, 154, 156–8, 166–9, 171, 195, 197, 205–7, 209, 235, 264–5, 276, 284, 303–4, 307, 310–14, 316–17, 320, 323, 326–9, 331, 337, 340, 342, 350, 356–7, 361–2, 364–7, 375, 380, 389–90

intellectuals 10, 14, 312, 322–3, 325, 330, 335, 345, 352, 362–4, 368, 382, 387
Labour Corps 303–5, 330, 346
nation 104, 284, 288, 325, 334, 341, 350, 358, 385, 387, 406, 422
National Council (NNC) 96–7, 102, 183, 255–6, 258, 265, 272, 290, 296, 305, 310, 312–13, 320–2, 324–5, 327–8, 330, 332–3, 335–45, 347, 350, 352–3, 356–60, 364–7, 370, 374–5, 385, 387, 391, 393–6, 405, 411, 417
nationalism 101, 104, 162, 284, 302, 306, 309, 370, 388
nationalist leaders 103, 125, 422
political issue 10, 124, 312, 313, 338, 367, 376–7, 381, 416
political movement 74, 105, 302, 324, 339, 371, 390–1, 396, 398, 407, 417, 419, 421, 423
politics 291, 310, 316, 323, 329, 367
rebels 10, 16, 86, 97, 99, 102, 107, 359, 397, 402, 407–10, 423
traditional religion 4, 16, 76, 107, 127, 131, 239, 247–8, 253–4, 277–8, 282, 403, 431
women 369–71, 376–7, 379

Nagaland
  Baptist Church Council
    (NBCC) 5–6, 108–9, 123–7,
    145, 149, 163, 177, 185,
    188, 201, 209, 241, 254,
    266–9, 316–19, 368, 373,
    377, 405, 416, 419–20,
    423
  Christian Revival Church 150
  dry state 127
  eastern 18, 189–90
  "India's little Vietnam" 359
  official tribes 26
  Liquor Total Prohibition Act
    (NLTP) 126–7
  State Archive 262
Nagaland 71, 101, 169, 171, 234,
  307, 327, 380, 406
Naga Memorandum, The 305,
  308–9
Naga Mothers' Association
  (NMA) 126
Naga National Rights, The 102,
  359, 395
Naga Nation, The 313, 346–7,
  357–8
Naga Path 261, 262, 277, 289,
  392
Naga tribes
  advanced 168, 236, 345
  chieftainship 165, 173, 262
  eastern 19, 167–8, 170–1, 175,
    184, 186, 190, 193, 196, 199
Naga Women's Federation (NWF)
  374–6, 378
Naked Nagas, The 15, 90, 169,
  236, 240
Nanyü 103
Narayan, Jayaprakash 319, 368,
  378

nationalism
  Assamese 346
  Naga 101, 104, 162, 284, 302,
    306, 309, 370, 388
National
  Socialist Council of Nagaland
    (Khaplang) 104, 113–14,
    250, 265, 268, 410, 418–19,
    422–3
  Socialist Council of Nagalim
    (Isak-Muivah) 9, 104, 265,
    268, 410, 418–19, 422–3
nationhood 358, 388, 396, 422
negotiations 25, 201, 318, 393
  political 318, 393
Nehru, Jawaharlal 86–9, 97,
  101, 259, 283–4, 287, 291,
  311–12, 320, 323–4, 356,
  358, 365–7, 380–1, 386,
  389–90, 399
Nepal 6, 139
Next Christendom, The 23
Nisier Angami 10, 309
Noklak 18, 114, 177–80, 182,
  184
North Cachar Hills 258, 365
North-East Frontier Agency
  (NEFA) 74, 87–8, 98, 120,
  166–7, 172, 325, 365, 395
North-East India 1, 3, 26, 105–6,
  112, 124, 134, 253–4, 265,
  271, 319, 322, 356, 386,
  401
  Christianity 265
  frontier 54
  insurgency 401

opium 57, 218, 225, 236, 244–6
  addiction 57, 245
  Akbari 57

eating 57, 244–5
epidemic 246
shop 245–6
Orunodoi 60–1, 346–7

Paik system 56
Papacy 3
Paupaise 277–8
Pawsey, Charles 326–30
Pentecostalism 6, 8, 144, 191, 249
People's Liberation Army (PLA) 387, 409, 411–14
Phek 20, 202, 204, 209, 248–9
Phichü 128–30
Phizo, A.Z. 19, 95–8, 103–4, 255–56, 284–93, 305, 311, 313, 320, 324, 329–45, 348–9, 351–3, 357–9, 362, 364–6, 370, 376, 379, 385, 388, 391–4, 396, 407–8, 417, 419
Phom 26, 140, 167, 233
pietism 39, 100, 144, 190, 193, 294
Pilgrim's Progress, The 309, 353, 371
Pochury Nagas 26, 209–11, 383
political
 agents 24, 48–9, 93, 148–9, 168–9
 aspirations 307, 313
 class 101, 302, 313–14
 consciousness 283, 307, 332, 347, 370, 373
 developments 27, 168, 179
 issue 124, 312–13, 338, 367, 376, 381, 416
 life 16, 24, 27, 375
 movement 74, 86, 105, 302,

 320, 324, 339, 347, 371, 390–1, 396, 398–9, 407, 417, 419, 421, 423
 negotiations 318, 393
 power 242, 388, 397
 struggle 102, 292, 338, 341
 training 387, 413
politico-religious
 indoctrination 410
 movement 250, 274
politics 29–30, 32, 60, 73, 106, 124–6, 129, 179, 200, 202, 216, 239, 242, 247, 265–7, 288, 291–2, 310, 316, 318, 323, 329, 339, 356, 365, 367, 373–4, 378, 386, 396, 418, 421–2
 denominational 265
polygamy 141, 218
pongyin 213, 220–1, 241–3
 anchen 221
 angh 213, 220–1, 241–3
poverty 18, 44, 116, 199, 298
Presbyterian mission 79, 89, 265
Protestant(s) 4–6, 22–3, 25, 29, 35, 38–9, 43–4, 49, 72, 76, 80, 82, 116, 239, 363
 missions 22–3, 35
 pietism 39
Protestantism 22, 40, 81–2, 107, 419

race 1, 61, 73, 89, 304, 310, 331, 338, 393
 martial 338, 393
 uncivilised 1
Races of Burma, The 73
Rammuny, Murkot 19, 311, 337–8, 340, 364, 375

INDEX

Rashtriya Swayamsevak Sangh (RSS) 8, 254, 281, 294, 300
refugees 80, 100, 328, 366
religiosity 43, 214, 276, 299, 418, 422–3
religious
  homogeneity 87, 104
  life 8, 24, 26, 124, 150, 164, 265, 267
  pluralism 296
  revivalism 22, 260, 277
  traditions 80, 81, 253
Rengmas 206, 209, 309
Rengma Nagas, The 26, 127, 147, 169, 203, 205–9, 345, 350
Representation of People Act 339
repression 105, 319, 381, 411, 416
  state 105, 319, 411
Return to the Naked Nagas 84, 189, 193, 202
revitalisation 260, 278
revivalism 22, 40, 260, 277, 288, 296
  cultural 277
  religious 22, 260, 277
revival period 190, 192–3
rice beer 20–1, 129, 174–5, 216
ritual(s) 5, 225, 232, 412
  water immersion 5
Rivenburg, S.W. 23, 42, 67, 127, 157–60, 203, 266, 292, 304, 308, 315, 329, 331–2, 348, 352
Roman Catholicism 141, 150
  Catholics 3–4, 104, 192, 405
Rongmei 250, 255, 258, 260, 273–4, 288, 295–6, 300–2

Rüzhükhrie 308–9

Sagaing region 71, 79, 91, 108–9, 113, 120, 178–9, 181–2, 184, 214, 221, 241
Sakhrie, T. 104, 305, 310, 314, 327, 332, 336, 340, 342, 344, 347, 348, 349, 350, 351, 352 – 9, 382, 387
salvation 5–6, 18, 22, 34, 48, 63, 164, 190–1, 217, 281–2, 429
Sangkap 185, 188, 192–3
Sangtam 19, 26, 140, 167, 171, 173, 193, 195–201, 204, 209–10, 344, 350
Sankaradeva 62–3
sanyasis 375
Savaging the Civilized 101, 380
school(s) 32–4, 42, 46, 53, 60, 65, 75, 90–2, 108, 111, 149, 152, 168, 171, 181–2, 199, 213, 215, 296, 307–9, 320, 341, 353, 369–70, 382, 429
  government-run 181
  high 181, 215, 222, 224, 308, 333, 372
  mission 10, 90, 92, 100, 121, 148–50, 152, 168, 181–2, 199, 233, 266, 277, 292, 305, 307–10, 312, 316–18, 320–1, 329, 333, 343, 345–6, 349, 353–5, 362, 371, 382, 384, 386–7
Scott, Michael 319, 330, 378–9
scriptures 6, 22, 149, 182, 224, 251, 386, 406
  infallible 22
  interpretation 6, 406

Second Great Awakening 39
Second Vatican Council 4
self-rule 74, 96, 168, 258, 284, 286, 317, 325, 343, 362, 374, 423
self-styled prophets 145, 191–2, 324, 424
Sema 71, 98, 171, 204, 237, 255, 304, 317, 350, 376, 415
Sema, Hokishe 255, 317, 376
Sema Nagas, The 204, 237, 304
Seng Khasi 298
Serampore 11, 48–50
Seventh-Day Adventists 141, 150
Shaiza, Rano 356, 370, 372–8, 380
Shillong Accord 292, 407–8, 417
Simon Commission 103, 265, 306, 308, 310
Sivasagar 31–2, 51, 56–7, 61, 65–6, 68, 76, 119, 121, 123, 132–5, 138, 154, 232, 368
social
   issues 11, 127
   life 16, 144, 202, 205, 229
   relationships 14, 187
   stratification 37
socialism 387, 418
society
   Burmese 92
   European 23
   Indian 17, 298
   multicultural 6
   Naga 10, 14, 16, 20, 100, 126, 160, 174, 201, 211, 239, 265, 291, 304, 306, 310,
330, 334, 351, 358, 361, 386–7, 422–3
   Scandinavian 14
Sola fide 5, 282
Sola scriptura 5
South Asia 58, 104
South East Asia 73–4, 84–5, 106, 112–15, 164, 288, 361, 388–9
spiritual
   awakening 143–4, 189, 193–4
   movement 289
spirituality 118, 151, 191, 297
Star of the Naga Hills, The 42, 128, 157–8, 304, 316, 331
Sukhai, Kaito 321, 330, 345, 382, 391, 393–9, 401, 408, 415
Sumi Nagas 4, 19, 21, 23, 26, 75, 102, 127, 138, 141–6, 149–51, 168–9, 171–6, 198, 203–4, 206, 235, 314, 317, 325, 330, 345, 383–4, 386, 389, 394–5, 401, 419, 421
Swu, Isak Chishi 104, 345, 402, 407, 411, 414, 417–23
Swu, Scato 345, 346, 384–6, 389, 394, 399

tattooing 14, 186, 221, 231, 240
teetotalism 20, 127
Thailand 6, 80, 108, 116, 139, 152, 177
Thangkam 273
Thehu 332
Thenkoh 238
Tikhir 19

Tingkao Raguang Chapriak (TRC) 296
Tingwang 276
trade 35, 47, 78, 84, 112, 135, 138, 183, 234, 245, 332
tradition(s)
 angh 245
 head-hunting 91, 98, 136, 161, 167, 169, 171, 185–6, 194, 213, 222, 231–2, 234–5, 240, 344
 literary 309
 musical 139
 oral 108, 118, 147, 264, 286, 291
 tattooing 14, 186, 231, 240
trans-Dikhu Mission, The 197
Treaty of Gauhati 57
tribal(s)
 dress 17
 identity 361
  religion, 64
  spirit worship 174
 theology 11
 warfare 136
tribe(s)
 barbarian 65
 cognate 120
 expansionist 26, 262
 free 18
 hill 18, 29, 33–4, 37, 47, 53, 57, 63, 68, 168, 310, 364, 367, 425–6
 "hill leaders union" 365
 Scheduled 120
 trans-Dikhu 18, 167, 171, 195–6
 unadministered 18, 196, 279
tribalism 115, 347, 396, 407

Tuensang 8, 18–19, 74, 98, 166–8, 170–3, 175, 177–9, 184–5, 187, 190, 192, 198–9, 201, 223, 241, 279–80, 282, 323, 346, 394
 Frontier Division 8, 98, 394

United Liberation Front of Asom (ULFA) 113
Unlawful Activities (Prevention) Act, 1967 113
U Nu 86–7, 312, 367
Upper Assam 28–9, 32, 35, 37, 42, 50–1, 54–6, 119–20, 138, 143–4, 170, 233, 317, 416

Vaishnavism 32, 37, 55, 106, 262
Vishva Hindu Parishad (VHP) 281, 294
Viet Minh 388
violence 10, 22, 31, 102, 106–7, 125, 185, 269–71, 319, 337, 341–2, 360, 369, 371, 376, 378, 391, 400–1, 403, 406
 Catholic and Protestant 22
 communal 271
Visions of T. Sakhrie, The 340, 350, 361, 362, 363
voluntary associations 40, 239

Wancho Naga 218
Ward, William (American missionary) 61, 66, 425
Ward, William (English missionary) 50, 425
warfare 1, 78, 97, 99, 101, 136, 172, 360, 371, 380, 382,

384, 387, 393–4, 397, 410,
 414, 423
guerrilla 97, 99, 382, 384,
 387, 393, 397, 410,
 414
inter-village 78
jungle 97, 101, 360, 371, 380,
 393–4, 423
modern 1, 97
tribal 136
Western
 civilisation 40
 culture 194, 238, 278
 education 81, 110
 Europe 14, 22, 109, 427
 imperialism 16, 24, 388
 religion 278–9, 299
Westernisation 81, 121, 301
"white man's religion" 4
Witter, W.E. 147–9
Wokha 11, 21, 138, 146–9, 151,
 319, 327
women 14, 16, 61, 98, 125, 129,
 131, 160, 162, 171, 189,
 192, 205, 216, 222, 228,
 231–2, 247, 249, 251, 273,
 276, 279, 283, 288, 319,
 328, 348, 353, 361, 368–9,
 399, 401, 423, 427
 Naga 14, 328, 348, 353,
  368–73, 376–7, 379
 tribal 283
 voices 376
World Hindu Conference 291
World
 War I (WWI) 303
 War II (WWII) 1, 3, 97, 111,
  129, 143, 207, 311, 320,
  327, 345–6, 384, 387, 389,
  392, 395

worship 2–3, 14, 16, 37, 51, 59,
 62–4, 87, 103, 107, 115,
 140, 142–3, 149, 172, 174,
 191, 205, 213–14, 238, 248,
 252–3, 293, 299
 hero 172
 idol 63, 107
 pattern 248, 253
 services 142–3, 205, 252
 spirit 174

Yahoi 246–55
 movement 250–1, 254
Yanthan, Khodao 96–7, 104,
 345–6, 391
Yimchunger 19, 26, 140, 167,
 172–7, 185, 189, 198, 346,
 395
 Naga Baptist mission centre
  175

Zapuzhülie 308–9, 371
zealotry 16
Zelhou Keyho 5–6, 109, 124–5
Zeliang, N.C. 293–8
Zeliang Nagas 26, 127, 203, 254,
 258–60, 263–4, 266, 272,
 278, 289–90, 293–301, 314,
 342
 culture 301
Zeliangrong 258–62, 273, 282,
 285, 288, 290, 294–5, 298,
 301
 Heraka Association (ZHA) 282,
  294–5, 298
 Heraka Palace Association
  (ZHPA) 282
Zeme 258, 260, 276–8, 289, 296,
 299–301
Zunheboto 21, 100, 144–5, 384

www.ingramcontent.com/pod-product-compliance
Lightning Source LLC
Chambersburg PA
CBHW020257240426
43673CB00039B/621